Advances in Credit Risk Modelling and Corporate Bankruptcy Prediction

The field of credit risk and corporate bankruptcy prediction has gained considerable momentum following the collapse of many large corporations around the world, and more recently through the sub-prime scandal in the United States. This book provides a thorough compendium of the different modelling approaches available in the field, including several new techniques that extend the horizons of future research and practice. Topics covered include probit models (in particular bivariate probit modelling), advanced logistic regression models (in particular mixed logit, nested logit and latent class models), survival analysis models, non-parametric techniques (particularly neural networks and recursive partitioning models), structural models and reduced form (intensity) modelling. Models and techniques are illustrated with empirical examples and are accompanied by a careful explanation of model derivation issues. This practical and empirically based approach makes the book an ideal resource for all those concerned with credit risk and corporate bankruptcy, including academics, practitioners and regulators.

Stewart Jones is Professor of Accounting at the University of Sydney. He has published extensively in the area of credit risk and corporate bankruptcy, and is co-editor of the leading international accounting and finance journal, *Abacus*.

David A. Hensher is Professor of Management at the University of Sydney. He is the author of numerous books and articles on discrete choice models, including *Stated Choice Methods* (Cambridge University Press, 2000) and *Applied Choice Analysis* (Cambridge University Press, 2005). He teaches discrete choice modelling to academic, business and government audiences, and is also a partner in Econometric Software, the developers of Nlogit and Limdep.

Quantitative Methods for Applied Economics and Business Research

Series Editor

PROFESSOR PHILIP HANS FRANSES

Erasmus University, Rotterdam

Researchers and practitioners in applied economics and business now have access to a much richer and more varied choice of data than earlier generations. Quantitative Methods for Applied Economics and Business Research is a new series aimed at meeting the needs of graduate students, researchers and practitioners who have a basic grounding in statistical analysis and who wish to take advantage of more sophisticated methodology in their work.

Published titles
Lusk and Shogren (eds.) *Experimental Auctions*

Advances in Credit Risk Modelling and Corporate Bankruptcy Prediction

Edited by

Stewart Jones and David A. Hensher

CAMBRIDGE
UNIVERSITY PRESS

CAMBRIDGE UNIVERSITY PRESS

Cambridge, New York, Melbourne, Madrid, Cape Town, Singapore, São Paulo, Delhi

Cambridge University Press
The Edinburgh Building, Cambridge CB2 8RU, UK

Published in the United States of America by Cambridge University Press, New York

www.cambridge.org
Information on this title: www.cambridge.org/9780521689540

First published 2008

Printed in the United Kingdom at the University Press, Cambridge

A catalogue record for this publication is available from the British Library

Library of Congress Cataloguing in Publication data
Advances in credit risk modelling and corporate bankruptcy prediction /
   [edited by] Stewart Jones, David A. Hensher.
     p.   cm.
   Includes bibliographical references and index.
   ISBN 978-0-521-86928-7 (hardback) – ISBN 978-0-521-68954-0 (pbk.)
   1. Credit–Management.   2. Risk management.   3. Bankruptcy–Forecasting.
   I. Jones, Stewart, 1964–   II. Hensher, David A., 1947–   III. Title.
   HG4026.A342 2008
   658.8'82–dc22
   2008017482

ISBN 978-0-521-86928-7 hardback
ISBN 978-0-521-68954-0 paperback

Contents

v

Figures

Tables

Contributors

Edward I. Altman is the Max L. Heine Professor of Finance Stern Business School, New York University.

Andreas Charitou is Professor of Accounting and Finance the University of Cyprus.

William H. Greene is Professor of Economics and Statistics Stern School of Business, New York University.

David A. Hensher is Professor of Management Faculty of Economics and Business, The University of Sydney.

Stewart Jones is Professor of Accounting Faculty of Economics and Business, The University of Sydney.

Neophytos Lambertides is Lecturer at Aston University, UK.

Marc J. Leclere is Assistant Professor of Accounting Department of Accounting College of Business Administration University of Illinois at Chicago.

Maurice Peat is Senior Lecturer of Finance Faculty of Economics and Business, The University of Sydney.

Rajendra P. Srivastava is Ernst & Young Distinguished Professor of Accounting and Director of the Ernst & Young Center for Auditing Research and Advanced Technology at the School of Business, University of Kansas.

Lenos Trigeorgis is Professor at the University of Cyprus and Visiting Professor at MIT.

Robert G. Walker is Professor of Accounting Faculty of Economics and Business, The University of Sydney.

Advances in the modelling of credit risk and corporate bankruptcy: Introduction

Stewart Jones and David A. Hensher

Credit risk and corporate bankruptcy prediction research has been topical now for the better part of four decades, and still continues to attract fervent interest among academics, practitioners and regulators. In recent years, the much-publicized collapse of many large global corporations, including Enron, Worldcom, Global Crossing, Adelphia Communications, Tyco, Vivendi, Royal Ahold, HealthSouth, and, in Australia, HIH, One.Tel, Pasminco and Ansett (just to mention a few), has highlighted the significant economic, social and political costs associated with corporate failure. Just as it seemed these events were beginning to fade in the public memory, disaster struck again in June 2007. The collapse of the 'sub-prime' mortgage market in the United States, and the subsequent turmoil in world equity and bond markets has led to fears of an impending international liquidity and credit crisis, which could affect the fortunes of many financial institutions and corporations for some time to come.

These events have tended to reignite interest in various aspects of corporate distress and credit risk modelling, and more particularly the credit ratings issued by the Big Three ratings agencies (Standard and Poor's, Moody's and Fitches). At the time of the Enron and Worldcom collapses, the roles and responsibilities of auditors were the focus of public attention. However, following the sub-prime collapse, credit-rating agencies have been in the spotlight. At the heart of the sub-prime scandal have been the credit ratings issued for many collateralized debt obligations (CDOs), particularly CDOs having a significant exposure to the sub-prime lending market. In hindsight, many rated CDOs carried much higher credit risk than was implied in their credit rating. As the gatekeepers for debt quality ratings, the 'Big Three' have also been criticized for reacting too slowly to the sub-prime crisis, for failing to downgrade CDOs (and related structured credit products) in a timely manner and for failing to anticipate the rapidly escalating default rates on sub-prime loans. The adequacy of historical default data (and the risk models based on these data) has also been questioned. As it turned out, historical default rates did not prove to be a reliable indicator of future default rates which surfaced during the sub-prime crisis. Officials of the EU have since announced probes into the role of the ratings agencies in the sub-prime crisis, which are likely to be followed by similar developments in the United States.

Distress forecasts and credit scoring models are being increasingly used for a range of evaluative and predictive purposes, not merely the rating of risky debt instruments and related structured credit products. These purposes include the monitoring of the solvency of financial and other institutions by regulators (such as APRA in Australia), assessment of loan security by lenders and investors, going concern evaluations by auditors, the measurement of portfolio risk, and in the pricing of defaultable bonds, credit derivatives and other securities exposed to credit risk.

This book has avoided taking the well-trodden path of many credit risk works, which have tended to be narrowly focused technical treatises covering specialized areas of the field. Given the strong international interest in credit risk and distress prediction modelling generally, this volume addresses a broad range of innovative topics that are expected to have contemporary interest and practical appeal to a diverse readership, including lenders, investors, analysts, auditors, government and private sector regulators, ratings agencies, financial commentators, academics and postgraduate students. Furthermore, while this volume must (unavoidably) assume some technical background knowledge of the field, every attempt has been made to present the material in a practical, accommodating and informative way. To add practical appeal and to illustrate the basic concepts more lucidly, nearly all chapters provide a detailed empirical illustration of the particular modelling technique or application being explained.

While we have covered several traditional modelling topics in credit risk and bankruptcy research, our goal is not merely to regurgitate existing techniques and methodologies available in the extant literature. We have introduced new techniques and topic areas which we believe could have valuable applications to the field generally, as well as extending the horizons for future research and practice.

The topics covered in the volume include logit and probit modelling (in particular bivariate models); advanced discrete choice or outcome techniques (in particular mixed logit, nested logit and latent class models); survival analysis and duration models; non-parametric techniques (particularly neural networks and recursive partitioning models); structural models and reduced form (intensity) modelling; credit derivative pricing models; and credit risk modelling issues relating to default recovery rates and loss given default (LGD). While this book is predominantly focused on statistical modelling techniques, we recognize that a weakness of all forms of econometric modelling is that they can rarely (if ever) be applied in situations where there is little or no prior knowledge or data. In such situations, empirical generalizations and statistical inferences may have limited application; hence alternative analytical frameworks may be appropriate and worthwhile. In this context, we present a mathematical and theoretical system known as 'belief functions', which is covered in Chapter 10. Belief functions are built around belief 'mass' and 'plausibility' functions and provide a potentially viable alternative to statistical probability theory in the assessment of credit risk. A further innovation of this volume is that we cover distress modelling for public sector entities, such as local government authorities, which has been a much neglected area of research. A more detailed breakdown of each chapter is provided as follows.

In Chapter 1, Bill Greene provides an analysis of credit card defaults using a bivariate probit model. His sample data is sourced from a major credit card company. Much of the previous literature has relied on relatively simplistic techniques such as multiple discriminant models (MDA) or standard form logit models. However, Greene is careful to emphasize that the differences between MDA, and standard form logit and probit models are not as significant as once believed. Because MDA is no more nor less than a linear probability model, we would not expect the differences between logit, probit and MDA to be that great. While MDA does suffer from some limiting statistical assumptions (particularly multivariate normality and IID), models which rely on normality are often surprisingly robust to violations of this assumption. Greene does stress, however, that the conceptual foundation of MDA is quite naive. For instance, MDA divides the universe of loan applicants into two types, those who *will* default and those who *will not*. The crux of the analysis is that at the time of application, the individual is as if 'preordained to be a defaulter or a nondefaulter'. However, the same individual might be in either group at any time, depending on a host of attendant circumstances and random factors in their own behaviour. Thus, prediction of default is not a problem of classification in the same way as 'determining the sex of prehistoric individuals from a fossilized record'.

Index function based models of discrete choice, such as probit and logit, assume that for any individual, given a set of attributes, there is a definable probability that they will actually default on a loan. This interpretation places all individuals in a single population. The observed outcome (i.e., default/no default), arises from the characteristics and random behaviour of the individuals. Ex ante, all that can be produced by the model is a *probability*. According to the author, the underlying logic of the credit scoring problem is to ascertain how much an applicant resembles individuals who have defaulted in the past. The problem with this approach is that mere resemblance to past defaulters may give a misleading indication of the individual default probability for an individual who has not already been screened for a loan (or credit card). The model is used to assign a default probability to a random individual who *applies* for a loan, but the only information that exists about default probabilities comes from previous loan *recipients*. The relevant question for Greene's analysis is whether, in the population at large, Prob[D=1|x] equals Prob[D=1|x and C=1] in the subpopulation, where '$C = 1$' denotes having received the loan, or, in our case, 'card recipient'. Since loan recipients have passed a prior screen based, one would assume, on an assessment of default probability, Prob[D=1|x] must exceed Prob[D=1|x, C=1] for the same x. For a given set of attributes, x, individuals in the group with $C = 1$ are, by nature of the prior selection, less likely to default than otherwise similar individuals chosen randomly from a population that is a mixture of individuals who will have $C = 0$ and $C = 1$. Thus, according to Greene, the *unconditional* model will give a downward-biased estimate of the default probability for an individual selected at random from the full population. As the author notes, this describes a form of censoring. To be applicable to the population at large, the estimated default model should condition specifically on cardholder status, which is the rationale for the bivariate probit model used in his analysis.

In Chapters 2 and 3, Stewart Jones and David Hensher move beyond the traditional logit framework to consider 'advanced' logit models, particularly mixed logit, nested logit and latent class models. While an extensive literature on financial distress prediction has emerged over the past few decades, innovative *econometric* modelling techniques have been slow to be taken up in the financial sphere. The relative merits of standard logit, MDA and to a lesser extent probit and tobit models have been discussed in an extensive literature. Jones and Hensher argue that the major limitation of these models is that there has been no recognition of the major developments in discrete choice modelling over the last 20 years which has increasingly relaxed the behaviourally questionable assumptions associated with the IID condition (independently and identically distributed errors) and allowed for observed and unobserved heterogeneity to be formally incorporated into model estimation in various ways.

The authors point out a related problem: most distress studies to date have modelled failure as a simplistic binary classification of failure vs. nonfailure (the dependent variable can only take on one of two possible states). This has been widely criticized, one reason being that the strict legal concept of bankruptcy may not always reflect the underlying economic reality of corporate financial distress. The two-state model can conflict with underlying theoretical models of financial failure and may limit the generalizability of empirical results to other types of distress that a firm can experience in the real world. Further, the practical risk assessment decisions by lenders and other parties usually cannot be reduced to a simple pay-off space of just failed or nonfailed. However, modelling corporate distress in a multi-state setting can present major conceptual and econometric challenges.

How do 'advanced' form logit models differ from a standard or 'simple' logit model?. There are essentially two major problems with the basic or standard model. First, the IID assumption is very restrictive and induces the 'independence from irrelevant alternatives' (IIA) property in the model. The second issue is that the standard multinomial logit (MNL) model fails to capture firm-specific heterogeneity of any sort not embodied in the firm-specific characteristics and the IID disturbances.

The mixed logit model is an example of a model that can accommodate firm-specific heterogeneity across firms through random parameters. The essence of the approach is to decompose the stochastic error component into two additive (i.e., uncorrelated) parts. One part is correlated over alternative outcomes and is heteroscedastic, and another part is IID over alternative outcomes and firms as shown below:

$$U_{iq} = \beta' x_{iq} + (\eta_{iq} + \varepsilon_{iq})$$

where η_{iq} is a random term, representing the unobserved heterogeneity across firms, with zero mean, whose distribution over firms and alternative outcomes depends in general on underlying parameters and observed data relating to alternative outcome i and firm q; and ε_{iq} is a random term with zero mean that is IID over alternative outcomes and does not depend on underlying parameters or data. Mixed logit models assume a general distribution for η and an IID extreme value type-1 distribution for ε.

The major advantage of the mixed logit model is that it allows for the complete relaxation of the IID and IIA conditions by allowing all unobserved variances and covariances to be different, up to identification. The model is highly flexible in representing sources of firm-specific observed and unobserved heterogeneity through the incorporation of random parameters (whereas MNL and nested logit models only allow for *fixed* parameter estimates). However, a relative weakness of the mixed logit model is the absence of a single globally efficient set of parameter estimates and the relative complexity of the model in terms of estimation and interpretation.

In Chapter 3, Jones and Hensher present two other advanced-form models, the nested logit model (NL) and the latent class multinomial logit model (LCM). Both of these model forms improve on the standard logit model but have quite different econometric properties from the mixed logit model. In essence, the NL model relaxes the severity of the MNL condition between subsets of alternatives, but preserves the IID condition across alternatives within each nested subset. The popularity of the NL model arises from its close relationship to the MNL model. The authors argue that NL is essentially a set of hierarchical MNL models, linked by a set of conditional relationships. To take an example from Standard and Poor's credit ratings, we might have six alternatives, three of them level A rating outcomes (AAA, AA, A, called the a-set) and three level B rating outcomes (BBB, BB, B, called the b-set). The NL model is structured such that the model predicts the probability of a particular A-rating outcome conditional on an A-rating. It also predicts the probability of a particular B-rating outcome conditional on a B-rating. Then the model predicts the probability of an A or a B outcome (called the c-set). That is, we have two lower level conditional outcomes and an upper level marginal outcome. Since each of the 'partitions' in the NL model are of the MNL form, they each display the IID condition between the alternatives within a partition. However, the variances are different between the partitions.

The main benefits of the NL model are its closed-form solution, which allows parameter estimates to be more easily estimated and interpreted; and a unique global set of asymptotically efficient parameter estimates. A relative weakness of NL is that it is analytical and conceptually closely related to MNL and therefore shares many of the limitations of the basic model. Nested logit only partially corrects for the highly restrictive IID condition and incorporates observed and unobserved heterogeneity *to some extent* only.

According to Jones and Hensher, the underlying theory of the LCM model posits that individual or firm behaviour depends on observable attributes and on latent heterogeneity that varies with factors that are unobserved by the analyst. Latent classes are constructs created from indicator variables (analogous to structural equation modelling) which are then used to construct clusters or segments. Similar to mixed logit, LCM is also free from many limiting statistical assumptions (such as linearity and homogeneity in variances), but avoids some of the analytical complexity of mixed logit. With the LCM model, we can analyse observed and unobserved heterogeneity through a model of discrete parameter variation. Thus, it is assumed that firms are implicitly sorted into a set of M classes, but which class contains any particular firm, whether known or not to that firm, is unknown to the analyst. The central behavioural model is a multinomial logit model (MNL) for discrete choice among J_q alternatives, by firm q observed in T_q choice situations. The LCM model can also yield some powerful improvements over the standard logit model. The LCM is a semi-parametric specification, which alleviates the requirement to make strong distributional assumptions about firm-specific heterogeneity (required for random parameters) within the mixed logit framework. However, the authors maintain that the mixed logit model, while fully parametric, is so flexible that it provides the analyst with a wide range within which to specify firm-specific, unobserved heterogeneity. This flexibility may reduce some of the limitations surrounding distributional assumptions for random parameters.

In Chapter 4, Marc Leclere discusses the conceptual foundations and derivation of survival or duration models. He notes that the use of survival analysis in the social sciences is fairly recent, but the last ten years has evidenced a steady increase in the use of the method in many areas of research. In particular, survival models have become increasingly popular in financial distress research. The primary benefits provided by survival analysis techniques (relative to more traditional techniques such as logit and MDA) are in the areas of censoring and time-varying covariates. Censoring exists when there is incomplete information on the occurrence of an event because an observation has dropped out of a study or the study ends before the observation experiences the event of interest. Time-varying covariates are covariates that change in value over time. Survival analysis, relative to other statistical methods, employs values of covariates that change over the course of the estimation process. Given that changes in covariates can influence the probability of event occurrence, time-varying covariates are clearly a very attractive feature of survival models.

In terms of the mechanics of estimation, survival models are concerned with examining the length of the time interval ('duration') between transition states. The time interval is defined by an origin state and a destination state and the transition between the states is marked by the occurrence of an event (such as corporate failure) during the observation period. Survival analysis models the probability of a change in a dependent variable Y_t from an origin state j to a destination state k as a result of causal factors. The duration of time between states is called event (failure) time. Event time is represented by a non-negative random variable T that represents the duration of time until the dependent variable at time t_0 (Y_{t_0}) changes from state j to state k. Alternative survival analysis models assume different probability distributions for T. As Leclere points out, regardless of the probability distribution of T, the probability distribution can be specified as a cumulative distribution function, a survivor function, a probability density function, or a hazard function. Leclere points out that non-parametric estimation techniques are less commonly used than parametric and semi-parametric methods because they do not allow for estimation of the effect of a covariate on the survival function. Because most research examines het-erogeneous populations, researchers are usually interested in examining the effect of covariates on the hazard rate. This is accomplished through the use of regression models in which the hazard rate or time to failure is the fundamental dependent variable. The basic issue is to specify a model for the distribution of t given x and this can be accomplished with para-metric or semi-parametric models. Parametric models employ distributions such as the exponential and Weibull whereas semi-parametric models make no assumptions about the underlying distribution. Although most appli-cations of survival analysis in economics-based research avoid specifying a distribution and simply employ a semi-parametric model, for purposes of completeness, the author examines parametric and semi-parameteric regres-sion models. To the extent that analysts are interested in the duration of time that precedes the occurrence of an event, survival analysis represents a valu-able econometric tool in corporate distress prediction and credit risk analysis.

In Chapter 5, Maurice Peat examines non-parametric techniques, in par-ticular neural networks and recursive partitioning models. Non-parametric techniques also address some of the limiting statistical assumptions of earlier models, particularly MDA. There have been a number of attempts to over-come these econometric problems, either by selecting a parametric method with fewer distributional requirements or by moving to a non-parametric approach. The logistic regression approach (Chapters 2 and 3) and the general hazard function formulation (Chapter 4) are examples of the first approach.

The two main types of non-parametric approach that have been used in the empirical literature are neural networks and recursive partitioning. As the author points out, neural networks is a term that covers many models and learning (estimation) methods. These methods are generally associated with attempts to improve computerized pattern recognition by developing models based on the functioning of the human brain, and attempts to implement learning behaviour in computing systems. Their weights (and other parameters) have no particular meaning in relation to the problems to which they are applied, hence they can be regarded as pure 'black box' estimators. Estimating and interpreting the values of the weights of a neural network is not the primary modelling exercise, but rather to estimate the underlying probability function or to generate a classification based on the probabilistic output of the network.

Recursive partitioning is a tree-based method to classification and proceeds through the simple mechanism of using one feature to split a set of observations into two subsets. The objective of the spilt is to create subsets that have a greater proportion of members from one of the groups than the original set. This objective is known as reducing the impurity of the set. The process of splitting continues until the subsets created only consist of members of one group or no split gives a better outcome than the last split performed. The features can be used once or multiple times in the tree construction process.

Peat points out that the distinguishing feature of the non-parametric methods is that there is no (or very little) a priori knowledge about the form of the true function which is being estimated. The target function is modelled using an equation containing many free parameters, but in a way which allows the class of functions which the model can represent to be very broad. Both of the methods described by the author are useful additions to the tool set of credit analysts, especially in business continuity analysis, where a priori theory may not provide a clear guide on the functional form of the model or to the role and influence of explanatory variables. Peat concludes that the empirical application of both of methods has demonstrated their potential in a credit analysis context, with the best model from each non-parametric class outperforming a standard MDA model.

In Chapter 6, Andreas Charitou, Neophytos Lambertides and Lenos Trigeorgis examine structural models of default which have now become very popular with many credit rating agencies, banks and other financial institutions around the world. The authors note that structural models use the evolution of a firm's structural variables, such as asset and debt values, to determine the timing of default. In contrast to reduced-form models, where default is modelled as a purely exogenous process, in structural models default is endogenously generated within the model. The authors examine the first structural models introduced by Merton in 1974. The basic idea is that the firm's equity is seen as a European call option with maturity T and strike price D on asset value V. The firm's debt value is the asset value minus the equity value seen as a call option. This method presumes a very simplistic capital structure and implies that default can only occur at the maturity of the zero-coupon bond. The authors note that a second approach within the structural framework was introduced by Black and Cox (1976). In this approach default occurs when a firm's asset value falls below a certain threshold. Subsequent studies have explored more appropriate default boundary inputs while other studies have relaxed certain assumptions of Merton's model such as stochastic interest rates and early default. The authors discuss and critically review subsequent research on the main structural credit risk models, such as models with stochastic interest rates, exogenous and endogenous default barrier models and models with mean-reverting leverage ratios.

In Chapter 7, Edward Altman explores explanatory and empirical linkages between recovery rates and default rates, an issue which has traditionally been neglected in the credit risk modelling literature. Altman finds evidence from many countries that collateral values and recovery rates on corporate defaults can be volatile and, moreover, that they tend to go down just when the number of defaults goes up in economic downturns. Altman points out that most credit risk models have focused on default risk and assumed static loss assumptions, treating the recovery rate either as a constant parameter or as a stochastic variable independent from the probability of default. The author argues that the traditional focus on default analysis has been partly reversed by the recent increase in the number of studies dedicated to the subject of recovery rate estimation and the relationship between default and recovery rates. The author presents a detailed review of the way credit risk models, developed during the last thirty years, treat the recovery rate and, more specifically, its relationship with the probability of default of an obligor. Altman also reviews the efforts by rating agencies to formally incorporate recovery ratings into their assessment of corporate loan and bond credit risk and the recent efforts by the Basel Committee on Banking Supervision to consider 'downturn LGD' in their suggested requirements under Basel II. Recent empirical evidence concerning these issues is also presented and discussed in the chapter.

In Chapter 8, Stewart Jones and Maurice Peat explore the rapid growth of the credit derivatives market over the past decade. The authors describe a range of credit derivative instruments, including credit default swaps (CDSs), credit linked notes, collateralized debt obligations (CDOs) and synthetic CDOs. Credit derivatives (particularly CDSs) are most commonly used as a vehicle for hedging credit risk exposure, and have facilitated a range of flexible new investment and diversification opportunities for lender and investors. Increasingly, CDS spreads are becoming an important source of market information for gauging the overall credit worthiness of companies and the price investors are prepared to pay to assume this risk. Jones and Peat point out that while credit derivatives have performed a range of important functions in financial markets, they have their detractors. For instance, there have been concerns levelled that credit derivatives represent a threat to overall financial stability – among other reasons, credit derivatives may result in credit risk being too widely dispersed throughout the economy and ultimately transfer risk to counterparties who are not necessarily subject to the same regulatory controls and scrutiny as banks. Furthermore, there have been some concerns raised that credit derivative markets are yet to be tested in a severe market downturn. In the context of these concerns, Jones and Peat explore some of the ramifications of the recent 'sub-prime meltdown' on world equity and bond markets, and credit derivative markets in particular. Finally, the authors examine credit derivative pricing models and explore some implications for the pricing of credit default swaps using alternative default probability frameworks. Using Time Warner as a case illustration, the authors find that differences between the structural model probabilities and default probabilities generated from the reduced-form approach (using the recovery rate suggested by the Basel II framework) are striking and worthy of future investigation.

In Chapter 9, Stewart Jones and Robert Walker address a much-neglected area of the distress prediction literature. The main focus of previous chapters in this volume has been on private sector corporations. In this context, 'distress' has been variously interpreted as being evidenced by voluntary or creditor-induced administration (bankruptcy), default on a loan repayment, failure to pay a preference dividend (or even a reduction in the amount of ordinary dividend payments), share issues specifically to meet shortfalls in working capital, financial reorganization where debt is forgiven or converted to equity, and a failure to pay stock exchange listing fees.

Against this background, Jones and Walker attempt to fill a gap in the distress literature by developing a quantitative modelling approach to explain and predict local government distress in Australia. As local government authorities typically do not fail per se (e.g., bankruptcy or loan default), a major objective for the authors has been to develop a pragmatic and meaningful measure of local government distress that can be readily operationalized for statistical modelling purposes.

Given the difficulties in finding an appropriate financial distress measure in local councils, Jones and Walker focus on constructing a proxy of distress linked to the basic operating objectives of local councils, which is to provide services to the community. The authors operationalize this concept of distress in terms of an inability of local governments to provide services at pre-existing levels to the community. In order to provide services to the community, local governments are expected to invest in infrastructure and to maintain legacy infrastructure. The authors use the estimates developed by local governments of the cost of restoring infrastructure to a 'satisfactory condition' as a measure of degrees of 'distress'. As such, the study uses a quantitative measure of distress, as opposed to the more limited (and less relevant) binary classification that characterizes private sector distress research. The authors examine both a *qualitative* and *quantitative* measures of service delivery and find that the qualitative measure provides a more explanatory and predictive indicator of distress in local government authorities. Using a latent class model (see also Chapter 3), Jones and Walker find that in terms of higher impacts on council distress, the profile of latent Class 1 (which they call 'smaller lower revenue councils'), are smaller councils servicing smaller areas that are relatively less affected by population levels, but are highly impacted by road maintenance costs, and lower revenue generation capacity (particularly rates revenue generation). In terms of higher impacts on council distress, latent Class 2 councils (which they call 'larger higher revenue councils') are larger councils servicing larger areas with higher population levels and lower full-time staff. These councils are less impacted by their rates revenue base, but are impacted by lower overall revenue generation capacity. Compared to Class 1 councils, Class 2 councils are relatively less impacted by road programme costs, and the carrying value of infrastructure assets. Jones and Walker also find that the classification accuracy of their LCM model is higher than a standard multiple regression model. However, an important direction for future research identified by the authors is the further development and refinement of useful and practical financial distress constructs for the public sector.

In Chapter 10, Rajendra Srivastava and Stewart Jones present a theoretical and mathematical framework known as the Dempster–Shafer theory of belief functions for evaluating credit risk. The belief function framework provides an alternative to probability-based models in situations where statistical generalizations may have very limited or no practical application. Srivastava and Jones posit that there are two basic concepts related to any kind of risk assessment. One deals with the potential loss due to the undesirable event (such as loan default). The other deals with the uncertainty associated with the event (i.e., the likelihood that the event will or will not occur). Further, there are two kinds of uncertainties. One kind arises purely because of the random nature of the event. For random events, there exist stable frequencies in repeated trials under fixed conditions. For such random events, one can use the knowledge of the stable frequencies to predict the probability of occurrence of the event. This kind of uncertainty has been the subject of several previous chapters in this volume which have espoused various statistical models of credit risk and corporate bankruptcy. The other kind of uncertainty arises because of a fundamental lack of knowledge of the 'true state of nature': i.e., where we not only lack the knowledge of a stable frequency, but also the means to specify fully the fixed conditions under which repetitions can be performed. Srivastava and Jones present a theoretical framework which can provide a useful alternative to probability-based modelling to deal with such circumstances. Using the belief function framework, the authors examine the nature of 'evidence', the representation of 'ignorance' and 'ambiguity', and the basis for knowledge in the credit ratings formulation process. To demonstrate the application of belief functions, the authors derive a default risk formula in terms of the *plausibility* of loan default risk being present under certain specified conditions described in their illustration. Using the authors' example, their default formula suggests that if default risk exists, then the only way it can be minimized is for the lender to perform effective ongoing review activities, ceteris paribus. Finally, Srivastava and Jones discuss some approaches to decision making using belief functions and apply this to perform an economic analysis of cost and benefit considerations faced by a ratings agency when default risk is present.

Finally, we wish to thank Nicky Orth for her patience and dedication in assisting with the preparation of this manuscript, and Ashadi Waclik for his capable research assistance.

Stewart Jones

David A. Hensher

7 September 2007

1 A statistical model for credit scoring

William H. Greene

Acknowledgements: I am grateful to Terry Seaks for valuable comments on an earlier draft of this paper and to Jingbin Cao for his able research assistance. The provider of the data and support for this project has requested anonymity, so I must thank them as such. Their help and support are gratefully acknowledged. Participants in the applied econometrics workshop at New York University also provided useful commentary. This chapter is based on the author's working paper 'A Statistical Model for Credit Scoring', Stern School of Business, Department of Economics, *Working Paper* 92–29, 1992.

1.1. Introduction

Prediction of loan default has an obvious practical utility. Indeed, the identification of default risk appears to be of paramount interest to issuers of credit cards. In this study, we will argue that default risk is overemphasized in the assessment of credit card applications. In an empirical application, we find that a model which incorporates the expected profit from issuance of a credit card in the approval decision leads to a substantially higher acceptance rate than is present in the observed data and, by implication, acceptance of a greater average level of default risk.

A major credit card vendor must evaluate tens or even hundreds of thousands of credit card applications every year. These obviously cannot be subjected to the scrutiny of a loan committee in the way that, say, a real estate loan might. Thus, statistical methods and automated procedures are essential. Banks and credit card issuers typically use 'credit scoring models'. In practice, credit scoring for credit card applications appears to be focused fairly narrowly on default risk and on a rather small set of attributes.[1] This

---

[1] We say 'appears to be' because the actual procedures used by credit-scoring agencies are not public information, nor in fact are they even necessarily known by the banks that use them. The small amount of information that we have was provided to us in conversation by the supporters of this study. We will return to this issue below.

study will develop an integrated statistical model for evaluating a credit card application which incorporates both default risk and the anticipated profit from the loan in the calculation. The model is then estimated using a large sample of applications and follow-up expenditure and default data for a major credit card company. The models are based on standard techniques for discrete choice and linear regression, but the data present two serious complications. First, observed data on default and expenditure used to fit the predictive models are subjected to a form of censoring that mandates the use of models of sample selection. Second, our sample used to analyse the approval decision is systematically different from the population from which it was drawn. This nonrepresentative nature of the data is remedied through the use of choice-based sampling corrections.

Boyes *et al.* (1989) examined credit card applications and account performance using data similar to ours and a model that, with minor reinterpretation, is the same as one of the components of our model. They and we reach several similar conclusions. However, in one of the central issues in this study, we differ sharply. Since the studies are so closely related, we will compare their findings to ours at several points.

This paper is organized as follows. Section 2 will present models which have been used or proposed for assessing probabilities of loan default. Section 3 will describe an extension of the model. Here, we will suggest a framework for using the loan default equation in a model of cost and projected revenue to predict the profit and loss from the decision to accept a credit card application. The full model is sketched here and completed in Section 5. Sections 4 and 5 will present an application of the technique. The data and some statistical procedures for handling its distinctive characteristics are presented in Section 4. The empirical results are given in Section 5. Conclusions are drawn in Section 6.

1.2. Models for prediction of default

Individual i with vector of attributes x_i applies for a loan at time 0. The attributes include such items as: personal characteristics including age, sex, number of dependents and education; economic attributes such as income, employment status and home ownership; a credit history including the number of previous defaults, and so on. Let the random variable y_i indicate whether individual i has defaulted on a loan ($y_1 = 1$) or has not ($y_1 = 0$) during the time which has elapsed from the application until y_1 is observed.

We consider two familiar frameworks for predicting default. The technique of discriminant analysis is considered first. We will not make use of this technique in this study. But one of the observed outcome variables in the data that we will examine, the approval decision, *was* generated by the use of this technique. So it is useful to enumerate its characteristics. We then consider a probit model for discrete choice as an alternative.

Linear discriminant analysis

The technique of discriminant analysis rests on the assumption that there are two populations of individuals, which we denote '1' and '0', each characterized by a multivariate normal distribution of the attributes, x. An individual with attribute vector x_i is drawn from one of the two populations, and it is needed to determine which. The analysis is carried out by assigning to the application a 'Z' score, computed as

$$Z_i = b_0 + bx_i. \tag{1.1}$$

Given a sample of previous observations on y_i and x_i, the vector weights, $b = (b_0, b_1)$, can be obtained as a multiple of the vector regression coefficients in the linear regression of $d_i = P_0 \, y_i - P_1 \, (1 - y_i)$ on a constant and the set of attributes, where P_1 is the proportion of 1 in the sample and $P_0 = 1 - P_1$. The scale factor is $(n-2)/e'e$ from the linear regression.[2] The individual is classified in group 1 if their 'Z' score is greater than Z (usually 0) and 0 otherwise.[3] The linearity (and simplicity) of the computation is a compelling virtue.

The assumption of multivariate normality is often held up as the most serious shortcoming of this technique.[4] This seems exaggerated. Techniques which rely on normality are often surprisingly robust to violations of the assumption, recent discussion notwithstanding.[5] The superiority of the discrete choice techniques discussed in the next section, which are arguably more appropriate for this exercise, is typically fairly modest.[6] Since the left-hand-side variable in the aforementioned linear regression is a linear function of y_i, $d_i = y_i - P_1$, the *calculated*[7] discriminant function can be

---

[2] See Maddala (1983, pp. 18–25).

[3] We forego full details on the technique since we shall not be applying it to our data nor will we be comparing it to the other methods to be described.

[4] See Press and Wilson (1978), for example.   [5] See Greene (1993), Goldberger (1983), and Manski (1989).

[6] See, for example, Press and Wilson (1978).

[7] We emphasize 'calculated' because there is no underlying counterpart to the probability model in the discriminant function.

construed as nothing more (or less) than a linear probability model.[8] As such, the comparison between discriminant analysis and, say, the probit model could be reduced to one between the linear probability model and the probit or logit model.[9] Thus, it is no surprise that the differences between them are not great, as has been observed elsewhere.[10]

Its long track record notwithstanding, one could argue that the under-pinning of discriminant analysis is naïve. The technique divides the universe of loan applicants into two types, those who *will* default and those who *will not*. The crux of the analysis is that at the time of application, the individual is as if preordained to be a defaulter or a nondefaulter. In point of fact, the same individual might be in either group at any time, depending on a host of attendant circumstances and random elements in their own behaviour. Thus, prediction of default is not a problem of classification the same way as is, say, determining the sex of prehistoric individuals from a fossilized record.

Discrete-choice models

Index-function-based models of discrete choice, such as the probit and logit models, assume that for any individual, given a set of attributes, there is a definable probability that they will actually default on a loan. This inter-pretation places all individuals in a single population. The observed outcome, default/no default, arises from the characteristics and random behaviour of the individuals. Ex ante, all that can be produced by the model is a prob-ability. The observation of y_i ex post is the outcome of a single Bernoulli trial.

This alternative formulation does not assume that individual attributes x_i are necessarily normally distributed. The probability of default arises con-ditionally on these attributes and is a function of the inherent randomness of events and human behaviour and the unmeasured and unmeasurable determinants which are not specifically included in the model.[11] The core of this formulation is an index function model with a latent regression,

$$D = \beta' x_i + \varepsilon_i. \tag{1.2}$$

The dependent variable might be identified with the 'propensity to default'. In the present context, an intuitively appealing interpretation of D^* is as a quantitative measure of 'how much trouble the individual is in'.

---

[8] For a detailed and very readable discussion, see Dhrymes (1974, pp. 67–77).

[9] See Press and Wilson (1978) for discussion.

[10] See Aldrich and Nelson (1984) or Amemiya (1985), for example.

[11] Our discussion of this modelling framework will also be brief. Greater detail may be found in Greene (1993, Chapter 21).

Conditioning variables x_i might include income, credit history, the ratio of credit card burden to current income, and so on. If D is sufficiently large relative to the attributes, that is, if the individual is in trouble enough, they default. Formally,

$$D_i^* = \beta' x_i + \varepsilon_i \tag{1.3}$$

so the probability of interest is

$$P_i = \text{Prob}[D_i = 1|X_i]. \tag{1.4}$$

Assuming that ε is normally distributed with mean 0 and variance 1, we obtain the default probability

$$\begin{aligned} \text{Prob}[D_i = 1|x_i] &= \text{Prob}[D > 0|x_i] \\ &= \text{Prob}[\varepsilon_i \leq \beta' x_i | x_i] \\ &= \Phi(\beta' x_i), \end{aligned} \tag{1.5}$$

where $\Phi(\cdot)$ is the standard normal CDF.[12] The classification rule is

$$\text{Predict } D_i = 1 \text{ if } \Phi(\beta' x_i) > P^*, \tag{1.6}$$

where P^* is a threshold value chosen by the analyst. The value 0.5 is usually used for P^* under the reasoning that we should predict default if the model predicts that it is more likely than not. For our purposes, this turns out to be an especially poor predictor. Indeed, in applications such as this one, with unbalanced data sets (that is, with a small proportion of ones or zeros for the dependent variable) this familiar rule may fail to perform as well as the naïve rule 'always (or never) predict $D=1$'.[13] We will return to the issue in detail below, since it is crucial in our analysis. The vector of marginal effects in the model is

$$\theta = \frac{\partial \text{Prob}[D_i = 1|x_i]}{\partial x_i} = \varphi(\beta' x_i)\beta, \tag{1.7}$$

where $\varphi(\cdot)$ is the standard normal density.[14] If the discriminant score function can be viewed as a 'model' (rather than as merely the solution to an optimization problem), the coefficients would be the counterparts. The usefulness of this is in determining which particular factors would contribute most to a rejection of a credit application. An example is given in Section 1.5.

---

[12] One might question the normality assumption. But, the logistic and alternative distributions rarely bring any differences in the predictions of the model. For our data, these two models produced virtually identical results at the first stage. However, only the probit form is tractable in the integrated model.

[13] For discussion, see Amemiya (1985).

[14] While the coefficients in logit and probit models often differ markedly, estimates of θ in the two models tend to be similar, indeed often nearly identical. See Greene (1993) and Davidson and Mackinnon (1993, Chapter 15.)

Censoring in the default data

Regardless of how the default model is formulated, in practice it must be constructed using data on loan recipients. But the model is to be applied to a broader population, some (possibly even most) of whom are applicants who will ultimately be rejected. The underlying logic of the credit-scoring problem is to ascertain how much an applicant resembles individuals who have defaulted in the past. The problem with this approach is that mere resemblance to past defaulters may give a misleading indication of the individual default probability for an individual who has not already been screened.

The model is to be used to assign a default probability to a random individual who *applies* for a loan, but the only information that exists about default probabilities comes from previous loan *recipients*. The relevant question for this analysis is whether, in the population at large, Prob $[D=1 \mid x]$ equals Prob $[D=1 \mid x$ and $C=1]$ in the subpopulation, where '$C=1$' denotes having received the loan, or, in our case, 'card recipient'. Since loan recipients have passed a prior screen based, one would assume, on an assessment of default probability, Prob $[D=1 \mid x]$ must exceed $[D=1 \mid x, C=1]$ for the same x. For a given set of attributes, x, individuals in the group with $C=1$ are, by nature of the prior selection, less likely to default than otherwise similar individuals chosen randomly from a population that is a mixture of individuals who have $C=0$ and $C=1$. Thus, the unconditional model will give a downward-biased estimate of the default probability for an individual selected at random from the full population. This describes a form of censoring. To be applicable to the population at large, the estimated default model should condition specifically on cardholder status.

We will use a bivariate probit specification to model this. The structural equations are

Default equation

$$D = \beta' x_i + \varepsilon_i$$
$$D_i = 1 \text{ if and only if } D > 0, \text{ and } 0 \text{ else.}$$

(1.8)

Cardholder equation

$$C = \Upsilon' v_i + w_i$$
$$C_i = 1 \text{ if and only if } C > 0, \text{ and } 0 \text{ else.}$$

(1.9)

Sampling rule

D_i and x_i are only observed if $C_i = 1$

C_i and V_i are observed for all applicants.

(1.10)

Selectivity

$$[\varepsilon_i, w_i] \quad N_2[0, 0, 1, 1, \rho_{ew}]. \tag{1.11}$$

The vector of attributes, v_i, are the factors used in the approval decision. The probability of interest is the probability of default given that a loan application is accepted, which is

$$\text{Prob}[D_i = 1 | C_i = 1] = \frac{\Phi_2[\beta' x_i, \Upsilon' v_i, \rho]}{\Phi[\Upsilon' v_i]} \tag{1.12}$$

where Φ_2 is the bivariate normal cumulative probability. If ρ equals 0, the selection is of no consequence, and the unconditional model described earlier is appropriate.

The counterparts to the marginal effects noted earlier are

$$\frac{\partial \Phi_2(\beta' x_i, \Upsilon_i, \rho)/\Phi(\Upsilon' v_i)}{\partial x_i} = \theta | C_i = 1. \tag{1.13}$$

The detailed expression for this derivative is given in Section 5. This model was developed by Wynand and van Praag (1981) and recently applied to an analysis of consumer loans by Boyes et al. (1989).[15]

1.3. A model for evaluating an application

Expenditure of a credit card recipient might be described by a linear regression model

$$S_i = \alpha' z_i + u_i. \tag{1.14}$$

Expenditure data are drawn *conditionally* on $c_i = 1$. Thus, with the cardholder data, we are able to estimate only

$$E[S_i \mid z_i, C_i = 1] = \alpha' z_i + E[u_i \mid C_i = 1, z_i]. \tag{1.15}$$

This may or may not differ systematically from

$$E[S_i | z_i] = \alpha' z_i. \tag{1.16}$$

---

[15] Boyes et al. treated the joint determination of cardholder status and default as a model of partial observability. Since cardholder status is generated by the credit scorer while the default indicator is generated later by the cardholder the observations are sequential, not simultaneous. As such, the model of Abowd and Farber (1982) might apply. But, the simpler censoring interpretation seems more appropriate. It turns out that the difference is only one of interpretation. The log-likelihood functions for Boyes et al.'s model (see their p. 6) and ours (see (1.26)) are the same.

The statistical question is whether the sample selection into cardholder status is significantly related to the expenditure level of the individuals sampled. The equations of the sample selection model (see Heckman 1979) user here are

Expenditure

$$S_i = \alpha' z_i + u_i. \tag{1.17}$$

Cardholder status

$$C = \Upsilon' v_i + w_i$$
$$C_i = 1 \text{ if and only if } C > 0, \text{ and } 0 \text{ otherwise.} \tag{1.18}$$

Sample selectivity

$$[u_i, w_i] N_2 [0, 0, \sigma, 1, \rho_{uw} \sigma_u]. \tag{1.19}$$

Selectivity corrected regression

$$
\begin{aligned}
E[S_i \mid C_i = 1] &= \alpha' z_i + E[u_i \mid C_i = 1] \\
&= \alpha' z_i + (-\rho_{uw} \sigma_u) \lambda_i \\
&= \alpha' z_i + \alpha_\lambda \lambda_i,
\end{aligned}
\tag{1.20}
$$

where

$$\lambda_i = \varphi(\Upsilon' v_i) / \Phi(\Upsilon' v_i).$$

Estimation techniques are discussed in Section 5.

Finally, it seems likely that even controlling for other factors, the probability of default is related to expenditures. The extension to (1.12) that we will examine is

$$\text{Prob}[D_i = 1 | C_i = 1, x_i, S_i] = \frac{-\Phi_2 [\beta' x_i + \delta S_1, \Upsilon' v_i, \rho]}{\Phi(\Upsilon' v_i)} \tag{1.21}$$

where

$$S_i = E[S_i | C_i = 1].$$

Expenditure, like the default probability, is only an intermediate step. Ultimately, the expected profitability of a decision to accept a loan application is a function of the default probability, the expected expenditure and the costs associated with administering the loan. Let

$$P_D = \text{Prob}[D_i = 1 | C_i = 1].$$

Then

$$E\big[\Pi(x_i, v_i, z_i) \mid C_i = 1\big] = E[S_i \mid C_i = 1]m \qquad \text{(merchant fee)}$$
$$+ E[S_i \mid C_i = 1](1 - P_D)(f - t) \quad \text{(finance change} - \text{T bill rate)}$$
$$- E[S_i \mid C_i = 1]P_D[1 - r(1 + q)] \quad \text{(losses from default)}$$
$$+ \text{fixed fees paid by cardholder}$$
$$- \text{overhead expenses for the account.}$$

The merchant fee, m, is collected whether or not the consumer defaults on their loan. This term would also include any float which is accrued before the merchant is reimbursed. The second term gives the finance charges from the consumer, which are received only if default does not occur. The third term includes the direct loss of the defaulted loan minus any ultimate recovery. The term denoted 'r' is the recovery rate and 'q' is the penalty assessed on recovered funds.

This is a simple model which involves spending, costs and the default probability. Obviously, there are elements missing. Finance charges paid by the cardholder are the most complicated element. Specific treatment would require a subsidiary model of timing of repayment and how the consumer would manage a revolving charge account.[16] For the present, we assume that the finance charge component, if any, is simply included in the term 'f' in (1.22). Variations of this value could be used to model different repayment schedules. The model estimated later is for a monthly expenditure, so the applicable figure could range from 0 to 1.5 per cent depending on what is assumed about the repayment schedule. The figure is then net of the opportunity cost of the funds, based, for example, on the return on a treasury bill. Admittedly, the model is crude. It is important to emphasize that the preceding model applies to purchases, not to revolving loans. That is, the consumer might well make their purchases, then take years to repay the loan, each month making a minimum repayment. The preceding model is much simpler than that; it is a single period model which assumes that all transactions occur, either full repayment or default, within the one year period of observation. Nonetheless, even in this simple formulation, a clear pattern emerges. Based on observed data and the description of the cost structure, consideration of the censoring problem and use of an integrated

---

[16] Of course, if the finance charges, themselves, were influential in the default rate, this would have also have to be considered. This seems unlikely, but either way, this complication is beyond the scope of this study. Our data contain no information about finance charges incurred or paid. We have only the expenditure levels and the default indicator.

model produces a prescription for considerably higher acceptance rates for loan applicants than are seen in our observed data.

1.4. Data used in the application

The models described earlier were estimated for a well known credit card company. The data set used in estimation consisted of 13,444 observations on credit card applications received in a single month in 1988. The observation for an individual consists of the application data, data from a credit reporting agency, market descriptive data for the five-digit zip code in which the individual resides, and, for those applications that were accepted, a twelve-month history of expenditures and a default indicator for the twelve-month period following initial acceptance of the application. Default is defined as having skipped payment for six months. A full summary of the data appears in Tables 1.1 and 1.2.

The choice-based sampling problem

The incidence of default amongst our sample of cardholders mimics reasonably closely the incidence of default among cardholders in the population. But, the proportion of cardholders in the sample is, by design, considerably larger than the population of applications that are accepted. That is, the rejection rate for applications in the population is much higher than our sample suggests. The sampling is said to be 'choice based' if the proportional representation of certain outcomes of the dependent variable in the model is deliberately different from the proportional representation of those outcomes in the population from which the sample is drawn. In our sample, 10,499 of 13,444 observations are cardholders, a proportion of 0.78094. But, in the population, the proportion of card applications which are accepted is closer to 23.2%. In view of the fact that we are using 'Cardholder' as a selection rule for the default equation, the sample is 'choice-based'. This is a type of non-random sampling that has been widely documented in other contexts, and has been modelled in a counterpart to the study by Boyes *et al.* (1989).

Choice-based sampling induces a bias in the estimation of discrete choice models. As has been shown by Manski and Lerman (1977) possible to mitigate the induced bias if one knows the true proportions that should apply in the sampling. These are listed in Table 1.3.

Table 1.1 Variables used in analysis of credit card default

Indicators

CARDHLDR	=	1 for cardholders, 0 for denied applicants.
DEFAULT	=	1 for defaulted on payment, 0 if not.

Expenditure

EXP1, EXP2, EXP3, ..., EXP12 = monthly expenditure in most recent 12 months.

Demographic and Socioeconomic, from Application

AGE	= age in years and twelfths of a year.
DEPNDNTs	= dependents, missing data converted to 1.
OWNRENT	= indicators = 1 if own home, 0 if rent.
MNTHPRVAD	= months at previous address.
PREVIOUS	= 1 if previous card holder.
ADDLINC	= additional income, missing data coded as 0.
INCOME	= primary income.
SELFEMPL	= 1 if self employed, 0 if otherwise.
PROF	= 1 if professional (airline, entertainer, other, sales, tech).
UNEMP	= 1 for unemployed, alimony, disabled, or other.
MGT	= 1 for management services and other management.
MILITARY	= 1 for non-commissioned and other.
CLERICAL	= 1 for clerical staff.
SALES	= 1 for sales staff.
OTHERJOB	= 1 for all other categories including teachers, railroad, retired, repair workers, students, engineers, dress makers, food handlers, etc.

Constructed Variables

INCOME	= income + aadlinc.
AVGEXP	= $(1/12)\Sigma_i \; EXPi$
INCPER	= income per family member = (income + additional income)/(1 + dependents).
EXP_INC	= average expenditure for 12 months/average month.

Miscellaneous Application Data

MTHCURAD	= months at current address.
CRDBRINQ	= number of credit bureau inquiries.
CREDMAJR	= 1 if first credit card indicated on application is a major credit card.
CREDDEPT	= 1 if first credit card indicated is a department store card.
CREDGAS	= 1 if first credit card indicated is a gasoline company.
CURTRADE	= number of current trade item accounts (existing charge accounts).
MTHEMPLOY	= months employed.

Types of Bank Accounts

BANKSAV	= 1 if only savings account, 0 otherwise.
BANKCH	= 1 if only checking account, 0 else.
BANKBOTH	= 1 if both savings and checking, 0 else.

Derogatories and Other Credit Data

MAJORDRG	= count of major derogatory reports (long delinquencies) from credit bureau.
MINORDRG	= count of minor derogatories from credit bureau.
TRADACCT	= number of open, active trade lines.

Table 1.1 (cont.)

Credit Bureau Data

CREDOPEN	= number of open and current trade accounts.
CREDACTV	= number of active trades lines.
CREDDEL30	= number of trade lines 30 days past due at the time of the report.
CRED30DLNQ	= number of 30 day delinquencies within 12 months.
AVGRVBAL	= dollar amount of average revolving balance.
AVBALINC	= average revolving balance divided by average monthly income.

Market Data

BUYPOWER	= buying power index.
PCTCOLL	= percent college graduates in 5 digit zip code.
MEDAGE	= median age in 5 digit zip code.
MEDINC	= median income in 5 digit zip code.
PCTOWN	= percent who own their own home.
PCTBLACK	= percent black.
PCTSPAN	= percent Spanish.
GROWTH	= population growth rate.
PCTEMPL	= 1987 employment percent.

Commerce Within 5 Digit Zip Code

APPAREL	= apparel store precent of retail sales in 5 digit zip code of residence.
AUTO	= auto dealer stores, percent.
BUILDMTL	= building material stores, percent.
DEPTSTOR	= department stores, percent.
DRUGSTOR	= drug stores, percent.
EATDRINK	= eating and drinking establishments, percent.
FURN	= furniture stores, percent.
GAS	= gas stations, percent.

The 'Weighted Endogenous Sampling MLE' (WESML) estimator is obtained by maximizing where the subscript 'i' indicates the ith individual. There are J possible outcomes, indexed by 'j', the indicator I_{ij} equals 1 if outcome or choice j is occurs for or is chosen by individual i, P_{ij} is the theoretical probability that individual i makes choice J, Ω_j is the sampling weight,

$$\Omega_j = W_j \,/\, w_j \tag{1.23}$$

and

W_j = the 'true' or population proportion of occurrences of outcome j

w_j = the sample counterpart to W_j. $\tag{1.24}$

(See Table 1.3.) Note that, in our application, this would give smaller weight to cardholders in the sample and larger weight to rejects than would the unweighted log-likelihood.

Table 1.2 Descriptive statistics for variables

Variable	Mean	Std. Dev.	Minimum	Maximum	Cases
CARDHLDR	.78094	.41362	0.0	1.000	13444
DEFAULT	.094866	.29304	0.0	1.000	10499
DB1	268.20	542.39	0.0	24650	10499
DB2	252.60	537.20	0.0	24030	10499
DB3	238.89	460.30	0.0	7965	10499
DB4	247.32	507.61	0.0	14240	10499
DB5	253.24	504.53	0.0	17870	10499
DB6	266.46	509.99	0.0	10310	10499
DB7	256.41	500.52	0.0	9772	10499
DB8	248.62	494.10	0.0	9390	10499
DB9	245.06	472.36	0.0	8377	10499
DB10	228.60	441.28	0.0	6926	10499
DB11	273.66	520.60	0.0	16820	10499
DB12	233.26	458.15	0.0	18970	10499
ADDLINC*	.41262	.91279	0.0	10.000	13444
BANKSAV	.033695	.18045	0.0	1.000	13444
BANKCH	.29753	.45719	0.0	1.000	13444
BANKBOTH	.66877	.47067	0.0	1.000	13444
AGE	33.472	10.226	0.0	88.67	13444
MTHCURAD	55.319	63.090	0.0	576.0	13444
CRDBRINQ	1.4080	2.2891	0.0	56.00	13444
CREDMAJR	.81308	.38986	0.0	1.000	13444
DEPNDNTS	1.0173	1.2791	0.0	9.000	13444
MTHMPLOY	60.648	72.240	0.0	600.0	13444
PROF	.11537	.31948	0.0	1.000	13444
UNEMP	.00052068	.022813	0.0	1.000	13444
MGT	.074308	.26228	0.0	1.000	13444
MILITARY	.022464	.14819	0.0	1.000	13444
CLERICAL	.088143	.28351	0.0	1.000	13444
SALES	.078325	.26869	0.0	1.000	13444
OTHERJOB	.62087	.48519	0.0	1.000	13444
MAJORDRG	.46281	1.4327	0.0	22.00	13444
MINORDRG	.29054	.76762	0.0	11.00	13444
OWNRENT	.45597	.49808	0.0	1.000	13444
MTHPRVAD	81.285	80.359	0.0	600.0	13444
PREVIOUS	.073341	.26071	0.0	1.000	13444
INCOME*	3.4241	1.7775	0.1300	20.000	13444
SELFEMPL	.057944	.23365	0.0	1.000	13444
TRADACCT	6.4220	6.1069	0.0	50.00	13444
INCPER*	2.1720	1.3591	0.03625	15.00	13444
EXP_INC	.070974	.10392	0.00009	2.038	13444
CREDOPEN	6.0552	5.2405	0.0	43.00	13444

Table 1.2 (cont.)

Variable	Mean	Std. Dev.	Minimum	Maximum	Cases
CREDACTV	2.2722	2.6137	0.0	27.00	13444
CRDDEL30	.055564	.26153	0.0	3.000	13444
CR30DLNQ	.36581	1.2494	0.0	21.00	13444
AVGRVBAL	5.2805	7.5904	0.0	190.0	13444
AVBALINC	46.570	42.728	0.0	2523	13444
BUYPOWER	.013963	.0090948	0.0	.1134	13444
PCTCOLL	10.729	8.5104	0.0	54.90	13444
MEDAGE	33.181	5.4232	0.0	65.00	13444
MEDINC*	2.8351	1.0437	0.0	7.500	13444
PCTOWN	53.983	28.549	0.0	100.0	13444
PCTBLACK	11.777	20.557	0.0	100.0	13444
PCTSPAN	7.7817	13.186	0.0	96.60	13444
GROWTH**	.0022462	.001877	− 0.06172	.7068	13444
PCTEMPL	40.993	108.01	0.0	5126	13444
APPAREL	2.4398	2.4312	0.0	33.30	13444
AUTO	1.4972	1.3235	0.0	33.30	13444
BUILDMTL	1.1293	1.2335	0.0	33.30	13444
DEPTSTOR	.15870	.25209	0.0	12.50	13444
EATDRINK	6.6657	3.9570	0.0	100.0	13444
FURN	1.8646	2.5164	0.0	100.0	13444
GAS	1.7654	1.7958	0.0	100.0	13444

*Income, Addlinc, Incper, and Medinc are in $10,000 units and are censored at 10.
**Population growth is growth/population.

Table 1.3 Sampling weights for choice-based sampling

Event	w = sample	W = Population	$\Omega = W/w$
D = 1, C = 1	996/13444	.232 × .103	.32255
D = 0, C = 1	9503/13444	.232 × .897	.29441
C = 0	2945/13444	.768	3.50594

After estimation, an adjustment must be made to the estimated asymptotic covariance matrix of the estimates in order to account for the weighting. The appropriate asymptotic covariance matrix is

$$V = H^{-1}BH^{-1},$$ (1.25)

where B is the Berndt *et al.* (1974) estimator and H is the inverse of the estimated expected Hessian of the log-likelihood. Both matrices in the expression are computed using the sampling weights given above.

1.5. Empirical results

Cardholder status

Table 1.4 presents univariate probit estimates of the cardholder equation both with and without the correction for choice-based sampling. We also show the results of applying the familiar prediction rule. The effect of the reweighting is quite clear in these tables. As might be expected, with the choice-based sampling correction, the predictions are more in line with the population proportions than with the distorted sample.

The cardholder equation is largely consistent with expectations. The most significant explanatory variables are the number of major derogatory reports and credit bureau inquiries (negative) and the number of open trade accounts (positive). What Table 1.7 reveals most clearly is the credit scoring vendor's very heavy reliance upon credit reporting agencies such as TRW. There is one surprising result. Conventional wisdom in this setting is that the own/rent indicator for home ownership is the single most powerful predictor of whether an applicant will be given a credit card. We find no evidence of this in these data. Rather, as one might expect, what explains acceptance best is a higher income, fewer dependents, and a 'clean' credit file with numerous accounts at the reporting agency. Surprisingly, being employed longer at one's current job appears not to increase the probability of approval, though being self-employed appears significantly to decrease it. We should note that the market descriptive data are interesting for revealing patterns in the default data. But, because they do not relate specifically to the individual, they could not be used in a commercial credit scoring model.

Expenditure

The expenditure equation is estimated using Heckman's sample selection correction and adjustment for the estimated standard errors of the coefficients. The selection mechanism is the univariate probit model for cardholder status. The equations of the model are given in (1.17) – (1.20). Details on the estimation method may be found in Heckman (1979) and Greene (1981, 1993). Parameter estimates and estimated asymptotic standard errors are given in Table 1.5. Note that the dependent variable in this equation is

Table 1.4 Weighted and unweighted probit cardholder equations

Variable	Choice based sampling		Unweighted	
	Coefficient	t-ratio	Coefficient	t-ratio
ONE	− 1.1175	− 9.090	0.1070	1.390
AGE	− 0.0021	− 0.806	− 0.0012	− 0.672
MTHCURAD	0.0010	2.547	0.0011	3.943
DEPNDNTS	− 0.0947	− 2.623	− 0.0957	− 4.079
MTHMPLOY	− 0.0002	− 0.410	− 0.0002	− 0.694
MAJORDRG	− 0.7514	− 13.922	− 0.7796	− 34.777
MINORDRG	− 0.0609	− 1.554	− 0.0471	− 2.005
OWNRENT	0.0514	0.947	− 0.0042	− 0.119
MTHPRVAD	0.0002	0.626	0.0001	0.767
PREVIOUS	0.1781	1.843	0.2089	2.967
INCOME	0.1153	4.353	0.1362	7.001
SELFEMPL	− 0.3652	− 3.711	− 0.3634	− 5.804
TRADACCT	0.0995	19.447	0.1099	25.573
INCPER	− 0.0167	− 0.476	− 0.0007	− 0.027
CREDOPEN	− 0.0276	− 3.550	− 0.0227	− 4.194
CREDACTV	0.0443	2.825	0.0341	3.074
CRDEL30	− 0.2720	− 2.658	− 0.2740	− 4.776
CR30DLNQ	− 0.0947	− 3.773	− 0.0891	− 6.732
AVGRVBAL	0.0095	2.949	0.0094	3.560
AVBALINC	− 0.0019	− 1.616	− 0.0010	− 2.573
BANKSAV	− 0.5018	− 4.012	− 0.5233	− 7.305
BANKBOTH	0.4630	9.579	0.4751	14.692
CRDBRINQ	− 0.1559	− 13.907	− 0.1719	− 23.469
CREDMAJR	0.3033	5.407	0.3092	8.652

Predicted Actual	0	1	TOTAL	Predicted Actual	0	1	TOTAL
0	.208	.011	**2945**	0	.110	.109	**2945**
1	.420	.361	**10499**	1	.020	.761	**10499**
TOTAL	**8448**	**4996**	**13444**	**TOTAL**	**1748**	**11696**	**13444**

average monthly expenditure, computed as the simple average of the twelve months beginning when the credit card was issued.

As might be expected, INCOME is the single most significant explanatory variable in the expenditure equation. The market variables which appear to be very significant are puzzling. Three, PCTOWN, PCTBLACK and PCTSPAN, given their relationship to average income, would seem to have the wrong sign.

Table 1.5 Estimated expenditure equation

Dependent Variable	= AVGEXP in $ per month
Observations	= 10499
Means of LHS	= 251.03
StdDev of residuals	= 315.60
Corrected Std. error	= 319.68
(This is a consistent estimate of σ_u)	
R-squared	= 0.0977
Adjusted R-squared	= 0.0952
Correlation of disturbance in regression and selection equation = − 0.204	

Variable	Coefficient	Std. Error	t-ratio
Constant	− 44.249	160.270	− 0.276
AGE	− 1.487	0.34655	− 4.291
DEPNDNTS	− 2.0829	2.79774	− 0.744
OWNRENT	− 1.9733	7.71648	− 0.256
INCOME	55.0379	2.05561	26.774
SELFEMPL	− 33.4684	14.3173	− 2.338
TRADACCT	1.5301	0.63709	2.402
PROF	71.8808	157.985	0.455
MGT	60.3144	158.096	0.382
MILITARY	9.0472	159.241	0.057
CLERICAL	25.8032	158.121	0.163
SALES	112.145	158.118	0.709
OTHERJOB	53.4139	157.770	0.339
BUYPOWER	375.513	380.930	0.986
PCTCOLL	1.7967	0.46231	3.886
MEDAGE	− 0.0889	0.61771	− 0.144
MEDINC	14.3057	3.95810	3.614
PCTOWN	− 0.5333	0.13336	− 3.999
PCTBLACK	0.5094	0.17949	2.838
PCTSPAN	0.6271	0.25991	2.413
GROWTH	0.00564	0.015846	0.356
PCTEMPL	− 0.01769	0.033207	− 0.533
APPAREL	0.78475	1.49578	0.525
AUTO	− 4.89992	2.56277	1.912
BUILDMTL	1.48865	2.63996	0.564
DEPTSTOR	− 6.61155	13.9866	− 0.473
EATDRINK	− 1.24421	0.82499	− 1.508
FURN	0.97996	1.15843	0.846
GAS	− 1.77288	1.99177	− 0.890
LAMBDA	65.4875	8.52960	7.678

Table 1.6 Average predicted expenditures

All Observations	$ 263.29
Cardholders	$ 251.03
Noncardholders	$ 307.03

But, since MEDINC is already in the equation, as well as the individual income, one must conclude that these variables are picking up some other effect.

The last variable in the equation is the selectivity correction described earlier. Its large t-statistic suggests that the sample selection correction is, indeed, warranted. The coefficient on LAMBDA estimates $-\rho_{uw}\sigma_u$. An estimate of σ_u is given at the top of the results, 319.68, so the implied estimate of ρ_{uw} is -0.204. The negative value is surprising given the criteria that are probably used to determine cardholder status. But, since INCOME, OWNRENT, etc., are already in the equation, it is unclear just what sign should have been expected.

Table 1.6 displays the average predicted expenditures for three groups of observations. The predicted expenditure is substantially higher for those whose applications were denied.

Default probability

Table 1.7 gives the probit estimates of the default equation. Predicted expenditure, FITEXP, is computed using (1.20). The 'selection' variable, λ_i, is computed using the leftmost coefficients in Table 1.4. The coefficients used in computing the linear function in (1.20) are given in Table 1.5. The single-equation unconditional model is given in the first three columns. The results agree with our conjecture that default rates might be related to expenditures, and the idea of cardholders 'getting in over their heads' comes to mind. Table 1.8 presents the full-information conditional estimates of the default equation based on (1.8) – (1.11) and (1.23) – (1.25) with the re-estimated cardholder equation. Estimates of the cardholder equation are given in Table 1.8.

Maximum likelihood estimates for the conditional model are obtained by maximizing[17]

---

[17] This is the same log-likelihood as maximized by Boyes *et al.* (1989). The second term in their formulation would be $\log[\Phi(d) - \Phi_2(d, c, \rho)]$, but this equals $\log[\Phi_2(-d, c, -\rho)]$, so the two are the same.

Table 1.7 Default model

Variable	Unconditional			Conditional			Partial
	Coeff.	Std.Err.	t-ratio	Coeff.	Std.Err.	t-ratio	
Basic Default Specification							
Constant	−1.1350	0.0984	−11.533	−1.3752	0.3945	−3.486	
AGE	−.0031	0.0023	−1.342	−0.0054	0.0094	−0.582	−.0018
MTHCURAD	0.0003	0.0003	1.069	0.0002	0.0013	0.153	−.0001
DEPNDNTS	0.0445	0.0294	1.512	−0.0217	0.1114	−0.195	.0073
MTHMPLOY	0.0007	0.0003	2.331	0.0007	0.0013	0.566	.0002
MAJORDRG	0.0592	0.0408	1.448	−0.2969	0.1985	−1.495	.0033
MINORDRG	0.0764	0.0296	2.586	0.1780	0.0993	1.793	.0488
OWNRENT	−0.0010	0.4312	−0.023	0.0908	0.1706	0.533	.0236
MTHPRVAD	0.0004	0.0002	1.817	0.0002	0.0009	0.274	.00002
PREVIOUS	−0.1507	0.0792	−1.902	−0.1112	0.3103	−0.358	−.0434
INCOME	−0.0168	0.0033	−5.608	−0.0072	0.0151	−0.476	.0062
SELFEMPL	0.0788	0.0850	0.927	−0.1969	0.3565	−0.552	−.0177
TRADACCT	0.0004	0.0044	0.109	0.0207	0.0205	1.009	−.0028
INCPER	−0.0228	0.0323	−0.706	−0.0545	0.1058	−0.515	−.0094
EXP_INC	−0.4761	0.1717	−2.774	−0.5790	0.5033	−1.150	−.1614
Credit Bureau							
CREDOPEN	0.0138	0.0063	2.195	0.0199	0.0199	0.0272	.0066
CREDACTV	−0.1218	0.0126	−9.657	−0.1500	−0.1500	0.0557	−.0424
CRDDEL30	0.2841	0.712	3.991	0.2829	0.2829	0.2766	.1120
CR30DLNQ	0.0806	0.0177	4.559	0.0446	0.0446	0.0757	.0225
AVGRVBAL	0.0011	0.0024	0.439	0.0156	0.0156	0.0123	.0038
AVBALINC	0.0039	0.00042	9.192	0.0008	0.0008	0.0021	.0004
Expenditure							
FITEXP	0.0014	0.0044	3.103	0.00064	0.0019	0.336	

Table 1.8 Estimated cardholder equation joint with default equation

	Coeff.	Std Error	t-ratio
Basic Cardholder Specification			
Constant	− 1.2734	0.1563	− 8.150
AGE	− 0.00002	0.0039	− 0.006
MTHCURAD	0.0015	0.0006	2.465
DEPNDNTS	− .1314	0.0487	− 2.700
MTHMPLOY	0.0003	0.0006	0.491
MAJORDRG	− 0.8230	0.0442	− 18.634
MINORDRG	0.0082	0.0462	0.178
OWNRENT	0.0129	0.0765	0.168
MTHPRVAD	0.0003	0.0004	0.698
PREVIOUS	0.1185	0.1283	0.924
INCOME	0.0156	0.0040	3.867
SELFEMPL	− 0.5651	0.1307	− 4.325
TRADACCT	− 0.0850	0.0064	13.352
INCPER	− 0.0550	0.0513	− 1.073
Credit Bureau			
CREDOPEN	− 0.0096	0.0109	− 0.876
CREDACTV	0.0060	0.0223	0.270
CRDDEL30	− 0.3167	0.1197	− 2.647
CR30DLNQ	− 0.0965	0.0317	− 3.048
AVGRBAL	0.0049	0.0050	0.974
AVBALINC	− .00014	0.0008	− 1.906
Credit Reference			
BANKSAV	− 0.4708	0.1731	− 2.719
BANKBOTH	0.5074	0.0694	7.310
CRDBRINQ	− 0.1473	0.0176	− 8.393
CREDMAJR	0.3663	0.0807	4.541
Correlation Between Disturbances			
ρ_{we}	0.4478	0.2580	1.736

$$
\begin{aligned}
\log{-}L &= \sum_{C=0} \Omega_i \log(\operatorname{Prob}[C_i = 0] + \sum_{C=1,D=0} \Omega \log(\operatorname{Prob}[D_i = 0 | C_i = 1]\operatorname{Prob}[C_i = 1]) \\
&\quad + \sum_{C=1,D=1} \Omega \log(\operatorname{Prob}[D_i = 1 | C_i = 1]\operatorname{Prob}[C_i = 1]) \\
&= \sum_{C=0} \Omega_i \log(1 - \Phi(\gamma' v_i)) + \sum_{C=1,D=0} \Omega_i \log \Phi_2[-(\beta' x_i + \delta \bar{S}_i), \Upsilon' v_i, -\rho] \\
&\quad + \sum_{C=1,D=1} \Omega_i \log \Phi_2(\beta' x_i + \delta \bar{S}_i, \Upsilon' v_i, \rho).
\end{aligned}
$$

Optimization and construction of the asymptotic covariance for the estimates can be based on the following results. Let $\Phi_2(d, c, \rho)$, and $\varphi_2(d, c, \rho)$ denote the cdf and density, respectively, of the bivariate normal distribution, then

$$\partial\Phi_2/\partial c = \varphi(c)\Phi\left[(d - \rho c)/(1 - \rho^2)^{1/2}\right] = g_c,$$
$$\partial\Phi_2/\partial\rho = \varphi_2,$$
$$\partial^2\Phi_2/\partial c^2 = -cg_c - \rho\varphi_2 - g/\Phi_2,$$
$$\partial^2\Phi_2/\partial c\partial d = \varphi_2 - g_c g_d/\Phi_2,$$
$$\partial^2\Phi_2/\partial c\partial\rho = \varphi_2\left(\left[\rho/(1 - \rho^2)^{1/2}\right](d - \rho c) - c - g_c/\Phi_2\right),$$
$$\partial^2\Phi_2/\partial\rho^2 = \varphi_2\{[\rho/(1 - \rho^2)](1 - (c^2 + d^2 - 2\rho cd)/(1 - \rho^2)) + \rho cd - \varphi_2/\Phi_2\}.$$

(1.26)

Terms that are symmetric in c and d are omitted.

Partial effects in the single equation model are obtained by multiplying the coefficients by $\partial\Phi(d)/\partial d = \varphi(d)$, which gives roughly 0.13 for these data. By this calculation, the most important behavioural variables in the equation appear to be MAJORDRG (0.0077), MINORDRG (0.0099), CRDDEL30C (0.0369), and CR30DLNQ (0.0104). These are counts, so the marginal effects are obtained directly. Note, in particular, the number of trade lines past due at the time of the application. An increase of one in this variable alone would be sufficient to raise the estimated default probability from an acceptable level (say 0.095) to well beyond the threshold (roughly 0.11). CPTF30, the number of 30 day delinquencies, is similarly influential. The marginal effects in the conditional probability, account for the selection equation. Let the joint probability be denoted

$$\text{Prob}[D = 1, C = 1] = \Phi_2[d, c, \rho],$$

(1.27)

where

$$d = \beta'x_i + \delta[\alpha'z + \alpha_\lambda\varphi(\Upsilon'v)/\Phi(\Upsilon'v)]$$

(1.28)

and

$$c = \Upsilon'v.$$

(See (1.20) and (1.21). Note that the term in square brackets in (1.28) is expected expenditure given cardholder status.) Let w denote the union of the variables in x (see (1.2)), v (see (1.9)), and z (see (1.14)). Then, reconfigure β, γ, and α conformably, with zeros in the locations where variables do not actually appear in the original equation. Thus,

Table 1.9 Estimated default probabilities

Group	Conditional	Unconditional
All observations	.1498	.1187
Cardholders	.1056	.0947
Non-cardholders	.3090	.2061
Defaulters	.1632	.1437
Nondefaulters	.0997	.0895

$$\frac{\partial \text{Prob}[D=1|C=1]}{\partial \mathbf{W}} = \frac{1}{\Phi(c)}\left[g_d \frac{\partial d}{\partial \mathbf{W}} + g_c \frac{\partial c}{\partial \mathbf{W}}\right] - \frac{\Phi_2(d,c,\rho)}{(\Phi(c))^2}\frac{\partial c}{\partial \mathbf{W}}. \qquad (1.29)$$

The outer derivatives g_d and g_c were defined earlier. The inner derivatives are

$$\partial c / \partial w = \Upsilon \qquad (1.30)$$

and

$$\partial d / \partial w = \beta + \delta[\alpha - \alpha_\lambda \lambda(c+\lambda)\Upsilon]. \qquad (1.31)$$

Inserting the sample means of the variables where required for the computation gives an estimate of approximately $+0.0033$. The rightmost column in Table 1.7, labelled 'Partial', gives a complete set of estimates of the marginal effects for the conditional default equation. It is clear that the coefficients themselves are misleading. In particular, the apparent effect of MAJORDRG turns out to be an effect of selection; increases in this variable appear to decrease default only because increases so heavily (negatively) influence the approval decision.

Predicted default probabilities

Table 1.9 shows the average of the predicated default probabilities computed with the models in Tables 1.7 and 1.8 for some subgroups of the data set.

The standard predictive rule, 'predict $y_i = 1$ if $\widehat{P}_i > 0.5$' predicts only 11 defaults, 6 of them incorrectly, in the sample of 10,499 observations which includes 996 defaults. Obviously, this is not likely to be useful. The problem is that the sample is extremely unbalanced, with only 10 per cent of the observations defaulting. Since the average predicted probability in the sample will equal the sample proportion, it will take an extreme observation to produce a probability as high as 0.5. Table 1.10 shows the effect with three alternative choices of the threshold value. The value 0.09487 is the sample proportion.

Table 1.10 Predictions for different thresholds

	Predict $D=0$			Predict $D=1$			
	.09487	.12	.15	.09487	.12	.15	
Actual							Total
0	5225	6464	7675	4278	3039	1828	9503
1	214	329	494	782	667	502	996
Total	5439	6793	8169	5060	3706	2330	10499

Expected profit

The final step in this part of the analysis is to construct the equation for expected profit from approving an application. The basis of the model is equation (1.22). We used the following specific formulation:

$$
\begin{aligned}
m &= 2\% + 10\%/52 && \text{(merchant fee)} \\
f &= 1.25\% && \text{(finance changes)} \\
t &= 1\% && \text{(opportunity cost of funds)} \\
r &= 50\% && \text{(recovery rate)} \\
q &= 2\% && \text{(penalty rate)} \\
\text{fee} &= \$5.25 && \text{(fee for card(s))} \\
o &= 0.2\% && \text{(overhead rate on loans).}
\end{aligned}
\tag{1.32}
$$

This assumes a 2.00 per cent merchant fee, 1.25 per cent finance charge, plus one week's float on repayment and an interest rate of 10 per cent. The net return on finance charges is only 3% per year, but the merchant fees are quite substantial. We assume a 50 per cent ultimate recovery rate on defaulted loans and a 2 per cent penalty rate. As before, we acknowledge the simplicity of the preceding. Nonetheless, it captures most of the important aspects of the calculation. Based on the estimated expenditure equation and conditional default mode, Table 1.11 lists the sample averages for $E[\Pi]$ for several subgroups.

The values in Table 1.11 are striking. It is clear that the results are being driven by the default probability. Figure 1.1 shows the behaviour of the model's predictions of estimated profits against the predicted default probability for the full sample of individual observations. The dashed vertical line in the figure is drawn at the sample average default rate of slightly under 10 per cent. The horizontal line is drawn at zero. The shading of the triangles shows the density of the points in the sample. The figure clearly

Table 1.11 Sample average expected profits

All Observations	− $4.41
Cardholders	$4.27
Defaulters	− $3.15
Nondefaulters	$5.06
Noncardholders	− $35.32

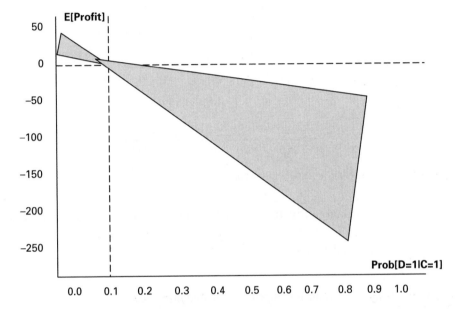

Figure 1.1   Model predictions of profits vs. default probabilities

shows that the model predicts negative profits for most individuals whose estimated default probability exceeds roughly ten per cent. The familiar rule of 0.5 for the threshold for predicting default is obviously far too high to be effective in this setting.

Figure 1 agrees strongly with Boyes *et al.*'s finding that applicants whose default probability exceeded nine per cent were generally associated with negative profits. We find exactly the same result. But they suggest at several points that higher balances are likely to be associated with higher expected earnings. Our results strongly suggest the opposite.

Figure 2 shows the behaviour of expected profits plotted against expected expenditure in the sample data. Clearly, beyond a surprisingly modest expenditure level, higher expenditures are generally associated with lower, not higher, profits. Our own results are easily explained. The expenditure

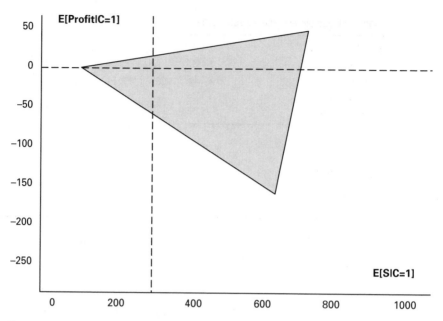

Figure 1.2   Expected profit vs. expected expenditure

level strongly influences the default probability in our model, and the profit equation is, in turn, heavily dependent on the default probability. The result is explored further in the next section.

Aggregate decisions rules for approving or denying credit

Consider a pool of applicants within which default probabilities will be widely distributed. For each individual in the pool, we can compute an expected profit, as in the preceding section, which will depend on both predicted default rate and predicted expenditure. The expected profit of a decision rule can then be obtained by summing the expected profits of those in the pool who are accepted by this rule. An equivalent procedure is to compute the 'normalized expected profit',

$$E^*[\Pi] = E_{P*}[\{E[\Pi_i]P^*\} \times AR(P^*)] \qquad (1.33)$$

where $AR(P^*)$ is the acceptance rate with a particular threshold probability. Obviously, $AR(P^*)$ increases monotonically with (P^*). However, $E[\Pi_i] \mid P^*$ falls with P^*. Because the acceptance rate is falling with P^*, the profits that will be obtained from a given pool need not rise with falling P^*. In short, a rule which decreases P^* attracts fewer and fewer better and better loans. Thus, the total, average loans times number of loans, may not rise.

Table 1.12 Normalized expected profits

P^*	Acceptance Rate	Sample Mean $E^*[\Pi_i]P^*$	Normalized Profit
0.00000	0.00000	0.00000	0.00000
0.00500	0.00885	21.89900	0.19384
0.01000	0.02581	20.29800	0.52391
0.02000	0.07461	17.41600	1.29933
0.03000	0.13292	15.54800	2.06667
0.04000	0.19154	14.19900	2.71961
0.05000	0.25082	13.12700	3.29249
0.06000	0.30861	12.22200	3.77187
0.07000	0.36180	11.45900	4.14583
0.08000	0.40970	10.79700	4.42353
0.09000	0.45425	10.19100	4.62931
0.10000	0.49636	9.62100	4.77543
0.11000	0.53689	9.07600	4.87285
0.11500	0.55437	8.83700	4.89900
0.12000	0.57200	8.59900	4.91865
0.12500	0.58710	8.38800	4.92460
0.13000	0.60257	8.17170	4.92405
0.13500	0.61871	7.94200	4.91383
0.14000	0.63262	7.74310	4.89850
0.15000	0.66096	7.32700	4.84288
0.16000	0.68826	6.91500	4.75933
0.17000	0.71259	6.52260	4.64791
0.18000	0.73408	6.18000	4.53663
0.19000	0.75268	5.85800	4.40919
0.20000	0.76986	5.42200	4.17418

In order to estimate the function in (1.33), we use the following steps. Compute for every individual in the pool (1) probability of acceptance, Prob $[C_i = 1]$ $\Phi[\gamma'v_i]$, (note that this is only for purposes of dealing with our censoring problem; it is not part of the structure of the model), (2) expected expenditure from (1.20), (3) probability of default from (1.21), and (4) expected profit from (1.33). For different values of P^* we compute the average value of $E^*[\Pi_i]$ for those individuals whose estimated default probability is less than P^*. We then multiply this sample means by the acceptance rate. Table 1.12 gives the result of this calculation. The last column shows that, by this calculation, there is an optimal acceptance rate. Figures 1.3 and 1.4 show the relationship between acceptance rate and normalized expected profit.

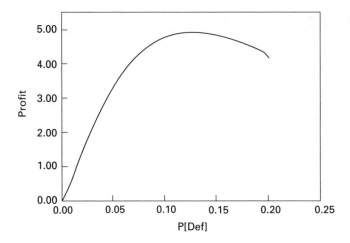

Figure 1.3   Normalized expected profits

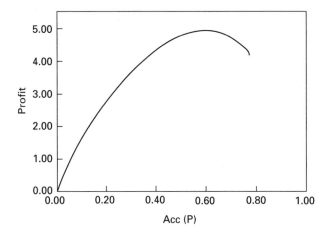

Figure 1.4   Profits vs. default probability

Table 1.12 suggests that a rule $P^* = 0.125$, or an acceptance rate of about 59% is optimal. This is a rule that allows a fairly high default rate, in exchange for higher expected profits. It also accepts some individuals with negative expected profits, since the default rate is not, alone, sufficient to ensure positive expected profit. This acceptance rate is noticeably higher than the value actually observed, which was roughly 25 per cent during the period in which these data were drawn.

Ranking attributes which contribute to a denial of credit

Denote by R^* the criterion, or 'rule' that has been used for the decision whether to approve or deny an application and by $R(w_i)$ the value of the criterion for a particular individual 'i' where w is the full vector of attributes and characteristics used in the calculation. In order to establish which factor contributed to an individual's failure to meet the benchmark, we need to determine the values of the factors which are consistent with meeting it. We can do so by sampling individuals who meet the benchmark and empirically determining sample means. We will do so by obtaining for a set of individuals, *all of whom are at or close to the benchmark*, the sample means of the attributes. This estimates $E[w \mid P = P^*]$. Denote the set of sample means $\overline{w}^*$.

If the sample is large enough (by which we surmise a few thousand observations), then it will be the case that $R^* \approx R(\overline{w}^*)$. Now, approximate the rule function evaluated at the particular with a linear Taylor series, expanding around the point of means that we have obtained:

$$R(w_i) - R^* \approx \sum_k [\partial R(\overline{w}^*)/\partial \overline{w}](w_{ik} - \overline{w})$$
$$= \sum_k \Psi_k(w_{ik} - \overline{w}).$$

Thus, the deviation of the individual's 'score' from the benchmark is expressed as a linear function of the deviations of their attributes from the benchmark attributes. If the decision rule is the default probability, then the elements of Ψ are the marginal effects in (1.28). Some of the numeric values are given in the last column of Table 1.7. If the expected profit is used, the calculation is only slightly more difficult. By combining terms, the expected profit may be written as

$$E[\Pi] = \Pi_0 + E[S](\Pi_1 + \text{Prob}[D = 1 | C = 1]),$$

so the extension to this function would be straightforward using results already given.

We will use the default probability for an illustration. For the example, we take as a cutoff our earlier-described optimal default probability rule of $R^* = P^* = 0.125$. Using the model presented in the previous sections, observation number 4805 in our sample has a predicted default probability of 0.165, so they would be rejected. (They were.) In order to obtain the means for the calculation, we use observations which have predicted default rates between 0.115 and 0.135. (With more data we could use a narrower range). This leaves about 800 observations of the original 13,444. The set of calculations listed above produces a default probability at the means of roughly $R = (\overline{w}^*) = 0.116$. The sample mean predicted default probability for these 800 observations is $R = 0.127$. (Recall, we have attempted to match 0.125, so this is quite close.) The difference between the computed default probability and the benchmark is $0.165 - 0.125 = 0.040$. The decomposition obtained as the sum of the term gives a value of 0.0414. The difference of -0.0014 would be the remainder term in the Taylor series approximation. The largest single term is associated with CPTF30, the 30 day delinquency count in the last 12 months. The average in the sample for this variable is 0.242. This individual had 4. The second largest contributor was the number of credit bureau inquiries, for which, once again, this individual (4) was well above the mean (1.23558).

1.6. Conclusions

The preceding has described a methodology for incorporating costs and expected profits into a credit-scoring model for loan approvals. Our main conclusion is the same as Boyes *et al*'s (1989). When expected return is included in the credit-scoring rule, the lender will approve applications that would otherwise be rejected by a rule that focuses solely on default probability. Contrary to what intuition might suggest, we find that when spending levels are included as a component of the default probability, which seems quite plausible, the optimal loan size is relatively small.

The model used for profit in this study is rudimentary. More detailed data on payment schedules would allow a more elaborate behavioural model of the consumer's repayment decisions. Nonetheless, it seems reasonable to expect similar patterns to emerge in more detailed studies. Since, in spite of our earlier discussion, we continue to find that default probability is a crucial determinant of the results, it seems that the greatest payoff in terms of model development would be found here. For example, with better and finer data, it would be possible to examine the timing default rather than simply its occurrence. The relationship between default probability and account size could also be further refined. Finally, our objective function for the lender, expected profit, is quite simple. The preceding is best viewed as merely a simulation. A more elaborate model which made use of the variation in expenditures from month to month or used the second moment of the distribution of profits might more reasonably characterize the lender's objectives.

Much of the modelling done here is purely illustrative. The equations are somewhat unwieldy. Credit-scoring vendors would still be required to manipulate the models with convenience, which would make a more critical specification search necessary. The obvious use of models such as ours is for processing initial applications, which can, in principle, be done at a leisurely pace. But an equally common application is the in-store approval for large purchases. For relatively small purchases this has been automated, and focuses simply on whether the account is already in arrears. But for very large purchases, which often require human intervention, credit card companies often rely on a decidedly ad hoc procedure, the gut reaction of an individual based on a short telephone call. A simple enough behavioural model which incorporates up-to-date information and behavioural characteristics might be of use in this situation.

REFERENCES

Abowd, J. and Farber, H., 'Job queues and the union status of workers', *Industrial and Labor Relations Review*, 35, 1982, 354–67.

Aldrich, J. and Nelson, F., *Linear Probability, Logit and Probit Models*, Beverly Hills, CA, Sage, 1984.

Amemiya, T., *Advanced Econometrics*, Cambridge, MA, Harvard University Press, 1985.

Berndt, E., Hall, R., and Hausman J., 'Estimation and inference in nonlinear structural models', *Annals of Economic and Social Measurement*, 3/4, 1974, 1263–78.

Boyes, W., Hoffman D., and Low, S., 'An econometric analysis of the bank credit scoring problem', *Journal of Econometrics*, 40, 1989, 3–14.

Davidson, R., and Mackinnon, J., *Estimation and Inference in Econometrics*, New York, Oxford University Press, 1993.

Goldberger, A., 'Abnormal selection bias', in S. Karlin, T. Amemiya, and Goodman L. (eds.), *Studies in Econometrics, Time Series, and Multivariate Statistics*, Stamford, CT, Academic, 1983.

Greene, W., 'Sample selection as a specification error: Comment', *Econometrica*, 49, 1981, 795–8.3.

Greene, W., *Econometric Analysis*, 2nd Edn, New York: Macmillan, 1993.

Heckman, J., 'Sample selection as a specification error', *Econometrica*, 47, 1979, 153–61.

Maddala, G., *Limited Dependent and Qualitative Variables in Econometrics*, Cambridge University Press, 1983.

Manski, C., 'Anatomy of the selection problem', *Journal of Human Resources*, 24, 1989, 341–60.

Manski, C. and Lerman, S., 'The estimation of choice probabilities for choice based samples', *Econometrica*, 45, 1977, 1977–88.

Press, J. and Wilson, S., 'Choosing between logistics regression and discriminant analysis', *Journal of the American Statistical Association*, 73, 1978, 699–705.

Wynand, P. and van Praag, B., 'The demand for deductibles in private health insurance: a probit model with sample selection', *Journal of Econometrics*, 17, 1981, 229–52.

2 Mixed logit and error component models of corporate insolvency and bankruptcy risk

David A. Hensher and Stewart Jones

2.1 Introduction

Mixed logit[1] is the latest among a new breed of econometric models being developed out of discrete choice theory (Train 2003). Discrete choice theory is concerned with understanding the discrete behavioural responses of individuals to the actions of business, markets and government when faced with two or more possible outcomes (or choices) (Louviere *et al.* 2000). Its theoretical underpinnings are derived from microeconomic theory of consumer behavior, such as the formal definition of agent preferences as inputs into a choice or outcome setting as determined by the utility maximization of agents. Given that the analyst has incomplete knowledge on the information inputs of the agents being studied, the analyst can only explain a choice outcome up to a probability of it occurring. This is the basis for the theory of random utility (see Louviere *et al.* 2000 for a review of the literature).[2] While random utility theory has developed from economic theories of consumer behaviour it can be applied to any unit of analysis (e.g., firm failures) where the dependent variable is discrete.[3]

---

[1] Mixed logit is also referred to in various literatures as random parameter logit (RPL), mixed multinomial logit (MMNL), kernel logit, hybrid logit and error components logit.

[2] In the theory of discrete choices, an essential departure from traditional microeconomic theory is the postulate that utility is derived from the properties or characteristics of things, rather than the goods per se. Discrete-choice theory incorporates the work of the standard Lancaster–Rosen model, but modifies this approach further by assuming that individuals maximize their utility on the basis of their *perceptions* of characteristics, rather than the characteristics per se (see Louviere *et al.* 2000 for an overview).

[3] Random utility theory (RUT) is a very general theory of how the analyst represents the preferences of agents where elements of information (known to the agents) are not observed by the analyst. While RUT has gained particular recognition within discrete-choice theory in recent years, RUT is not restricted to choice theory and can be implemented in a wide range of possible decision contexts.

The concept of behavioural heterogeneity (individual variations in tastes and preferences), and how this impinges on the validity of various theoretical and empirical models has been the subject of much recent attention in this literature.[4] However, econometric techniques to model heterogeneity have taken time to develop, despite a long-standing recognition that failure to do so can result in inferior model specification, spurious test results and invalid conclusions (Louviere *et al.* 2000; Train 2003). Starting with the simple binary logit model, research progressed during the 1960s and 1970s to the multinomial logit (MNL) and nested logit models, the latter becoming the most popular of the generalized logit models. Although more advanced choice models such as mixed logit existed in conceptual and analytical form in the early 1970s, parameter estimation was seen as a practical barrier to their empirical usefulness. The breakthrough came with the development of simulation methods (such as simulated maximum likelihood estimation) that enabled the open-form models such as mixed logit to be estimated with relative ease (e.g., Stern 1997).

Mixed logit and its variants (such as the error component logit model) have now supplanted simpler models in many areas of economics, marketing, management, transportation, health, housing, energy research and environmental science (Train 2003). This can largely be explained in terms of the substantial improvements delivered by mixed logit over binary logistic and MNL models.

Considering the case of firm failures, the main improvement is that mixed logit models include a number of additional parameters which capture observed and unobserved heterogeneity both within and between firms.[5] For a mixed logit model, the probability of failure of a specific firm in a sample is determined by the mean influence of each explanatory variable with a fixed parameter estimate within the sampled population, *plus*, for any random parameters, a parameter weight drawn from the distribution of individual firm parameters estimated across the sample. This weight is randomly allocated to each sampled firm unless there are specific rules for mapping individual firms to specific locations within the distribution of firm-specific parameters.[6] In contrast, the probability of failure for an individual firm using a binary logistic or MNL model is simply a weighted

---

[4] The modelling of behavioural heterogeneity has been important in many fields of inquiry, including recent economics literature (see Jones and Hensher 2004).

[5] In addition to fixed parameters, mixed logit models include estimates for the standard deviation of random parameters, the mean of random parameters and the heterogeneity in the means (discussed further below and in Section 2.4).

[6] The moments of an individual firm's coefficient cannot be observed from a single data point, but rather estimated by assuming a distribution for the coefficients of any particular attribute across all firms in the sample (see Train 2003, pp. 262–263).

function of its fixed parameters (i.e., assumption of homogeneous preferences) with all other behavioural information assigned (incorrectly) to the error term.[7] As noted by Hensher and Greene (2003), parameter estimation in the mixed logit model maximizes use of the behavioural information embedded in any dataset appropriate to the analysis. Ultimately, these conceptual advantages afford the analyst with a substantially improved foundation for explanation and prediction.[8] The important theoretical advantages of the mixed logit model are further considered in the formal specification and analysis of the model which now follows.

The main value of progressively moving to less restrictive models is the ability to distinguish between a larger number of behaviourally meaningful influences that can explain a firm status in respect of the choice outcome of interest, be it distress levels (e.g., nonfailure, insolvency, distressed merger, outright failure), or takeover (e.g., firms not subject to any takeover activity, friendly takeover targets, hostile takeovers targets) or other comparisons of states of interest.

Mixed logit reveals new ways in which we can enrich our models, for the sole purpose of gaining a greater understanding of the role that factors internal and external to the firm play in explaining the status of a firm in terms of alternative states observed in the market place. The increased behavioural richness is designed to both improve predictive performance as well as provide greater confidence in the responsiveness of firms to changes in the regime of particular variables such as market prices, cash flow, earnings ratios and so on.

We begin with a systematic build-up of the mixed logit model from first principles, followed by a discussion of the simulation methods used to estimate these open-form models and the array of useful outputs. An empirical example is used to illustrate the extended capabilities of mixed logit.

2.2 Building up to a mixed logit regime

Like any random utility model of the discrete choice family of models, we assume that a sampled firm $(q = 1, \ldots, Q)$ faces a 'choice' amongst $i = 1, 2, \ldots, I$

---

[7] A fixed parameter essentially treats the standard deviation as zero such that all the behavioural information is captured by the mean. Standard logit models assume the population of firms is homogeneous across attributes with respect to domain outcomes (i.e., levels of financial distress). For instance, the parameter for a financial ratio such as total debt to total equity is calculated from the sample of all firms (thus it is an average firm effect), and does not represent the parameter of an individual firm.

[8] A variety of studies have now demonstrated the superior forecasting accuracy of mixed logit compared to standard logit (see for example Brownstone *et al.* 2000).

alternatives in each of T occasions. Within the context of financial distress, since firms do not *choose* to fail per se, we prefer to use the phrase *outcome domain* (or simply outcome) as the descriptor of the observed *choice* outcome. A firm q is assumed to recognize the full set of alternative outcomes in occasion t and to focus on business strategies designed to result in the delivery of the outcome associated with the highest utility (i.e., non-failure). The (relative) utility associated with each outcome i as evaluated by each firm q in occasion t is represented in a discrete outcome model by a utility expression of the following general form:

$$U_{itq} = \beta_{itq}X_{itq} + \varepsilon_{itq}. \tag{2.1}$$

X_{itq} is a vector of explanatory variables that are observed by the analyst (from any source) and include observed attributes of the alternative outcomes, observed characteristics of the firm and descriptors of the decision context in occasion t; β_{itq} and ε_{itq} are not observed by the analyst and are treated as stochastic influences.

To provide an intuitive explanation of how equation (2.1) operates in an outcome setting, think of the task as being one of representing sources of variance that contribute to explaining a specific outcome. For a specific firm, equation (2.1) has variance potential associated with the coefficient attached to each observed characteristic (i.e., β), to each observed characteristic itself (i.e., X) and the unobserved effects term (ε). We could expand this equation out to reflect these sources of variance for three characteristics, defining the subscripts 'O' as observed and 'U' as unobserved, as (dropping the q and t subscripts) (see Jones and Hensher, 2004):

$$U_i = (\beta_{O1}X_{O1} + \beta_{U1}X_{U1}) + (\beta_{O2}X_{O2} + \beta_{U2}X_{U2})$$
$$+ (\beta_{O3}X_{O3} + \beta_{U3}X_{U3}) + \varepsilon_i. \tag{2.2}$$

Each characteristic is now represented by a set of observed and unobserved influences. In addition, each parameter and characteristic can itself be expressed as some function of other influences, giving more depth in the explanation of sources of variance. As we expand the function out, we reveal deeper parameters to identify. In the most restrictive (or simplistic) versions of the utility expression, we would gather all the unobserved sources together and replace (2.2) with (2.3):

$$U_i = \beta_{O1}X_{O1} + \beta_{O2}X_{O2} + \beta_{O3}X_{O3}$$
$$+ (\beta_{U1}X_{U1} + \beta_{U2}X_{U2} + \beta_{U3}X_{U3} + \varepsilon_i). \tag{2.3}$$

and would collapse the unobserved influences into a single unknown by assuming that all unobserved effects cannot be related in any systematic way with the observed effects:

$$U_i = ß_{O1}X_{O1} + ß_{O2}X_{O2} + ß_{O3}X_{O3} + \varepsilon_i. \tag{2.4}$$

Furthermore, by defining a utility expression of the form in (2.4) for each alternative outcome i and imposing a further assumption that the unobserved influences have the same distribution and are independent across alternatives, we can remove the subscript i attached to ε. What we have is the utility expressions of a multinomial logit (MNL) model, assumed for illustrative purposes only to be linear additive in the observed characteristics (see Chapter 3). This intuitive discussion has highlighted the way in which an MNL model restricts, through assumption, the opportunity to reveal the fuller range of potential sources of influence on utility as resident throughout the full dimensionality of equation (2.2). Explaining these fuller sources is equivalent to explaining the broader set of sources of observed and unobserved heterogeneity on an outcome domain.

The word *heterogeneity* has special and important relevance in the development of advanced logit models. The main value of moving to less restrictive models is the ability to distinguish between a larger number of potential sources of *observed* and *unobserved* heterogeneity in such a way that we can establish the (unconfounded) contribution of these sources. When we talk of heterogeneity, we often make a distinction between that which can be attributed to differences in the role that measured explanatory variables play across individual firms in influencing outcomes, and that which varies across outcomes that may be linked to observed and/or unobserved influences that vary both within and across firms. The observed sources can be captured in many ways, but the common way is to align them with specific characteristics of firms and of outcomes. Statistically speaking, heterogeneity is another word for variance within the relevant domain, which includes the utility distribution associated with a particular characteristic across individual firms in a sample (often referred to as observed heterogeneity and captured in random parameters), and the standard deviation associated with a specific outcome (often referred to as unobserved heterogeneity and captured through error components). We discuss this in more detail below.

A condition of the MNL model is that ε_{itq} is independent (between outcome alternatives) and identically distributed (i.e., same or constant variance across alternative outcomes) (IID) extreme value type 1. IID is clearly restrictive in that it does not allow the error or random component of different alternative outcomes to have different variances (i.e. degrees of unobserved heterogeneity) and also to be correlated. We would want to be able to take this into account in some way in recognition that we are unlikely to capture all sources of explanation through the observed explanatory variables. One way to do this is to partition the stochastic component into two additive (i.e., uncorrelated) parts. One part is correlated over alternative outcomes and heteroscedastic, and another part is IID over alternative outcomes and firms as shown in equation (2.5) (ignoring the t subscript for the present).

$$U_{iq} = \text{\ss}'X_{iq} + \left(\eta_{iq} + \varepsilon_{iq}\right) \tag{2.5}$$

where η_{iq} is a random term with zero mean whose distribution over firms and alternative outcomes depends in general on underlying parameters and observed data relating to outcome i and firm q; and ε_{iq} is a random term with zero mean that is IID over alternative outcomes and does not depend on underlying parameters or data.

There is a lot of technical jargon in the previous sentence, which needs clarification. We can illustrate the meaning in the context of an explanatory variable, the gearing ratio (or total debt to total equity ratio). We start with recognition that there are potential gains to be made by accounting for differences in the role that the gearing ratio plays in influencing each sampled firm's observed outcome state. That is, instead of having a single (fixed) parameter attached to the gearing ratio variable (often called a mean estimate), we allow for the possibility of a distribution of parameter estimates, captured through the mean and standard deviation parameters of the distribution. The actual shape of the (analytical) distribution is not important at this stage, but the recognition of a distribution suggests the presence of heterogeneity across the sample firms in terms of the role that the gearing ratio plays in contributing to a firm being in one of the outcome states (e.g. nonfailure or failure). We can express this heterogeneity symbolically for a single variable (i.e., the gearing ratio) as

$$\text{\ss}_{qk} = \text{\ss}_k + \eta_{qk} \tag{2.6}$$

where η_{qk} is a random term whose distribution over firms depends on underlying parameters that define the standard deviation (or variance) of the selected analytical distribution (e.g., normal or triangular) as well as the possibility of correlation between pairs of explanatory variables. Note that since β_{qk} may be a state-specific constant (for $J-1$ outcomes), η_{qk} may also vary across outcomes and, in addition, may induce correlation across outcomes. Since we have no way of knowing where on the analytical distribution a specific firm is located, without further information, the value of η_{qk} is appended to the random component as shown in (2.6). That is, each firm has a value for η_{qk} but it is not known other than that it is a random assignment on the distribution. There is a vector of η_{qk} to capture the set of explanatory variables that are given random parameters instead of a fixed parameter treatment.

However, if we were to have additional information that suggests some specific link between this additional information and a possible location on the distribution, then we are moving away from full random allocation (referred to as random heterogeneity) to degrees of systematic heterogeneity. For example, suppose that the influence of the gearing ratio on firm failure is linked to whether a firm is in the resource sector or not, and its size in terms of turnover, then this would be captured through a re-specification of (2.6) as

$$ß_{qk} = ß_k + \delta_k' \mathbf{z}_q + \eta_{qk} \tag{2.7}$$

where the additional input is $\mathbf{z}_q$, a vector of observed data of membership of the resources sector and turnover. A popular distribution in discrete-choice analysis for the remaining random component, ε, is the extreme value type 1 (EV1) distribution. The name is intriguing but before explaining it, we should write out the form of this distribution as

$$\text{Prob}\left(\varepsilon_j \leq \varepsilon\right) = \exp(-\exp-\varepsilon) \tag{2.8}$$

where 'exp' is shorthand for the exponential function. Distributions are analytical constructs that we hope bear a good relationship to the role of information captured in the distribution in explaining actual choices. While we can never be totally sure we have got the 'best' behavioural representation through a specific distribution, we do have statistical tests to provide some broad-based clues. The phrase 'extreme value' arises relative to the normal distribution. The essential difference between the EV1 and normal distributions is in the tails of the distribution where the extreme values reside. With a small choice set such as two alternatives this may make little difference because the resulting differences in the outcome probabilities between the normal and EV1 is usually negligible. When one has an increasing number of alternatives, however, one gets many very small outcome probabilities and it is here that differences between the distributions can be quite noticeable. For example an outcome probability of 0.02 compared to 0.04 is significant, and when aggregated across a population can amount to sizeable differences in overall outcome shares.

We now have the essential elements to move forward in building the mixed logit model, where the emphasis is on deriving a model that can take the range of inputs, observed or unobserved by the analyst, and build them into a model to establish their influence on the 'choice' amongst outcome states. Given the existence of unobserved influences on outcome states, the analyst does not have full information on what influences each firm's membership of a particular outcome state, and hence identification of choice outcomes exists only up to a probability of its occurrence. The formal derivation of the mixed logit model takes as its starting position the MNL model, which is the specification arrived at by the imposition of the IID condition and EV1 distribution on ε. What we have added (at least initially, in what we might term the random parameter version of mixed logit) is the η term (equation 2.6). This term has a value representing the importance role of each explanatory variable for each firm, and hence the incidence of these values, defined by the selection of an analytical distribution such as normal, is captured through its density. The density of η is denoted by $f(\eta|\Omega)$ where Ω are the fixed parameters that describe this density such as the mean and covariance, where the latter includes the standard deviation (i.e., variances) and the correlation (i.e., covariances). For a given value of η, the conditional probability for outcome i is logit, since the remaining error term is IID extreme value:

$$L_i(\eta) = \exp(\beta'X_i + \eta_i) / \sum_j \exp(\beta'X_j + \eta_j). \tag{2.9}$$

Equation (2.9) is the simple multinomial logit model, but with the proviso that, for each sampled firm, we have additional information defined by η_q. This is where the use of the word 'conditional' applies – the probability is conditional on η_q. This additional information influences the choice outcome.

Since η is not observed, the (unconditional) outcome probability in this logit formula, integrated over all values of η weighted by the density of η, is

$$P_i = \int L_i(\eta) f(\eta|\Omega) d\eta. \tag{2.10}$$

Models of this form are called *mixed logit*[9] because the outcome probability $L_i(\eta)$ is a mixture of logits with f as the mixing distribution (see Revelt and

---

[9] The proof in McFadden and Train (2000) that mixed logit can approximate any choice model including any multinomial probit model is an important message. The reverse cannot be said: a multinomial probit model cannot approximate any mixed logit model, since multinomial probit relies critically on normal distributions. If a random term in utility is not normal, then mixed logit can handle it and multinomial probit cannot.

Train 1998, Train 2003, Jones and Hensher 2004, Hensher *et al.* 2005) The mixing distribution is typically assumed to be continuous;[10] meaning that η can have an infinite set of values, that are used to obtain mixed logit probability through weighted averaging of the logit formula, evaluated at different values of η, with the weights given by the density $f(\eta|\Omega)$. The weighted average of several functions is known, in the statistical literature, as a mixed function, and the density that provides the weights is called a mixing distribution (Train 2003).

The probabilities do not exhibit the well known independence from irrelevant alternatives property (IIA). That is, the ratio of any two outcome probabilities (e.g., states A and B) is determined by all of the data including that associated with states other than A and B. Different substitution patterns are obtained by appropriate specification of *f*. For example, if two outcomes are deemed to be more similar in terms of how a change in the gearing ratio impacts on the probabilities of each outcome state (i.e., a unit change in the gearing ratio of insolvency draws proportionally more from distressed merger than nonfailure), then we can recognize this by imposing a covariance term to capture the correlation between the two alternatives in terms of the gearing ratio, setting it to zero between each of these close states and the other state. Importantly, we are now moving to the realm of behavioural hypotheses, which is appropriate, rather than relying on the model to totally guide the analyst. The mixed logit model widens the number of testable hypotheses in contrast to models such as MNL and nested logit.

The identification of the parameter estimates in a mixed logit model is complex. The log likelihood must be formulated in terms of observables. The unconditional probability (equation 2.10) is obtained by integrating the random terms out of the probability. As η_i may have many components, this is understood to be a multidimensional integral. The random variables in η_i are assumed to be independent, so the joint density, $g(\eta_i)$, is the product of the individual densities. The integral will, in general, have no closed form.[11] However, the integral is an expected value, so it can be approximated by simulation. Assuming that η_{ir}, $r = 1, \ldots, R$ constitutes a random sample from the underlying population η_i, under certain conditions (see Train 2003), including that the function $f(\eta_i)$ be *smooth*, we have the property that

$$\text{plim} \frac{1}{R} \sum_{r=1}^{R} f(\eta_{ir}) = E(f(\eta_i)). \tag{2.11}$$

[10] A discrete mixing distribution results in a latent class model.

[11] That is, we cannot, analytically derive a specific function form in which the outcome probabilities can be obtained directly from the right-hand-side function without integration each time there is a change.

This result underlies the approach to estimation of all mixed logit model variants. A random number generator or intelligent draws, such as Halton draws, are commonly used to produce the random samples. For each sampled firm, the simulated unconditional probability for their observed outcome is

$$\text{Prob}_s(y_i = j) = \frac{1}{R}\sum\nolimits_{r=1}^{R} \frac{\exp(\beta'_{ir}x_{ji})}{\sum_{m=1}^{J}\exp(\beta'_{ir}x_{mi})}$$

$$= \frac{1}{R}\sum\nolimits_{r=1}^{R} \text{Prob}(y_i = j, \eta_{ir})$$

(2.12)

where β_{ir} is the representation of equation (2.7), and η_{ir} is a random draw from the population generating η_i. The simulated log likelihood is then

$$\log L_S = \sum\nolimits_{i=1}^{N} \log \text{Prob}_S(y_i = j).$$

(2.13)

This function is then to be maximized with respect to the structural parameters underlying equation (2.7). To illustrate how the elements of η_{ir} are drawn, we begin with a random vector $\mathbf{w}_{ir}$ which is either K independent draws from the standard uniform [0,1] distribution or K Halton draws from the mth Halton sequence, where m is the mth prime number in the sequence of K prime numbers beginning with 2. The Halton values are also distributed in the unit interval. This primitive draw is then transformed to the selected analytical distribution. For example, if the distribution is normal, then the transformation is

$$\eta_{k,ir} = \Phi^{-1}(w_{k,ir}).$$

(2.14)

The random sequence used for model estimation must be the same each time a probability or a function of that probability, such as a derivative, is computed in order to obtain replicability. In addition, during estimation of a particular model, the same set of random draws must be used for each firm every time. That is, the sequence $\eta_{i1}, \eta_{i2}, \dots, \eta_{iR}$ used for firm i must be the same every time it is used to calculate a probability, derivative or likelihood function. If not, the likelihood function will be discontinuous in the parameters, and successful estimation becomes unlikely.

To be more concrete let us take the gearing ratio and give it a random parameter treatment, with an assumed normal distribution. Let us assume we have 100 firms each represented by one observation. For each firm we draw a value of the normal and assign it to each firm. We begin with an initial parameter estimate obtained from an MNL model. Since MNL only has a fixed parameter, we take this as the mean of the distribution for a random parameter and assign (arbitrarily) a standard deviation of unity.

Given the initial start values for each parameter, an iterative process locates the most likely population level parameter estimates for the data, based on minimizing (towards zero) the log-likelihood of the model. The log-likelihood function for the mixed logit model is calculated using

$$L(\beta|x,y) = \sum_{q=1}^{Q}\sum_{t=1}^{T}\sum_{j=1}^{J} y_{jtq} \log \overline{P}_{jtq}(x_{jtq}|\beta), \tag{2.15}$$

where β represents a vector of parameters (what we are trying to estimate), y_{jtq} is a choice index such that $y_{jtn} = 1$ if alternative j was selected by firm q in outcome situation t, or is zero otherwise and $\overline{P}_{jtq}$ is the average (over draws; see below) probability of firm q choosing alternative outcome j given the observed data, x, in choice situation t and the estimated parameters in the vector β. In each iteration, a series of R draws are taken for each of the random parameter distributions across each of the choice observations in the data set. Let the initial parameter estimate be distributed such that $\beta_1 \sim N(-0.5,1)$. Most software packages begin by first generating R values between zero and one, where the number R is specified by the analyst. These R values are treated as probabilities which are then translated into the parameter draws by drawing corresponding values from the inverse of the cumulative distribution function of the random parameter distribution specified by the analyst. For example, assuming we randomly generate a value between zero and one of 0.90, from the cumulative probability distribution assuming $\beta \sim N(-0.5,1)$, this value translates to a parameter draw of 0.78.

Conventional simulation-based estimation uses a random number to produce a large number of draws from a specified distribution. The central component of the standard approach is draws from the standard continuous uniform distribution, $U[0,1]$. Draws from other distributions are obtained from these draws by using transformations. In particular, where u_i is one draw from $U[0,1]$, for the triangular distribution:

$$\eta_i = \sqrt{2u_i} - 1 \text{ if } u_i \leq 0.5, \; \eta_i = 1 - \sqrt{2u_i - 1} \text{ otherwise.} \tag{2.16}$$

Given that the initial draws satisfy the assumptions necessary, the central issue for purposes of specifying the simulation is the number of draws. Results differ on the number needed in a given application, but the general finding is that when simulation is done in this fashion, the number is large. A consequence of this is that for large-scale problems, the amount of computation time in simulation-based estimation can be extremely long.

Procedures have been devised in the numerical analysis literature for taking 'intelligent' draws from the uniform distribution, rather than random

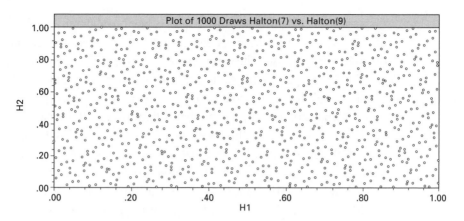

Figure 2.1   Bivariate scatter plot of Halton (7) and Halton (9)

ones (See Train 1999 and Bhat 2001). These procedures reduce the number of draws needed for estimation (by a factor of 90% or more) and reduce the simulation error associated with a given number of draws. Using Halton sequences, Bhat (2001) found that 100 Halton draws produced lower simulation error than 1,000 random numbers. The sequence of Halton values is efficiently spread over the unit interval as illustrated in Figure 2.1 for two sequences of Halton draws based on $r=7$ and $r=9$.

For the second and subsequent iterations, different moments of the random parameter distributions are determined. In particular, the mean and standard deviation parameter at each subsequent iteration is derived by taking the first and second derivatives of the log-likelihood function of the model based on the previous iteration. The parameter estimates in each new iteration are calculated by adding the $K \times 1$ vector of parameter estimates from the previous iteration with the $K \times 1$ step change vector. K represents the number of parameters in the model, including the standard deviation parameters. Once the new parameter estimates have been determined, the entire estimation process is repeated, using the same random or Halton sequences as per previous iterations. The process is terminated when some convergence criterion is met (typically, all values in the step function vector are less than some very small value; that is, the parameter estimates will not significantly change from the previous iteration).

Thus far we have focused on the inclusion of additional behavioural sources of observed and unobserved heterogeneity, without being explicit about whether such heterogeneity is best captured through the way we parametrize the role of each explanatory variable, and/or in the way that we capture differences in unobserved heterogeneity for alternatives. Despite the appeal of capturing as much of the behavioural heterogeneity at the level of each explanatory variable, be it through an outcome-specific specification of each parameter for the same variable or through a generic specification (i.e., common parameter estimates across two or more alternatives), there is a limit, subject to the quality of the data, as to how many parameters can be random. Experience suggests that the number will vary according to the amount of variation in the levels of each variable and the selection of the analytical distribution.[12] There will, however, always been an amount of 'residual' variance that is best allowed to be free, in contrast to being 'forced' into the IID condition. This additional variance in a mixed logit model is associated with a set of error components, one for each alternative. These error components can be correlated or uncorrelated within the set of alternatives, and may be structured as a nest to allow for differential correlation according to the way in which alternatives are related to each other.

An additional layer of individual heterogeneity may now be added to the model in the form of the error components (see Hensher *et al.* 2007). The full model with all components is

$$\text{Prob}(y_{it} = j)$$
$$= \frac{\exp\left[\alpha_{ji} + \beta_i' \mathbf{x}_{jit} + \Sigma_{m=1}^{M} d_{jm}\theta_m \exp(\gamma_m' \mathbf{he}_i) E_{im}\right]}{\sum_{q=1}^{J_i} \exp\left[\alpha_{qi} + \beta_i' \mathbf{x}_{qit} + \Sigma_{m=1}^{M} d_{qm}\theta_m \exp(\gamma_m' \mathbf{he}_i) E_{im}\right]} \quad (2.17)$$

with terms that are not already defined given below. $(\alpha_{ji}, \beta_i) = (\alpha_j, \beta) + \Gamma\Omega_i v_i$ are random outcome-specific constants and variable-specific parameters; $\Omega_i = \text{diag}(\sigma_1, \ldots, \sigma_k)$; and β, α_{ji} are constant terms in the distributions of the random parameters. Uncorrelated parameters with homogeneous means and variances are defined by $\beta_{ik} = \beta_k + \sigma_k v_{ik}$ when $\Gamma = \mathbf{I}$, $\Omega_i = \text{diag}(\sigma_1, \ldots, \sigma_k)$, and v_i is random unobserved taste variation, with mean vector $\mathbf{0}$ and covariance matrix $\mathbf{I}$. This model accommodates correlated parameters with homogeneous means through defining $\beta_{ik} = \beta_k + \Sigma_{s=1}^{k} \Gamma_{ks} v_{is}$ when $\Gamma \neq \mathbf{I}$, and $\Omega_i = \text{diag}(\sigma_1, \ldots, \sigma_k)$, with Γ defined as a lower triangular matrix with ones on the diagonal that allows correlation across random parameters when $\Gamma \neq \mathbf{I}$. An additional layer of firm heterogeneity can be added to the model in the form of the error components. The firm-specific underlying random error components are introduced through the term E_{im}, $m = 1, \ldots, M$, $E_{im} \sim N[0,1]$, given $d_{jm} = 1$ if E_{im}

---

[12] We have found that constrained distributions that permit one sign on the parameter across its range together, as appropriate, with limits on the variance, often enable model convergence with fewer iterations (or even convergence at all). What this does, however, is move the estimate towards a fixed estimate while recognizing that the amount of heterogeneity assumed through unconstrained distributions simply does not exist.

appears in the utility expression for outcome state j and 0 otherwise, and θ_m is a dispersion factor for error component m. γ_m defines parameters in the heteroscedastic variances of the error components, and $\mathbf{he}_i$ are firm outcome-invariant characteristics that produce heterogeneity in the variances of the error components,

The probabilities defined above are conditioned on the random terms, $\mathbf{V}_i$ and the error components, $\mathbf{E}_i$. The unconditional probabilities are obtained by integrating v_{ik} and E_{im} out of the conditional probabilities: $P_j = E_{\mathbf{v}, \mathbf{E}}[P(j|\mathbf{v}_i, \mathbf{E}_i)]$. This is a multiple integral which does not exist in closed form. The integral is approximated by sampling *nrep* draws from the assumed populations and averaging (as discussed above; see Bhat 2003, Revelt and Train 1998, Train 2003 and Brownstone *et al.* 2000 for discussion). Parameters are estimated by maximizing the simulated log likelihood

$$\log L_s = \sum_{i=1}^{N} \log \frac{1}{R} \sum_{r=1}^{R} \Pi_{t=1}^{T_i}$$

$$\frac{\exp\left[\alpha_{ji} + \beta'_{ir}\mathbf{x}_{jit} + \Sigma_{m=1}^{M} d_{jm}\theta_m \exp(\gamma'_m \mathbf{he}_i) E_{im,r}\right]}{\sum_{q=1}^{J_i} \exp\left[\alpha_{qi} + \beta'_{ir}\mathbf{x}_{qit} + \Sigma_{m=1}^{M} d_{qm}\theta_m \exp(\gamma'_m \mathbf{he}_i) E_{im,r}\right]} \qquad (2.18)$$

with respect to $(\beta, \Gamma, \Omega, \theta)$, where $R =$ the number of replications, $\beta_{ir} = \beta + \Gamma\Omega_i v_{ir}$ is the rth draw on β_i, $\mathbf{V}_{ir}$ is the rth multivariate draw for individual firm i, and $E_{im,r}$ is the rth univariate normal draw on the underlying effect for firm i. The multivariate draw v_{ir} is actually K independent draws. Heteroscedasticity is induced first by multiplying by Ω_i, then the correlation is induced by multiplying $\Omega_i v_{ir}$ by Γ.

The outcome-specific constants in (2.18) are linked to the EV1 type distribution for the random terms, after accounting for unobserved heterogeneity induced via distributions imposed on the observed variables, and the unobserved heterogeneity that is outcome-specific and accounted for by the error components. The error components account for unobserved (to the analyst) differences across firms in the intrinsic 'preference' for a choice outcome. The parameter associated with each error component is $\beta^*\sigma$, neither of which appears elsewhere in the model. We induce meaning by treating this parameter pair as θ which identifies the variance of the outcome-specific heterogeneity. What we are measuring is variation around the mean.[13]

---

[13] The idea that beta is the coefficient on the unmeasured heterogeneity might be strictly true, but the concept does not work in other models that have error components in them, so we should not try to impose it here. For example, in the linear model, we have an unmeasured variable epsilon, and we write the model $y = a + x'b + $ sigma*epsilon where, strictly speaking, epsilon is the unmeasured heterogeneity and sigma is the coefficient. But, sigma is the standard deviation of the unmeasured heterogeneity, not the 'coefficient' on the unmeasured heterogeneity.

This model with error components for each outcome is identified. Unlike other specifications (e.g., Ben-Akiva *et al.* 2001) that apply the results to identifying the scale factors in the disturbances in the marginal distributions of the utility functions, the logic does not apply to identifying the parameters on the explanatory variables; and in the conditional distribution we are looking at here, the error components are acting like variables, not disturbances. We are estimating the θ parameters as if they were weights on such variables, not scales on disturbances, and hence the way that the conditional distribution is presented. The parameters are identified in the same way that the β of the explanatory variables are identified. Since the error components are not observed, their scale is not identified. Hence, the parameter on the error component is $(\delta_m \sigma_m)$, where σ_m is the standard deviation. Since the scale is unidentified, we would normalize it to one for estimation purposes, with the understanding that the sign and magnitude of the weight on the component are carried by θ. But, neither is the sign of δ_m identified, since the same set of model results will emerge if the sign of every draw on the component were reversed – the estimator of δ would simply change sign with them. As such, we normalize the sign to plus. In sum, then, we estimate $|\delta_m|$, with the sign and the value of σ_m normalized for identification purposes.

2.3 Empirical application of the mixed logit model[14]

Jones and Hensher (2004) introduce a three-state financial distress model. They use an ordered mixed logit analysis for model estimation and prediction. However, the mixed logit model used in their study is more rudimentary than the error component logit model described in this chapter. Here, we extend their study to include other important manifestations of corporate distress observable in business practice, notably distressed mergers (discussed below) (see Clark and Ofek 1994). We also test a wider range of explanatory covariates than Jones and Hensher (2004), including market prices and macroeconomic variables. Further, while Jones and Hensher (2004) only test an ordered mixed logit model, this paper focuses on *unordered* failure outcomes. Ordered and unordered discrete outcome models have distinct conceptual and econometric properties. An unordered model specification is more appropriate when the set of alternative

---

[14] This empirical illustration is based on Hensher *et al.* (2007) 'An Error Component Logit Analysis of Corporate Bankruptcy and Insolvency Risk in Australia', *The Economic Record*, 83:260, pp. 86–103. This material was reproduced with permission from Blackwell Publishing, the publishers of the *The Economic Record*.

outcomes representing the dependent variable does not follow a natural ordinal ranking.[15] Given that most economic and finance-related problems which utilize a discrete outcome dependent variable involve unordered outcomes, the illustration provided in this study is particularly instructive in this respect.

This study describes financial distress in four (unordered) states as follows:

State 0: nonfailed firms.

State 1: insolvent firms. Insolvent firms are defined as: (i) loan default, (ii) failure to pay Australian Stock Exchange (ASX) annual listing fees as required by ASX Listing Rules; (iii) a capital raising *specifically* to generate sufficient working capital to finance continuing operations; and (iv) a debt/equity restructure due to a diminished capacity to make loan repayments.

State 2: financially distressed firms who were delisted from the ASX because they were subject to a merger or takeover arrangement.

State 3: firms who filed for bankruptcy followed by the appointment of receiver managers/liquidators.[16] For purposes of this study, States 0–3 are treated as mutually exclusive states within the context of an *unordered* model.

The inclusion of firms subject to mergers and takeovers represents a development on previous distress research, which has not previously considered this restructuring alternative in various models of firm failure (Clark and Ofek 1994; Bulow and Shoven 1978; Pastena and Ruland 1986). Unlike legal bankruptcy, mergers are a relatively common event. Mergers have been rationalized as a restructuring alternative to avoid bankruptcy, which can be a trade-off between going-concern value and liquidation value. A motivation for mergers and takeovers is that the indirect costs of bankruptcy can be very high (Altman 1984), and can reduce the going-concern value of the firm, such as loss of credibility and reputation for firms under administration (Pastena and Ruland 1986; Sutton and Callaghan 1987). Mergers involving financially distressed companies can be an effective means to avoid many of the detrimental consequences of bankruptcy and ultimately increase shareholder value (Opler and Titman 1995). Clark and Ofek (1994) set out a procedure for identifying financially distressed firms requiring restructuring through merger. They use several other events to classify firms

---

[15] Lau (1987) improved on the methodology of dichotomous prediction models by using a five-state model, but the study has a number of limitations. For instance, the MNL approach selected is not robust to violations of the IID and IIA assumptions which are corrected for in this study.

[16] This sample includes three major forms of bankruptcy proceeding available under the legislative provisions of the Australian *Corporations Act* (2001): (i) voluntary administration (first introduced in Australia in June 1993 under the *Corporate Law Reform Act*, 1992); (ii) liquidation and (iii) receivership. Most failed firms in the sample were in categories (i) and (ii).

as targets for a merger restructuring, such as management turnover, reduction in a firm's dividend, asset restructuring, qualified audit opinions, and financial distress. A similar examination was performed in our own study but we also include firms with severe deficiencies in working capital-resulting in a need for a major capital-raising effort (either through share issues or unsecured loans).[17]

Inclusion of distressed mergers presents an opportunity to further examine the explanatory and predictive power of advanced models across greater and more diverse states of financial distress observable in practice. Testing predictive capability becomes ever more challenging as we increase the number of failure alternatives, as greater demands are placed on the discriminatory power of the models to capture potentially subtle variations across the financial distress states – these samples tend to be *very* small in absolute terms, relative to the sample of nonfailed firms.

2.4 Sample selection

We develop two samples for the purposes of model estimation and validation. A sample of nonfailed and distressed firms in states 0, 1, 2 and 3 was collected between the years 1992 and 2004. The full sample was then randomly allocated to an estimation and holdout sample. To avoid the backcasting problem identified by Ohlson (1980), data were collected for each firm *prior* to the announcement of failure to the market. Failure announcement dates are ascertained from the ASX's Signal G releases.[18] To avoid oversampling problems and error rate biases associated with matched-pair designs we use a sample which better approximates actual takeover rates in practice (Zmijewski 1984). This procedure produced a final useable sample for the estimation sample of 2,259 firm years, with 1,871 firm years in the nonfailed state 0; and 280, 41 and 67 firm years in states 1, 2 and 3 respectively.[19] A final

---

[17] However, we avoided Clark and Ofek's definition of 'financial distress' because it would require us using specific ratios and/or financial variables also used as covariates to estimate and test distress models used in this study.

[18] Signal G disclosures are regulated by the ASX Listing Rule 3.1 which identifies the types of information which Australian companies must disclose to the market on a timely basis. Examples include: the appointment of a receiver or liquidator; information relating to mergers and takeovers; capital reorganizations; loan defaults; share issues; failure to pay listing fees and any other information which could have a material affect on the value of a company's securities (see also Sections 674 and 675 of the Corporations Act, 2001). Information for release to the market must be lodged by companies with the ASX's company announcement office (CAO), which is then immediately released to the market under Signal G (see Explanatory Note, ASX Listing Rules, Chapter 3, 97,575; and Chapter 15 of the listing rules). Because all Signal G market releases are electronically dispatched (in 'real time'), an accurate determination could be made whether a firm's financial statements were released before or after the announcement of failure.

[19] To avoid over sampling problems and error rate biases associated with matched pair designs (see Zmijewski 1984), a sample of failed and nonfailed firms was used which better approximates actual fail rates in practice.

useable sample for the validation sample included 2,192 firm years in state 0; and 242, 37 and 123 firm years in states 1, 2 and 3 respectively. The sample of nonfailed firms is drawn over the same time period range as the firms in states 1, 2, and 3, and the proportion of failed to nonfailed firms sampled is approximately equal across each of the years the data are collected. Checks were made to ensure that the nonfailed/insolvent/merger/failed firms identified in states 0, 1, 2 and 3 for the estimation sample are not also included in the validation sample. Only publicly listed firms on the ASX are included in the estimation and validation samples. Furthermore, only firms who report cash flow information under requirements of the Approved Australian Accounting Standard AASB 1026 'Statement of Cash Flows' were included in both samples.[20]

With respect to the sample of insolvent and merger firms, the same data collection procedures were used as with failed firms. The financial report prior to the indication of the firm's solvency problem or merger announcement was used for estimation purposes. Whether a firm experienced a solvency problem or distressed merger as defined in this study was ascertained from the analysis the ASX's Signal G releases, as was the case with failed firms.

Explanatory variables

To illustrate the performance of the error component logit model, we draw together a range of financial and market-based measures used in prior research (examples include Altman *et al.* 1977, Ohlson 1980, Zemjewski 1984, Casey and Bartczak 1985, Gentry *et al.* 1985, Jones 1987, Altman 2001, Jones and Hensher 2004). Financial variables include: operating cash flows to total assets; cash flow record (a dummy variable indicating the number of consecutive annual periods of negative operating cash flows reported by a sampled firm); total debt to gross cash flow; cash resources to total assets; working capital to total assets; total debt to total equity; total liabilities to total equity; interest cover ratio; earnings before interest and taxes to total assets; return on total assets; sales turnover; and retained earnings to total assets. Following the work of Hribar and Collins (2002), this study uses the actual reported cash flows of firms extracted from the firm's published *Statement of Cash Flows*, as opposed estimates of cash flows widely used in previous research.[21]

---

[20] The Australian cash flow standard *Approved Australian Accounting Standard* AASB 1026 'Statement of Cash Flows' was issued by the AASB in 1991, with a mandatory operative date of June 1992.

[21] Previous research has indicated that estimates of operating cash flows (using balance sheet reconstruction methods) can be poor proxies for the operating cash flow number reported in the *Statement of Cash Flows* (see Hribar and Collins 2002 for detailed discussion).

Market price variables are also becoming increasingly important predictors of corporate distress (see, e.g., Clark and Weinstein 1983, Dichev 1998, Frino *et al.* 2007). This research finds that impending corporate failures are rarely complete surprises to the market – that is, stock prices largely anticipate corporate collapses well before the announcement of failure. For instance, Frino *et al.* (2005), find that stock prices and bid–ask spreads 'impound' a solvency deterioration signal in financially struggling firms up to two years before the public announcement of failure. Market variables tested in this study include excess market returns and the market value of equity to total book value of debt, the latter variable being a widely used market proxy for firm solvency in many structural models of default risk (see Altman 2001). Due to the relative lack of liquidity in many Australian stocks, we could not generate reliable parameter estimates using a market model such as the capital asset pricing model (CAPM). A more common measure used in Australian capital market research is market-adjusted returns, calculated by subtracting the return to the All Ordinaries Accumulation Index (AOAI) from the sample firm's return expressed as a price relative (see, e.g., de Silva Rosa *et al.* 2004). Other variables tested in this study include firm size (proxied by the natural log of total assets) and age of the firm (a dummy variable indicating the number of years in which a firm has been in existence). We also examine industry variables classified across four major sectors: the old economy sector; the new economy sector; the resources sector and the financial services sector.[22] Finally, we test three state variables relating to general economic conditions in Australia over the sample period. These variables related to stock market conditions, general interest rates and growth in the economy over the sample period. The stock market condition variable is a dummy variable coded '1' if the ASX All Ordinaries index experienced a collapse of more than 20% in any one year over the sample period, zero otherwise; the general interest rates variable is a dummy variable coded '1' if interest rates increased by 2% or more in any given year over the sample period, zero otherwise; and the growth in the economy variable was coded '1' if the Australian GDP contracted for at least two consecutive quarters over the sample period, zero otherwise (a widely used definition for economic recession). A list of variables tested in the study is provided in Table 2.1.

---

[22] Firms in the New Economy sector are classified according to the ASX industry classification guidelines, outlined in the ASX Market Comparative Analysis (2004). These are: (i) health and biotechnology; (ii) high technology; (iii) internet firms; and (iv) telecommunications. The resources sector is classified by the ASX as: (i) gold companies; (ii) other metals and (iii) diversified resources. Financial services are defined by the ASX as banks and finance houses, insurance companies and investment and financial services companies. Old economy firms are defined as all firms not being in the new economy, resources and financial services sectors.

Table 2.1 Definition of variables

Variable acronym		Definition
Expected sign	**Financial variables**	
+	Netopta	Net operating cash flow by total assets
−	Cdebtc	Total debt by gross operating cash flow
+	Cpta	Cash, deposits and marketable securities by total assets
−	NegCFO2	A dummy variable coded 1 if a firm had two consecutive annual periods of negative operating cash flows and zero otherwise
−	NegCFO3	A dummy variable coded 1 if a firm had three consecutive annual periods of negative operating cash flows and zero otherwise
−	NegCFO4	A dummy variable coded 1 if a firm had four consecutive annual periods of negative operating cash flows and zero otherwise
+	Workcta	Working capital (current assets – current liabilities) by total assets
−	Cgear	Total debt by total equity
−	Tlte	Total liabilities to total equity
+	Nicover	Reported EBIT by annual interest payments
+	Ebitta	Reported EBIT by total assets
+	Roa	Return on assets
+	Csalesta	Total sales revenue by total assets
+	Creta	Retained earnings by total assets
	Market variables	
+	Excess market returns	Calculated by subtracting the return to the All Ordinaries Accumulation Index (AOAI) from the sample firm's return expressed as a price relative. Excess returns are calculated using monthly price data *for each month* up to four years prior to failure.
	Contextual variables	
	Industry classification	
−	New_econ	If a new economy firm coded 1, 0 otherwise
−	Resource	If a resources firm coded 1, 0 otherwise
+	Old_econ	If an old economy firm coded 1, 0 otherwise
+	Finance	If a financial services firm coded 1, 0 otherwise
	Size variable	
+	Logta	Natural log of total assets
	Age variable	
−	Age	A dummy variables coded 1 if a firm was established in the previous six years, zero otherwis
	State variables	
−	ASX_Coll	Stock market collapse over the sample period (1 = yes; zero otherwise). Stock market collapse defined by $>= 20\%$ drop in the ASX All Ords.

Table 2.1 (cont.)

Variable acronym		Definition
–	Int_Inc	Significant increase in interest rates over the sample period (1 = yes; zero otherwise). Defined by $> = 2\%$ increase in interest rates over a one year period.
–	Recen_Var	Significant contraction in economy over sample period (1 = yes; zero otherwise). Defined by at least two consecutive quarters of GDP contraction.

Results

We estimate a multinomial error component logit model and a standard MNL model to identify the statistically significant influences on the probability of firm financial distress. Panels A–D of Table 2.2 summarize the overall model system for both the error component logit model and the standard MNL model. Panel A reports the fixed-parameter estimates for both models while Panel B reports the random-parameter and latent-error component estimates for the final multinomial error component logit model. Panel C displays the log-likelihood at convergence and the sample sizes for both models. Finally, Panel D reports the descriptive statistics for the significant covariates found in Panels A and B of Table 2.2.

The models reported in Table 2.2 are specified as a set of mutually exclusive *unordered* outcomes. Since not all explanatory variables vary across the alternatives (but are associated with a known outcome), to identify each model we needed to constrain the parameters of each variable to equal zero for at least one of the alternatives. This specification relies on the variability across the sample to establish the influence of each firm variable on the outcome probability.

Different sets of financial variables associated with the utility functions of each alternative (i.e. nonfailure, insolvency, distressed merger and outright failure) are specified in order to test their statistical influence on the response outcome. In unordered models, the utility functions specified by the researcher may not be the same for each alternative. Different attributes may enter into one or more utility expressions, with a general constraint that no single attribute can appear in all utility expressions simultaneously (see Hensher *et al.* 2005).

Generally, variables that enter the models are determined on the basis of prior literature (discussed above) and on examining correlations and hypothesized

Table 2.2 Panel A: Fixed parameter estimates and *t*-values for final multinomial error component logit and standard MNL models

Variables	Alternative	Multinomial error component logit	Standard multinomial logit (MNL)
Fixed parameters:			
Insolvency constant	Insolvency	− 5.77	− 2.77
		(− 5.32)	(− 26.9)
Distressed Merger	Distressed Mergers	− 12.91	− 7.26
constant		(− 5.00)	(− 5.02)
Outright failure	Outright failure	− 2.343	− .747
constant		(− .76)	(− .558)
Four periods of	Nonfailure	− 4.800	− 1.85
negative CFO		(− 4.48)	(− 9.77)
Age of Firm	Nonfailure	1.412	.455
		(2.62)	(2.47)
Excess market returns	Nonfailure	Random parameter	.001
			(1.83)
Cash resources to	Nonfailure	Random parameter	− .021
total assets			(− 4.75)
Retained earnings to	Insolvency, Distressed	− .0149	− .005
total assets	merger, Outright failure	(− 4.68)	(− 9.5)
Working capital to	Distressed Mergers	.0117	.0026
total assets		(1.185)	(.517)
Age of Firm	Distressed mergers	− 1.906	− 1.35
		(− 2.088)	(− 1.82)
Log of total assets	Distressed mergers	Random parameter	.154
			(1.92)
Log of total assets	Outright failure	Random parameter	− .183
			(− 2.35)
Cash resources to	Outright failure	− .031	− .025
total assets		(− 2.67)	(− 3.28)
Total debt to	Outright failure	.006	.0054
operating cash flow		(1.36)	(2.44)
MNL interactions:			
EMR and financial	Nonfailure		− .0045
sector dummy			(− 2.06)
Cpta and financial	Nonfailure		.0111
sector dummy			(1.58)
Cpta and new	Nonfailure		− .0138
economy			(− 2.58)

Note: t-values in parentheses.

Table 2.2 Panel B: Random parameter and latent error component estimates and *t*-values for final multinomial error component logit

Variables	Alternative	Multinomial error component logit
Random parameters:		
Excess market returns	Nonfailure	.028
		(3.69)
Cash resources to total assets	Nonfailure	.065
		(2.08)
Log of total assets	Distressed Merger	.168
		(3.62)
Log of total assets	Outright failure	− .372
		(− 1.806)
Heterogeneity in means:		
Cash resources to total assets	Nonfailure	− .122
New Economy		(− 2.92)
Standard Deviation of Random Parameters:		
Excess market returns	Nonfailure	.059
		(4.21)
Cash resources to total assets	Nonfailure	.209
		(4.0)
Log of total assets	Distressed Merger	.169
		(3.62)
Log of total assets	Outright failure	.167
		(2.58)
Heteroscedasticity in random parameters:		
Excess market returns	Nonfailure	.696
Financial services		(1.79)
Cash resources to total assets	Nonfailure	− .90
Financial services		(− 1.74)
Standard deviation of latent error component effects:		
SigmaK01	Nonfailure	3.15
		(2.95)
SigmaK02	All but nonfailure	2.55
		(2.53)
Heterogeneity in variance of latent error component effects:		
K01 by old economy	Nonfailure	− 1.22
dummy		(− 1.60)

Note: t-values in parentheses. Standard MNL logit only has fixed parameter estimates.

signs among the covariates (highly correlated variables were removed from the analysis).[23] We searched for a behaviourally and statistically coherent model based on the expectations of prior literature. We note that some variables are expected to have a stronger impact in the utility expressions of some alternatives relative to others. For example, from prior literature (and anecdotal evidence in business takeover practice), we expect variables such as rate of return on assets, sales revenue, working capital, debt to equity and stock price performance to be critical in distressed mergers, as acquirers of distressed companies are often looking for poorly managed companies (proxied by lower rates of return and stagnant sales growth) with good residual value left in the underlying assets which can be acquired at attractive prices.

Likewise, we would expect operating cash flows, debt to cash flow ratios and cash resources to be particularly important variables in the insolvency category, whereas prior literature has shown that all of these variables (including size and age of the firm) are potentially important influences on outright failures.

Random parameters are also selected based partly on the expectations of prior literature and partly on the expected behavioural relationships among certain covariates. For instance, we expected a high degree of heteroscedasticity in some explanatory variables relative to others across the sample. For example, stock price returns are expected to be more volatile across some distress categories relative to others (particularly outright failures and distressed mergers vs. non-failures). Failed companies tend to have much smaller market capitalizations and are relatively illiquid – hence small volume and price movements can have a dramatically greater impacts on overall sample averages relative to firms with larger market capitalizations. This is also true for operating cash flows, which tends to be smaller in absolute terms and more volatile in each of the distress categories relative to the nonfailure category.

Furthermore, firm size tends to be associated with considerable heteroscedasticity across our distress states – outright failures and insolvent companies tend to have much smaller market capitalizations and total asset sizes relative to nonfailed firms (some distressed mergers, however, can involve quite large companies). Decomposition of means and variances (the interaction of random parameter means and variances with contextual factors) was also based on prior findings in the literature. For example, we

---

[23] Pearson product moment correlations for all explanatory variables is available on request.

Table 2.2 Panel C: Log-likelihood at convergence and sample sizes for final multinomial error component logit and standard MNL models

	Multinomial error component logit	Standard multinomial logit (MNL)
Log-likelihood at zero	− 3131.64	− 3131.64
Log-likelihood at convergence	− 1036.90	− 1088.57
Sample size	2259	2259

Table 2.2 Panel D: Descriptive statistics for significant covariates reported in panels A and B

Variables	Alternative	Mean	Standard deviation
Excess market returns	Nonfailure	13.46	64.33
Cash resources to total assets	Nonfailure	12.59	22.70
Four periods of negative CFO	Nonfailure	.032	.177
Retained earnings to total assets	Insolvency	− 207.84	226.08
Retained earnings to total assets	Distressed merger	− 36.45	53.68
Working capital to total assets	Distressed merger	17.43	34.35
Log of total assets	Distressed merger	17.35	.889
Log of total assets	Outright failure	14.35	1.67
Retained earnings to total assets	Outright failure	− 95.77	194.24
Cash resources to total assets	Outright failure	11.84	16.99
Total debt to operating cash flow	Outright failure	12.21	27.33
Firm age (in existence six years or less)	Outright failure	.054	.229

would expect certain industries to be associated with higher failure rates relative to others, which led us to specifically test for these effects (see Jones and Hensher 2004).

It can be seen from Table 2.2 (Panel C) that the error component logit model has delivered a very good overall goodness of fit. The log-likelihood (LL) has decreased from 3131 (assuming no information other than random shares) to − 1036.9. The improvement in the log-likelihood ratio is less pronounced for the standard MNL model, with the LL showing a decrease to -1088.57. To ensure MNL comparability with error component logit, where possible, we introduce three interactions (two with the finance dummy and one with the new economy dummy variable) that are 'equivalent' to the decomposition of the mean and standard deviation of random parameters. Using an LL ratio test (which compares the LL ratio of the error component logit model and standard MNL model at convergence adjusted for number of parameters in each model) we can calculate the likelihood ratio as $-2 \times (1088.57 - 1036.9) = -103.34$ at 6 degrees of freedom. This is chi-square distributed and at any level of significance the error component logit model is a significant improvement over standard MNL.

Both models are estimated from the full set of variables in the data set. However, a similar set of variables are found to be statistically significant in both the error component logit and standard MNL models. These variables include the firm age proxy (a dummy variable coded '1' if the firm was established in the past 6 years or less, '0' otherwise); whether a firm had four periods of consecutive net operating cash flow losses (a dummy variable coded '1' if yes, '0' otherwise); cash resources to total assets (for the outright failure alternative); and retained earnings to total assets. However, each model also reveals some different influences. For instance, the total debt to operating cash flows variable is significant in the MNL model, but the firm age variable is significant for the error component logit model (for the distressed merger alternative).

The MNL model is *only* represented by fixed-parameter estimates including three interactions between financial and contextual variables (see Panel A of Table 2.2). A fixed parameter treats the standard deviation as zero such that all the behavioural information on the marginal utility of a variable is assumed to be captured by the mean, either as a stand-alone variable or an interaction with firm-specific characteristics. Essentially this assumes that the population of firms have homogeneous preferences (i.e. fixed marginal utilities) with respect to the role of a variable on the failure states or homogeneity within a segment as described by a firm-specific characteristic (in the MNL model herein they are finance and new economy dummy variables' interaction with excess market return and cash resources to total assets). For instance, the parameter for a financial ratio, such as excess market returns, is estimated from the sample of all firms as an average firm effect, and does not allow for the possibility of a distribution of preferences across the sample.

In contrast, the error component logit model has several additional parameters which capture both observed and unobserved heterogeneity between and within firms. As can be seen in Panel B of Table 2.2, random and systematic firm-specific heterogeneity is represented in the error component logit model by the standard deviation of random parameters, heterogeneity in the mean of random parameters, decomposition in the standard deviation of random parameters, alternative-specific latent error component effects and their decomposition. Panel B of Table 2.2 indicates that there are four statistically significant random parameters associated with three variables – excess market returns, cash resources to total assets and the firm size proxy – each specified as an unconstrained normal distribution, except for the natural logarithm of firm size in state 2 (i.e. distressed merger) which was a constrained normal in which the standard deviation parameter is set equal to the mean parameter. This latter restriction was found to be the best representation of random firm-specific heterogeneity, implying that an unconstrained normal tended to force a spread of firm-specific heterogeneity which was too thin at the tails and impacting on the overall statistical significance of the distribution.[24] If the researcher only relies on a simple multinomial (or binary logit) model, the opportunity to identify the presence of firm-specific heterogeneity would be lost (by being inappropriately assigned to the IID random component as occurs for a standard MNL model).

Overall, these findings suggest that the standard deviation beta for excess market returns, cash resources to total assets and the firm size proxy provide important information to establish *the extent* of *random* preference heterogeneity (or marginal utility) in the sampled population for these variables. A search for sources of *systematic* preference heterogeneity, through interaction of contextual effects with the mean and/or standard deviation betas of the random parameter, has identified further statistically significant impacts. For example, we find that for the random parameter variable 'cash resources to total debt', the interaction of the mean beta with the new economy dummy variable suggests that membership of the new economy has a differential influence on the role of these variables to the failure outcome. Given a positive sign on the mean estimate and negative sign of the new economy decomposition, the marginal utility decreases for new economy firms relative to non-new economy firms.

---

[24] There is an active debate on the merits of constrained vs. unconstrained distributions. It is important to recognise that the imposed distributions are analytical approximations to a true behavioural profile. An unconstrained distribution 'forces' maximum spread of potential firm-specific heterogeneity to satisfy the lack of a priori assumption on the standard deviation (or spread). Constrained distributions have merit but as we reduce the standard deviation by assumption we are forcing the firm-specific heterogeneity towards zero. We have found in numerous studies that a standard deviation equal to the mean or twice the mean appears to capture the firm-specific heterogeneity within acceptable bounds of statistical significance.

A similar conclusion can be reached from analysis of the heteroscedasticity in the variance of random parameters (see Panel B). One positive and one negative parameter have been found with the interaction between the finance sector dummy variable and, respectively, the standard deviation beta for excess market returns and cash resources to total assets. This suggests that the subsample of firms that are in the finance sector display a greater amount of preference heterogeneity (i.e. higher standard deviation or variance) than exists for the sample as a whole (or for the non-finance sector) with respect to excess market returns, and conversely a lesser amount of preference heterogeneity with respect to cash resources to total assets. Ignoring the impact of these significant interactions would lead, *ceteris paribus*, in prediction, to narrowing the distribution of the marginal utility of excess market returns and inflating the distribution of marginal utility for cash resources to total assets for finance firms and respectively widening and narrowing them for all other samples firms not in this industry group.

Alternative groupings of the four state outcomes are evaluated to identify additional sources of unobserved heterogeneity that can be attributed to specific states. We find that the three failure states (1,2,3) vs. non-failure provide the statistically significant differentiation as error component effects, with no cross-state effects. If we had not established such additional state-specific differential variance then this would have been absorbed into the extreme value distribution as IID. What we find is that the standard deviation of the latent error component effect for the nonfailure state is greater than that for the three failure states; highlighting the presence of a greater amount of unobserved preference heterogeneity associated with the nonfailure state after accounting for sources of preference heterogeneity via a set of variable specific random parameters and the constant marginal utility effects of an additional set of explanatory variables.

In addition to identifying and accounting for the random distribution of unobserved state-specific heterogeneity, we have been successful in establishing one source of systematic variability in such heterogeneity. We find a marginally significant effect for the decomposition of the nonfailure state latent error component effect into old economy vs. new economy. Firms in the old economy have a narrower distribution of unobserved state-specific heterogeneity contributing to the utility of firm nonfailure compared to new economy firms. Although the effect is not strong, it serves to illustrate the value in searching for systematic, in contrast to random, sources of firm-specific heterogeneity that can be associated with the overall distribution of relative utility of a specific state in contrast to competing states.

Table 2.2 Panel E: Direct elasticies for final multinomial error component logit and standard MNL models

Variables	Alternative	Multinomial error component logit	Standard multinomial logit (MNL)
Excess market returns	Nonfailure	.0188 (.4067)	.000049
Cash resources to total assets	Nonfailure	.0322 (.4198)	.00057
Four periods of negative CFO	Nonfailure	− .231 (.8148)	− .097
Retained earnings to total assets	Insolvency	− .440 (1.079)	− .139
Retained earnings to total assets	Distressed merger	− .752 (2.11)	− .232
Working capital to total assets	Distressed merger	.132 (.298)	.029
Log of total assets	Distressed merger	.737 (1.34)	.023
Log of total assets	Outright failure	− 1.62 (2.87)	.031
Retained earnings to total assets	Outright failure	− .701 (1.92)	− .214
Cash resources to total assets	Outright failure	− .370 (.536)	− .298
Total debt to operating cash flow	Outright failure	.0421 (.163)	.036
Firm age (in existence six years or less)	Outright failure	.0427	.013
Sample size		2259	2259

Note: Standard deviation of elasticities in parentheses.

Analysis of model elasticities

A direct interpretation of the behavioural meaning of parameter estimates reported in Panels A and B of Table 2.2 is not possible given the logit transformation of the outcome dependent variable required for model estimation. We therefore provide the elasticities (Panel E of Table 2.2) defined as the influence that a percentage change in an explanatory variable (or its functional presence) has on the percentage change in the probability of selecting a particular outcome, *ceteris paribus.* We do not expect the elasticities to have the same sign as the utility parameters, and indeed they are complex functions of a number of parameters when random parameter decomposition is present. Hence the statistical significance of a utility parameter does not imply the same significance for the elasticity (see Hensher *et al.* 2005 for details).

The direct[25] elasticities reported in Panel E all appear to have logical and consistent signs for both the error component logit and standard MNL models. For example, the excess market returns variable for the nonfailure category has a positive direct elasticity, indicating that a percentage increase in this variable *increases* the probability of nonfailure, *ceteris paribus*. This result is consistent with established literature that deteriorating financial health is impounded into stock prices (through lower excess market returns) of struggling companies well before the announcement of failure to the market. In this case, excess market returns are statistically significant 14 months prior to the actual failure announcement by firms, which is generally consistent with previous literature (see Frino *et al.* 2007).

The variable NegCFO4 (whether a firm has four consecutive periods of negative operating cash flows) is negative, suggesting that firms with consecutive cash flow losses have an increased probability of financial distress (or reduced probability of nonfailure). The direct elasticities appear consistent and logical on the distress outcome alternatives as well. For instance, retained earnings to total assets has a negative direct elasticity on the insolvency alternative, suggesting that higher levels of a sampled firm's retained earnings reduce the probability of insolvency, *ceteris paribus* (which is intuitive, as positive retained earnings are accumulated from previous years' *positive* earnings results of firms). Another example is the total debt to operating cash flow variable, which has a positive direct elasticity on the outright failure alternative, suggesting that increasing this variable increases the probability of outright failure, *ceteris paribus*. This result is also expected as higher levels of this ratio indicate higher external indebtedness and/or a reduced capacity to service debt with available operating cash flows. Interestingly, the firm size proxy (log of total assets) indicates a negative direct elasticity on the outright failure alternative (suggesting that larger firms have a lower probability of outright failure, ceteris paribus) but a positive elasticity on the distressed merger category (suggesting that larger firms have a higher probability of entering a distressed merger, *ceteris paribus*). The firm age variable indicates a positive direct elasticity on the outright failure alternative, indicating that if a firm has been in existence six years or less, the

---

[25] Cross-elasticities are not reported but are available from the authors on request.

probability of outright failure increases. This result is consistent with pre-vailing literature that suggests that smaller and more recently established firms generally have a relatively higher likelihood of failure than larger more established firms (Altman 2001). The fact that larger firms are more likely to enter a distressed merger is consistent with the view that such mergers are motivated by an attempt to salvage residual value in the assets of distressed businesses, which is more likely for larger businesses (which also tend to be more established and therefore have higher residual assets) than for smaller entities (see Altman *et al.* 2005).

It can be seen from Panel D that the direct elasticities are generally much stronger for the error component logit model than the standard MNL model. For example, a one per cent increase in the excess market returns variable increases the probability of nonfailure by 0.0188% for the error component logit model, but only increases the probability by 0.000049% for the MNL model (other extreme differences in the elasticity effects are revealed on the cash resources to total assets, for the nonfailure alternative and retained earnings to total assets, for the insolvency alternative). While the error component logit elasticity is stronger than the standard MNL model, we acknowledge that even for the error component logit model the economic impact of the excess return variable is still quite small in absolute terms (e.g., a 10% change in excess return covariate only changes the probability of nonfailure by 0.2%). However, it needs to be borne in mind that our sample is based on failure frequency rates (and insolvency and distressed merger rates) that are much closer to actual failure rates observable in practice. Our model's elasticities tend to be smaller in absolute terms because they are derived from probabilities and parameter estimates which are based on a *very* high proportion of nonfailures relative to each of the distress categories (i.e., a much larger change in an elasticity is needed to move a company (in probability terms) from the nonfailure category to one of the distress states).[26] Furthermore, as many failed and distress firms in our sample tend to have very small market capitalizations (as well as very thin trading liquidity), large changes in stock price will not necessarily have a significant impact on financial distress levels.[27]

---

[26] Much previous bankruptcy research has used matched-pair samples or samples that do not resemble actual failure rates in practice (Zmijewski 1984). Consequently, the elasticities of these models are likely to overstate the behavioural impact of covariates on the probability of distress.

[27] In an extreme case, a distressed firm's stock price can go from 1 cent to 2 cents on very small trading volume (a 100% increase) but this ostensibly large increase is likely to have little impact on the overall distress level of the firm.

Only for two of the covariates are the direct elasticities for the error component logit and MNL models reasonably comparable – for instance, a one per cent increase in the cash resources to total assets variable (for the outright failure alternative) reduces the probability of failure by 0.37% for the error component logit model, but reduces the probability of failure by 0.29% for the MNL model. Furthermore, a one per cent increase in the total debt to operating cash flow increases the probability of outright failure by 0.0421% for the error component logit model, and increases this probability by 0.036% for the MNL model.

Forecasting accuracy of the error component logit model

Having evaluated the model-fit information and direct elasticities, we now turn to the prediction outcomes. Calculating probability outcomes for a error component logit model is considerably more complex than for a standard MNL model because it has an open form solution and a wider range of parameters estimates which collectively contribute to the outcome probability. In deriving the probability outcomes for the error component logit model we note that some explanatory variables are a composite function of a mean parameter, a distribution around the mean and decomposition of the mean and variance by some contextual effect (in our case it is the new economy and financial services industry effects). In addition to fixed parameters, each individual firm is 'located' in parameter space on the normal distribution for the four random parameter variables in Table 2.2 (Panel B). The specification in Equation (2.7) for the attribute *cash resources to total assets* (CPTA) and excess market returns (EMR) are:

Marginal utility of CPTA = {0.065 − 0.122 × new_econ + 0.209 × [exp(− 0.90*financial services)] × N }
Marginal utility of EMR = {0.028 + 0.059 × [exp(− 0.696*financial services) × N] }

where N is normal distribution.

Consistent with the approach adopted in the discrete choice literature, we focus on a sample enumeration method which recognizes that the estimated model is based on a sample drawn from a population and the application of the model must preserve the full distribution of information obtained from the model system (see Train 2003). This includes the outcome probabilities. Thus we aggregate the probabilities associated with each outcome across the entire sample to obtain the predicted values. Implementing a sample enumeration strategy on our holdout sample, we can evaluate the predictive performance of the error component logit model. We find that the error component logit model has a high level of predictive accuracy on a holdout sample across most of the alternatives. The error component logit model is 99% accurate in predicting the nonfailure outcome (84.5% actual vs. 85.2% predicted), 91% accurate in predicting the insolvency outcome (9.3% actual vs. 10.2% predicted), 76.3% accurate in predicting distressed merger outcome (1.42% actual vs. 1.56% predicted) and 56% accurate in predicting the outright failure outcome (4.74% actual vs. 2.65% predicted).[28] The MNL tends to do a fairly good job at predicting the state shares for dominant states such as nonfailure (i.e., 84.5% actual vs. 81.34% predicted) but was found to be slightly worse in predicting shares for the states that are infrequently observed. For instance, the MNL model predicted the insolvency category (9.3% actual vs. 11.9% predicted) and the outright failure category (4.74% actual vs 3.1% predicted), with less accuracy than the error component logit model, but both models produced almost identical predictions on the distressed merger category.

Notwithstanding the relatively strong predictive accuracy of the error component logit model, we reiterate our earlier comments that selecting a model based solely on prediction capability of a holdout sample is to deny the real value of models in evaluating the behavioural responses in the market to specific actions, planned or otherwise, as represented by the elasticities linked to specific explanatory variables. Elasticities are arguably the most important behavioural outputs, although confidence in sample-based predictions of state shares adds to the overall appeal of an empirical model as a policy tool. A behaviourally relevant model should be able to predict with confidence what is likely to happen when one or more explanatory variables take on new values in real markets.

2.5 Conclusion

Over the past four decades, the corporate distress literature has tended to rely on simplistic choice models, such as linear discriminant models and binary logit/probit models. There are two major limitations with this literature. First, the archetypical two-state failure model only provides a very limited representation of the financial distress spectrum that corporations typically face in the real world. Secondly, simple-form discrete models suffer

---

[28] A simple mixed logit model with only a mean and standard deviation on each random parameter produced overall shares of 84.24, 11.1, 1.94 and 2.69 per cent for states 0,1,2 and 3 respectively (hence, the model is slightly less accurate than the error component logit model in predicting smaller shares or the actual states of distress).

from a number of limiting statistical assumptions which can, under some conditions at least, seriously impair their explanatory and predictive performance. More recently, the discrete-choice literature has shifted to model specifications which have increasingly relaxed the rigid assumptions associated with the IID and IIA conditions in a manner that is computationally tractable, behaviourally rich and practical.

This chapter has set out a more general discrete-choice model than the popular nested logit specification. The nested logit approach is limiting in that is not capable of accounting for the potential correlation induced through repeated observations on one or more pooled data sets. Nor does it recognize the role that various sources of heterogeneity play in influencing choices outcomes, either via the random parametrization of observed attributes and via parametrization of error components associated with a single or sub-set of alternatives (alternative-specific heterogeneity).

The unified mixed logit model presented herein is capable of allowing for these influencing dimensions, observed or unobserved) in addition to accounting for scale differences (that are equivalent to the scale revealed in the NL model). The empirical example illustrates the additional outputs from the unified mixed logit model and the differences in key behavioural outputs.

We find that the error component logit and MNL models are represented by a similar group of significant covariates which are also statistically coherent in terms of the expected sign of their parameter estimates and direct elasticities. Further, the variables having the greatest overall statistical influence on the failure outcome are broadly consistent with previous academic and professional literature. These variables include: firm size, firm age, retained earnings to total assets, operating cash flow performance, working capital to total assets, cash resources to total assets, total debt to operating cash flows and excess market returns. However, financial-based variables (including the firm size proxy) appear to have the greatest overall association with the failure outcome, relative to market-based variables, firm age and macro-economic factors (none of which are found to be significant in either the error component logit or MNL models reported in Table 2.2). In addition to these effects, the error component logit model has identified further contextual impacts as interactions or decompositions of the means and standard deviation of random parameters, and identified state-specific random and systematic firm-specific heterogeneity.

Notwithstanding some general consistencies with the estimated error component logit and MNL models, our results suggest that, in a four-state unordered failure setting at least, the error component logit model provides much improved explanatory power (but more limited additional predictive performance) over a standard logit specification. For instance, the model-fit statistics are statistically superior for the error component logit model. Furthermore, the direct elasticities of the error component logit model are generally stronger than the MNL model, which suggests that the covariates in the error component model have a stronger overall behavioural response on the domain outcome when changed in real markets. The overall predictive accuracy of the error component logit model on a holdout sample is impressive (better than 97% accurate overall), notwithstanding that the model is a little less effective in predicting the outright failure category relative to the nonfailure, insolvency and distressed merger categories. The predictive performance of the error component logit model provides us with a level of assurance that use of a more complex and behaviourally appealing model form will not necessarily result in significant trade-offs with a loss in predictive performance.

REFERENCES

Altman, E., Haldeman, R. and Narayan, P., 'ZETA analysis: a new model to identify bankruptcy risk of corporations', *Journal of Banking and Finance*, June, 1977, 29–54.

Altman, E. I., 'A further empirical investigation of the bankruptcy cost question', *Journal of Finance*, 39(4), 1984, 1067–89.

Altman, E. I, *Bankruptcy, Credit Risk and High Yield Junk Bonds*, New York, Blackwell, 2001.

Altman, E. I., Resti, R. and Sironi, P., *Recovery Risk*, London, Risks Books, 2005.

Australian Accounting Standards Board, *Approved Australian Accounting Standard AASB 1026: Statement of Cash Flows*. Melbourne, Australian Accounting Research Foundation, 1992.

Australian Corporations Act, Cwt (http://www.asic.gov.au/asic/ASIC), 2001.

Australian Stock Exchange, *Market Comparative Analysis*, Sydney (http://www.asxtra.asx.com.au) 2004.

Bhat, C. R. 'Quasi-random maximum simulated likelihood estimation of the mixed multinomial logit model', *Transportation Research*, 35B, 2001, 677–95.

Bhat, C. R., 'Simulation estimation of mixed discrete choice models using randomized and scrambled Halton sequences', *Transportation Research B*, 37(9), 2003, 837–55.

Ben-Akiva, M., Bolduc, D. and Walker, J., 'Specification, identification and estimation of the logit kernel (or continuous mixed logit) model', *MIT Working Paper*, Department of Civil Engineering, 2001.

Brownstone, D., Bunch, D. S. and Train, K., 'Joint mixed logit models of stated and revealed preferences for alternative-fuel vehicles', *Transportation Research*, 34B, 2000, 315–38.

Bulow, J. I., and Shoven, J. B. 'The bankruptcy decision', *Bell Journal of Economics*, 9(2), 1978, 437–56.

Casey, C., and Bartczak, N., 'Using operating cash flow data to predict financial distress: some extensions', *Journal of Accounting Research*, 23, 1985, 384–401.

Clark, K. and Ofek, E., 'Mergers as a means of restructuring distressed firms: and impirical investigation', *Journal of Financial and Quantitative Analysis*, 29, 1994, 541–65.

Clark, T. A. and Weinstein, M. I., 'The behaviour of the common stock of bankrupt firms', *Journal of Finance*, 38, 1983, 489–504.

De Silva Rosa, R., Nguyen T. and Walter, T., 'Market returns to acquirers of substantial assets', *Australian Journal of Management*, 29, 2004, 111–34.

Dichev, I. D., 'Is the risk of bankruptcy a systematic risk', *Journal of Finance*, 53, 1998, 1131–48.

Frino, A., Jones, S. and Wong, J., '*Market behaviour around bankruptcy announcements: Evidence from the Australian Stock Exchange*', *Accounting and Finance*, 47(4), 2007, pp. 713–30.

Gentry, J., Newbold, P. and Whitford, D., 'Classifying bankrupt firms with funds flow components', *Journal of Accounting Research*, 23, 1985, 146–60.

Hensher, D. A. and Greene, W. H., 'Mixed logit models: state of practice', *Transportation*, 30 (2), 2003, 133–76.

Hensher, D. A., Rose, J. and Greene, W. H., *Applied Choice Analysis: A Primer*, Cambridge University Press, 2005.

Hensher, D. A., Jones, S. and Greene, W. H. 'An error component logit analysis of corporate bankruptcy and insolvency risk in Australia', *The Economic Record*, 83:260, 2007, 86–103.

Hribar, P. and Collins, D., 'Errors in estimating accruals: implications for empirical research', *Journal of Accounting Research*, 40, 2002, 105–34.

Jones, F., 'Current techniques in bankruptcy prediction', *Journal of Accounting Literature*, 6, 1987, 131–64.

Jones, S. and Hensher, D. A., 'Predicting firm financial distress: a mixed logit model', *The Accounting Review*, 79, 2004, 1011–38.

Lau, A. H., 'A five-state financial distress prediction model', *Journal of Accounting Research*, 25, 1987, 127–38.

Louviere, J. J., Hensher, D. A. and Swait, J. F., *Stated Choice Methods and Analysis*, Cambridge University Press, 2000.

McFadden, D. and Train K., 'Mixed MNL models for discrete response', *Journal of Applied Econometrics*, 15, 2000, 447–70.

Ohlson, J., 'Financial ratios and the probabilistic prediction of bankruptcy', *Journal of Accounting Research*, 18, 1980, 109–31.

Opler, T. and Titman, S., *Financial distress and capital structure choice. Working Paper*, Boston College, 1995.

Pastena, V. and Ruland, W., 'The merger/bankruptcy alternative', *The Accounting Review*, 61, 1986, 288–301.

Revelt, D. and Train, K., 'Mixed logit with repeated choices: households' choices of appliance efficiency level', *Review of Economics and Statistics*, 80, 1998, 1–11.

Stern, S., 'Simulation-based estimation', *Journal of Economic Literature*, 35, 1997, 2006–39.

Sutton, R. I. and Callaghan, A. L., 'The stigma of bankruptcy: spoiled organizational image and its management', *Academy of Management Journal*, 30, 1987, 405–36.

Train, K. 'Halton sequences for mixed logit', *Working Paper*, Department of Economics, University of California, Berkeley, 1999.

Train, K., *Discrete Choice Methods with Simulation*, Cambridge University Press, 2003.

Zmijewski, M. 'Methodological issues related to the estimation of financial distress prediction models', *Journal of Accounting Research*, 22(3), 1984, Supplement, 59–82.

3 An evaluation of open- and closed-form distress prediction models: The nested logit and latent class models

Stewart Jones and David A. Hensher

3.1. Introduction

As was seen in Chapter 2, the discrete choice literature has witnessed tremendous advances over the past decade. A range of sophisticated choice models have been developed and applied throughout the social sciences. Only very recently has this literature been applied to accounting and finance-related research (see Jones and Hensher 2004). Essentially, the discrete-choice literature has developed down two distinct paths: one is towards open-form (simulation based) choice models, the most prominent of which is the mixed logit model and extensions such as the error component logit model. The other approach has developed down the path of closed-form models[1] (also called generalized extreme value or GEV models), the most prevalent of which are the multinomial nested logit and latent class MNL models. Both open- and closed-form models have a number of unique advantages as well as some limitations associated with their use, hence the issue of their comparative performance is an important empirical question in evaluating the full potential of these models in accounting research. In this chapter, we compare the explanatory and predictive performance of the open-form mixed logit model with two sophisticated and widely used closed-form models, multinomial nested logit and latent class MNL (see Train 2003).

Chapter 2 provided an illustration of the performance of the open-form mixed logit model (with error components) in the context of financial distress prediction. We highlighted the improvement in explanatory and

---

[1] In simple terms, a closed-form solution enables the modeler to establish changes in outcome probabilities without having to perform numerical or analytical calculations involving either taking derivatives or simulating draws, as in the case of open-form models such as mixed logit (see Jones and Hensher 2004, 2007).

predictive power delivered by mixed logit relative to the more simplistic standard logit model widely used in much previous accounting research. The major advantages of open-form models (such as mixed logit model) is that they allow for the *complete* relaxation of the behaviourally questionable assumptions associated with the IID condition (independently and identically distributed errors) and incorporate a number of additional parameters which capture firm-specific observed and unobserved heterogeneity both between and within firms. Inclusion of these heterogeneity parameters[2] can allow for a high level of behavioural richness and definition to be specified into model estimation which is generally not possible with closed-form models.[3]

Notwithstanding the potential usefulness of mixed logit models in accounting research, open-form models have some unique limitations, many of which are not shared by closed-form models. The most obvious limitation is the relatively high level of complexity and computational intensity involved in the estimation and interpretation of open-form models. For instance, estimation of random parameter coefficients in a mixed logit model requires complex and often time-consuming analytical calculations, which involves integration of the logit formula over the distribution of unobserved random effects across the set of alternatives. Outcome probabilities cannot be calculated precisely because the integral does not have a closed form in general, hence they must be approximated through simulation (see Stern 1997). Unlike closed-form models which guarantee a unique globally optimal set of parameter estimates, the mixed logit model (due to the requirement to use simulated random draws) can produce a range of solutions, only one of which is globally optimal (see Louviere *et al.* 2000, Train 2003).[4] The open-form mixed logit model also presents a major challenge in that random parameters possess a distribution which is unknown, thus necessitating strong assumptions to be made about the distribution of random

---

[2] In addition to fixed-parameter estimates, mixed logit models can include up to four heterogeneity parameters: random-parameter means, random-parameter variances, heterogeneity in means and the decomposition in variances parameter.

[3] These potentially important behavioral influences are effectively treated as 'white noise' effects in the error structure of simple closed-form models. Nested logit captures some of these influences by accommodating error structure correlation among pairs of alternatives, whereas the latent class MNL model captures these influences by including one or more discrete unobserved variables in model estimation (see discussion in Section 2).

[4] As explained in Chapter 2, the mixed logit model has a likelihood surface that is capable of producing local optima in contrast to a single unique global optimum from MNL. Using the MNL parameter estimates as starting values produces a global solution since it begins the gradient search at a location of the nonlinear surface that tends to be the best starting location for determining the global optimum.

parameters.[5] These factors can add considerable complexity (and an element of subjective judgement) in the application of open-form models.

Closed-form models are extensively used in the discrete-choice literature partly because they avoid many of the problems associated with the estimation and interpretation of open-form models. Unlike open-form models, closed-form models do not require use of simulation algorithms to solve intractable multidimensional integrals (see Bhat 2003, Train 2003). The main benefit of a closed-form solution model is that parameter estimates and probability outcomes are generally easier to estimate. This is especially true as the number of attributes and alternatives increases. It is now well documented in the literature that mixed logit models can become very unstable beyond a certain number of alternatives and attributes levels[6] (see Hensher *et al.* 2005 for discussion). Closed-form models are also much more straightforward to interpret, as all parameters are fixed or point estimates.[7] The behavioural influence of explanatory variables can be represented by a number of parameters in a mixed logit model (of which fixed-parameter estimates are only one potential source of behavioural influence on the domain outcome).

Given the prevalent use of advanced closed-form models in the literature and their potentially important practical value and appeal, no evaluation of the potential usefulness of discrete-choice models in accounting can be said to be complete without a rigorous empirical evaluation of the comparative performance of open- and closed-form models. Testing the empirical performance of advanced closed-form models will establish whether they can be considered a complementary and/or alternative modelling technique to both open-form models and/or the more commonly used standard logit model. The empirical comparison in Chapter 2 is restricted to standard logit, i.e. multinomial logit (MNL), which is the *most basic* form of discrete model in the social sciences (Train 2003). While mixed logit is the most advanced open-form model (for both ordered and unordered outcomes), the nested logit and latent class MNL models are the most advanced of the closed-form models, particularly for unordered outcomes (Hensher *et al.* 2005). The

---

[5] Random parameters can take a number of predefined functional forms, the most common being normal, triangular, uniform and lognormal (see Hensher and Jones 2007).

[6] This is particularly true for models incorporating more than 8 alternatives and 30 attributes (Louviere *et al.* 2000).

[7] A fixed parameter treats the standard deviation as zero such that all the behavioural information on the marginal utility of a variable is captured by the mean. Essentially this assumes that the population of firms have homogeneous preferences (i.e. fixed marginal utilities) with respect to the role of a variable on the distress states.

nested logit model[8] and latent class MNL models have all the practical benefits of a closed-form solution model, but are conceptually superior to the standard logit because model specification is better able to handle the highly restrictive IID condition and both model forms allow for the incorporation of unobserved heterogeneity, at least to some extent (see discussion in Section 2) (Stern 1997, Hensher *et al.* 2005). An opportunity therefore exists to identify and illustrate the usefulness of other potentially powerful discrete-choice models and their application to financial distress prediction.

The remainder of this chapter is organized as follows. Section 2 discusses the conceptual basis and econometric properties of the multinomial nested logit and latent class MNL models. Section 3 outlines the research methodology. Section 4 provides the empirical results, which is followed by concluding comments in Section 5.

3.2. Closed-form models: The multinomial nested logit and latent class MNL models

In this section, we briefly outline the conceptual and econometric properties of two of the most powerful and widely used closed-form choice models in the discrete-choice literature, the nested logit and latent class MNL models.

The nested logit model

Similar to the mixed logit model, the nested logit model represents a methodological improvement over standard logit which has been used extensively in previous financial distress research (see, e.g., Ohlson 1980, Jones 1987, Lau 1987, Ward 1994). The nested logit model (also referred to in some literature as hierarchical logit and tree extreme logit) is more flexible than standard logit in dealing with the restrictive IID condition because through partitioning (or nesting), potential differences in sources of unobserved heterogeneity can be investigated (see Jones and Hensher 2007).

To gain a better understanding on what the IID assumption means behaviourally in the context of a nested logit model, we take a closer look at

---

[8] More recently, the generalized nested logit (GNL) has been developed. The GNL model provides a higher level of flexibility in estimating correlation or 'nesting' structures between pairs of alternatives. The GNL model can closely approximate any multi-level nested logit model but takes into account differences in cross-elasticities between pairs of alternatives (see Koppelman and Sethi 2000). However, while we estimated a GNL model on our sample, we could not improve on the predictive accuracy of the nested logit model results reported in this study (see Table 3.3 results).

the structure of the variance–covariance matrix in which the sources of unobserved influences reside. The IID assumption implies that the variances associated with the component of a random utility expression describing each alternative (capturing all of the *unobserved* influences on a set of outcomes) are identical, and that these unobserved effects are not correlated between all pairs of alternatives. If we have three alternatives, this can be shown as a 3 by 3 variance–covariance matrix (usually referred to as a covariance matrix) with three variances (the diagonal elements) and $J^2 - J$ covariances (i.e., the off-diagonal elements). The IID assumption implies that the off-diagonal terms are all zero and the diagonal terms of identical (hence not subscripted). Given constant variance we can normalize the variance by setting it equal to 1.0:

$$\begin{bmatrix} \sigma^2 & 0 & 0 \\ 0 & \sigma^2 & 0 \\ 0 & 0 & \sigma^2 \end{bmatrix}. \tag{3.1}$$

The most general variance–covariance matrix allows all elements to be unique (or free) as presented by the matrix in (2) for three alternatives:

$$\begin{bmatrix} \sigma_{11}^2 & \sigma_{12}^2 & \sigma_{13}^2 \\ \sigma_{21}^2 & \sigma_{22}^2 & \sigma_{23}^2 \\ \sigma_{31}^2 & \sigma_{32}^2 & \sigma_{33}^2 \end{bmatrix}. \tag{3.2}$$

There are $J^*(J-1)/2$ unique off-diagonal elements in the above matrix. For example, the second element in row 1 equals the second element in column 1. The mixed logit model (discussed in Chapter 2) is an example of a discrete-choice model that can test for the possibility that pairs of alternatives in the choice set are correlated to varying degrees, which is another way of stating that the off-diagonal elements for pairs of alternatives are non-zero.

When we relax the MNL's assumption of equal or constant variance, then we have a model called the heteroscedastic extreme value (HEV) or heteroscedastic logit (HL) model. The covariance matrix has zero-valued off-diagonal elements and uniquely subscripted diagonal elements as shown in (3), with one of the variances normalized to 1.0 for identification:

$$\begin{bmatrix} \sigma_{11}^2 & 0 & 0 \\ 0 & \sigma_{22}^2 & 0 \\ 0 & 0 & \sigma_{33}^2 \end{bmatrix}. \tag{3.3}$$

The degree of estimation complexity increases rapidly as we move away from the standard logit form and relax assumptions on the main and off-diagonals of the variance–covariance matrix. The most popular non-IID model is the nested logit (NL) model. It relaxes the severity of the MNL condition between subsets of alternatives, but preserves the IID condition across alternatives within each nested subset.

The popularity of the NL model stems from its inherent similarity to the MNL model. It is essentially a set of hierarchical MNL models, linked by a set of conditional relationships. To take an example from Standard and Poor's credit ratings, we might have six alternatives, three of them level A rating outcomes (AAA, AA, A, called the a-set) and three level B rating outcomes (BBB, BB, B, called the b-set). The NL model is structured such that the model predicts the probability of a particular A-rating outcome conditional on an A-rating. It also predicts the probability of a particular B-rating outcome conditional on a B-rating. Then the model predicts the probability of an A or a B outcome (called the c-set). That is, we have lower-level conditional choices and upper-level marginal choices. This two-level nested logit model can be generalized to any number of levels to account for differences in variances of unobserved effects amongst the alternatives:

$$\begin{bmatrix} \sigma_a^2 & 0 & 0 \\ 0 & \sigma_a^2 & 0 \\ 0 & 0 & \sigma_a^2 \end{bmatrix} \begin{bmatrix} \sigma_b^2 & 0 & 0 \\ 0 & \sigma_b^2 & 0 \\ 0 & 0 & \sigma_b^2 \end{bmatrix} \begin{bmatrix} \sigma_c^2 & 0 \\ 0 & \sigma_c^2 \end{bmatrix}. \tag{3.4}$$

Since each of the 'partitions' in the NL model are of the MNL form, they each display the IID condition between the alternatives within a partition. However, the variances are different between the partitions. Furthermore, and often not appreciated, some correlation exists between alternatives within a nest due to the common linkage with an upper level alternative (Louviere *et al.* 2000). For example, there are some attributes of the set of A rating alternatives that might be common due to both being forms of A rating. Thus the combination of the conditional choice of an A-rating outcome and the marginal choice of the A-rating set invokes a correlation between the alternatives within a partition.

The IID condition assumes a constant variance and zero covariance for the variance–covariance matrix. The nested logit model recognizes the possibility that each alternative may have information in the unobserved influences of each alternative, which in turn has a role to play in determining a choice outcome that is different across the alternative branches.[9] This difference implies that the variances might be different (i.e., specific

---

[9] Within the context of financial distress, since firms do not *choose* to fail per se, we use the phrase *outcome domain* (or simply outcome) as the descriptor of the observed *choice* outcome.

alternatives $(j = 1, \ldots, J)$ do not have the same distributions for the unobserved effects, denoted by ε_j). Differences might also imply that the information content could be similar amongst subsets of alternatives and hence some amount of correlation could exist among these subsets (i.e., nonzero and varying covariances for pairs of alternatives).[10]

The presence of these possibilities is equivalent to relaxing IID *to some extent*. We would only totally relax these conditions if we allowed all variances and covariances to be different, up to identification, as in the case of the mixed logit model (see Chapter 2).

Deriving the nested logit model

In contrast to the relatively general mixed logit model described in Chapter 2, the nested logit model restricts the revelation of heterogeneity through differential variances in the unobserved effects, preserving the IID condition within partitions of the full set of alternatives. All parameters are fixed (i.e., they have no standard deviation estimates). The model form is shown in equation (3.5) for a model in which we partition the alternatives into subsets, each having constant variance amongst the alternatives but different between the subsets. The notation refers to the levels in a nested structure (lowest level represents the actual or elemental alternatives $(k = 1, \ldots K)$, the next level up is the branch level with branches $j = 1, \ldots, J$; and the top level of a three-level nest is the limb level with limbs $I = 1, \ldots, I$. The choice probabilities for the *elemental alternatives* are defined as (see Hensher *et al.* 2005)

---

[10] A practical illustration might help clarify the basic concept of a nested logit model (see Hensher and Jones 2007). Consider a travel mode choice setting where consumers must choose between taking a bus or train or car to work. Let us assume that 'comfort' is an important attribute influencing choice, but that it has not been measured (and thefore not included as an attribute in the model). Its exclusion may be due to the difficulty of measuring comfort (it can mean many things to different people). However, it is likely that when we investigate the meaning of comfort in a little more detail we find that 'comfort' has a similar meaning for bus and train compared to car travel (i.e. the comfort level between a bus and train could be similar as both modes of transport are public, may requiring having to stand, no access to the comforts of a private vehicle, such as music, climate control, etc.). Already we have made a statement that indicates that the information in the e_j associated with bus and train is possibly more similar than the information in the e_j associated with car (note comfort is the e_j or the unobserved influence because it is not formally measured). If 'comfort' was deemed to be the only unobserved information influencing the choice outcome, then we can safely suggest that the e_j for bus and train are likely to be correlated to some degree (due to common element of comfort) and even have a similar variance (possibly identical) for bus and train which is different to the variance of car. Another way of thinking about this is to assume we can separate out two components of comfort for bus and train; one part that is unique to bus and unique to train and another part that is common to them because they are both forms of public transport. It is this common element that engenders the correlation. Nested logit is a choice method specifically designed to recognize the possibility of different variances across the alternatives and some correlation amongst subsets of alternatives.

$$P(k|j,i) = \frac{\exp[\mathbf{b}'\mathbf{x}(k|j,i)]}{\sum\limits_{l=1}^{K|j,i} \exp[\mathbf{b}'\mathbf{x}(l|j,i)]} \tag{3.5}$$

where $k|j,i$ is the elemental alternative k in branch j of limb i, $K|j,i$ is the number of elemental alternatives in branch j of limb i, and the inclusive value for branch j in limb i is

$$IV(j|i) = \log \sum_{k=1}^{K|j,i} \exp[\mathbf{b}'\mathbf{x}(k|j,i)]. \tag{3.6}$$

The *branch level* probability is

$$p(j|i) = \frac{\exp\{\lambda(j|i)[\mathbf{a}'\mathbf{y}(j|i) + IV(j|i)]\}}{\sum\limits_{m=1}^{J|i} \exp\{\lambda(m|i)[\mathbf{a}'\mathbf{y}(m|i) + IV(m|i)]\}} \tag{3.7}$$

where $j|i$ is branch j in limb i, $J|i$ is number of branches in limb i, and

$$IV(i) = \log \sum_{j=1}^{J|i} \exp\{\lambda(j|i)[\mathbf{a}'\mathbf{y}(j|i) + IV(j|i)]\}. \tag{3.8}$$

Finally, the *limb level* is defined by

$$p(i) = \frac{\exp\{\gamma(i)[\mathbf{c}'\mathbf{z}(i) + IV(i)]\}}{\sum\limits_{n=1}^{I} \exp\{\gamma(n)[\mathbf{c}'\mathbf{z}(n) + IV(n)]\}} \tag{3.9}$$

where I is the number of limbs in the three-level tree and

$$IV = \log \sum_{i=1}^{I} \exp\{\gamma(i)[\mathbf{c}'\mathbf{z}(i) + IV(i)]\}. \tag{3.10}$$

To be able to identify the model, we have to normalize (or scale) certain parameters. The parameters are scaled at the lowest level (i.e. for $\mu'(k|j,i) = \mu(j|i) = 1$).

Equations (3.6), (3.8) and (3.10) need special comment, given their importance in identifying the compliance of the nested structure with the underlying behavioural rule of (random) utility maximization. If we assume that the attributes of elemental alternatives influence the choice between composite alternatives (a testable assumption) at the branch level, then we need to include this information in the utility expressions for each composite alternative. The linkage is achieved through an index of expected maximum utility (EMU), known more commonly as the inclusive value index (IV). This information resides in the utility expressions associated with the elemental alternatives which are used to derive the standard MNL model by imposition of an IID condition for the unobserved influences.

To establish the expected maximum utility we have to take the MNL form and search over the entire utility space in which the choice probabilities of each alternative are identified.[11] A formal derivation is given in Louviere *et al.* [2000, p. 188]. Mathematically EMU is equal to the natural logarithm of the denominator of the MNL model associated with the elemental alternatives. The form is shown in equation (3.10) for the A choice set, comprising elemental alternatives A, AA, AAA (see matrix equation (3.4)):

$$\text{EMU}(A, AA, AAA) = \log\{\exp V_A + \exp V_{AA} + \exp V_{AAA}\}$$
$$\text{EMU}(A, AA, AAA) = \log\{\ \}. \tag{3.11}$$

A similar index exists for the B choice set:

$$\text{EMU}(B, BB) = \log\{\exp V_B + \exp V_{BB}\}. \tag{3.12}$$

These two indices are easily calculated once the MNL models are estimated for the lowest level of the nested structure. The next step is to recognize this as information relevant to the choice between the A-set and the B-set. This is achieved by including the EMU index in the utility expressions for the relevant composite alternative as just another explanatory variable, as shown in equation (3.7).

The numerical value of the parameter estimate for IV is the basis of establishing the extent of dependence or independence between the linked choices. It has been shown in many publications that this parameter estimate is inversely proportional to the variance of the unobserved effects associated with the MNL specification at the level below a branch. Louviere *et al.* (2000, pp. 142–3) show that the variance is defined as

$$\sigma^2 = \frac{\pi^2}{6\lambda^2} \tag{3.13}$$

where Π^2 is a constant (equal to 3.14159), and λ is an unknown, referred to as the scale parameter. The scale parameter (squared) describes the profile of the variance of the unobserved effects associated with an alternative. A scale parameter exists at each level of a nested structure and hence this parametrization enables us to establish the extent to which the variances differ

---

[11] That is, for all values of V_j for all elemental alternatives associated with a composite alternative. This is equivalent to using integration within a 1, 0 bound with respect to changes in V_j.

between sets of alternatives. Clearly if they do not differ then the nest can collapse to an MNL model. For identification, we have to normalize on either the upper- or lower-level scale parameter. Any value of the unconstrained λ would be judged against 1.0 for deviations from MNL. Furthermore, the IV parameter estimate must lie in the 0–1 range for the nested structure to be compliant with utility maximization.

The nested logit model is estimated using the method of full information maximum likelihood. Although nested models can be estimated sequentially it is preferable to estimate them simultaneously so that the parameter estimates associated with the inclusive value indices are asymptotically efficient (given that the IV index itself is a derivative of a parametrized expression).

The latent class MNL model

The latent class model (LCM) for the analysis of individual heterogeneity has a history in several literatures, however the early development of LCM has been attributed to Lazarsfeld (1950). The LCM model proposed in this chapter is in some respects a semi-parametric variant of the MNL that resembles the mixed logit model. In Chapter 2 we assumed the mixing distribution $f(\beta)$ is a continuous variable. However, if we assume β takes on a finite distinct set of values, we have in effect a latent class model. It is somewhat less flexible than the mixed logit model in that it approximates the underlying continuous distribution with a discrete one; however, it does not require the analyst to make specific assumptions about the distributions of parameters across firms (i.e., normal, triangular, lognormal or other – see Hensher and Jones 2007 for a review). Thus, each model has its limitations and virtues. A comparison of the strengths and challenges of the standard MNL model, the mixed logit model, the nested logit model and the LCM model is outlined Table 3.1.

The underlying theory of the LCM model posits that individual or firm behaviour depends on observable attributes and on latent heterogeneity that varies with factors or latent classes that are unobserved by the analyst. A simple illustration is proposed by Goodman (2002). Consider the simplest of cases of a cross-classification of analysis of two dichotomous variables which has a two-way 2×2 cross-classification table $[X, Y]$; where the two rows of the 2×2 table correspond to the two classes of the dichotomous variable X, and the two columns of the 2×2 table correspond to the two classes of the dichotomous variable Y. Let P_{ij} denote the probability that an

Table 3.1 Summary of major strengths and challenges of different logit models

	Classical MNL	Nested Logit	Mixed Logit	Latent Class-MNL
Major Strengths	• *Closed-form solution* • *Provides one set of globally optimal parameter estimates* • *Simple calculation* • *Widely understood and used in practice* • *Easy to interpret parameter estimates* • *Easy to calculate probability outcomes* • *Less demanding data quality requirements*	• *Closed-form solution* • *Provides one set of globally optimal parameters* • *Relatively easy to interpret parameter estimates* • *Relatively easy to calculate probability outcomes* • *Partially corrects for IID condition* • *Incorporates firm-specific observed and unobserved heterogeneity to some extent (especially the covariance extension)*	• *Allows for complete relaxation of IID condition* • *Avoids violation of the IIA condition* • *High level of behavioural definition and richness allowed in model specification* • *Includes additional estimates for random parameters, heterogeneity in means and decompositions in variances (these influences are effectively treated as 'white noise' in basic models)*	• *Closed-form solution* • *Semi-parametric specification* • *Like mixed logit, this model form is free from many limiting statistical assumptions, such as homogeneity in variances and normality assumptions* • *Incorporates firm-specific observed and unobserved heterogeneity through 'latent class' constructs* • *Less complex interpretation than mixed logit*
Major Challenges	• *Highly restrictive error assumptions (IID condition)* • *Violates the IIA assumption* • *Ignores firm-specific*	• *Only partially corrects for IID condition* • *Analytically very closely related to basic MNL model (thus shares many of the limitations of MNL)*	• *Open-form solution (requires analytical integration and use of simulated maximum likelihood to estimate model parameters)*	• *Lacks flexibility in specification of firm-specific unobserved* • *Model estimation can be time consuming due to computational intensity*

- observed and unobserved heterogeneity which can lead to inferior model specification and spurious interpretation of model outputs
- Parameters are point estimates with little behavioural definition
- Often provide good aggregate fits but can be misleading given simple form of the model
- Tends to be less behaviourally responsive to changes in attribute levels

- Does not capture potential sources of correlation across nests
- Judgement required in determining which alternatives can be appropriately partitioned into nests (nested logit requires well separated nests to reflect their correlation)

- Lack of a single set of globally optimal parameter estimates (i.e., due to the requirement for simulated maximum likelihood)
- Assumptions must be imposed for the distribution of unobserved influences
- Complex interpretation
- Model estimation can be time consuming due to computational intensity
- High quality data constraints

- Assumption that manifest variables within latent classes are independent can be unrealistic
- High quality data constraints

Source: Jones and Hensher (2007).

observation will fall in the ith row ($i=1,2$) and jth column ($j=1,2$) of this 2×2 table. If the variables X and Y are statistically independent, we have the following simple relationship (i.e., the assumption of local independence):

$$P_{ij} = P_i^X P_j^Y \tag{3.14}$$

where P_i^X is the probability that an observation will fall in the ith class on variable X (the ith row of the 2×2 table), and P_i^Y is the probability that an observation will fall in the jth class (the jth column of the 2×2 table) on variable Y with

$$P_i^X = P_{i+} = \sum_j P_{ij}, \; P_j^Y = P_{i+} = \sum P_{ij}. \tag{3.15}$$

A practical application of this simple concept is provided by Lazarsfeld and Henry (1968). Suppose that a sample of 1,000 people are asked whether they read journal X and Y with the survey responses appearing as follows:

	Read X	Did not read X	Total
Read Y	260	140	400
Did not read Y	240	360	600
Total	500	500	1000

It can be readily see that the two variables (reading X and reading Y) are strongly related (the chi square test is statistically significant), and therefore X and Y are not independent of each other. Readers of X tend to read Y more often (52%) than non-readers of X (28%). When reading X and Y is independent, then $P(X\&Y) = P(X)^*P(Y)$. However, 260/1000 is not 400/1000*500/1000. Thus reading X and Y is dependent on each other. However, adding the education level of respondents generates the following table:

High education	Read X	Did not read X	Total	Low education	Read X	Did not read X	Total
Read Y	240	60	300	Read Y	20	80	100
Did not read Y	160	40	200	Did not read Y	80	320	400
Total	400	100	500	Total	100	400	500

And again if reading X and Y are independent, then $P(A\&B) = P(A)^*P(B)$ for each education level.

Note that $240/500 = 300/500 * 400/500$ and $20/500 = 100/500 * 100/500$. Hence, when we examine separately the high- and low-educated people, there is no relationship between the two journals (i.e., reading X and Y are independent within educational level). The educational level accounts for the difference in reading X and Y. When variables X and Y are not statistically independent, (3.14) does not hold. If X and Y are key variables of interest to the analyst, the analyst would be interested in measuring the degree of non-interdependence (or correlation) between X and Y. While there are many measures of association and correlation that can reveal the magnitude of non-interdependence between X and Y, they cannot determine whether the relationship between X and Y is spurious: that is, whether the apparent relationship between X and Y can be explained away (or even explained more fully) by some other variable, say Z, where this variable may be *unobserved* or *latent*. Most methods, such as regression, correlation analysis and standard logit measure apparent or manifest effects. Latent class models allow us to probe these relationships more deeply.

Let us now consider a simple illustration with firm failures. A statistically significant relationship between firm size (S) (measured by market capitalization) and corporate failure (F) is often observed in this research (i.e., smaller public companies on average tend to have a higher propensity to fail than larger public companies). However, it is possible that any number of latent effects or factors could influence this relationship. Let us consider one such factor, which we call firm financial performance (P). It is possible that P could be driving both S and F (so P is an antecedent variable to both S and F), in which case S and F are conditionally independent of each other given the level of P (see Figure 3.1(a)), see Goodman 2002. That is, higher-performing companies tend to be associated with higher stock prices and therefore higher market capitalizations (i.e., these firms are larger on average); furthermore, firms with better overall financial performance tend to have a lower probability of failure relative to poorer-performing firms). Hence, the apparent relationship between S and F could be spurious.

Another possible scenario is that firm size (S) could also be driving financial performance (P) which in turn drives F, in which case P is an intervening variable as shown in Figure 3.1(b). In this case, larger firms tend to have higher market concentrations, greater access to capital and consumer markets and greater economies of scale in production which could lead to superior overall financial performance. Again, S and B are conditionally independent, given the level of P. It is also possible that S and P could also be reciprocally affecting each other relation where S drives P. Again, S and F are conditionally independent.

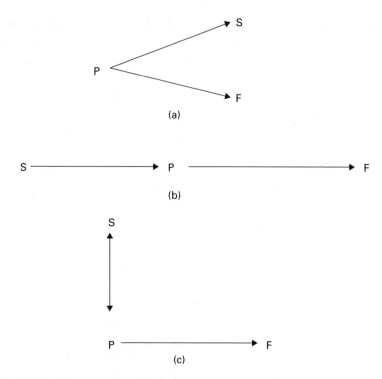

Figure 3.1   Latent effects on corporate failure

An application to latent class MNL to corporate bankruptcy prediction

Consistent with the discussion above, we propose to apply the LCM to analyse firm specific heterogeneity through a model of discrete parameter variation. Thus, it is assumed that firms are implicitly sorted into a set of Q classes, but which class contains any particular firm is unknown to the researcher. When the dependent variable is ordinal or nominal, the central behavioural model is a multinomial logit model for discrete outcomes among J_i alternatives, by firm i observed in T_i outcome situations,

Prob [alternative j by firm i in outcome situation t |class q]

$$
= \frac{\exp(\mathbf{x}'_{it,\,j}\beta_q)}{\sum_{j=1}^{J_i} \exp(\mathbf{x}'_{it,\,j}\beta_q)} \tag{3.16}
$$
$$
= \mathrm{F}(i,t,j|q).
$$

The number of observations and the size of the outcome set may vary by firm. In principle, the outcome set could vary by outcome situation as well. The conditional probability for the specific outcome made by a firm can be formulated in several ways; for convenience, we allow y_{it} to denote the specific outcome alternative for firm i, so that the model provides

$$P_{it|q}(j) = \text{Prob}(v_{it} = j|\text{class} = q) \tag{3.17}$$

For convenience, we simplify this further to $P_{it|q}$. We have used a generic notation for the density of the random variable of interest to suggest that this formulation will provide a means of extending the latent class model to other frameworks, though we restrict our attention herein to the discrete-choice model. Note that this is a 'panel data' sort of application in that we assume that the same firm is observed in several outcome situations.

We assume that given the class assignment, the T_i events are independent. (This is a possibly strong assumption, especially given the nature of our data. In fact, there is likely to be some correlation in the unobserved parts of the random utilities. The latent class does not readily extend to auto-correlation, so we have left this aspect for further research.) Thus, for the given class assignment, the contribution of firm i to the likelihood would be the joint probability of the sequence $\mathbf{y}_i = [y_{i1}, y_{i2}, \ldots y_{iT}]$. This is

$$P_{i|q} = \prod_{t=1}^{T_i} P_{it|q}. \tag{3.18}$$

The class assignment is unknown. Let H_{iq} denote the prior probability for latent class q for firm i (we consider posterior probabilities below). Various formulations have been used this (see Greene 2003). For our bankruptcy data, a particularly convenient form is the multinomial logit:

$$H_{iq} = \frac{\exp\left(\mathbf{z}_i'\theta_q\right)}{\sum_{q=1}^{Q} \exp\left(\mathbf{z}_i'\theta_q\right)}, q = 1, \ldots Q, \cdot\theta_Q\ q = 1, \ldots, Q, \theta_q = 0 \tag{3.19}$$

where $\mathbf{z}_i$ denotes a set of observable characteristics which enter the model for class membership. Roeder *et al.* (1999), using this same formulation, denote $\mathbf{z}_i$ the 'risk factors'. The Qth parameter vector is normalized to zero to secure identification of the model (Greene 2003). There may be no such covariates, in which case, the only element in $\mathbf{z}_i$ would be the constant term, '1', and the latent class probabilities would be simple constants which, by construction, sum to one. The likelihood for firm i is the expectation (over classes) of the class-specific contributions:

$$P_i = \sum_{q=1}^{Q} H_{iq} P_{i|q}. \tag{3.20}$$

The log-likelihood for the sample is

$$\ln L = \sum_{i=1}^{N} \ln P_i = \sum_{i=1}^{N} \ln\left[\sum_{q=1}^{Q} H_{iq}\left(\prod_{t=1}^{T_i} P_{it|q}\right)\right]. \tag{3.21}$$

Maximization of the log-likelihood with respect to the Q structural parameter vectors, β_q, and the $Q-1$ latent class parameter vectors, θ_q, is a conventional problem in maximum likelihood estimation. Greene (2003) discusses the mechanics and various aspects of estimation. In comparison to more familiar maximum likelihood problems, this is a relatively difficult optimization problem, though not excessively so. For a given choice of Q, the choice of good starting values seems to be crucial. The asymptotic covariance matrix for the full set of parameter estimators is obtained by inverting the analytic second derivatives matrix of the log-likelihood function.

An issue to be confronted is the choice of Q, the number of latent classes. This is not a parameter in the interior of a convex parameter space, so one cannot test hypotheses about Q directly. If there is a known Q^* that is greater than the 'true' Q, then it is possible to 'test down' to Q by using, for example likelihood ratio tests. A model with $Q+1$ classes encompasses one with Q if the parameters in any two of the $Q+1$ classes are forced to equality. This does move the problem up one level, since the Q^* must now be assumed known, but testing down from a specified Q^* is straightforward. ('Testing up' from a small Q (one) is not valid, since the estimates obtained for any model that is too small are inconsistent.) Roeder et al. (1999) suggest using the Bayesian Information Criterion or BIC:

$$\text{BIC(model)} = \ln L + \frac{(\text{model size}) \ln N}{N}. \tag{3.22}$$

With the parameter estimates of θ_q in hand, the prior estimates of the class probabilities are $\hat{H}_{iq}$. Using Bayes' theorem, we can obtain a posterior estimate of the latent class probabilities using

$$\hat{H}_{q|i} = \frac{\hat{P}_{i|q}\hat{H}_{iq}}{\sum_{q=1}^{Q} \hat{P}_{i|q}\hat{H}_{iq}}. \tag{3.23}$$

The notation $\hat{H}_{q|i}$ is used to indicate the firm-specific estimate of the class probability, conditioned on their estimated outcome probabilities, as distinct from the unconditional class probabilities which enter the log-likelihood function. A strictly empirical estimator of the latent class within which the individual resides would be that 1 associated with the maximum value of $\hat{H}_{q|i}$. We may also use these results to obtain posterior estimates of the firm-specific parameter vector

$$\hat{\beta}_i = \sum_{q=1}^{Q} \hat{H}_{q|i}\hat{\beta}_q. \tag{3.24}$$

The same result can be used to estimate marginal effects in the logit model:

$$\sigma_{km,itj|q} = \frac{\partial \ln F(i,t,j|q)}{\partial x_{it,km}} = x_{it,km}[1(j=k) - F(i,t,k|q)]\beta_{m|q} \qquad (3.25)$$

for the effect on firm i's choice probability j in choice situation t of attribute m in outcome probability k. The posterior estimator of this elasticity is

$$\hat{\sigma}_{km,tj|i} = \sum_{q=1}^{Q} \hat{H}_{q|i} \hat{\sigma}_{km,\ ji|q}. \qquad (3.26)$$

An estimator of the average of this quantity over data configurations and firms would be

$$\hat{\bar{\sigma}}_{km,\ j} = \frac{1}{N} \sum_{i=1}^{N} \frac{1}{T_i} \sum_{t=1}^{T_i} \hat{\sigma}_{km,tj|i}. \qquad (3.27)$$

3.3. Empirical illustration of the nested logit and latent class models

For the purposes of illustration, we use the same sample and four state unordered failure model described in Chapter 2.[12] To demonstrate the predictive performance of our models, we also test a broad range of financial measures used in prior research over the last three decades (examples include Altman *et al.* 1977, Ohlson 1980, Zemjewski 1984, Casey and Bartczak 1985, Gentry *et al.* 1985, Jones 1987). Among other explanatory variables Chapter 2 examined the predictive value of reported cash flow from operations (CFO), whereas most previous bankruptcy research have used some estimate of CFO (see, e.g., Casey and Bartczak 1985). An interesting question is whether reported cash flow predicts corporate insolvency and bankruptcy better than estimated cash flow. This chapter extends the covariates used in Chapter 2 to include both estimated and reported CFO. To examine this proposition, we test two CFO estimates: (i) crude 'add back' method and (ii) a more sophisticated and widely used measure which adjusts net income for working capital changes (Hirbar and Collins 2002). For the accrual-based measures, we test various ratios based on: cash position; working capital; profitability and earnings performance; turnover, financial structure; and debt servicing capacity. These variables, including their definitions, are summarized in the Appendix. An examination of the partial correlations

---

[12] This illustration is based on Jones, S. and Hensher, D. A., 'Modelling Corporate Failure: A Multinomial Nested Logit Analysis for Unordered Outcomes', *The British Accounting Review*, vol.39:1, pp. 89–107. The illustration has been reproduced with permission from the publishers.

indicates generally very weak correlations across most of our covariates.[13] In particular, we find that correlations among ratios based on reported CFO and the sophisticated estimate of CFO are quite weak, suggesting that reported CFO is providing distinct or unique information from the sophisticated estimate of CFO. Furthermore, correlations between the crude estimate of CFO (estc1_ta, estc1_de) and the sophisticated estimate (including reported CFO) are also noticeably weak, suggesting that the sophisticated estimate of CFO provides distinct information relative to crude measures of cash flow, a finding consistent with previous literature (Gombola and Ketz 1983, Thode *et al.* 1986, Bowen *et al.* 1987). Correlations between many measures based on CFO (both reported and estimated) and accrual-based measures were found to be almost orthogonal, suggesting that our predictor variables are all providing distinct and unique information. We also use the contextual variables described in Chapter 2.

3.4. Empirical results

Table 3.2 summarizes the overall model system for the nested logit, latent class and mixed logit models (Panel A). All models reported in Table 3.2 are specified as a set of mutually exclusive *unordered* outcomes. Since all explanatory variables do not vary across the alternatives (but are associated with a known outcome), to identify each model we needed to constrain the parameters of each variable to equal zero for at least one of the alternatives. This specification relies on the variability across the sample to establish the influence of each firm variable on the outcome probability. Different sets of financial variables associated with the utility functions of each alternative (i.e. nonfailure, insolvency, distressed merger and outright failure) are specified in order to test their statistical influence on the response outcome.

It can be seen from Table 3.2 (Panel A) that the nested logit model has delivered a very good overall goodness of fit. The log-likelihood (LL) has decreased from -5977 (assuming no information other than random shares) to -1763. The improvement in the log-likelihood ratio is less impressive for the standard MNL model, with the LL showing a more modest decrease to -3688. The model-fit for nested logit was statistically much better than a standard MNL model. Using an LL ratio test (which compares the LL

---

[13] A full correlation matrix of all variables used on the study is available on request. The illustration of the nested logit model is based on Hensher and Jones (2007).

Table 3.2 Model fit summary, parameter estimates (random and fixed) for final nested logit, latent class MNL and mixed logit model

Panel A: Parameter Estimates and Model-fit Statistics for Advanced Discrete-Choice Models

Variables	Acronym	Alternative	Mixed Logit	Nested Logit	Latent Class MNL – 3 classes
Total debt to CFO	Cdebtc	Nonfailure	−.01113 (−4.375)	−.01296 (−5.69)	−.2046 (−2.91) −.0017 (−.13) .0086 (1.13)
Two periods of negative CFO	Negcash2	Nonfailure	−	−.7856 (−7.28)	−.6571 (−1.42) .3931 (1.77) −3.851 (−12.4)
Total liabilities to total equity	TLTA	Nonfailure	−.001562 (−2.048)	−.00083 (−3.02)	−.0087 (−1.28) .0561 (7.67) −.0643 (−11.7)
Insolvency constant	IC	Insolvency	−3.156 (−29.115)	−3.753 (−38.34)	−3.6803 (−7.09) −2.6641 (−14.69) −7.398 (−17.5)
New Economy dummy	New_Econ	Insolvency	−	.4240 (2.27)	−.9306 (−.40) −.2869 (−.69) 1.301 (5.03)
Distressed Merger constant	DMC	Distressed Mergers	−3.640 (−17.02)	−18.64 (−2.23)	−3.008 (−6.61) −4.162 (−14.0) −9.012 (−18.9)
Outright Failure constant	OFC	Outright Failures	−4.400 (−35.07)	−19.07 (−2.25)	−4.326 (−8.47) −5.155 (−10.75) −7.122 (−17.67)
Total debt to total assets	Cgear	Outright Failures	.0011 (3.766)	.005 (3.25)	.0101 (3.32) −.0548 (−.66) −.0142 (−3.97)
Net CFO to total assets	Netopta	Nonfailure	.009 (4.99)		
Estimated latent class probabilities:					
Class 1					.1235 (4.36)
Class 2					.6743 (14.38)
Class 3					.2022 (7.97)
IV parameters:					
IV		Nonfailed		Fixed (1.0)	
IV		Insolvent		Fixed (1.0)	
IV		Distressed Merger		.2 (2.14)	
Random Parameters					
Working capital to total assets	Workcta	Nonfailed	.0149 (2.84)		

Table 3.2 (cont.)

Variables	Acronym	Alternative	Mixed Logit	Nested Logit	Latent Class MNL – 3 classes
Cash resources to total assets	Cpta	Distressed Merger	−.25370 (−2.11)		
Sales to total assets	Csalesta	Insolvency	−.02640 (−2.99)		
Heterogeneity in Means					
Working capital*	Work*	Nonfailed	−.02563		
New Econ	New_Econ		(−2.63)		
Log-likelihood at zero			−5977	−5977	−5977
Log-likelihood at convergence			−854	−1763	−1677

Panel B – Marginal Effects for Advanced Discrete-Choice Models

Variables	Acronym	Alternative	Mixed Logit	Nested Logit	Latent Class MNL – 3 classes
Total debt to CFO	Cdebtc	Nonfailed	−.383*	−.085*	−.802*
		Insolvent	.465	.051	.326
		Distressed Merger	.370	.029	.350
		Outright Failure	.596	.037	.261
Two periods of negative CFO	Negcash2	Nonfailed	–	−.517*	−.278*
		Insolvent	–	.310	.857
		Distressed Merger	–	.174	.142
		Outright Failure		.221	.409
Total liabilities to total equity	TLTE	Nonfailed	−.194	−.002	−.108
		Insolvent	.068	.001	.139
		Distressed Merger	.082	.005	.349
		Outright Failure	.138*	.008*	1.31*
Total debt to total assets	Debtta	Nonfailed	−.351*	−.006*	−.250*
		Insolvent	.419	.003	1.55
		Distressed Merger	.197	.002	.235
		Outright Failure	.332	.002	.481

Table 3.2 (cont.)

Variables	Acronym	Alternative	Mixed Logit	Nested Logit	Latent Class MNL – 3 classes
Working capital to total assets	Workcta	Nonfailed	.15*		
		Insolvent	−.783		
		Distressed Merger	−.190		
		Outright Failure	−.140		
Cash resources to total assets	Cpta	Nonfailed	.052		
		Insolvent	−.012		
		Distressed Merger	−.167*		
		Outright Failure	−.18		
Sales to total assets	Csalesta	Nonfailed	.08		
		Insolvent	−.09*		
		Distressed Merger	−.107		
		Outright Failure	−.21		
Net CFO to total assets	Netopta	Nonfailed	.357*		
		Insolvent	−.956		
		Distressed Merger	−.299		
		Outright Failure	−.539		
New economy effect	New_econ	Nonfailed		−.133	−.216
		Insolvent		.189*	.312*
		Distressed Merger		−.105	−.028
		Outright Failure		−.147	−.812
Sample Size			5310	5310	5310

*Indicates direct effects

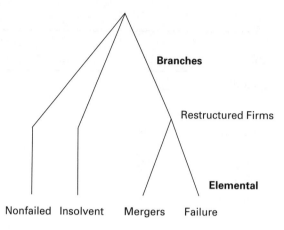

Figure 3.2   Nested tree structure for states of financial distress

ratio of the nested logit and standard MNL models at convergence adjusted for number of parameters in each model) we can calculate the likelihood ratio as $-2^*(1767-3688) = -3842$ at four degrees of freedom. This is chi-square distributed and at any level of significance the nested logit model is a statistically significant improvement over standard MNL.

Table 3.2 indicates that the overall model-fit was better again for the latent class model. The LL has decreased from -5977 (assuming no information other than random shares) to -1677. However, the model-fit summary appears to be best for the mixed logit model, where the LL ratio has decreased from -5977 (assuming no information other than random shares) to -854.[14]

The two-level nested logit structure shown in Figure 3.2 is found in our analysis to provide the best model-fit for our four-state distress sample (which includes nonfailed firms, insolvent firms, mergers and outright failures, described in detail in Section 3.3).

The basic test for determining the best tree structure for a nested logit model is the overall goodness-of-fit measure (the log-likelihood at convergence).[15] In searching for the best tree structure, we followed a methodology suggested by Hensher *et al.* (2005), which involves specification of the nested logit model in which each branch has only one alternative – this is the degenerate nested logit (or NL-DG). While nonfailed and insolvency represent independent (degenerate branch) alternatives, there is a hierarchy which

---

[14] Application of Vuong test (see Vuong 1989) (a formal test of differences in model-fits between non-nested discrete choice models) indicates that the mixed logit has the best model-fit statistics relative to all other models.

[15] However, establishing eligible trees that produce the 'best' tree in terms of compliance with global utility maximization and lowest log-likelihood involves investigating a large number of potential candidate trees.

establishes groupings which we describe in Figure 3.2, for convenience, as the 'restructured' firms (i.e. distressed mergers and outright failures). In Figure 3.2, there is one conditional outcome where the probability of a distressed merger or outright failure is conditional on whether a firm falls under the 'restructure' category.

The numerical value of the parameter estimate for IV is the basis of establishing the extent of differential variance between the alternatives associated with a specific branch and the alternatives in one or more other branches. It can be seen in Table 3.2 (Panel A) that the IV parameter has a value of 0.2. A t-test of a difference to 1.0 (the restricted IV index parameter value for the degenerate branches, equivalent to an MNL condition) also indicates that nested logit is preferred to a standard MNL model.[16]

The results in Table 3.2 indicate that four financial variables (total debt to reported CFO; two periods of consecutive negative reported CFO[17]; total liabilities to total equity; and total debt to total assets) had the strongest statistical impact on the response outcome for the nested logit. Interestingly, no measures based on estimated CFO were found to be significant in the advanced-choice models, a finding which corroborates a growing body of literature confirming the superiority of reported cash flows over estimated measures in many areas of empirical accounting research (Hribar and Collins 2002).

The latent class model has also generated significant results. An important issue in estimating an LCM is specifying number of classes. A 1-class model makes the standard homogeneity assumption that an MNL holds true for all cases (the explanatory variables are independent or what is equivalent the IID condition for the error structure). It is crucial to determine the right number of classes – typically, more classes will result in models that better fit the data, but can cause the model to become unstable; but specifying too few could result could ignore important class differences. Typically, a number of models will be estimated on different class number assumptions, and the model fit statistics and significant of the latent class parameters evaluated using different number of classes. We found that the log-likelihood function and BIC values improved most when a 3-class model was specified. This model also generated a number of significant latent class parameters. Further

---

[16] It should be noted that if all states in Figure 3.2 were independent (in the sense of no correlation between the alternatives, i.e. mergers and failures were separate branches such as nonfailures and insolvent firms) we would have no need for a nested logit model, as all domain outcomes would be independent and a standard MNL model specification would be appropriate.

[17] A dummy variable coded '1' if yes, and '0' for otherwise.

analysis indicates that the classes have a differential impact on different variables with respect to the outcome alternative. For example, class 1 has a stronger statistical impact on the total debt to CFO variable, whereas class 3 has a stronger impact on the 'two periods of negative CFO' variable.

The mixed logit model is represented by a similar set of variables for fixed-parameter estimates,[18] but unlike the closed-form models (which are only represented by fixed-parameter estimates) the mixed logit model has three statistically significant random parameter variables (working capital to total assets, cash resources to total assets and sales revenue to total assets) and a statistically significant heterogeneity in means parameter (which indicates a contextual affect with the new economy dummy and the working capital to total assets variable).

A direct interpretation of the parameter estimates reported in Panel A of Table 3.2 is not possible given the logit transformation of the outcome-dependent variable required for model estimation. We therefore provide the marginal effects (Panel B of Table 3.2), defined as the derivatives of the probabilities, and which have substantive behavioural meaning. A marginal effect is the influence a one unit change in an explanatory variable has on the probability of selecting a particular outcome, *ceteris paribus*.[19] The marginal effects need not have the same sign as the utility parameters. Hence the statistical significance of a utility parameter does not imply the same significance for the marginal effect (see Hensher *et al.* 2005 for details).

It is noteworthy that the direct and indirect marginal effects reported in Table 3.2 all appear to have logical and consistent signs across all models. For example, the total debt to CFO variable has a negative marginal effect for the nonfailure category (indicating that a 1 unit increase in this variable *reduces* the probability of nonfailure), but has a positive marginal effect on all the distress categories (indicating that a 1 unit increase in this variable will *increase* the probability of each of the financial distress outcomes, *ceteris paribus*). However, it can be seen from Panel B that the direct and indirect marginal effects are generally stronger for the mixed logit and latent class MNL models across most variables. For example, looking at the direct

[18] Although the ratio of net operating cash flows to total assets is significant as a fixed parameter estimate in the mixed logit model, the dummy variable representing two consecutive periods of negative operating cash flow performance was not found to be significant.

[19] This holds for continuous variables only. For dummy (1,0) variables, the marginal effects are the derivatives of the probabilities given a change in the level of the dummy variable and thus represent the influence of a change in level of the variable upon the probability of choosing a given outcome, *ceteris paribus*. The marginal effects need not have the same sign as the utility parameters.

marginal effects, a 1 unit increase in the total debt to CFO variable reduces the probability of nonfailure by 0.383% for the mixed logit model, and reduces the probability of nonfailure by 0.802% for the latent class model, but only reduces the probability of nonfailure by 0.085% for the nested logit model. Likewise, a 1 unit increase in the total liabilities to total equity variable reduces the probability of nonfailure by .194% for the mixed logit model, and reduces the probability of nonfailure by 0.108% for the latent class model, but only reduces the probability of nonfailure by 0.002% for the nested logit model.

For the nested logit and latent class MNL models, the variable with the strongest overall statistical influence on the distress outcome is two periods of negative cash flow variable (negcash2). For this variable, the statistical influence is strongest with the nested logit model (two periods of negative cash flow performance reduces the probability of nonfailure by 0.517%, or, looking at the indirect marginal effects, increases the probability of insolvency, distressed merger and an outright failure by 0.31%, 0.174% and 0.221% respectively, *ceteris paribus*).

Finally, it can be seen that the mixed logit model is represented by a number of additional variables (including fixed parameter estimates, random parameters and heterogeneity in means parameters) which have a statistical influence on the outcome dependent variable. The mixed logit model has one fixed-parameter estimate that is not represented in the other two models (net operating cash flow to total assets). The marginal effects of this variable are fairly strong relative to other variables in the model, and indicate that a 1 unit increase in this ratio increases the probability of nonfailure by 0.357% (but reduces the probability of an insolvency, distressed merger and an outright failure by 0.956%, 0.299% and 0.539% respectively, *ceteris paribus*). Furthermore, Panel B reports the marginal effects for the random-parameter variables. Among the random-parameter variables, the strongest marginal effects are found on the working capital to total assets variable. Here, a 1 unit increase in this variable increases the probability of nonfailure by 0.15% (but reduces the probability of insolvency, distressed merger and an outright failure by 0.783%, 0.19% and 0.14% respectively, *ceteris paribus*).

Forecasting accuracy of open- vs. closed-form models

Having evaluated the model-fit information and marginal effects for each model, we now turn to the prediction outcomes. The nested logit and latent class MNL models are closed form, and hence deriving the probabilities is a straightforward exercise. For the nested logit model, probabilities are derived by inputting the financial and contextual variables of Table 3.2 into the elemental and branch expressions of equations (3.4), (3.5) and (3.6) above. Similarly, for the latent class MNL model, financial and contextual variables are inputted into equation (3.7) to derive probability outcomes. As indicated in Chapter 2, calculating probability outcomes for mixed logit is considerably more complex because it has an open-form solution. In deriving the probability outcomes for the mixed logit model some explanatory variables are a composite function of a mean parameter, a distribution around the mean and decomposition of the mean and variance by some contextual effect (in our case it is the new economy effect). In addition to fixed parameters, each individual firm is 'located' in parameter space on the normal distribution for the three random-parameter variables in Table 3.2 (Panel A) as follows.

Preference Distribution for working capital to total assets $= 0.0023 - 0.2563$ *New_Econ $+ 0.0149^{*}$normal density
Preference Distribution for cash resources to total assets $= .0035–0.2537^{*}$normal density
Preference Distribution for sales revenue to total assets $= 0.005675 - 0.0264^{*}$normal density.

Consistent with the approach adopted in the discrete-choice literature, we focus on a sample enumeration method which recognizes that the estimated model is based on a sample drawn from a population and the application of the model must preserve the full distribution of information obtained from the model system. This includes the outcome probabilities. Thus is it essential to aggregate the probabilities associated with each outcome across the entire sample to obtain the predicted values. Implementing a sample enumeration strategy on our hold out sample, we can compare the predictive performance of the standard MNL, nested logit, latent class MNL and mixed logit models.

Table 3.3 displays the forecasting accuracy of all advanced models reported in Table 3.2 using our validation sample. The results suggest that all advanced models have a high level of predictive accuracy on a holdout sample. Consistent with the ordered MNL results reported by Jones and Hensher (2004), the forecasting results for the unordered MNL analysis are found to be much inferior to the advanced models illustrated in Table 3.3, and hence are not reported here. Based on the pooled observations, it can be seen from Table 3.3 that the latent class MNL model has the highest overall predictive accuracy on a holdout sample. The latent class model is 90.4%

Table 3.3 Forecasting performance of final multinomial nested logit, latent class MNL and mixed logit models across distress states 0–3

Model	POOLED DATA (Reporting Periods 1–5)							
	Nonfailure (0)		Insolvent (1)		Merger (2)		Outright Failure (3)	
	Actual	Predicted	Actual	Predicted	Actual	Predicted	Actual	Predicted
Nested Logit	95.02%	95.66%	1.89%	1.59%	1.41%	1.31%	1.68%	1.44%
Latent Class	95.02%	95.41%	1.89%	1.71%	1.41%	1.36%	1.68%	1.52%
Mixed Logit	95.02%	95.51%	1.89%	1.51%	1.41%	1.62%	1.68%	1.40%
	1st Reporting Period Prior to Failure							
Nested Logit	95.09%	95.85%	2%	1.6%	1.42%	1.19%	1.49%	1.36%
Latent Class	95.09%	95.72%	2%	1.66%	1.42%	1.23%	1.49%	1.39%
Mixed Logit	95.09%	95.99%	2%	1.62%	1.42%	1.21%	1.49%	1.31%
	3rd Reporting Period Prior to Failure							
Nested Logit	94.5%	95.52%	2.31%	1.90%	1.29%	1.08%	1.9%	1.5%
Latent Class	94.5%	95.28%	2.31%	1.99%	1.29%	1.14%	1.9%	1.61%
Mixed Logit	94.5%	95.71%	2.31%	1.88%	1.29%	1.09%	1.9%	1.42%
	5th Reporting Period Prior to Failure							
Nested Logit	95.28%	96.30%	1.9%	1.40%	1.35%	1.09%	1.47%	1.21%
Latent Class	95.28%	95.88%	1.9%	1.54%	1.35%	1.20%	1.47%	1.38%
Mixed Logit	95.28%	96.52%	1.9%	1.36%	1.35%	1.02%	1.47%	1.19%

accurate in predicting the insolvency category (the comparable prediction accuracies are 84.12% for nested logit and 79.89% for mixed logit). For the distressed merger category, the latent class model is 96.4% accurate (comparable accuracies rates are 92.9% for nested logit and 87% for mixed logit). Finally, for the outright failure category, the latent class model is 90.4% predictively successful (the comparable prediction accuracies are 85.7% for nested logit and 83.3% for mixed logit).

Five reporting periods from failure, the latent class model is 81% accurate in predicting the insolvency state (comparable predictions are 73.6% and 71.5% for the nested logit and mixed logit models respectively), and 88.8% accurate in predicting the distressed merger state (comparable accuracy rates are 78.9% and 75.5% for nested logit and mixed logit respectively). Finally, five reporting periods from failure the latent class model is 93.8% accurate in predicting the outright failure state (comparable predictive accuracy rates are 82.3% and 80.9% for the nested logit and mixed logit models respectively).

3.5. Conclusions

The literature on discrete-choice modelling has evolved down two distinct paths. One is towards open-form (simulation based) discrete-choice models and the other is towards closed-form models. Chapter 2 introduced the open-form ordered mixed logit model; this modelling approach has a number of unique advantages but some limitations associated with their use and interpretation. Open-form models are potentially very powerful because they allow for a complete relaxation of the highly restrictive IID condition and provide a high level of flexibility and contextual richness in the specification of firm-specific observed and unobserved heterogeneity both between and within firms. However, with this added flexibility and sophistication comes a potential price: complex interpretation and a certain level of analytical intractability. For instance, estimation of random parameters in a mixed logit model requires complex analytical calculations to identify changes in outcome probabilities through varying levels of attributes over outcome alternatives. Mixed logit estimation involves the use of analytically intractable integrals which can only be approximated using simulation methods (see Stern 1997). Furthermore, unlike closed-form models which guarantee a unique globally optimal set of parameter estimates, the mixed logit model (due to the requirement to use simulated random draws) can produce a range of solutions, only one of which is globally optimal. The open-form mixed logit model also presents interpretative difficulties in that random parameters have a distribution which is unknown to the researcher. This necessitates strong assumptions (and a level of subjective judgment) to be made about the distribution of random parameters. While none of these issues represent insurmountable problems, they do involve added layers of complexity when it comes to interpreting and applying open-form models.

Advanced closed-form models are potentially important because they avoid many of the problems and pitfalls associated with estimation and interpretation of open-form models. Closed form models, such as nested logit and latent class MNL, are relatively simple to estimate, interpret and apply in contrast to open-form models. Practitioners in the main who use discrete-choice methods, prefer to use closed-form models, especially the nested logit and latent class models because of their relative simplicity in estimation. Furthermore, these models are particularly attractive in settings where there are large numbers of outcome alternatives (see Bhat 2003).

Nested logit is conceptually superior to standard models such as MNL because through partitioning (or nesting), the nested logit model partially corrects for the restrictive IID condition and enables potential differences in sources of unobserved heterogeneity to be investigated. The latent class MNL model is also more powerful than standard logit because it includes one or more discrete unobserved variables in model estimation. The latent class model is a semi-parametric specification, which alleviates the requirement to make strong distributional assumptions about firm-specific heterogeneity within a mixed logit framework. However, similar to mixed logit, a major strength of the latent class model is that it is free from many restrictive econometric assumptions (such as the IID condition on the error term).

The results of this research confirm the general superiority of all major classes of advanced discrete-choice model discussed in this study relative to the standard logit model widely used in previous research. After adjusting for the number of parameters, the model-fit for the nested logit, latent class MNL and mixed logit models are significantly better than MNL. Furthermore, the out-of-sample forecasting accuracy of these models is much superior to standard logit.

However, in a predictive context, in aggregate, we do not find compelling evidence for the superiority of open-form models (mixed logit) over advanced closed-form models such as multinomial nested logit and latent class MNL. In fact, the latent class model appears to have the highest overall out-of-sample predictive accuracy (nested logit was also slightly more predictively accurate than mixed logit). However, the mixed logit model had the greatest overall explanatory power (in terms of improvement in the log-likelihood function) compared to nested logit or latent class MNL.

We conclude that both open- and closed-form models can both have much potential value in the prediction of corporate insolvency and bankruptcy. Given the strong predictive performance of nested logit and latent class MNL, and the many appealing properties associated with closed-form models, these models may represent an effective practical alternative to mixed logit in the modelling of discrete outcomes, especially when the number of attributes and outcome alternative grows to a level where mixed logit models can become extremely unstable.

On the face of it this appears to be a conclusion more in favour of the use of closed-form models over open-form models. After all, why should researchers use a more complex model form unless it is able to perform appreciably better than a simpler model This may well be true if prediction is the sole focus of the research exercise. If the researcher's interest is as much on understanding behavioural relationships among explanatory variables on a deeper analytical level, mixed logit may be better equipped for this task. A major strength of mixed logit is that it instils greater behavioural realism into discrete-choice analysis as well as providing greater insight into the role and influence of covariates – observed and unobserved – on the domain outcome. This is partly achieved through the parametrization of measures which capture firm-specific observed and unobserved heterogeneity (such as random parameters and decomposition of random parameters means and variances). Closed-form models, no matter how sophisticated, are generally not designed to accommodate such a rich and flexible specification of behavioural heterogeneity in model specification.

Appendix

Definition of Variables

Variable Acronym	Definition
CFO Variables	
Netopta	Net operating cash flow by total assets
Netoptr	Net operating cash flow by sales revenue
Cfcover	Net operating cash flow by annual interest payments
Cdebtc	Total debt by gross operating cash flow
Negcash2	Two annual periods of negative CFO, coded $1 =$ yes; $0 =$ no
Negcash3	Three annual periods of negative CFO; coded 1 equal yes; $0 =$ no
Estimated CFO Measures	
Estc1	Crude estimate of CFO (net income + depreciation, amortization and depletion)
Estc2	Sophisticated estimate of CFO (Net Income before Extraordinary items + Depreciation + Annual Deferred Taxes − Annual Change in Current Assets − Cash + Annual Change in Current Liabilities − Current Maturities of Long-Term Debt)
Estc1_ta	Crude estimate of CFO by total assets
Estc1_de	Total debt by Crude estimate of CFO
Estc2_ta	Sophisticated estimate of CFO by total assets
Estc2_de	Total debt by sophisticated estimate of CFO

Accrual Based Measures

Cpta	Cash, deposits and marketable securities by total assets
Cpcl	Cash, deposits and marketable securities by current liabilities
Current	Current assets by current liabilities
Workcta	Working capital (current assets − current liabilities) by total assets
Cgear	Total debt by total equity
Tlte	Total liabilities to total equity
Debtta	Total debt to total assets
Cmardeb	Market value of equity by total debt
Nicover	Reported EBIT by annual interest payments
Ebitta	Reported EBIT by total assets
Roe	Return on equity
Roa	Return on assets
Crg	Annual growth in sales revenue
Csalesta	Total sales revenue by total assets
Creta	Retained earnings by total assets
Re1yr	Annual growth in retained earnings
Negreta2	Two annual periods of negative retained earnings; coded 1 = yes; 0 = no
Negreta3	Three annual periods of negative retained earnings; coded 1 = yes; 0 = no

Contextual Variables

Industry Classification

New_econ	If a new economy firm coded 1, 0 otherwise
Resource	If a resources firm coded 1, 0 otherwise
Old_econ	If an old economy firm coded 1, 0 otherwise
Finance	If a financial services firm coded 1, 0 otherwise

Size Variable

Logta	Natural log of total assets

REFERENCES

Altman, E., Haldeman, R. and Narayan, P., 'ZETA analysis: a new model to identify bankruptcy risk of corporations', *Journal of Banking and Finance*, 1(1), 1977, 29–54.

Bhat, C., 'Econometric choice formulations: alternative model structures, estimation techniques, and emerging directions', *Working Paper*, Department of Engineering, University of Texas, 2003.

Bowen, R. M., Burgstahler, D. and Daley, L. A., 'The incremental information content of accrual versus cash flows', *The Accounting Review*, 62(4), 1987, 713–26.

Casey, C. J., and Bartczak, N. J., 'Using operating cash flow data to predict financial distress: some extensions', *Journal of Accounting Research*, 23(1), 1985, 384–401.

Gentry J., Newbold P. and Whitford, D. T., 'Classifying bankrupt firms with funds flow components', *Journal of Accounting Research*, 23(1), 1985, 146–60.

Gombola, M. J., and Ketz, E. J., 'A note on cash flow classification patterns of financial ratios', *The Accounting Review*, 58(1), 1983, 105–14.

Goodman, L. A., 'Latent class analysis: the empirical study of latent types, latent variables, and latent structures', in Hagenaars, J. A. and McCutcheon, A. L. (eds.), *Applied Latent Class Analysis*, Cambridge University Press, 2002, pp. 3–56.

Greene, W. H., *Econometric Analysis*, 3rd edition, New york, Prentice-Hall, 2003.

Hensher, D. and Jones, S., 'Forecasting corporate bankruptcy: optimizing the performance of the mixed logit model', *Abacus*, 43:3, 2007, 241–64.

Hensher, D. A., Rose J. and Greene, W., *Applied Choice Analysis: A Primer*. Cambridge University Press, 2005.

Hribar, P., and Collins, D. W., 'Errors in estimating accruals: implications for empirical research', *Journal of Accounting Research*, 40(1), 2002, 105–34.

Jones, F. L., 'Current techniques in bankruptcy prediction', *Journal of Accounting Literature*, 6, 1987, 131–64.

Jones, S. and Hensher, D. A., 'Predicting firm financial distress: a mixed logit model', *The Accounting Review*, 79, 2004, 1011–39.

Jones, S. and Hensher, D. A., 'Evaluating the behavioural performance of alternative logit models: An Application in Corporate Takeovers Research', *Journal of Business Finance and Accounting*, 34(7), 2007, 1193–220.

Koppelman, F. and Sethi, V., Closed form discrete choice models, in Hensher, D. A. and Button, K. (eds.), *Transport Modeling*, Handbooks in Transport, Vol 1, Oxford, Elsevier, 2000.

Lazarsfeld, P. F., 'The logical and mathematical foundation of latent structure analysis', in S. A. Stouffer, L. Guttman, E. A. Suchman, P. F. Lazarsfeld, S. A. Star and J. A. Clausen (eds.), *Studies in Social Psychology in World War II: Vol 4. Measurement and Prediction*, Princeton University Press, 1950, pp. 362–472.

Lazarsfeld, P. F., and Henry, N. W., *Latent Structure Analysis*, Boston, MA, Houghton Mifflin, 1968.

Lau, A. H. L., 'A five-state financial distress prediction model', *Journal of Accounting Research*, 25(1), 1987, 127–38.

Louviere, J. J., Hensher, D. A. and Swait, J. F., *Stated Choice Methods and Analysis*, Cambridge University Press, 2000.

Ohlson, J. A., 'Financial ratios and the probabilistic prediction of bankruptcy', *Journal of Accounting Research*, 18(1), 1980, 109–31.

Roeder K., Lynch K., and Nagin D. S., 'Modeling uncertainty in latent class membership: a case study in criminology', *Journal of the American Statistical Association*, 94, 1999, 766–76.

Stern, S., 'Simulation-based estimation', *Journal of Economic Literature*, 35(4), 1997, 2006–39.

Thode, S. F., Drtina, R. E. and Largay, J. A., 'Operating cash flows: a growing need for separate reporting', *Journal of Accounting, Auditing & Finance*, 1(1), 1986, 46–57.

Train, K., *Discrete Choice Methods with Simulation*, Cambridge University Press, 2003.

Vuong, Q, 'Likelihood ratio tests for model selection and non-nested hypotheses', *Econometrica*, 57, 1989, 307–34.

Ward, T., 'An empirical study on the incremental predictive ability of Beaver's naïve operative flow measure using four-state ordinal models of financial distress', *Journal of Business Finance & Accounting*, 21(4), 1994, 547–62.

Zmijewski, M. E., 'Methodological issues related to the estimation of financial distress prediction models', *Journal of Accounting Research*, 22(3), Supplement, 1984, 59–82.

4 Survival analysis and omitted dividends

Marc J. LeClere

4.1. Introduction

Survival analysis is a set of statistical methods designed for the analysis of time to event data. Its origins can be traced back to interests in population mortality in the late 1600s (e.g., see Graunt 1676) and its designation as '*survival analysis*' reflects early applications in demography and biological science predominantly concerned with the ability of individuals or organisms to survive a given period of time until death.[1] Although the use of survival analysis in the social sciences is fairly recent, the last ten years have seen an increase in the use of the method in economics-based research as researchers have begun to develop an interest in the duration of time that precedes the occurrence of an event.

Survival analysis models are concerned with examining the length of the time interval ('*duration*') between transition states (Blossfeld *et al.* 1989). The time interval is defined by an origin state and a destination state and the transition between the states is marked by the occurrence of an event during the observation period. An event is a qualitative change that occurs to an individual, organization, political party, society, or other collective (hereafter 'individual') as it changes from one discrete state to another discrete state as the result of a substantive process.[2] The majority of survival analysis

---

[1] Although the statistical method is often called survival analysis, a large number of other descriptors serve to identify the same method. Survival analysis is also called event history analysis, lifetime analysis, reliability analysis, failure time analysis, duration analysis or transition analysis, depending upon the discipline or application in which the method is used.

[2] In most applications of survival analysis, the research question examines an event that is well-defined and available (e.g., marriage, birth, bankruptcy, job termination). It is not an exaggeration to say that survival analysis models are rarely used unless the event itself is readily identifiable by a natural transition between states. However, survival analysis can be employed in situations where the researcher defines the event. Allison (1995) suggests that researchers can create events when a quantitative variable experiences a large change or crosses a threshold. Jaggia and Thosar (2005) provide an illustration of an artificially constructed event by modelling the duration of time that it takes an IPO to achieve various cumulative market-adjusted rate of returns.

models examine the occurrence of a single event that transitions an individual across discrete states although there are models in which the event represents a transition to one of several states, repeated transitions from states, or where the event occurs many times. Regardless of the approach, the idea that underlies all the models is that there is a substantive process that drives the transition between states. The transition can occur at any point along the time path and the transition is influenced by certain influences or factors. Understanding the factors provides insights into the substantive process.

The most common applications of survival analysis in economics-based literature have been in the areas of financial distress and initial public offerings (IPOs). Survival analysis is well-suited to examining both issues. Financial distress at its most basic level is a transition. In the terminology of survival analysis, firms which are not experiencing financial distress are in an origin state and they transition to a destination state as the result of an event termed 'financial distress'. Financial distress can be represented by the occurrence of a formal event such as the declaration of bankruptcy or it can be represented by a user-defined event such as the occurrence of a loss or a skipped dividend payment. Survival analysis would model the duration between some pre-determined origin state and financial distress. Initial public offerings represent the first sale of a company's stock to the public. The IPO itself represents the origin and the event can be any number of occurrences that the researcher is interested in. The event may represent failure, the delisting of the firm from the exchange on which the IPO occurred, or the acquisition of the firm by another firm. Regardless of the event, the interest lies in the duration between the IPO and the event.

The purpose of this paper is to provide an overview of survival analysis and provide an illustration of the method with a specific application in the area of credit risk. The specific application references omitted dividend payments. Section 1 examines survival distributions. Section 2 presents an overview of the benefits of survival analysis relative to other statistical methods. Section 3 discusses non-parametric estimation while section 4 examines parametric and non-parametric regression models. Section 5 presents an empirical application of several models. Section 6 provides a summary and discusses the future potential of survival analysis models in research.

4.2. Survival distributions

Survival analysis models the probability of a change in a dependent variable Y_t from an origin state j to a destination state k as a result of causal factors (Blossfeld and Rohwer 1995). The duration of time between states is called event (failure) time. Event time is represented by a non-negative random variable T that represents the duration of time until the dependent variable at time t_0 (Y_{t_0}) changes from state j to state k.[3] Alternative survival analysis models assume different probability distributions for T. Regardless of the probability distribution of T, the probability distribution can be specified as a cumulative distribution function, a survivor function, a probability density function, or a hazard function. The cumulative distribution function is

$$F(t) = P(T \le t) = \int_0^t f(x)\mathrm{d}x. \tag{4.1}$$

It represents the probability that T is less than or equal to a value t and denotes the probability that the event occurs before some time t. $F(t)$ is also called the lifetime distribution or failure distribution (Elandt-Johnson and Johnson 1980). If T represents the first occurrence of an event (e.g., age at onset of disease or age at first marriage) then $F(t)$ represents the distribution of event or failure time.

The survival function (sometimes referred to as the reliability function, cumulative survival rate, or survivorship function) is the complementary function of $F(t)$ and is represented as

$$S(t) = P(Tt). \tag{4.2}$$

It represents the probability that the event time is greater than a value t. The survival function indicates that survival time is longer than t (the event has not occurred at time t) or that the individual survives until time t. The survival function is a monotonic non-increasing left-continuous function of time t with $S(0) = 1$ (since event time cannot be negative) and $S(\infty) = \lim_{t \to \infty} F(t) = 0$. As time elapses, the function approaches 0, since the event (e.g., death) will occur for all individuals. In event histories it is more common to employ the survival function rather than the cumulative distribution function because it is more intuitive to think of individuals

---

[3] T denotes event time but is alternately called the lifetime, the age at death, the age at failure, age or survival time.

surviving an event to a certain point in time rather than not surviving the event (Blossfeld and Rohwer 1995).

The probability density function is defined as

$$f(t) = \lim_{\Delta t \to 0} \frac{P(t \le T < t + \Delta t)}{\Delta t} = \frac{dF(t)}{dt} = -\frac{S(t)}{dt} \tag{4.3}$$

and it represents the unconditional instantaneous probability that failure occurs in the period of time from t to $t + \Delta t$ per unit width Δt. Before taking the limit, $P(t \le T \le t + \Delta t)$ represents the probability that the event occurs in the time period between t and Δt and $f(t)$ is proportional to this probability as the interval becomes very small. The density function is also known as the unconditional failure rate or the curve of deaths.

The hazard function is represented as

$$\lambda(t) = \lim_{\Delta t \to 0} \frac{P(t \le T < t + \Delta t | T \ge t)}{\Delta t} = \frac{f(t)}{1 - F(t)} \tag{4.4}$$

and it defines the instantaneous rate of failure at $T = t$ conditional upon surviving to time t.[4] The hazard function quantifies the probability of failure for individuals that have survived until time t and effectively removes individuals who have experienced the event prior to t from consideration. The hazard function is sometimes referred to as a hazard rate because it is a dimensional quantity that has the form number of events per interval of time (Allison 1995). It provides a local, time-related description of the behaviour of the process over time by providing a measure of the risk of failure per unit of time and represents the propensity of the risk set at time t to change from the origin state to the event state $(Y_t = j \to Y_t = k)$ (Blossfeld and Rohwer 1995). Because time is continuous, the probability that an event will occur exactly at time t is 0 so the hazard function is expressed as the probability that an event will occur in the small interval between t and Δt (Allison 1995). The hazard function is not a conditional probability because it can be greater than 1. The best approximation of the conditional probability $P(t \le T < | T \ge t)$ is $\lambda(t)\Delta t$ for very small values of t (Blossfeld et al. 1989). The hazard function provides information concerning future events if the individual survives to time t in that the reciprocal of the hazard function $1/\lambda(t)$ denotes the expected length of time until the event occurs (Allison 1995). The hazard function may increase, decrease, or remain constant over time depending upon the underlying process.

---

[4] The hazard function is alternatively referred to as the intensity function, intensity rate, risk function, hazard rate, failure rate, conditional failure rate, transition rate, mortality rate or force of mortality, and symbolized as $\lambda(t)$ $r(t)$ or $h(t)$. In economics, the reciprocal of the hazard rate is called Mill's ratio.

Because the cumulative distribution function, survivor function, probability density function, and hazard function all describe a continuous probability distribution, each can be defined in terms of the other (Kalbfleisch and Prentice 1980, Lee 1980, Allison 1995). If you know $F(t)$, then equations (4.1) and (4.2) provide

$$S(t) = 1 - F(t) \tag{4.5}$$

because survival and non-survival probabilities add to 1 and equation (4.4) provides

$$\lambda(t) = \frac{f(t)}{S(t)}. \tag{4.6}$$

If $S(t)$ is known, $f(t)$ can be determined since

$$f(t) = \frac{\mathrm{d}}{\mathrm{d}t} F(t) \tag{4.7}$$

and

$$f(t) = \frac{\mathrm{d}}{\mathrm{d}t}(1 - S(t)) = -S'(t) \tag{4.8}$$

and equation (4.6) provides $\lambda(t)$. If $\lambda(t)$ is known, then substituting equation (4.8) into equation (4.6) provides

$$\lambda(t) = -\frac{S'(t)}{S(t)} = -\frac{\mathrm{d}}{\mathrm{d}t} \log_e S(t), \tag{4.9}$$

integration provides

$$S(t) = \exp\left[-\int_0^t \lambda(x)\mathrm{d}x \right] \tag{4.10}$$

and equations (4.6) and (4.10) provide that

$$f(t) = \lambda(t) \exp\left[-\int_0^t \lambda(x)\mathrm{d}x \right]. \tag{4.11}$$

4.3. Benefits of survival analysis

Unique to survival analysis models is the manner in which the models address censored observations and time-varying covariates. Censoring occurs when complete information is not available on the occurrence of a specific

Table 4.1 IPO date and qualified audit opinion

Date of IPO	End date	Time	Qualified audit opinion	Censor
01-01-1990	12-30-1993	48	1	0
05-03-1991	12-30-1999	103	0	1
10-09-1992	12-30-1999	87	0	1
11-03-1992	12-30-1996	86	0	1
03-05-1993	12-30-1998	69	1	0

event. In a survival analysis study, individuals are in origin states and are observed for the occurrence of a specific event such as marriage, tenure, job termination, or bankruptcy. For example, in studies modelling the timing of first birth, women who have not given birth to a child are in an origin state termed nulliparous. When a woman gives birth to the first child, the event ('first birth') has occurred, and the woman is no longer in the origin state. Time spent in the origin state is defined as the duration of time preceding the birth of the child and a time origin. Depending upon the research question of interest or perhaps data availability, time origin might be defined as birth, age of menarche, age of marriage, or date of last contraceptive use.

In some studies, all the individuals under observation might actually be followed until the event of interest occurs. But many times a study ends before the event of interest occurs, subjects are lost or drop out of a study, or retrospective gathering of data focuses on a finite observation period. In this case censoring is said to occur. Censoring occurs when knowledge of the time that the individual spends in the origin state is incomplete and the exact duration of time ('lifetime') is known for only a portion of a sample. As an example, assume that a researcher is interested in the survival times of firms undertaking an initial public offering (IPO) where survival is defined as the number of months between the IPO and the issuance of a qualified audit opinion. Assume that a sample of firms undertaking an IPO is selected beginning with the year 1990. Firms are followed for ten years through 1999 and for simplicity assume that the firms are all calendar year firms. Tables 4.1 provides hypothetical data for five observations. Column 1 provides the date of the IPO, column 2 provides the end date, and column 3 provides the number of months that the firm is followed. The firm is followed until it receives a qualified audit opinion, until the end of the ten years, or until the firm is lost to observation. The column 'qualified audit opinion' records the presence or absence (1–0) of a qualified audit opinion and 'censor' records whether the firm completed the study without receiving a qualified audit opinion or was lost to observation (censor = 1). Firms that received a qualified audit opinion over the course of the study are not censored (censored = 0). As an example, observation 1 had its IPO on January 1, 1990 and it received a qualified audit opinion at the end of 1993. The firm had been followed for 48 months before the event occurred. Observation 2 was followed for 103 months until the end of the study's observation period by which time it had not received a qualified audit opinion. Observation 4 was followed for 87 months. It was lost to observation at the end of 1996 and it is censored.

The goal of the study would be to build a model that determines the effect of various covariates on firm survival time from the date of the IPO. But the problem is that for some of the observations, survival time is incomplete and conventional statistics do not apply. If the censored observations are ignored and are treated as measures of survival time, sample statistics are not measures of the survival time distribution but measures of a survival time distribution and a distribution based on survival times and censoring (Hosmer and Lemeshow 1999). For the five observations, the average survival time is 78.3 months. But this is not average survival time but rather a lower bound of average survival time; on average, the firms survived almost 79 months. For observations 2, 3, and 4, we know the exact survival time. These firms survived an average of 92 months. But firms 1 and 5 are censored. We know they survived, on average, at least 58.5 months. The benefit of survival analysis models is that they use methods of estimation (generally either maximum or partial likelihood) that incorporate information from censored and uncensored observations to provide consistent parameter estimates (Allison 1995). In contrast to survival analysis, regression analysis (either OLS or logistic) is unable to incorporate information from censored observations into the estimation process.

The second major issue which survival analysis addresses concerns the value of covariates over the observation period. Covariates can be time-invariant or time-varying.[5] Time-invariant covariates do not change during the duration that precedes the occurrence of an event. For instance, in the case of individuals, some covariates such as sex and blood-type never change over time. Other covariates might change over time, but the change is so insignificant that the covariate may be regarded as time-invariant. As an

---

[5] Time-varying covariates are sometimes referred to as time-dependent covariates.

example, if a survival analysis model employed industry as a covariate, although industry membership occasionally changes, industry changes might be viewed as so rare that industry membership is regarded as constant. On the other hand, time-varying covariates change during the course of the observation period. For individuals, covariates such as income, job status, education, family status, and wealth generally do change over time. In the case of firms, covariates such as income, size, and financial statement ratios change over time as well.

When modelling the duration of time that precedes the occurrence of an event, the value of a covariate along the time path affects the probability of event occurrence. The major contribution of survival analysis methods in this area is that the estimation procedures consider changes in the value of covariates over time. Cross-sectional studies only examine the level of a variable at a given point in time. A cross-sectional analysis employs a 'snap-shot' methodology because it only views the individual at a 'snap-shot' in time. Survival analysis, relying on longitudinal data rather than cross-sectional data, incorporates changes in the covariates over time in the estimation process.

4.4. Non-parametric estimation

The most basic approach to describe the distribution of survival times consists of non-parametric descriptive methods. Non-parametric methods make no assumption about the distribution of event times (T) but instead focus on providing descriptive information about the survival function of event times (Lee 1980). Non-parametric or distribution-free methods for analysing survival data have been favoured by biostatisticians (Allison 1995). Although non-parametric methods of estimation are used less frequently than parametric and semi-parametric methods, the methods are appropriate when a theoretical distribution is not known. Prior to fitting a theoretical distribution, non-parametric methods are useful for preliminary examination of data, suggesting functional form, and assessing homogeneity (Kiefer 1988, Allison 1995).

The most common technique for non-parametric estimation of the survivorship function is the Kaplan–Meier estimator. For the period under observation, assume time begins at t_0, ends at t_e, and the period $[0,t_e]$ is divided into M intervals $[0,t_1)$, $[t_1,t_2)$, $\ldots$, $[t_{m-1},t_e]$ where the intervals are so small that the probability of more than one event in an interval is almost nonexistent (Elandt-Johnson and Johnson 1980). The event times are ordered such that $t_1 < t_2 < \cdots t_e$ where $e \leq n$ (Blossfeld, et al. 1989). The risk set at any given point is R_i and it represents the number of individuals or firms that survived until time t_i (or in actuality, survived until the moment of time just before t_i) (Elandt-Johnson and Johnson 1980). Defining

$$\phi_i = \begin{cases} 1 \text{ if death occurs in } [t_{i-1}, t_i) \\ 0 \text{ otherwise} \end{cases} \tag{4.12}$$

and q_{i-1} as the conditional probability of death in $[t_{i-1}, t_i)$ given that the individual is alive at t_{i-1}, then $L_i \propto (q_{i-1})^{\phi_i} (p_{i-1})^{R_i - \phi_i}$ provides

$$\hat{\lambda}_{i-1} = \begin{cases} \frac{1}{R_i} \text{ if event occurs in } [t_{i-1}, \downarrow_f t_i) \\ 0 \text{ otherwise} \end{cases}. \tag{4.13}$$

as the unbiased maximum likelihood estimator of the hazard function (Elandt-Johnson and Johnson 1980). The probability of surviving beyond the current period is

$$\hat{p}_{i-1} = 1 - \hat{\lambda}_{i-1} = \begin{cases} \frac{R_i - 1}{R_i} \text{ if event occurs at } t_i \\ 1 \text{ otherwise} \end{cases} \tag{4.14}$$

and the survival function is

$$\hat{S}(t_i) = \hat{P}_i = \hat{P}_0 \, \hat{P}_1 \ldots \hat{P}_{i-1}, \tag{4.15}$$

where $\hat{S}(0) = \hat{P}_0 = 1$ (Elandt-Johnson and Johnson 1980). Because an event may not occur in some time interval t_i, $p_{i-1} = 1$ and time divisions without an event do not enter into the estimate of the survivor function. The interest is therefore only on the ordered time periods where an event occurs, $t'_i < t'_2 < \cdots < t'_j \cdots < t'_K$, where K signifies the number of events at a distinct time point (Elandt-Johnson and Johnson 1980). Defining $\Re_j$ as the risk set at t'_j, the product-limit estimator or Kaplan–Meier estimator of $S(t)$ is

$$S(t) = \begin{cases} 1 & \text{for } t' < t_1 \\ \prod\limits_{j=1}^{i} \frac{R_{j-1}}{R_j} & \text{for } t'_1 \leq t < t'_{i+1}, \ i = 1, 2, \ldots K - 1 \\ \prod\limits_{j=1}^{K} \frac{R_{j-1}}{R_j} & \text{for } t \geq t'_k. \end{cases} \tag{4.16}$$

Equation (4.16) states that for any time period t before an event occurs, the probability of surviving to t'_1 is equal to one. For any other time period except where $t \geq t'_k$, the survivor function is equal to the product of the conditional probabilities of surviving to R_j given survival to R_{j-1}. If the time period is greater than or equal to t'_k, the survivor function depends on the nature of censored observations. If there is no censoring (no events occur in or after t'_k) then $S(t)$ equals 0. But if there are right-censored observations, $S(t)$ is undefined. The Kaplan–Meier estimator facilitates comparisons across sub-groups, estimates of the standard error of the survivor function allow the calculation of confidence intervals, and several test statistics exist for comparing survivor functions generated by the product-limit estimator (Lee 1980, Blossfeld and Rohwer 1995).

4.5. Regression models

Non-parametric estimation of the survival function is useful for preliminary analysis but it does not allow for an estimation of the effect of a covariate on the survival function. Because most research examines heterogeneous populations, researchers are usually interested in examining the effect of covariates on the hazard rate (Kalbfleisch and Prentice 1980, Lawless 1982, Blossfeld *et al.* 1989). This is accomplished through the use of regression models in which the hazard rate or time to failure is the fundamental dependent variable.

When non-parametric methods of estimation are employed, data gathering involves obtaining failure or duration data for each subject. Expanding the method of estimation to a regression model requires that covariates be gathered for each subject in the sample. Upon completion of data gathering, there is a vector of covariates where $\mathbf{x} = (x_1, \ldots, x_s)$ for a process with failure time $T < 0$. The basic issue is to specify a model for the distribution of t given $\mathbf{x}$ and this can be accomplished with parametric or semi-parametric models. Parametric models employ distributions such as the exponential and Weibull while semi-parametric models make no assumptions about the underlying distribution. Although most applications of survival analysis in economics-based research avoid specifying a distribution and simply employ a semi-parametric model, for purposes of completeness, parametric regression models are briefly discussed.

Parametric regression models

Parametric regression models are heavily influenced by the specification of the error term. The simplest form of a parametric regression model is the exponential regression model where

$$T = e^{\beta X} X \, \varepsilon \tag{4.17}$$

where survival time is represented by T and the error term is assumed to follow the exponential distribution. The model is linearized as

$$Y = \beta X + \theta \tag{4.18}$$

where $Y = \ln(T)$ and $\theta = \ln(\varepsilon)$ and the distribution of the error terms follows the Gumbel distribution with $G(0,1)$ (Hosmer and Lemeshow 1999). Alternatively, an additional parameter can be introduced to yield a log-Weibull model where

$$Y = \beta X + \sigma X \theta \tag{4.19}$$

and the distribution of $\sigma x \theta$ is $G(0,\sigma)$.

Parametric survival models are estimated using the maximum likelihood method. Maximum likelihood estimation is used because it produces estimators that are consistent, asymptotically efficient, and asymptotically normal. If data are gathered for a sample of n individuals ($i = 1, \ldots, n$), the data will consist of t_i, the time of the event (or if the observation is censored, the time of censoring), an indicator variable, δ_i, representing the present ($\delta_i = 0$) or absence ($\delta_i = 1$) of censoring, and a vector of covariates, $\mathbf{x}_i = x_1 \ldots x_{ik}$. In the absence of censored observations, the probability of observing the entire data is the product of the probabilities of observing the data for each specific individual. Representing the probability of each observation by its probability density function provides the likelihood function $L = \prod_{i=1}^{n} f_i(t_i)$, where L represents the probability of the entire data. If censoring is present, then the likelihood function becomes $L = \prod_{i=1}^{n} [f_i(t_i)]^{\delta_i} [S_i(t_i)]^{1-\delta_i}$. The likelihood function effectively combines uncensored and censored observations in that if an individual is not censored, the probability of the event is $f_i(t_i)$, and if the individual is censored at t_i, the probability of the event is $S_i(t_i)$, the survivorship function evaluated at t_i. Taking the natural log of L, the objective is to maximize the expression $\log(L) = \sum_{i=1}^{n} \delta_i \ln f_i(t_i) + \sum_{i=1}^{n} (1 - \delta_i) \ln S(t_i)$. Once the appropriate distribution has been specified, the process reduces to using a numerative method such as the Newton–Raphson algorithm to solve for the parameters.

Semi-parametric models

Although parametric models are an improvement over life tables and the Kaplan–Meier estimator, they still have limitations. Foremost among these problems are the necessity to specify the behaviour of the hazard function over time, finding a model with an appropriate shape if the hazard function is nonmonotonic, and a cumbersome estimation process when the covariates change over time (Allison 1984). The difficulties encountered with the parametric models are resolved with the proportional hazards models.[6] The proportional hazards model is represented as

$$\lambda_i(t) = \lambda_0(t)e^{x\beta}. \tag{4.20}$$

The model states that the hazard rate for any individual is the product of an arbitrary unspecified baseline hazard $(\lambda_0(t))$ rate and an exponentiated set of covariates. It is this lack of specificity of a base-line hazard function that makes the model semi-parametric or distribution-free. If a specific form were specified for $\lambda(t)$, a parametric model would result. $\lambda_0(t)$ may be thought of as the hazard function for an individual that has a value of 0 for each of the covariates and for whom $e^{x\beta} = 1.$[7] The regression model is written as

$$\log \lambda_i(t) = \alpha(t) + \beta_1 x_{i1} + \cdots + \beta_k x_{ik} \tag{4.21}$$

where $\alpha(t) = \log \lambda_0(t)$ (Allison 1984). The model is called the proportional hazards model because it has the property that different units have hazard functions that are proportional (Lawless 1982). This means that the ratio of the hazard function for two units with independent covariates does not vary with t. For two individuals, i and j, equation (4.20) can be expressed as the ratio of two hazard functions such that

$$\frac{\lambda_i(t)}{\lambda_j(t)} = e^{\{\beta_1(x_{i1}-x_{j1})+\cdots+\beta_k(x_{ik}-x_{jk})\}}. \tag{4.22}$$

---

[6] The proportional hazards model is frequently referred to as Cox's regression or Cox's proportional hazards regression model since it was proposed by Cox (1972).

[7] The conditional density function is

$$f(t;x) = \lambda_0(t)e^{x\beta}e^{-\int_0^t \lambda_0(u)e^{x\beta}du}$$

and the conditional survivorship function is

$$S(t;x) = S_0(t)^{e^{x\beta}}$$

where

$$S_0(t) = e^{-\int_0^t \lambda_0(u)du}$$

represents the baseline survivor function for an individual with $e^{x\beta} = 1$ (Lawless 1982).

The hazard for any individual is a fixed proportion of the hazard of any other individual at any point in time.

The uniqueness of the proportional hazards model is the manner in which the β parameters are estimated in the absence of knowledge of $\lambda(t)$. Cox (1972) referred to this estimation procedure as the method of partial likelihood. The method of partial likelihood begins by assuming that there is a group of individuals, $R(t_{(i)})$, that are at risk of failure just before the occurrence of $t_{(i)}$. If only one failure occurs at $t_{(i)}$, the conditional probability that the failure occurs to individual i, given that individual i has a vector of covariates x_i, is represented by

$$\frac{\lambda\left(t_{(i)}|x_{(i)}\right)}{\sum\limits_{l\in R\left(t_{(i)}\right)} \lambda\left(t_{(i)}|x_l\right)} = \frac{\lambda_0 e^{x_i\beta}}{\sum\limits_{l\in R_{\left(t_{(i)}\right)}} \lambda_0 e^{x_l\beta}} = \frac{e^{x_i\beta}}{\sum\limits_{l\in R_{\left(t_{(i)}\right)}} e^{x_l\beta}}. \tag{4.23}$$

Equation (4.23) is the hazard function for individual i at a specific point in time, $t_{(i)}$, divided by the sum of the hazard functions for all individuals in the risk set just before the occurrence of time $t_{(i)}$. Because λ_0 is common to every term in the equation it is eliminated. The partial likelihood function is obtained by taking the product of equation (4.23) over all k points in time such that

$$L(\beta) = \prod_{i=1}^{k} \left(\frac{e^{x_i\beta}}{\sum\limits_{l\in R_i} e^{x_l\beta}}\right)^{\delta_i}. \tag{4.24}$$

Equation (4.24) does not depend on $\lambda_0(t)$ and can be maximized to provide an estimate of $\hat{\beta}$ that is consistent and asymptotically normally distributed (Kalbfleisch and Prentice 1980, Lawless 1982, Namboodiri and Suchindran 1987). Although the proportional hazards model does not require the specification of a hazard function, it does not provide for tests about the shape of the hazard function (Allison 1995). This limitation is overcome with the use of a piecewise exponential model. The idea behind the piecewise exponential model is that the time scale is divided into intervals. Within each interval, the hazard is constant but the hazard is allowed to vary across time intervals. The time scale has J intervals and the cutpoints are defined as $a_0, a_1, \ldots, a_J$ with $a_0 = 0$ and $a_J = \infty$. Each individual has a hazard function of the form

$$\lambda_i(t) = \lambda_i e^{\beta X_i} \qquad \text{for } a_{j-1} \le t < a_j \tag{4.25}$$

or

$$\log \lambda_i(t) = \alpha_j + \beta X_i \qquad\qquad (4.26)$$

where $\alpha_j = \log \lambda_j$ (Allison 1995). This allows the intercept to vary across intervals.

4.6. Survival analysis and credit risk

The use of survival analysis in financial distress research can be traced to its first application in a paper by Lane, Looney *et al.* (1986). In the intervening twenty years the method has seen an increased use in accounting and finance research. The most common applications of survival analysis in economics-based research involve financial distress and IPO offerings. LeClere (2000) provides a review of the applications of survival analysis in the financial distress literature. Research papers discussed include Lane *et al.* (1986), Whalen (1991), Chen and Lee (1993), Abdel-Khalik (1993), Bandopadhyaya (1994), Audretsch and Mahmood (1995), Wheelock and Wilson (1995), Kim *et al.* (1995), Helwege (1996), Henebry (1996), Hill *et al.* (1996), Lee and Urrutia (1996), George *et al.* (1996), and Hensler *et al.* (1997). Readers are encouraged to see LeClere (2000) for a review of that literature. Recent papers that the reader should consult include Jain and Kini (1999), Ongena and Smith (2001), Manigart *et al.* (2002), Moeller and Molina (2003), Turetsky and McEwen (2001), Cameron and Hall (2003), Audretsch and Lehmann (2005), Jain and Martin (2005), Wheelock and Wilson (2005) and Yang and Sheu (2006).

Financial distress

An interest in the ability of accounting information to predict financial distress generates considerable research in accounting and finance. Early works by Altman (1968) and Beaver (1966, 1968a, 1968b) represent the emergence of a large body of literature that examines the relation between accounting ratios and other financial information and the phenomenon of financial distress.[8] The majority of the research studies in the financial distress area employ either multiple discriminant analysis or a qualitative response model with a dichotomous dependent variable such as probit or

---

[8] Foster (1986), Zavgren (1983) and Griffen (1982) contain reviews of the literature.

logistic regression. These models provide the posterior probability that a firm will fail or not fail for a given set of financial characteristics. The majority of financial distress research has chosen to ignore the time to failure and provides no information on the process of financial distress. A common approach in financial distress study employing logistic regression as a statistical technique would typically used data one or two years prior to failure. The resulting model could be used to predict whether a firm would fail in one or two years. But the interest in building a model of financial distress is conditioned on the fact that creditors, regulators and other interested parties need models that provide an indication of failure well in advance of actual failure. Models that omit event time from the modelling process may not provide a warning of failure with enough lead time to be of use.

Financial distress: The case of omitted dividend payments

A large amount of literature in corporate finance has examined firm dividend policy. This body of research has examined the information content of dividends as well as dividend payout policy. With respect to firm dividend policy, some research has focused on the relationship between financial distress and changes in firm dividend policy (see e.g., DeAngelo and DeAngelo 1990). This paper provides an insight into firm dividend policy by using survival analysis to examine the relationship between financial distress and a firm's decision to omit dividend payments. For purposes of this illustration, financial distress is assumed to occur when a firm that has demonstrated long-term profitability incurs a loss and the interest lies in the duration of time between the firm reporting the loss and the omission of a cash dividend.

The sample of firms and related data was obtained from the annual Compustat Industrial and Research files maintained at Wharton Data Research Services. The potential sample of firms began with an initial sample of 9,240 firms for the years 1991–5. Firms were eliminated if they were not from the manufacturing, mining, retailing and nonfinancial service sectors.[9] This criteria eliminated 5,335 firms. Firms were also eliminated if they did not report income before extraordinary items (data item #18) or pay dividends on common stock (data item #21) for a five year period. This eliminated 3,253 firms. The final sample consisted of 652 firms with positive

---

[9] The sample includes firms from SIC codes 1000–3999, 5300–5999, and 7000–9999.

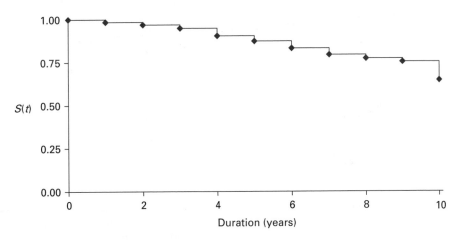

Figure 4.1   Kaplan–Meier estimator of survival function of omitted dividend payments

income and dividend payments for the five year periods 1991–5, 1992–6, 1993–7, 1994–8, and 1995–9. Firms could only enter the sample once. Firms were followed until they omitted a dividend payment on common stock or the end of 2005. The final sample consisted of 206 firms that experienced the event (omitted dividend payments) and 446 censored observations.

DeAngelo and DeAngelo (1990) document that the common explanations among firms as to why firms cut or omit dividend payments include current or expected losses, low or declining earnings, cash conservation, the need to fund new investment and high debt payments. The potential predictors of firm dividend cuts considered in this paper are the current ratio ('liquidity'), the ratio of long-term debt to equity ('leverage'), the ratio of income to total assets ('profitability'), the ratio of free cash flow to total assets ('free cash flow'), and the log of sales ('size'). Leverage is assumed to have a negative effect on the survival rate while the other four variables are assumed to have a positive effect on the survival rate. When firms are financially distressed, they are assumed to omit dividend payments in order to make debt and interest payments. However, firms with higher levels of liquidity, profitability, free cash flow and size are assumed to be in a better position to maintain dividend payments.

Figure 4.1 presents an estimate of the survival function of omitted dividend payments using the Kaplan-Meier estimator. The survival function has a gradual slope and after ten years about 25% of the firms have omitted a dividend payment and 75% of the firms have managed not to omit a

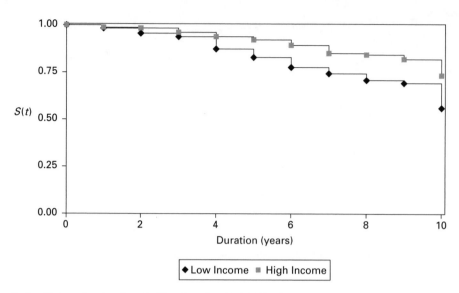

Figure 4.2   Kaplan–Meier estimator of survival function of omitted dividend payments stratified by income/assets

dividend payment. The survival curve has a gradual slope and the decision to omit dividend payments is not clustered in any one period of time. Figure 4.2 presents survival curves stratified by profitability. Firms were grouped on the basis of the median value of the ratio in year 1. The high-income group has ratio values above the median value and the low-income group has ratio values at or below the median value. It is obvious that the high-income group's survival curve is above the survival curve of the low-income group. All conventional tests of equality over the strata indicate that the two groups are significantly different. Survival curves (not presented) were examined for liquidity, leverage, size and free cash flow based upon similar strata. Survival curves were not significantly different for liquidity or size but were significantly different for leverage and free cash flow. The survival curves provide some preliminary evidence that profitability, leverage, and free cash flow influence the duration of time that elapses before a firm omits a dividend payment. Although the Kaplan–Meier estimator provides an indication that some of the variables influence the duration between the firm loss and an omitted dividend payment, there are a couple of problems inherent in its use. First, it only provides an initial indication that the specific variables have an effect on duration but it provides no information on the actual influence that the variable has on duration. Second, it provides no information on the collective effect of the variables in

Table 4.2 Survival analysis models

All data items in this note refer to Compustat data items. [a]Ratio of current assets (data item #4) to current liabilities (data item #5), [b]ratio of long-term debt (data item #9) to the sum of common equity (data item #60) and preferred stock – carrying value (data item #130), [c]ratio of ordinary income become extraordinary items (data item #18) to total assets (data item #6), [d]natural log of sales (data item #12), [e]ratio of operating activities – net cash flow (data item #308) less capital expenditures (data item #128) to total assets (data item #6). Missing data values were set to yearly mean values.

	Expected sign	Model 1	Model 2	Expected sign	Model 3	Model 4
Variable						
Intercept					1.6420	1.7806
Liquidity[a]	–	−0.1144*	−0.0766	+	0.0930	0.0542*
Leverage[b]	+	0.0305	0.0004	–	−0.0269	−0.0162
Profitability[c]	–	−6.3997***	−6.9190***	+	5.5639***	3.0850***
Size[d]	–	−0.1644***	−0.1220***	+	0.1421***	0.0805***
Free cash flow[e]	–	−1.7158	−2.3262**	+	1.2625	0.8592
Scale					1.0000	0.4816
Shape					1.0000	2.0762
Likelihood ratio		46.00***	119.46***		−508.72***	−137.83***

* Indicates significance at the .10 level
** Indicates significance at the .05 level
*** Indicates significance at the .01 level

a multivariate setting. Some of the variables appear to be significant in a univariate setting but that may not be the case in a multivariate setting.

Table 4.2 presents four survival analysis models. For each variable in the models, the table presents the variables, their expected sign, the coefficients, the significance of the coefficients, and the likelihood ratio. The likelihood ratio is a test for the overall significance of the models. Models 1 and 2 are non-parametric and models 3 and 4 are parametric. Model 1 is a Cox proportional hazards model with time-invariant covariates. The covariates in model 1 are fixed at their year 1 values. For example, for a firm that reported income and dividends for the years 1991–5 and entered the sample because of a loss in 1996, the values of each of the covariates are fixed at their 1996 value. Model 2 is a Cox proportional hazards model with time-dependent covariates. In model 2, the covariates are allowed to change over the estimation period. Model 3 is an exponential regression model and model 4 is a Weibull regression model.

Regardless of the model, the results are generally consistent across all four models. Profitability and size are significant at the 0.01 level in all four models. Liquidity is significant in only two of the models and then only at the 0.10 level. Free cash flow is only significant in model 2 but is significant at the 0.05 level. Leverage is not significant in any of the models. It appears that the decision to omit dividend payments in the face of financial distress in heavily influenced by firm profitability and size given that these effects are consistent across models. A comparable statement cannot be made for the other variables since their effect is not consistent across models.

Models 1 and 2 are proportional hazard models. Equation (4.21) shows that the dependent variable in the proportional hazards model is the log of the hazard rate. Consequently, the coefficients indicate the effect of a covariate on the hazard rate. Negative (positive) coefficients indicate that the covariate reduces (increases) the hazard rate and increases (decreases) survival time. The basic difference between models 1 and 2 is that model 1 is estimated with time-invariant covariates while model 2 is estimated with time-dependent covariates. This is a substantial difference. In model 1, the covariates are fixed at the start of the observation period and are assumed not to change over time. The assumption is that the covariates for a given firm remain constant while the firm is in the observation period regardless of whether it fails or is censored. In model 2, the covariates are allowed to change across time. In each year that the firm is in the sample, the covariate is set at its value for that particular year. The difference in covariates probably accounts for the slight differences in the models. Liquidity is significant in model 1 but not model 2. This suggests that firms with high current ratios at the start of the observation period have a longer survival time (omit dividend payments later) than other firms but the current ratio on a year by year basis has no effect on survival time. On the other hand, free cash flow is not significant in model 1 but is significant in model 2. Free cash flow at the start of the observation period has no effect on survival time, but across time, free cash flow does influence survival time on a year by year basis. Generally, with firm financial statement data, it is probably more realistic to assume that the variable's current year value influences the occurrence of the event rather than the value of the variable set at the origin.

The results in models 3 and 4 are consistent with models 1 and 2. Equations (4.18) and (4.19) show that the dependent variable is the log of time rather than the log of the hazard rate. Consequently, the signs of the coefficients change between non-parametric and parametric models because the coefficients now show the effect on survival time rather than the hazard rate. Positive (negative) coefficients indicate that the covariate increases (decreases) survival time and decreases (increases) the hazard rate. Because the models are parametric regressions, they contain the shape and scale parameters. The shape parameter of a hazard function determines the manner in which the probability that a firm omits dividend payments changes over time. The scale parameter provides an indication how this probability differs across firms at a given point in time. Because an exponential model implies a constant hazard across time, the scale parameter in model 3 is forced equal to 1. In model 4, the scale parameter, since it is greater than 1, implies that the hazard rate decreases with time. Across all four models, the duration between financial distress and the omission of a dividend appears to be heavily influenced by firm profitability and size.

4.7. Summary

This chapter provides an introduction to survival analysis and illustrates its use with an application in the area of omitted dividend payments. Survival analysis is a statistical method that in recent years has been increasingly used in the areas of financial distress and IPO offerings. The primary benefits provided by survival analysis techniques are in the areas of censoring and time-varying covariates. Censoring exists when incomplete information exists on the occurrence of an event because an observation has dropped out of a study or the study ends before the observation experiences the event of interest. Time-varying covariates are covariates that change in value over time. Survival analysis, relative to other statistical methods, employs values of covariates that change over the course of the estimation process. Given that changes in covariates influence the probability of event occurrence, time-varying covariates are an attractive feature of survival analysis models. To the extent that researchers in accounting and finance are interested in the duration of time that precedes the occurrence of an event, they are urged to utilize survival analysis in their future research.

REFERENCES

Abdel-Khalik, A. R., 'Discussion of "Financial Ratios and Corporate Endurance: A Case of the Oil and Gas Industry"', *Contemporary Accounting Research*, 9(2), 1993, 695–705.

Allison, P. D., *Event History Analysis*, Beverly Hills, CA, Sage, 1984.

Allison, P. D., *Survival Analysis Using the SAS System: A Practical Guide.* Cary, NC, SAS Institute Inc, 1995.

Altman, E., 'Financial ratios, discriminant analysis, and the prediction of corporate bankruptcy', *Journal of Finance*, 23(4), 1968, 587–690.

Audretsch, D. B. and Lehmann, E. E., 'The effects of experience, ownership, and knowledge on IPO survival: empirical evidence from Germany', *Review of Finance and Accounting*, 4(4), 2005.

Audretsch, D. B. and Mahmood, T., 'New firm survival: new results using a hazard function', *The Review of Economics and Statistics*, 77(1), 1995, 97–103.

Bandopadhyaya, A., 'An estimation of the hazard rate of firms under Chapter 11 protection', *The Review of Economics and Statistics*, 76(2), 1994, 346–50.

Beaver, W., 'Financial ratios as predictors of failure', *Journal of Accounting Research*, 4, Supplement, 1966, 71–111.

Beaver, W., 'Alternative accounting measures as predictors of failure', *The Accounting Review*, 43(1), 1968a, 113–22.

Beaver, W., 'Market prices, financial ratios, and the prediction of failure', *Journal of Accounting Research*, 7, 1968b, 179–99.

Blossfeld, H. P., Hamerle, A. and Mayer, K. U., *Event History Analysis Statistical Theory and Application in the Social Sciences.* Hillsdale, NJ, Lawrence Erlbaum Associates, 1989.

Blossfeld, H. P. and Rohwer, G., *Techniques of Event History Modeling.* Mahwah, NJ, Lawrence Erlbaum Associates, 1995.

Cameron, A. C. and Hall, A. D., 'A Survival Analysis of Australian Equity Mutual Funds', *Australian Journal of Management*, 28(2), 2003, 209–26.

Chen, K. C. W. and Lee, C. J., 'Financial ratios and corporate endurance: a case of the oil and gas industry', *Contemporary Accounting Research*, 9(2), 1993, 667–94.

Cox, D. R., 'Regression models and life-tables', *Journal of the Royal Statistical Society B*, 34(2), 1972, 187–220.

DeAngelo, H. and DeAngelo, L., 'Dividend policy and financial distress: an empirical investigation of troubled NYSE firms', *The Journal of Finance*, 45(5), 1990, 1415–31.

Elandt-Johnson, R. C. and Johnson, N. L., *Survival Models and Data Analysis*, New York, Wiley, 1980.

Foster, G., *Financial Statement Analysis*, New York, Prentice-Hall, 1986.

George, C. R., Spiceland, J. D. and George, S. L., 'A longitudinal study of the going-concern audit decision and survival time', *Advances in Quantitative Analysis of Finance and Accounting*, 4, 1996, 77–103.

Graunt, J., *Natural and Political Observations made upon the Bills of Mortality*, Cambridge University Press, 1676.

Griffen, P. A., *Usefulness to Investors and Creditors of Information Provided by Financial Reporting: A Review of Empirical Accounting Research*, Stamford, CT, Financial Accounting Standards Board, 1982.

Helwege, J., 'Determinants of savings and loan failures: estimates of a time-varying proportional hazard function', *Journal of Financial Services Research*, 10(4), 1996, 373–92.

Henebry, K. L., 'Do cash flow variables improve the predictive accuracy of a Cox proportional hazards model for bank failure?', *The Quarterly Review of Economics and Finance*, 36(3), 1996), 395–409.

Hensler, D. A., Rutherford, R. C. and Springer, T. M., 'The survival of initial public offerings in the aftermarket', *The Journal of Financial Research*, 20(1), 1997, 93–110.

Hill, N. T., Perry, S. E. and Andes, S., 'Evaluating firms in financial distress: an event history analysis', *Journal of Applied Business Research*, 12(3), 1996, 60–71.

Hosmer, D. W. J. and Lemeshow, S., *Applied Survival Analysis*, New York, Wiley, 1999.

Jaggia, S. and Thosar, S., 'Survival analysis with artificially constructed events', *Review of Finance and Accounting*, 4(4), 2005.

Jain, B. A. and Kini, O., 'The life cycle of initial public offering firms', *Journal of Business, Finance, and Accounting*, 26(9/10), 1999, 1281–307.

Jain, B. A. and Martin, J., C. L., 'The association between audit quality and post-IPO performance: a survival aalysis approach', *Review of Finance and Accounting*, 4(4), 2005, 46–71.

Kalbfleisch, J. D. and Prentice, R. L., *The Statistical Analysis of Failure Time Data*, New York, Wiley, 1980.

Kiefer, N. M., 'Economic duration data and hazard functions', *Journal of Economic Literature*, 26(2), 1988, 646–79.

Kim, Y., Anderson, D. R., Amburgey, T. L. and Hickman, J. C., 'The use of event history analysis to examine insurer insolvencies', *The Journal of Risk and Insurance*, 62(1), 1995, 94–110.

Lane, W. R., Looney, S. W. and Wansley, J. W., 'An application of the Cox proportional hazards model to bank failure', *Journal of Banking and Finance*, 10(4), 1986, 511–31.

Lawless, J. F., '*Statistical Models and Methods for Lifetime Data*', New York, Wiley, 1982.

LeClere, M. J., 'The occurrence and timing of events: survival analysis applied to the study of financial distress', *Journal of Accounting Literature*, 19, 2000, 158–89.

Lee, E. T., *Statistical Methods for Survival Data*, Belmont, CA, Wadsworth, 1980.

Lee, S. H. and Urrutia, J. L., 'Analysis and prediction of insolvency in the property-liability insurance industry: a comparison of logit and hazard models', *The Journal of Risk and Insurance*, 63(1), 1996, 121–30.

Manigart, S., Baeyens, K. and Van Hyfte, W., 'The survival of venture capital backed companies', *Venture Capital*, 4(2), 2002, 103–24.

Moeller, T. and Molina, C. A., 'Survival and default of original issue high-yield Bonds', *Financial Management*, Spring, 2003, 83–107.

Namboodiri, K. and Suchindran, C. M., *Life Tables and Their Applications*, Orlando, FL, Academic, 1987.

Ongena, S. and Smith, D. C., 'The duration of bank relationships', *Journal of Financial Economics*, 61, 2001, 449–75.

Turetsky, H. F. and McEwen, R. A., 'An empirical investigation of firm longevity: a model of the *ex ante* predictors of financial distress', *Review of Quantitative Finance and Accounting*, 16, 2001, 323–43.

Whalen, G., 'A proportional hazards model of bank failure: an examination of its usefulness as an early warning tool', *Economic Review*, 27(1), 1991, 1–31.

Wheelock, D. C. and Wilson, P. W., 'Explaining bank failures: deposit insurance, regulation, and efficiency', *The Review of Economics and Statistics*, 77(4), 1995, 689–700.

Wheelock, D. C. and Wilson, P. W., 'The Contribution to On-Site Examination Ratings to an Empirical Model of Bank Failures', *Review of Finance and Accounting*, 4(4), 2005, 107–30.

Yang, C. and Sheu, H., 'Managerial ownership structure and IPO survivability', *Journal of Management and Governance* 10, 2006, 59–75.

Zavgren, C. V., 'The prediction of corporate failure: the state of the art', *Journal of Accounting Literature*, 2, 1983, 1–38.

5 Non-parametric methods for credit risk analysis: Neural networks and recursive partitioning techniques

Maurice Peat

5.1. Introduction

In all credit analysis problems, a common factor is uncertainty about the continuity of the business being analysed. The importance of business continuity in credit analysis is reflected in the focus, by both academics and practitioners, on constructing models that seek to predict business continuity outcomes (failure or distress). There are two types of modelling exercise that can be useful to decision makers. The first are models that generate the probability of default, an important input to expected loss calculations. The second are classification models, which are used in credit-granting decisions. In this chapter we will look at two non-parametric approaches, neural networks for the generation of default probabilities and classification and recursive partitioning for classification. Each method and its implementation will be presented along with a numeric example.

There is an extensive literature that documents problems in empirical default prediction see Zmijewski (1984), Lennox (1999) or Grice and Dugan (2001). One of the earliest issues was the distributional assumptions that underlie parametric methods, particularly in relation to multiple discriminant analysis (MDA) models. There have been a number of attempts to overcome the problem, either by selecting a parametric method with fewer distributional assumptions or by moving to a non-parametric method. The logistic regression approach of Ohlson (1980) and the general hazard function formulation of Shumway (2001) are examples of the first approach. The two main types of non-parametric approach that have been used in the empirical literature are neural networks (O'Leary (1998) provides a survey of 15 studies that have used this approach) and recursive partitioning, which was introduced by Marais *et al.* (1984).

To understand the non-parametric approach we begin with a traditional regression model

$$y_i = f(\beta, x_i) + \varepsilon_i \tag{5.1}$$

where β is a vector of parameters to be estimated, x_i is a vector of features and the errors ε_i are assumed to be iid. The function $f(\bullet)$ which relates the average value of the response y to the factors is specified in advance as a linear function. The general non-parametric approach to regression is written in the same form

$$y_i = f(x_i) + \varepsilon_i \tag{5.2}$$

but the function $f(\bullet)$ is not specified. The object of non-parametric regression methods is to estimate the function $f(\bullet)$ directly from the data, rather than estimate parameter values. Because it is difficult (computationally intensive) to fit the general non-parametric model in cases where there are a large number of factors, a number of restricted models have been developed. The most common is known as the additive regression model

$$y_i = \alpha + f_i(x_{i1}) + f_2(x_{i2}) + \cdots + f_m(x_{im}) + \varepsilon_i \tag{5.3}$$

where the partial regression functions $(f_j\bullet)$ are assumed to be smooth and are estimated from the data. Allowing the additive model to include derived features $V_j = w_i'x$ leads to the projection pursuit regression model

$$y_i = \sum_{j=1}^{m} f_j\left(w_j^T x_i\right). \tag{5.4}$$

In these models the functions $f_j(\bullet)$ are estimated along with the directions w_j using an appropriate numerical approach.

Credit analysts deal with two different general functions; in expected loss problems probabilities are the primary interest. In the case of default probability estimation the function of interest is the probability density function, conditioned on the observed characteristics (features) of the firms included in the estimation. The feature vectors from class k are distributed according to a density $p_k(x)$, that is a case drawn at random from the population with feature vector x will have probability $p_k(x)$ of being a member of group k.

When the analyst is making categorizing decisions the function of interest is a classifier, which assigns members of the population to a group based on their observed features. A classifier is a relation which uses the $C(\bullet)$ features of a population member to assign them to one of the groups,

$$C : X \to G.$$

The features of the Ith population member are grouped into a feature vector, denoted x_i which is an element of the feature space X. The set $G = \{1, \ldots, K\}$ are the population groups.

The classifier is constructed to minimize a loss function, which is driven by the number of correct classifications. To estimate the accuracy of a classifier a measure of its misclassification rate is needed. One approach to measuring the misclassification rate is to classify cases from the same population as the learning sample (with known group membership) which were not used in the construction of C. The number of these cases which are misclassified provides a performance measure, which is an estimate of the true misclassification rate, for the constructed classifier. The utility of the classifier is determined by its ability to correctly classify members of the population which were not used in its construction; this is known as generalizability.

A subset of the population, for which group membership is known, is used to construct the classifier, $C(\bullet)$. The population subset used in the construction of the classifier is known as a learning sample in the neural network and recursive partitioning literatures; and in statistics it is known as the estimation sample.

The probability estimation and classification problems are related. After a probability density function is estimated the resulting probabilities can be used to partition the interval $(0, 1)$ into regions that are associated with the population groups. When a classifier has been constructed, counts of the members of the population classified into each group provide an estimate of the discrete conditional probability distribution. The nature of the decision problem and the data available will be important in determining the choice of approach.

One of the best-known classifiers in distress prediction is derived from the Altman MDA model (1968):

$$C(x_i) = \left\{ \begin{array}{l} \text{fail: if } 2X_1 + 1.4X_2 + 3.3X_3 + 0.6X_4 + 0.999X_5 < 2.65 \\ \text{continuing: if } 2X_1 + 1.4X_2 + 3.3X_3 + 0.6X_4 + 0.999X_5 \geq 2.65 \end{array} \right\}$$

where the features used are financial ratios: X_1 is Working Capital/Total Assets (WCTA), X_2 is Retained Earnings/Total Assets (RETA), X_3 is Earnings Before Interest and Taxes/Total Assets (EBITTA), X_4 is the Market

Value of Equity/Total Debt (MARDEB) and X_5 is Sales/Total Assets (SALESTA). This classifier is the result of a two-stage process, in the first stage a parametric (MDA) model is estimated, giving the linear equations in the example. In the second stage a cut-off value for the output from the MDA model, which minimizes the misclassification rate, is found: the value is 2.65 in the example.

The exploration of non-parametric methods begins with the presentation of the neural network approach.

5.2. Estimating probabilities with a neural network

Neural networks is a term that covers many models and learning (estimation) methods. These methods are generally associated with attempts to improve computerized pattern recognition by developing models based on the functioning of the human brain; and attempts to implement learning behaviour in computing systems.

A neural network is a two-stage model that is commonly represented in the form of a network diagram. Figure 5.1 represents the most common neural network, known as the single hidden layer back-propagation network. The example has three inputs, one hidden layer and two output classes.

The network in Figure 5.1 can be represented in functional form. The derived features z_j are a function of the sum of weighted combinations of the inputs x_j,

$$Z_j = f_i\left(\alpha_j^T x\right), \; j = 1 \ldots M. \tag{5.5}$$

The outputs y_k are then a function of weighted combinations of the derived features z,

$$H_k = \beta_k^T Z, \; k = 1 \ldots K$$
$$F_k(x) = g_k(H_k), \; k = 1 \ldots K. \tag{5.6}$$

Combining these elements gives the function

$$F_k(x) = g_k\left(\sum_{k=1}^{K} \beta_K f_j \sum_{j=1}^{m} \alpha_j^T x_j\right) \tag{5.7}$$

where M is the number of input factors and K is the number of output classes. To operationalize this general function the component functions

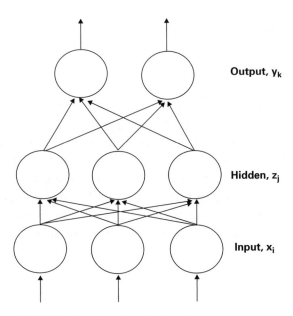

Figure 5.1   Single hidden layer neural network structure

$g_k(\bullet)$ and $g_k(\bullet)$ have to be specified. The logistic function (sigmoid)

$$f(x) = \frac{1}{1 + e^x} \tag{5.8}$$

is commonly chosen, as it is a smooth and differentiable function. The output function $g_k(\bullet)$ allows for a final transformation of the outputs. The identity function $g_k(H_k) = H_k$ is the most commonly used transformation. When a neural network is used for K group classification an output function that produces positive values that sum to one (probabilities of group membership) is useful: the softmax function

$$g_k(H_k) = \frac{e^{H_k}}{\sum\limits_{l=1}^{k} e^{H_l}} \tag{5.9}$$

is often used as the output function. When the functions $f_j(\bullet)$ and $g_k(\bullet)$ are specified in this way the neural network is a member of the class of additive non-linear regression models.

    A neural network constructed from logistic activation functions and identity or softmax output functions gives a smooth and continuous functional representation. A squared error loss function, E, based on $F_k(x)$

will therefore be smooth and continuous:

$$E = \sum_{i=1}^{N} (y_i - F_k(x_i))^2. \tag{5.10}$$

The smoothness property allows for the generic approach of steepest decent (see Judd 1998 Ch. 4.4) to be applied to the minimization of the error function. The derivatives of the error function with respect to the weights (the gradients of the problem) can be derived by application of the chain rule. The numerical values of the gradients are calculated in two stages, a forward pass through the network to calculate the error and a back pass through the network to numerically estimate the derivatives. The derivative of the error function with respect to the output layer weights is given by

$$\frac{\partial E_i}{\partial \beta_{km}} = -2(y_i - F_k(x_i))g_k'\left(\beta_k^T Z_i\right)z_{mi}. \tag{5.11}$$

The derivative of the error function with respect to the hidden weights is

$$\frac{\partial E_i}{\partial \alpha_{ml}} = -\sum_{k=1}^{K} 2(y_i - F_k(x_i))g_k'\left(\beta_k^T Z\right)\beta_{km} \, f_j'\left(\alpha_m^T x_i\right)x_{il}. \tag{5.12}$$

With these derivatives a gradient decent weight update, from iteration (r) to $(r+1)$ has the form

$$\beta_{km}^{(r+1)} = \beta_{km}^{(r)} - \lambda_\theta \sum_{i=1}^{N} \frac{\partial E_i}{\partial \beta_{km}^{(r)}}$$

$$\alpha_{km}^{(r+1)} = \alpha_{km}^{(r)} - \lambda_\theta \sum_{i=1}^{N} \frac{\partial E_i}{\partial \alpha_{ml}^{(r)}} \tag{5.13}$$

where λ_r is the learning rate parameter, its value in the range $[0,1]$. The learning rate is the step size and the derivatives are the directions in the gradient decent. The derivatives can be rewritten in error form

$$\frac{\partial E_i}{\partial \beta_{km}} = \delta_{ki} z_{mi}$$

$$\frac{\partial E_i}{\partial \alpha_{ml}} = \phi_{mi} x_{il} \tag{5.14}$$

where

$$\delta_{ki} = -2(y_i - F_k(x_i))g'_k\left(\beta_k^T Z_i\right) \tag{5.15}$$

and

$$\phi_{mi} = -\sum_{k=1}^{K} 2(y_i - F_k(x_i))g'_k(\beta_k^T Z)\beta_{km}\, f'_j(\alpha_m^T x_i) \tag{5.16}$$

are the errors, which satisfy the back-propagation equations:

$$\phi_{mi} = f'_j(\alpha_m^T x_i) \sum_{k=1}^{K} \beta_{km}\delta_{ki}. \tag{5.17}$$

The weight updates are implemented by firstly fixing the weights at their iteration (r) values and calculating the output values $F_k(x_i)$. In the back pass the errors δ_{ki} and ϕ_{mi} are calculated. These errors are then used to calculate the gradients used in the update equations. The update equations as specified are a form of batch learning, with the updates being calculated using all of the observations in the learning sample. In the batch case the learning rate λ_θ is held constant and the updating procedure proceeds until the change in the error function is less than a user-specified tolerance.

The weights can also be updated on an observation-by-observation basis (which is analogous to the recursive least squares approach to regression analysis). Using the method in this way allows the method to handle large learning samples and for the weights to be updated as new observations are made. The weight update equations become

$$
\begin{aligned}
\beta_{km}^{(r+1)} &= \beta_{km}^{(r)} - \lambda_\theta \frac{\partial E_i}{\partial \beta_{km}^{(r)}} \\
\alpha_{km}^{(r+1)} &= \alpha_{km}^{(r)} - \lambda_\theta \frac{\partial E_i}{\partial \alpha_{ml}^{(r)}}.
\end{aligned}
\tag{5.18}
$$

The observations are processed one at a time and the weights are updated at each observation, the updating procedure proceeds until the change in the error function is less than a user-specified tolerance. A training epoch refers to one run through the learning sample; the process finding the error minimizing weights usually requires many epochs. To ensure convergence in observation-by-observation updating the learning parameter λ_θ should decrease to zero as θ increases; this is accomplished by setting $\lambda_\theta = 1/\theta$, where θ is the number of the current training epoch.

The back-propagation method, like all gradient decent methods, can be slow to converge due to the local direction that is used in the weight updating step not being the globally optimal direction. In practice the weights are found by applying extensions to the steepest decent approach, such as quasi-Newton or conjugate gradient methods, which make use of curvature information to select directions which accelerate convergence to the global minimum.

Neural networks are a member of the class of non-linear additive models, with a well-defined estimation method. Their use can help to overcome the problems associated with the use of models with strong assumption about functional form and data properties. They can also produce both probabilities and categorical outputs. In this section we will look at some of the practicalities of estimating a neural network classifier and also consider how choices about the network architecture are made.

The back-propagation method of fitting a neural network requires two sets of inputs; firstly, it needs initial weight values for the weight updating procedure; it also requires a learning sample. With the logistic activation function the settings of the initial weight values will affect the characteristics of the network. Setting the weights close to zero causes the logistic function to behave like a linear function, which causes the network to closely approximate an additive linear function. As the weights are updated away from zero the degree of non-linearity increases. Individual units in the network, whose weights are moved away from zero, introduce local non-linearity into the network as needed. The common practice of selecting random weight values close to zero takes advantage of this characteristic and leads to networks which add non-linearity as needed. Starting the back-propagation algorithm with large weights starts with a highly non-linear structure, then attempts to reduce the level of non-linearity; this approach often leads to poor results.

The values of the input features will also influence the scale of the weights (α) in the input layer, and ultimately through the forward error calculation, the values of the outputs from the network. To ensure that all inputs are treated equally by the back-propagation algorithm they are standardized to have zero mean and unit standard deviation. Standardizing in this way allows the weights to be chosen at random from a uniform distribution that is close to zero. When the input factors are standardized it is common to select the initial weight values from a uniform distribution on the interval $[-0.7, 0.7]$.

In regression analysis it is possible to improve the fit, that is to increase the R^2, by adding further explanatory variables. The resulting regression equation will fit the estimation sample well, but result in poor out-of-sample fit. Such a regression equation has been over-fitted. Measures such as adjusted R^2 are commonly used to measure the goodness-of-fit for regression equations. These measures trade off error for parsimony by including a penalty based on the number of fitted parameters in the model. Stepwise regression methods make use of these measures, usually adjusted R^2, to sequentially build a regression equation. The forward approach repeatedly adds the explanatory variable that results in the largest decrease in the error, and backwards methods begin with all the variables included then repeatedly remove the variable that reduces the error measure by the greatest amount until the improvement in the error measure is possible.

These procedures aim to produce a model that contains the smallest number of variables to describe the explanatory variable. As a neural network is an additive non-linear regression we can treat the nodes as an explanatory variable and use a forward or backward approach to the determination of the best structure for the neural network. In a constructive (forward) approach nodes are added to the neural network until the error measure cannot be improved. A pruning (backward) approach either physically removes nodes from the network or uses a penalty function to force the weights of nodes which are not needed to zero, effectively removing the node from the network.

5.3. Sample collection and explanatory variables

A numerical experiment using simple feed-forward neural networks will be described. For convenience the variables used in Altman (1968), described above, will be used in all examples. The issue of appropriate variables to include in the classification relation is not addressed here. Data for listed Australian companies in 2001 and 2002 are used. Companies are categorized as continuing or having suffered a broad failure. A broad failure includes firms that liquidated (either forced liquidation or voluntary liquidation), defaulted on debt, failed to pay listing fees, raised working capital specifically to meet short-term liquidity problems or engaged in a debt and equity restructure. Data for the year 2001 will be used to construct all models whereas data from 2002 are used as an independent test sample.

To investigate the stability and generalizability of neural networks a number of networks were constructed. The Altman variables were first standardized and initial starting values for the weights were randomly selected as discussed above. The probability values estimated were used to classify the firms in both samples. With standardized inputs a cut-off value of 0.5 is used to convert probabilities to categories. Translating from probabilities to categories allows for the computation of the commonly

Table 5.1 Neural network model fits

One hidden layer Networks number of hidden units	SSE	In-sample Misclassification rate	Out-of-Sample Misclassification rate
2	66.921611	13.1215%	11.7221%
3	65.534135	13.2597%	11.2880%
4	67.043856	13.2597%	11.4327%
5	66.367042	13.1215%	11.4327%
6	65.737018	13.3978%	11.7221%
7	66.098848	13.1215%	11.5774%
8	66.256525	13.1215%	11.2880%
9	66.735611	13.2597%	11.4327%
10	67.260748	13.8122%	10.8538%
MDA (non-standardized data)		15.2893%	15.4624%

reported misclassification rate statistics and facilitates comparisons with the tree-based approach.

5.4. Empirical results for the neural network model

Table 5.1 reports the results for a sequence of single hidden-layer networks. Networks with an increasing number of hidden units were constructed, and the sum square errors, in sample misclassification rates and out-of-sample misclassification rates are reported. The network with seven hidden nodes performs best on the in-sample data set, achieving a misclassification rate of 13.12%. The seven hidden-node network achieves a misclassification rate of 11.58% on the 2002 sample, demonstrating that the network generalizes well. The flatness of the misclassification rate against the number of nodes graph shows that there is no clearly superior network; O'Leary (1998) notes that studies based on the Altman variables have typically selected 5 or 10 hidden units, opting for multiples of the number of input variables rather than an optimization over the number of units.

The out-of-sample performance of all of the networks is consistent; their performance is no worse than the performance of the network on the training sample. This suggests that neural network methods can help to overcome problems of generalizability that have been documented. The performance of all the networks estimated compares favourably with the 15.3% in-sample misclassification rate of a traditional MDA model estimated with the 2001 data.

The next section describes the tree-based approach to classification and provides a numerical exploration of the method.

5.5. Classifying with recursive partitioning

The tree-based approach to classification proceeds through the simple mechanism of using one feature to split a set of observations onto two subsets. The objective of the spilt is to create subsets that have a greater proportion of members from one of the groups than the original set. This objective is known as reducing the impurity of the set. The process of splitting continues until the subsets created only consist of members of one group or no split gives a better outcome than the last split performed. The features can be used once or multiple times in the tree construction process.

Sets which cannot be split any further are known as terminal nodes. The graphical representation of the sequence of splits forms a decision tree. In these graphs a set that is split is represented by a circle and known as an internal node. Sets that cannot be split further are denoted by a box and known as terminal nodes.

It is possible to proceed with the splitting process until each terminal node contains only one observation. Such a tree will correctly classify every member of the sample used in the construction of the tree but it is likely to perform poorly in classifying another sample from the population. This is the problem of generalization, the trade-off between the accuracy of a classifier on the data used to construct it and its ability to correctly classify observations that were not used in its construction.

The standard approach to tree construction is to grow, through the splitting process, a tree which is over-fitted. This tree is then pruned by working from the terminal nodes back up the tree, removing parts of the tree, based on changes in the overall classification accuracy of the tree. Using a combination of tree growing and pruning an optimal, in terms of misclassification rate, tree is found.

Tree construction involves three steps: splitting a set into two, deciding when a set cannot be split further and assigning the terminal sets to a class. To select the best binary split at any stage of tree construction, a measure of the impurity of a set is needed. The best possible split would result in the two subsets having all members form a single population group. The worst possible split results in two subsets each consisting of equal numbers from each of the population groups. In non-separable cases the subsets resulting from a split will contain members from each of the population groups. A general split using feature x_i, of a set τ of the form $x_i > c$ results in two subsets τ_L and τ_R (a left and right subset containing members from each group) with the following allocation of elements of the original set:

		Group 1	Group 2	
Left (τ_L)	$x_i \le c$	$n_{1,1}$	$n_{1,2}$	$n_{1,.}$
Right (τ_R)	$x_i > c$	$n_{2,1}$	$n_{2,2}$	$n_{2,.}$
		$n_{.,1}$	$n_{.,2}$	

Let $Y = 1$ if the member of the set τ is from group 2 and $Y = 0$ otherwise. From this contingency table the probability that a member of the right set comes from group 2 is $P[Y = 1|\tau_R] = n_{1,2}/n_{1,.}$ and the probability that a member of the left subset is from group 2 is $P[Y = 1|\tau_L] = n_{2,2}/n_2$. The impurity of a subset (τ) is defined as a non-negative function of the probability $P[Y = 1|\tau]$, the proportion of group 1 members in the set τ. The least impure set will contain all members from one of the groups $P[Y = 1|\tau] = 0/1$. The most impure set will have equal numbers of members from each group, $P[Y = 1|\tau] = 0.5$. An impurity function is defined as

$$i(\tau) = \phi(P[Y = 1|\tau]) \tag{5.19}$$

where $\phi \geqslant 0$ and for any $p \in (0,1)$, $\phi(p) = \phi(1 - p)$ and $\phi(0) = \phi(1) < \phi(p)$. A common measure of the impurity of the subsets formed by splitting is based on information theory. It is known as the cross entropy measure, for the left subset

$$i(\tau_L) = -\frac{n_{11}}{n_{1.}}\log\left(\frac{n_{11}}{n_{1.}}\right) - \frac{n_{12}}{n_{1.}}\log\left(\frac{n_{12}}{n_{1.}}\right). \tag{5.20}$$

For the right subset it is

$$i(\tau_R) = -\frac{n_{21}}{n_{2.}}\log\left(\frac{n_{21}}{n_{2.}}\right) - \frac{n_{22}}{n_{2.}}\log\left(\frac{n_{22}}{n_{2.}}\right). \tag{5.21}$$

The measure of the overall effectiveness of a split is

$$\Delta I(s, \tau) = i(\tau) - P(\tau_L)i(\tau_L) - P(\tau_R)i(\tau_R) \tag{5.22}$$

where τ is the set being split with simple split s. The $P(\tau_L)$ and $P(\tau_R)$ are the probabilities that an element of falls into τ_L or τ_R respectively. From the table above $P(\tau_L) = n_{1,.}/(n_{1,.} + n_{2,.})$ and $P(\tau_R) = n_{2,.}/(n_{1,.} + n_{2,.})$. The improvement measure is calculated for all possible splits of each factor. The split that leads to the greatest value of $\Delta I(s, \tau)$ is chosen. The best split for each of the subsets created is then chosen by the same method. This process is continued until there is no split with $\Delta I(s, \tau) > 0$, all the members of the subset created are from the same group or some minimum number of set members has been reached. Any node that cannot be split is known as a terminal node. A property of the splitting procedure is that the number of possible splits decreases as the depth of the tree increases. Eventually there are no splits that reduce impurity further and the tree-growing procedure stops. When the splitting process terminates there is no further split which reduces the impurity of the terminal nodes, or every member of the training set has been correctly classified. The process results in a tree that is larger than is warranted and leads to a downward bias is the estimated misclassification rate for the tree.

The standard approach to this over-fitting problem is to implement a pruning procedure on the large tree that is generated in the splitting step (see Breiman *et al.*, Ch. 3). Taking the large tree and removing a node and all its descendant nodes (pruning) upwards from the terminal nodes produces a sequence of sub-trees that ends up with a one-node tree. Each of the sub-trees is assigned a cost measure, which is minimized to find the best sub-tree. The most common cost measure is known as cost complexity

$$R_\alpha(T) = R(T) + \alpha|\bar{T}| \tag{5.23}$$

where α is the complexity parameter which penalizes trees with a large number of terminal nodes, $|\bar{T}|$. $R(T)$ is the cost of the tree; in classification problems this is taken to be the misclassification cost of the tree.

The pruning process works by finding the weakest link in the current tree and removing all nodes below the identified node in the tree. For each possible sub-tree determine the value of α which equates the cost complexity measure of the tree which includes the nodes being evaluated and the tree that has the nodes removed. This value is given by

$$\alpha = \frac{R(T) - R(t)}{|\bar{t}| - 1} \tag{5.24}$$

where $R(T)$ is the cost complexity measure of the full tree, $R(T)$ is the cost complexity measure of the tree with the nodes removed and $|\bar{t}|$ is the number of nodes that have been removed. The sub-tree that corresponds to the lowest value of α will be removed from the tree, the node at the top of the sub-tree that is removed is known as the weakest link. After the sub-tree has been removed from the tree the overall misclassification cost of the pruned tree is calculated.

The process is repeated with the pruned tree being used as the new starting tree. The procedure leads to a sequence of nested sub-trees of decreasing size, corresponding to a sequence of increasing α_n:

$$t_{\alpha_0} \subset t_{\alpha_1} \subset t_{\alpha_2} \subset \cdots \subset t_{\alpha_m} \tag{5.25}$$

each with a corresponding misclassification cost. The sub-tree with the smallest misclassification cost is chosen from this sequence as the optimal tree. When a test sample is available the sub-trees are applied to the test sample to determine the misclassification cost. In the absence of a test sample a cross-validation process is employed to calculate the cost of each of the sub-trees.

5.6. Empirical results for the recursive partitioning model

The results from a numerical experiment with the recursive partitioning algorithm described above are presented in Table 5.2. Note that the untransformed data were used for these exercises. The number of terminal nodes, in sample misclassification rate and out-of-sample misclassification rate is reported for each tree constructed.

The results for the full tree grown from the data highlight the problem of over-fitting in tree-based classifiers. The final tree has 45 terminal nodes and an impressive in-sample misclassification rate of 6.06%. However, the out-of-sample misclassification rate is substantially higher at 14.5%. A sequence of pruned trees was then constructed using $\alpha = 0.5, 1.0, 1.5, 2.0$. The number of terminal nodes in the constructed sub-trees is seen to decrease as the value of α increases. As the number of nodes in the pruned trees decreases, the in-sample misclassification rate increases. However, the out-of-sample misclassification rate is steadily declining as the size of the tree decreases. These example trees clearly demonstrate the trade-off between generalizability and in-sample performance when constructing tree-based classifiers. With $\alpha = 2.0$ a manageable tree, with eight terminal nodes, is generated with in-sample and out-of-sample misclassification rates that are comparable and both models lower the misclassification rate from the MDA model. These results also demonstrate the importance of an independent test sample in the construction

Table 5.2 Classification tree results

Tree	Number of Terminal nodes	In-sample Misclassification rate	Out-of-sample Misclassification rate
Full	45	6.0610%	14.4509%
$\alpha = 0.5$	28	6.4740%	13.7283%
$\alpha = 1.0$	24	7.0250%	13.0058%
$\alpha = 1.5$	15	8.6780%	12.2832%
$\alpha = 2.0$	8	10.6100%	11.8497%

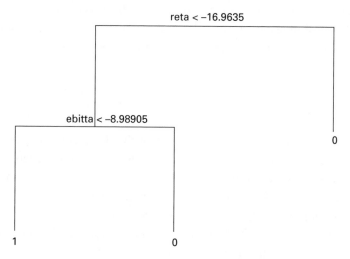

Figure 5.2   Classification tree with two splits and three terminal nodes

of a tree-based classifier. Based on the training sample it is probable that an over-fitted tree, that does not generalize well, will be selected.

As trees are generated by a sequence of binary splits on features they can be restated as a set of rules. Trees recast in this form provide important information for credit analysts and regulators who need to select companies for review and explain their decisions. The sequence of questions that define the splits in the tree can be converted to a set of if–then–else rules. The simple tree in Figure 5.2, generated with $\alpha = 14$, is shown rewritten as rules in Table 5.3. Rule one describes the split at the root node of the tree, rules two and three describe the split at the first node of the tree. Equipped with this set of rules an analyst can quickly categorize a firm, and provide an

Table 5.3 Classification tree in rules form

Rule1	IF	RETA $\geqslant$ -16.9635
	THEN	code $= 0$
Rule2	IF	EBITTA < -8.98905
	AND	RETA < -16.9635
	THEN	code $= 1$
Rule3	IF	EBITTA $\geqslant -8.98905$
	AND	RETA < -16.9635
	THEN	code $= 0$

explanation of the basis for the decision. The in-sample misclassification rate of this simple tree is 14.46%, indicating that use of this simple rule would be more accurate than the benchmark MDA model.

5.7. Conclusion

In this chapter, two non-parametric approaches for credit analysis have been described and applied. The distinguishing feature of these methods is that there is no (or very little) a priori knowledge about the form of the true function which is being estimated. The target function is modelled using an equation containing many free parameters, but in a manner which allows the class of functions which the model can represent to be very broad.

Neural networks are one of the non-parametric models that have been analysed. Because their weights (and other parameters) have no particular meaning in relation to the problems to which they are applied, they can be regarded as pure 'black box' estimators. Estimating and interpreting the values of the weights of a neural network is not the primary goal of this model system. The primary goal is to estimate the underlying probability function or to generate a classification based on the probabilistic output of the network. Classification trees are the second non-parametric model that was presented. The decision tree that is generated by the tree-growing and pruning algorithm provides an estimated two group classifier. This method provides both classification of cases and a set of derived rules that describe the classifier. The numerical exploration of both of these methods has demonstrated their potential in a credit analysis context, with the best model from each class outperforming a standard MDA model. Both of these techniques are valuable additions to the tool set of credit analysts, especially in business continuity analysis, where a priori theory does not necessarily provide a clear guide on functional form or the role and influence of explanatory variables.

REFERENCES

Altman, E. I., 'Financial ratios, discriminant analysis and the prediction of corporate bankruptcy', *Journal of Finance*, 23(4), 1968, 589–609.

Breiman, L., Friedman, J., Olshen, R. and Stone, C., *Classification and Regression Trees*, London, Chapman and Hall, 1984.

Grice, J. S. and Dugan, M. T., 'The limitations of bankruptcy prediction models: some cautions for the researcher', *Review of Quantitative Finance and Accounting*, 17, 2001, 151–66.

Judd, K. J., *Numerical Methods in Economics*, MIT Press, 1998.

Lennox, C., 'Identifying failing companies: a revaluation of the logit, probit and DA approaches', *Journal of Economics and Business*, 51, 1999, 347–64.

Marais, L., Patell, J. and Wolfson, M., 'The experimental design of classification models: an application of recursive partitioning and bootstrapping to commercial bank loan classifications', *Journal of Accounting Research*, 22, Supplement, 1984, 87–118.

Ohlson, J. A., 'Financial ratios and the probabilistic prediction of bankruptcy', *Journal of Accounting Research*, 18(1), 1980, 109–31.

O'Leary, D. E., 'Using neural networks to predict corporate failure', *International Journal of Intelligent Systems in Accounting, Finance & Management*, 7, 1998, 187–97.

Shumway, T., 'Forecasting bankruptcy more accurately: a simple hazard model', *Journal of Business*, 74(1), 2001, 101–24.

Zmijewski, M. E., 'Methodological issues related to the estimation of financial distress prediction models', *Journal of Accounting Research*, 22, Supplement, 1984, 59–82.

6 Bankruptcy prediction and structural credit risk models

Andreas Charitou, Neophytos Lambertides and Lenos Trigeorgis[*]

6.1. Introduction

Default is triggered by a firm's failure to meet its financial obligations. Default probabilities and changes in expected default frequencies affect markets participants, such as investors and lenders, since they assume responsibility for the credit risk of their investments. The lack of a solid economic understanding of the factors that determine bankruptcy makes explanation and prediction of default difficult to assess. However, the accuracy of these predictors is essential for sound risk management and for evaluation of the vulnerability of corporations and institutional lenders. In recognition of this, the new capital adequacy framework (Basel II) envisages a more active role for banks in measuring the default risk of their loan books. The need for reliable measures of default or credit risk is clear to all.

The accounting and finance literature has produced a variety of models attempting to predict or measure default risk. There are two primary types of models that describe default processes in the credit risk literature: structural models and reduced-form models. Structural models use the evolution of a firm's structural variables, such as asset and debt values, to determine the timing of default. Merton's model (1974) is considered the first structural model. In Merton's model, a firm defaults if, at the time of servicing the debt at debt maturity, its assets are below its outstanding debt. A second approach within the structural framework was introduced by Black and Cox (1976). In this approach default occurs when a firm's asset

[*] A. Charitou is Professor at the University of Cyprus. N. Lambertides is Lecturer at Aston University, UK. L. Trigeorgis is Professor at the University of Cyprus and visiting Professor at MIT. We would like to thank I. Karamanou, C. Louca, S. Martzoukos, G. Nisiotis for useful comments. Address for correspondence: Department of Business Administration, University of Cyprus, P.O.Box 20537, Nicosia, CY 1678, Cyprus. E-mail: charitou@ucy.ac.cy, lambertn@aston.ac.uk, lenos@ucy.ac.cy.

value falls below a certain threshold. In contrast to the Merton approach, default can occur at any time.

Reduced-form models do not consider the relation between default and firm value explicitly. In contrast to structural models, the timing of default is not determined based on the value of the firm but as the first jump in an exogenously given jump process. The parameters governing the default hazard rate are inferred from market data.[1] Prior to 1977, various bankruptcy prediction studies were conducted for non-financial firms based primarily on linear discriminant analysis. This research was originated with Beaver's (1966) univariate analysis model and culminated with the Zeta model of Altman *et al.* (1977). During this period, researchers attempted to improve the accuracy of multi-ratio predictive models by optimizing a set of predictor variables. After the mid-1970s, researchers focused primarily on the problems associated with the then prevailing methodological approaches (e.g., see Eisenbeis 1977). Related studies from this period include Altman (1968), Beaver (1968), Edmister (1972), Wilcox (1973), Menash (1984) and Zmijewski (1984). Despite the criticisms expressed in these later studies, the main conclusion of this body of research was that financial ratios provided a significant indication of the likelihood of financial distress. However, later efforts to overcome the methodological difficulties associated with MDA resulted in greater use of the logit model which relied on less restrictive assumptions than MDA (e.g., see Ohlson 1980 and Zavgren 1983).

Structural default models relate the credit quality of a firm and the firm's economic and financial conditions. Thus, in contrast to reduced-form models where default is determined exogenously, in structural models default is endogenously generated within the model. Also, the treatment of recovery rates for reduced-form models is exogenously specified, whereas in structural models recovery rates are determined by the value of the firm's assets and liabilities at default.

The literature on structural credit risk models was initiated by Merton (1974), who applies option pricing theory to the modelling of a firm's debt (see Table 6.1). In Merton's model, the firm's capital structure is assumed to be composed of equity and a zero-coupon bond with maturity T and face value D. The basic idea is that the firm's equity is seen as a European call option with maturity T and strike price D on asset value V. The firm's debt value is the asset value minus the equity value seen as a call option. This

---

[1] For a review of reduced form models see Elizalde (2005a).

method presumes a very simplistic capital structure and implies that default can only occur at the maturity of the zero-coupon bond.

Black and Cox (1976) introduced the first paper of the so-called 'first passage' models. First-passage models specify default as the first time the firm's asset value hits a specified lower barrier, allowing default to take place at any time up to debt maturity. The default barrier V, exogenously given as in Black and Cox (1976) and Longstaff and Schwartz (1995), acts as a safety covenant that protects bondholders. Alternatively, it can be determined endogenously as a result of the stockholders' attempt to choose the default threshold which maximizes the value of the firm, as in Leland (1994) and Leland and Toft (1996).

Prior structural models considered both deterministic interest rates (Black and Cox 1976, Geske 1979, Leland 1994, Leland and Toft 1996) as well as stochastic interest rates (Ronn and Verma 1986, Kim, Ramaswamy and Sundaresan 1993, Nielsen *et al.* 1993, Longstaff and Schwartz 1995, Briys and de Varenne 1997, Hsu *et al.* 2004).

In first-passage models, default occurs the first time the asset value goes below a certain lower threshold and the firm is liquidated immediately after the default event. In more recent models, a default event does not immediately cause liquidation, but it represents the beginning of a liquidation process which might or might not lead to liquidation once it is completed. This is consistent with Chapter 11 of the US Bankruptcy Law where the firm remains in control of the business throughout the reorganization process. As a consequence, equity has some value even when the firm is insolvent. However, the company's management is subject to detailed supervision by the courts, which may potentially limit its discretion to raise financing, sell assets, or even set the level of salaries of managers. We refer to these models as 'liquidation process models'.

Nowadays, various researchers attempt to incorporate more real-life features into structural models, namely, 'State-dependent models' together with 'liquidation process models'. Although these models make good theoretical sense, they have not been subjected to extensive empirical testing. State-dependent models assume that some of the parameters governing the firm's ability to generate cash flows or its funding costs are state dependent, where states can represent the business cycle (recession versus expansion) or the firm's external debt rating.

This study proceeds as follows: section 2 discusses the standard Merton option model and the related prediction models. Section 3 summarizes and critically evaluates the main structural credit risk models available in the literature. Section 4 provides empirical illustration and finally section 5 provides summary and conclusions.

6.2. The standard Merton option model and related bankruptcy prediction models

The basic reasoning behind the standard option model (e.g., Merton, 1974, 1977) is that the equity of a levered firm can be viewed as a European call option to acquire the value of the firm's assets (V) by paying off (i.e., having as exercise price) the face value of the debt (B) at the debt's maturity (T). From this perspective, a firm will be insolvent if the market value of the firm's assets falls below what the firm owes to its creditors at debt maturity (i.e., when $V_T < B$). In that event, equityholders will default on the debt (file for bankruptcy) and simply hand over the firm's assets to its creditors and walk away free, protected by their limited liability rights. The probability of default at debt maturity in this case, $\text{Prob}(V_T < B) = N(-d2)$, is driven by the five primary option pricing variables: (i) the natural logarithm of the book value of total liabilities ($\ln B$) due at maturity representing the option's exercise price, (ii) the natural logarithm of the current market value of the firm's assets ($\ln V$), (iii) the standard deviation of percentage firm value changes (σ), (iv) the time to the debt's maturity (T) representing the option's expiration, and (v) the difference between the expected asset return (μ) and the firm's payout yield (interest and dividend payments as proportion of asset value, D).

The standard Merton option model is fairly parsimonious in that it uses only the aforementioned five primary option variables. A version of the Merton model has been adapted by Vasicek (1984) and has been applied by KMV Corporation, Hillegeist *et al.* (2004) and Bharath and Shumway (2005). Other option-related studies include Vasicek (1984), Cheung (1991), Kealhofer *et al.* (1998), and Core and Schrand (1999). The standard Merton model, however, focuses on default at maturity only and does not allow for real-world considerations, such as cash constraints or liquidity problems that may cause involuntary, early bankruptcy (even when the firm is still a viable concern). This problem is exacerbated by the assumption of a single, zero-coupon debt issue.[2]

---

[2] Kealhofer and Kurbat (2001) argue that the KMV–Merton models capture all the information in traditional agency ratings and information included in traditional accounting variables.

The possibility of early default, and differences between insolvency and illiquidity, have been analysed previously in various types of capital structure models: static ones (e.g., Leland and Toft 1996), dynamic ones (e.g., Goldstein *et al.* 2001) and strategic ones, in which shareholders can renegotiate the debt without formally defaulting (e.g., Mella-Barral and Perraudin 1997). These 'structural' models of optimal capital structure have implications for critical default boundaries (below which shareholders should default whenever debt service payments are due) and for expected default probabilities. Leland (2004) compares the different implications for critical default boundaries and the relative performance of two structural models: the exogenous default boundary approach, represented by the standard Merton model, and the endogenous model where equityholders must decide whether it is worth meeting promised debt payments to continue or defaulting, as in Leland and Toft (1996).

A number of other studies have addressed empirically the relevance of market versus accounting-based variables in explaining bankruptcy. Shumway (2001) uses a hazard model approach (reduced-form model) based on accounting variables identified previously by Altman (1968) and Zmijewski (1984) and finds that half of these variables are statistically unrelated to default probability. Shumway (2001) develops a simple hazard model that uses all available information to determine each firm's bankruptcy risk at each point in time (see Kiefer 1988, Lancaster 1990). He suggests that while static models produce biased and inconsistent bankruptcy probability estimates, the hazard model is consistent in general and unbiased in some cases. Estimating hazard models using accounting variables previously employed by Altman (1968), Zmijewski (1984) and Shumway (2001) finds that half of these variables are statistically unrelated to bankruptcy probability. Shumway's (2001) model, using three market-driven variables to identify failing firms, outperforms alternative models in out-of-sample forecasts. Shumway (2001), as well as Chava and Jarrow (2001) and Hillegeist *et al.* (2004), conclude that adding market variables to the previously identified accounting variables helps improve forecasting accuracy.

Hillegeist *et al.* (2004) extend Shumway by using Merton's option model in a discrete hazard framework to examine the predictive ability of the Altman and Ohlson accounting-based variables. They find that traditional accounting-based measures of bankruptcy risk do not add incremental information beyond the standard option variables. They do not examine the probability of default at an intermediate stage. Their results may be more a consequence of the poor performance of the accounting-based variables, rather than of the superiority of their (hazard) model.

Charitou and Trigeorgis (2006) take a different approach, showing that adding cash flow coverage (CFC) proxying for the probability of inter-mediate default (due to liquidity problems) to the basic option-based financial variables that drive the probability of terminal (as well as voluntary intermediate) default, brings about incremental explanatory power. Their approach is analogous to the endogenous structural model approach, in that they also account for the equityholders' intermediate option to default voluntarily. They also account for the possibility of early involuntary default through the inclusion of the option-motivated cash flow coverage variable based on their compound-option extension. Liquidity is not discussed explicitly in the above papers; for example, no liquidity variable is used to calibrate the models in Leland (2004) or in the KMV model that practi-tioners reference routinely.

Vassalou and Xing (2004) also rely on the Merton option pricing model. They examine the effect of default risk on equity returns. They estimate default likelihood indicators for individual firms using equity data and report that size and book-to-market are default effects. Instead of using the face value of debt at maturity similar to the default point of Merton (1973, 1974) they adopt the arbitrary default boundary used by KMV without actually counting for the probability of intermediate default. However, concerning the estimation of the expected asset return in the probability of default, their method often provides negative expected growth rates which seem inconsistent with the asset pricing theory.

Moreover, Bharath and Shumway (2005) examine the accuracy and contribution of KMV–Merton model in bankruptcy prediction. They sug-gest that the KMV–Merton model is widely applied by researchers and practitioners without knowing very much about its statistical properties. They examine the accuracy and contribution of the default forecasting KMV–Merton model and how realistic its assumptions are. Comparing the KMV–Merton model to a similar but much simpler alternative, they find that it performs slightly worse as a predictor in hazard models and in out-of-sample forecasts. They report that the KMV–Merton model does not pro-duce a sufficient statistic for the probability of default, suggesting that it can be improved and it is possible to have a model with better predictive properties. Their approach seems possible to generate sufficient statistics similar to KMV–Merton model without solving the simultaneous nonlinear equations. Their interesting methodology may change the whole concept of the BSM model and it should motivate further research on this issue.

Similarly, Du and Suo (2004) examine the empirical performance of credit rating predictions based on Merton's (1974) structural credit risk model and find that Merton's default measure is not a sufficient statistic of equity market information concerning the credit quality of the debt issuing firm. They also conclude that structural models hardly provide any significant additional capability when they are used for forecasting credit ratings. Duffie and Wang (2004) show that KMV–Merton probabilities have significant predictive power in a model of default probabilities over time, which can generate a term structure of default probabilities. Additionally, Campbell *et al.* (2004) estimate hazard models that incorporate both KMV probabilities and other variables for bankruptcy, finding that the KMV probability seems to have relatively little forecasting power after conditioning on other variables.

6.3. Main structural credit risk models

In this section we discuss and critically evaluate the main structural credit risk models, namely: (a) the Merton (1974) standard option-pricing model, (b) models with stochastic interest rate, (c) exogenous default barrier models, (d) models with mean-reverting leverage ratio and (e) endogenous default barrier models.

The standard option-pricing model of business default

The core concept of the structural models, which originated from the seminal work of Merton (1974), is to treat a firm's equity and debt as contingent claims written on the firm's asset value. Default is triggered when the underlying asset process reaches the default threshold or when the asset level is below the face value of the debt at maturity date. The total market value of the firm's assets at time t, V_t, is assumed to follow a standard diffusion process of the following form:

$$\mathrm{d}V_t/V_t = (\mu - D)\mathrm{d}t + \sigma\mathrm{d}z \tag{6.1}$$

where μ denotes the expected total rate of return on the firm's asset value (subsequently 'expected asset return' μ) reflecting the business prospects (equal to the risk-free rate, r, plus an asset risk premium), D is the total payout rate by the firm to all its claimants (including dividends to equity-holders and interest payments to debtholders) expressed as a percentage of V, σ is the business volatility or standard deviation of a firm's asset returns (percentage asset value changes), and dz is an increment of a standard Wiener process. Equity is seen as a European call option on the firm's asset value. It is assumed that the issuing firm has only one outstanding zero-coupon bond and hence that firm does not default prior to debt maturity. The model assumes that the risk-free interest rate, r, a firm's asset volatility, σ_v and asset risk premium, π_v, are constant.

Merton (1974, 1977) has shown that any claim whose value is contingent on a traded asset (portfolio) with value V, having a payout D and time to maturity $\tau\,(\equiv T-t)$ must satisfy a certain fundamental partial differential equation. Each individual contingent claim (corporate liability) is uniquely represented by specifying its particular terminal and boundary conditions, along with the payout it receives. Consider the case of the simple firm assumed in Merton's model, with only stockholders' equity of market value E and a single issue of coupon-paying debt (of market value MD). The promised face value of the bond, B, is due at maturity T, $\tau\,(\equiv T-t)$ years from now. On the debt's maturity $(t=T)$, $\tau=0$, equity will be worth either $(V-B)$ or zero, whichever is best for the equityholders, i.e. $E(V, 0)=$ Max$(V-B, 0)$.[3] The equity of such a levered firm is analogous to a European call option on the value of the firm's assets, V, with exercise price equal to the bond's promised payment, B, and time to expiration equal to the debt's maturity (T).

The market value of stockholders' equity (to voluntarily default at maturity) is given by the Black–Scholes solution for a European call option (on firm value V, after a transformation of variables) adjusted for a constant dividend-like payout D (see Merton 1973 and Black and Scholes 1973):

$$E(V, \tau) \;=\; Ve^{-D\tau}N(d_1) \;-\; Be^{-r\tau}N(d_2) \tag{6.2}$$

where

$$d_2 \;=\; \{\ln(V/B) + [(r-D) - 1/2\sigma^2]\,\tau\}\,/\,\sigma\sqrt{\tau}; \; d_1 = d_2 + \sigma\sqrt{\tau}$$

---

[3] On the debt's maturity (T), if the value of the firm exceeds the face value of the debt, $V_T > B$, the bondholders will receive the full promised payment, B, and the equityholders will receive any residual claims, $V-B$. If $V_T < B$, the stockholders will find it preferable to exercise their limited liability rights, i.e., default on the promised payment and instead surrender the firm's assets V to its bondholders and receive nothing.

$N(d) = $ (univariate) cumulative standard normal distribution function (from $-\infty$ to d)

$B = $ face value (principal) of the debt

$V = $ value of a firm's assets

$\sigma = $ standard deviation of firm value changes (returns in V)

$\tau (\equiv T - t) = $ time to debt's maturity

$r = $ risk-free interest rate

The first term in (6.2) is the discounted expected value of the firm if it is solvent (assuming a constant dividend payout D). $N(d_2)$ in the second term of (6.2) is the (risk-neutral) probability the firm will be solvent at maturity, i.e., $\text{Prob}(V_T > B)$, in which case it will pay off the debt principal B (with a present value cost of $B\,e^{-r\tau}$). Analogously, $1 - N(d_2)$ or $N(-d_2)$ in (6.2) represents the (risk-neutral) probability of voluntary default at the debt's maturity.

It is worth noting that while the value of the option depends on the risk-neutral probability of default (where d_2 depends on the value of the risk-free rate, r), the actual probability of default at the debt's maturity depends on the future value of the firm's assets and hence on the expected asset return, μ. This is obtained simply by substituting the expected return on assets, μ, for the risk-free rate, r, in the above equation for d_2, i.e.

Prob. voluntary default (on principal B at maturity T)

$$= \text{Prob}(V_T < B) = 1 - N(d_2) = N(-d_2) \tag{6.3}$$

where $-d_2(\mu) = -\{\ln(V/B) + [(\mu - D) - 1/2\sigma^2]\tau\}/\sigma\sqrt{\tau}$.

The above standard option model has some interesting implications for the determinants of corporate distress. The probability of (voluntary) business default at the debt's maturity depends on the five primary option variables influencing $-d_2(\mu)$ in (10.3). Namely, the actual probability of default, Prob $(V_T < B)$, measured by $N(-d_2)$ or simply by $-d_2(\mu)$, is higher when:

(1) the current firm value V ($\ln V$) is low;
(2) the face value of the debt B due at maturity ($\ln B$) is high – alternatively, when $\ln(V/B)$ is low (or the firm's leverage B/V is high);
(3) the volatility of the firm's asset return σ is high;
(4) the (average) maturity of the debt τ is higher initially, and then declines;[4]

---

[4] In general the (European) option is not monotonic in time to maturity. $\partial C/\partial T$ depends on $(r - \delta - 0.5\sigma^2)$, so its sign depends on the relative magnitude of $r - \delta$ vs. $0.5\sigma^2$, as well as on T. This may be shifting over time. For practical purposes a change in sign might occur after several years. Furthermore, in practice firms facing financial difficulties

(5) the difference between the expected asset return, μ, and the firm's payout D (i.e., $\mu - D$) is lower.

The two unobserved variables, firm value (V) and firm volatility (σ), can be estimated from market data based on the following two relations:

$$E = Ve^{-D\tau}N(d_1) - Be^{-r\tau}N(d_2)$$
$$\sigma_E = [N(d_1)e^{-Dr}(V/E)]\sigma \tag{6.4}$$

with d_1, d_2 as defined above. The first equation is the Black–Scholes option pricing formula for equity E adjusted for a dividend payout on firm value D, see equation (6.2). The second is the relation between equity return volatility (σ_E) and firm (asset) return volatility (σ) connected via the equity/option elasticity. Using the identity that the total value of the firm equals the market value of equity plus the market value of debt ($V = E + MD$), the above can be rearranged into the following set of simultaneous equations for the market value of debt (MD) and firm volatility:

$$MD = \frac{E(1 - e^{-D\tau}N(d_1))}{e^{-D\tau}N(d_1)} + \frac{Be^{-r\tau}N(d_2)}{e^{-D\tau}N(d_1)}$$
$$\sigma = \frac{\sigma_E}{N(d_1)e^{-D\tau}}\left(\frac{E}{E+MD}\right). \tag{6.5}$$

The KMV model assumes equity is like a (perpetual) option on the firm's asset value which can trigger default when it goes below a given default point. Unlike the original Merton model which focuses exclusively on default on the principal payment (total liabilities) at maturity, both KMV and Charitou and Trigeorgis (2006) recognize that involuntary default may be triggered by nonpayment of any other scheduled payment, either interest expense or principal repayment. To account for the probability of intermediate involuntary default, KMV adjust downwards the default boundary at maturity, based on their proprietary database and experience, to (current liabilities $+ 0.5 \times$ long-term liabilities). Charitou and Trigeorgis (2006) instead preserve the original (theoretically motivated) default boundary as being (a duration-weighted average of) total liabilities and explicitly capture the possibility of earlier involuntary default separately, via the cash flow coverage (CFC) variable. KMV focus primarily on a distance to default measure, which they define as $(V - \text{default point})/V\sigma$, and focus on

---

are likely to have more difficulty in maintaining long-term debt, and so, by necessity, the sample of bankrupt firms may be associated with a lower duration of debt than healthy firms.

estimating a default probability over the next (one up to five) year(s). They use a proprietary historical default database to derive an empirical distribution relating a given distance to default (e.g., for a firm being d standard deviations away from default) to a default probability. They do so as an indirect way to capture a presumed adjustment in firms' liabilities as they approach default.[5]

Bharath and Shumway (2005) develop a new, simpler predictor without solving the nonlinear equations. The market value of the firm (V) constitutes the summation of the value of firm equity (E) and firm's face value of its debt (B), $V = E + B$, as observed by the market, assuming that the market is efficient and well informed. They suggest that since firms are close to default they have very risky debt, and the risk of their debt is correlated with their equity risk. Thus, they approximate the volatility of each firm's debt as

$$\sigma_B = 0.05 + 0.25\sigma_E,$$

and the total volatility of the firm as

$$\sigma_V = \frac{E}{E+B}\sigma_E + \frac{B}{E+B}\sigma_B \equiv \sigma_{BS}.$$

They also set the expected return on the firm's assets equal to the firm's stock return over the previous year, $\mu = r_{t-1}$ (in order to capture some of the same information that is captured by the KMV–Merton iterative procedure) and calculate their distance to default equal to

$$DD_{BS} = \frac{\ln(V/B) + (\mu - 0.5\sigma_{BS}^2)T}{\sigma_{BS}\sqrt{T}}$$

and the probability of default to $N(-DD_{BS}) = N\{-\frac{\ln(V/B)+(\mu-0.5\sigma_{BS}^2)T}{\sigma_{BS}\sqrt{T}}\}$.

Their alternative model is easy to compute – it does not require solving the equations simultaneously. It retains the structure of the KMV–Merton distance to default and expected default frequency. It also captures approximately the same quantity of information as the KMV–Merton probability.

---

[5] The KMV approach estimates the asset value and asset volatility of the borrowing firm based on the option pricing model, data including equity prices and contractual liabilities, and information about the borrower's size, industry, profitability and geographical location. KMV also sets a default-trigger value of assets, which increases in the borrower's book liabilities. In the determination of the default barrier, short-term liabilities are weighted roughly twice as much as long-term liabilities. It is assumed that default occurs as soon as the lender incurs economic loss. KMV's model uses estimates of the borrower's asset value, asset volatility, and default boundary to derive a firm-specific probability of default. The model is calibrated using historical default rates and credit spreads. If KMV's proprietary data sources have value added and/or the future resembles the past, it might produce better out-of-sample forecasts of default rates. Crosbie and Bohn (2002), Crouhy *et al.* (2001) and Leland (2004) provide a more detailed description of the KMV approach.

Modelling stochastic interest rates

Merton's (1974) model can be extended to the case where the risk-free interest rate is stochastic. For example, consider the case the interest rate follows the Vasicek (1977) process,

$$dr = k_r(\bar{r} - r)dt + \sigma_r dW_t^r \tag{6.6}$$

where k_r is the rate of mean reversion, $\bar{r}$ is the long-term mean, and σ_r is the short-rate volatility, W_t^r is a standard Brownian motion, and the instantaneous correlation between dW_t^u and dW_t^r is $\rho_{ur}dt$. All parameters are assumed to be constant. After some adjustments, Merton's model can be explicitly solved for a European call option with stochastic interest rate that can be easily adopted in default risk forecasting models.

Exogenous default barrier models

In exogenous default models the threshold level of asset value, V^*, is unspecified, typically set in accordance with aggregate historical data. When the fraction of assets lost in default is γ and the face value of debt B, then V^* is set so that $(1-\gamma)V^*/B$ equals the estimate of debt recovery rate after default. Models in this category typically assume that debt has infinite maturity. This assumption enables analytic tractability but makes it impossible to capture the empirical regularity that borrowers are less likely to default over a given horizon if they have to repay the debt principal further in the future.

Black and Cox (1976) treat firm's equity similar to a down-and-out call option on firm asset value. In this model, the firm defaults when its asset value hits a pre-specified default barrier, V^*, which can be a constant or a time-varying variable. The default barrier is assumed to be exogenously determined. When the risk-free interest rate, asset payout ratio, asset volatility and risk premium are all assumed to be constant, the cumulative default probability over a time interval $[t, t+r]$ can be determined as

$$
\begin{aligned}
DP_{BC}(t, t+r) = N\left(-\frac{\ln\left(\frac{V_t}{V^*}\right) + (\mu_v - \delta - \sigma_v^2/2)\tau}{\sigma_v\sqrt{\tau}}\right) \\
+ \exp\left(-\frac{2\ln\left(\frac{V_t}{V^*}\right)(\mu_v - \delta - \sigma_v^2/2)}{\sigma_v^2}\right) N\left(-\frac{\ln\left(\frac{V_t}{V^*}\right) - (\mu_v - \delta - \sigma_v^2/2)\tau}{\sigma_v\sqrt{\tau}}\right)
\end{aligned}
\tag{6.7}
$$

Longstaf and Schwartz (1995), subsequently LS, extend the Black–Cox
model to the case when the risk-free interest rate is stochastic following the
Vasicek (1977) process. In this model, the default boundary, V^*, is again
pre-determined. When default occurs bondholders receive a fraction $(1 - \omega)$
of the face value of the debt, B, at maturity. In the original LS model
the payout ratio of the asset value process is assumed zero, the asset risk
premium is assumed to be constant, and the interest rate risk premium is
of an affine form in r_t. In the LS model, the default boundary is presumed
to be a monotonic function of the amount of outstanding debt. Since
asset value follows geometric Brownian motion increasing exponentially
over time while the debt level remains constant, there is an exponential
decline in expected leverage ratios. However, this is not consistent with
empirical observations that most firms keep stable leverage ratios (e.g. see
Wang, 2005).

Mean-reverting leverage ratio

Collin-Dufresne and Goldstein (2001) extend this to a general model that
generates mean-reverting leverage ratios. In their model, the risk-free
interest rate is assumed to follow the Vasicek process, while the log-default
threshold is assumed to follow the process

$$\mathrm{d}\ln V_t^* = k_l[\ln V_t - v - \phi(r_t - \bar{r}) - \ln V_t^*]\mathrm{d}t. \tag{6.8}$$

Empirical evidence suggests that equity risk premiums tend to move
countercyclically and are negatively correlated with returns on broad equity
indices. Huang and Huang (2003) postulate a negative correlation between
the risk premium and unexpected shocks to the return on assets of the
typical borrower. Specifically, (1) is augmented by

$$\mathrm{d}\lambda_\tau = \kappa_\lambda(\bar{\lambda} - \lambda_\tau)\mathrm{d}t + \sigma_\lambda\mathrm{d}W_t^\lambda, \tag{6.9}$$

where $\mathrm{corr}(\mathrm{d}W_t^\lambda, \mathrm{d}w_t) \equiv \sigma_{\lambda v} < 0$.

A higher λ, implying a higher long-run drift in the value of assets, *ceteris
paribus* lowers the probability of default. The impact of λ is stronger the
larger is the mean-reversion parameter k_λ. In addition, since $\sigma_{\lambda v} < 0$, a
negative value of $\mathrm{d}W_t$, which puts upward pressure on the probability of
default, tends to be counteracted by an increase of the drift in the value of
assets.

Endogenous default barrier models

'Endogenous default' models allow the borrower decide when to default. The framework differs mainly in the assumptions underlying the default decision. Anderson *et al.* (1996) allow debtors to rearrange and adjust the terms of the debt contract. In contrast, renegotiation is not possible in the Leland and Toft (1996) (hereafter LT) model, in which borrowers service their debt as long as doing so is justified by the expected future return on equity. The two models differ also in their assumptions regarding the time to maturity of debt contracts. Anderson *et al.* (1996) assume perpetual bonds, while Leland and Toft (1996) assume that the firm continuously issues debt of a constant but finite time to maturity.

In the Anderson *et al.* model, at the time of default, creditors can either liquidate the borrowing firm and seize its assets net of bankruptcy costs or accept the terms of a new debt contract. Since liquidation of the firm is the worst possible outcome for equityholders, they have an incentive to agree to a post-default contract acceptable to creditors. To rule out arbitrage opportunities in this setup, the value of debt must increase continuously in the value of assets. No-arbitrage imposes a smooth switch between the pre-default and post-default value of debt. On the one hand, given a fixed bankruptcy cost, K, incurred only if creditors liquidate the firm, the post-default value of debt is set by equityholders so as to equal $V_t - K$. This renders creditors indifferent between re-contracting and liquidating. On the other hand, the pre-default value of debt is an increasing function of the firm's assets and is shifted upwards by a higher risk-neutral drift (a higher r and/or a lower δ), a higher debt principal, P, a higher coupon rate, c, a lower asset volatility, σ, and a lower monitoring cost, m. When the value of assets equal the equilibrium default trigger, the post- and pre-default value of debt is the same. A decline in bankruptcy costs, K, enhances the post-default value of debt, decreases debtors' bargaining power, and induces them to wait longer before renegotiating (set a lower). In contrast, an upward shift in the pre-default value of debt induces debtors to negotiate a more advantageous contract earlier (set a higher value of V^*).

Leland (1994) and Leland and Toft (1996) assume that the firm defaults when asset value reaches an endogenous default boundary. To avoid default a firm would issue equity to service its debt; at default, the value of equity goes to zero. The optimal default boundary is chosen by shareholders to maximize the value of equity at the default-triggering asset level. Leland (1994) assumes that the term structure, dividend payout rate and asset risk premium are constant. In the event of default, equityholders receive nothing while debt holders receive a fraction $(1 - \omega)$ of firm assets. Under these assumptions, the value of a perpetual bond that pays semi-annual coupons at an annual rate c and the optimal default boundary can be determined analytically.

Leland and Toft (1996) relax the assumption of infinite maturity of the debt, while maintaining the same assumptions for the term structure of interest rates and the fraction of loss upon default. In their model, the borrower forfeits its equity value as soon as it does not fulfil a contracted obligation. Thus, the willingness to service debt increases (i.e., the default trigger V^* decreases) in the value of equity. *Ceteris paribus*, the value of the firm decreases in the default costs, which are assumed to be an exogenous fraction α of assets. In contrast, since it has an infinite horizon, the value of the firm is insensitive to the time to maturity, T, of continuously re-issued debt contracts. The value of finitely lived debt decreases in α (but by less than the value of the firm). The value of debt decreases in T, which if it rises heightens the risk of default before the contract matures. The value of equity (the default trigger V^*) decreases (increases) in default costs but increases (decreases) in the time to debt maturity.

6.4. Empirical illustration

In this section we present empirical evidence on the application of the Merton model. Our sample consists of 109 distressed U.S. firms that filed for bankruptcy during the 1995–2000 period and an equivalent sample of healthy firms. Matched healthy firms must be from the same industry with similar asset size in the years prior to bankruptcy filing. We use Compustat database to collect all relevant data required to compute the five primary option variables (see Charitou and Trigeorgis 2006 for more details). Similar to the KMV–Merton procedure, the market value of the firm (V) and the firm standard deviation (σ) were calculated by solving simultaneous equations.[6]

We apply logistic regression methodology to test the significance of the standard option-pricing model using the five primary option variables.

---

[6] The sample is first divided into training and testing sub-samples. The training sub-sample consists of 142 firms and the testing sample consists of 76 firms. Based on the estimated coefficients and by using the inverse logit probability we calculate the (predicted) default probabilities in order to examine the power of the model based on the out-of-sample firms.

Specifically, Table 6.3 presents the results of the following model:

Prob. default $= f(\ln V, \ln B, \sigma, T, r - D)$.

This model uses the five primary option variables that account for default at debt maturity only. The natural logarithm of the current market value of the firm's assets, $\ln V$, is expected to have a negative relation with the probability of default since the greater the current worth of the firm's assets, the lower the probability of default at maturity. In contrast, the natural logarithm of the book value of total liabilities, $\ln B$, is expected to have positive relation with default probability since the higher the principal amount owed at maturity (the exercise price of the equityholders' option), the greater the probability of default. The standard deviation (σ) of % changes in firm value is also positively correlated with default since the greater the firm's volatility, the greater the value of equityholders' default option. The relation of average time to debt's maturity (T) (measured as the average duration of all out-standing debt maturities) and default may be unclear since the default option at first increases with maturity but beyond some point it may decline. Similarly, the difference between the expected asset return and the firm's payout rate, $r - D$, is not expected to have a constant relation with default.

Consistent with option theory, the model is statistically significant at the 1% level (based on the −2 log-likelihood test) one year prior to bankruptcy filing. All individual primary option variables are statistically significant (mostly at 1%). As expected, the probability of default is higher the lower the value of the firm ($\ln V$), the higher the amount of debt owed ($\ln B$), and the higher the firm volatility (σ). The coefficient of the average debt maturity (T) is negative, probably because firms in financial distress have more difficulty in raising long-term debt and so they tend to hold more short-term loans. As expected, the explanatory power of the model, as measured by the pseudo-R^2, is quite high (22%). Interestingly, the model seems to correctly classify 75% of the sample firms (as measured by the testing result).

The model seems to perform well in out-of-sample tests, especially when investigating default at debt maturity only. Recent studies (Bharath and Shumway 2005) show that the KMV–Merton model does not produce a sufficient statistic for the probability of default; suggesting that it can be improved. Charitou and Trigeorgis (2006) extended the above model by taking into consideration intermediate default as well.[7]

---

[7] For an in-depth discussion and empirical application of this model see Charitou and Trigeorgis (2006).

6.5. Conclusions

This study reviews prior research on credit risk analysis mainly focusing on structural models. Structural default models relate the credit quality of a firm and the firm's economic and financial conditions. Thus, in contrast to reduced-form models where default is given exogenously, in structural models, default is endogenously generated within the model. We present the revolution of the structural models commencing with the seminal work of Merton (1974). Merton's model considers a firm as failure if, at the time of servicing the debt at maturity, its assets are below its outstanding debt. The basic idea is that the firm's equity is seen as a European call option with maturity T and strike price D on asset value V. The firm's debt value is the asset value minus the equity value seen as a call option. This method presumes a very simplistic capital structure and implies that default can only occur at the maturity of the zero-coupon bond. In this chapter, we also evaluate subsequent research on the main structural credit risk models, such as models with stochastic interest rates, exogenous and endogenous default barrier models and models with mean-reverting leverage ratios.

Appendix

Table 6.1 Summary of main structural credit risk models

Model	Description
Merton (1974)	$E(V, \tau) = Ve^{-D\tau}N(d_1) - Be^{-r\tau} N(d_2)$
Black and Cox (1976)	Exogenous Default Barrier – Constant Interest Rate
Longstaff and Schwartz (1995)	Exogenous Default Barrier – Stochastic Interest Rate
Leland and Toft (1996)	Endogenous Default Barrier
Hillegeist et al. (2004)	Hazard model with Merton (1974) theory
KMV model	Distance to default = $(V -$ default point$)/V_\varsigma$
Bharath and Shumway (2005)	KMV–Merton model – without solving simultaneous equations

In the Merton model a firm's equity is treated as a European call option written on the firm's asset value. It is assumed that the issuing firm has only one outstanding bond, and thus the firm does not default prior to the debt maturity date. In addition, the term structure of risk-free interest rate r, firm's asset volatility σ_V and asset risk premium π_V are assumed to be constant.

Black and Cox (1976) treat the firm's equity as a down-and-out call option on firm's value. In their model, firm defaults when its asset value hits a pre-specified default barrier, V^*, which can be either a constant or a time-varying variable. The default barrier is assumed to be exogenously determined.

Longstaf and Schwartz (1995) extend the Black–Cox model to the case when the risk-free interest rate is stochastic and follows the Vasicek (1977) process. The default boundary, V^*, is pre-determined.

Leland and Toft (1996) assume that firm defaults when its asset value reaches an endogenous default boundary. They relax the assumption of the infinite maturity of debt while keeping the same assumptions for the term structure of interest rate and the fraction of loss upon default. In the LT model, the borrower forfeits its equity value as soon as it does not fulfil a contracted obligation.

Hillegeist *et al.* (2004) extend Shumway model by using Merton option theory in a discrete hazard model and examine the predictive ability of the Altman and Ohlson accounting-based variables.

The KMV model assumes equity is like a (perpetual) option on the firm's asset value which can trigger default when it goes below a given default point. Unlike the original Merton model which focuses exclusively on default on the principal payment (total liabilities) at maturity, KMV model recognizes that involuntary default may be triggered by nonpayment of any other scheduled payment, either interest expense or principal repayment. To account for the probability of intermediate involuntary default, KMV adjust downward the default boundary at maturity, based on their proprietary data base and experience, to (current liabilities $+ 0.5 \times$ long-term liabilities).

Bharath and Shumway (2005) develop a new, simpler predictor without solving the non-linear equations. They approximate the volatility of each firm's debt as $\sigma_B = 0.05 + 0.25\sigma_E$, the total volatility of the firm as $\sigma_{BS} = (E/V)\sigma_E + (B/V)\sigma_B$, and $DD_{BS} = \frac{ln(V/B) + (\mu - 0.5\sigma_{BS}^2)T}{\sigma_{BS}\sqrt{T}}$.

Table 6.2 Structural models following Merton (1974)

Structural Model	Authors	Year	Characteristics
Merton (1974)	Merton	1974	Standard option-pricing Constant r, σ, π_v, $T =$ Debts maturity
Exogenously default barrier	Black and Cox	1976	Equity as Down-and-out call option Non-stochastic interest rate
Exogenously default barrier	Longstaff and Schwartz	1995	Extends Black and Cox (1976) Stochastic Interest Rates (Vasicek, 1977)
Exogenously default barrier	Collin-Dufrense and Goldstein	2001	Mean reverting leverage ratio Extends Longstaff and Schwartz (1995)
Exogenously default barrier	Huang and Huang	2003	Mean revert. lev. Ratio, Neg. correl. Risk premium and unexpected shocks to return
Endogenously default barrier	Leland	1994	Constant term structure, dividend payout rate, asset risk premium
Endogenously default barrier	Leland and Toft	1996	Continuously debt issuing of constant but finite time to maturity
Endogenously default barrier	Anderson *et al.*	1996	Perpetual bonds
Merton's ext.	Vasicek	1984	Stochastic interest rate
Merton's ext.	KMV		Empirical model – historic data
Merton's ext.	Hillegeist *et al.*	2004	Hazard model
Dynamic models	Goldstein *et al.*	2001	Dynamic capital structure choice and corporate bond pricing
Strategic models	Mella-Barral and Perraudin	1997	Optimal capital structure (shareholders can renegotiate the debt without defaulting)
Merton's ext.	Charitou and Trigeorgis	2006	Voluntary and involuntary intermediate default model
KMV–Merton's ext.	Bharath and Shumway	2005	Extends KMV–Merton's model without solving the simultaneous equations

This table presents the major structural models commencing by the seminal work of Merton (1974). The first column presents the form of the structural model, the second and third columns relate to the authors and year of publication, respectively, and the last column notes some model characteristics.

Table 6.3 Logistic regression for primary option variables

Model	One year prior to failure	
	Coef.	Signif.
ln(V)	−1.209	(0.000)***
ln(B)	1.292	(0.000)***
σ	1.651	(0.024)**
T	−0.102	(0.043)**
$r - D$	−5.236	(0.001)***
Const.	0.812	(0.357)
Model signif.	(0.000)***	
Pseudo-R^2 (%)	22.0	
Training (%)	71.9	
Testing (%)	75.44	
Type I (%)	29.67	
Type II (%)	19.44	
Pair of companies	76	

***, ** significant at 1%, 5% level (respectively)

This table presents multivariate logistic regression results for the primary option variables one year prior to bankruptcy filing. ln(V): ln of current market firm value; ln(B): ln of book value of total liabilities; σ: standard deviation of firm value changes; T: average time to debt's maturity; $r - D$: expected return on asset value minus firm payout.

REFERENCES

Altman E., 'Financial ratios, discriminant analysis and the prediction of corporate bankruptcy', *Journal of Finance*, September, 1968, 589–609.

Altman, E. I., Haldeman, R. and Narayanan, P., 'ZETA analysis: A new model to identify bankruptcy risk of corporations', *Journal of Banking and Finance*, 10, 1977, 29–54.

Anderson, R. W., Sundaresan, S. and Tychon, P., 'Strategic analysis of contingent claims', *European Economic Review*, 40, 1996, 871–81.

Beaver, W., 'Financial ratios as predictors of failure', *Journal of Accounting Research*, 1966, 71–111.

Bharath, S. T. and Shumway, T., 'Forecasting default with the KMV–Merton model', *Working Paper*, University of Michigan, 2005.

Black, F. and Scholes, M., 'The pricing of options and corporate liabilities', *Journal of Political Economy*, May/June, 1973, 637–654.

Black, F., and Cox, J. C., 'Valuing corporate securities: some effects of bond indenture provisions', *Journal of Finance*, 31, 1976, 351–67.

Briys, E. and de Varenne, F., 'Valuing risky fixed rate debt: an extension', *Journal of Financial and Quantitative Analysis*, 31, 1997, 239–48.

Campbell, J. Y., Hilscher, J. and Szilagyi, J., 'In search of distress risk', *Working Paper*, Harvard University, 2004.

Charitou, A. and Trigeorgis, L., 'The probability of intermediate default in explaining financial distress: an option-based approach', *Working Paper*, University of Cyprus, 2006.

Chava, S. and Jarrow R., 'Bankruptcy prediction with bankruptcy effects, market versus accounting variables, and reduced form credit risk models', *Working Paper*, Cornell University, 2001.

Cheung J., 'A review of option-pricing theory in accounting research', *Journal of Accounting Literature*, 10, 1991, 51–84.

Collin-Dufresne, P. and Goldstein, R., 'Do credit spreads reflect stationary leverage ratios?', *Journal of Finance*, 56, 2001, 1929–57.

Core, J. and Schrand, C., 'The effect of accounting-based debt covenants on equity valuation', *Journal of Accounting and Economics*, 27(1), 1999, 1–34.

Crouhy M., Galai D. and Mark R., *Risk Management*, New York, McGraw-Hill, 2001.

Crosbie P. and J. Bohn, *Modeling Default Risk*, 2002, KMV.

Du, Yu, and Wulin Suo, 'Assessing credit quality from equity markets: Is a structural approach a better approach?', *Working Paper*, Queen's University, 2004.

Duffie, D. and Ke Wang, 'Multi-period corporate failure prediction with stochastic covariates', *Working Paper*, Stanford University, 2004.

Edmister, R. O., 'An empirical test of financial ratio analysis for small business failure prediction', *Journal of Financial and Quantitative Analysis*, 7, 1972, 1477–93.

Eisenbeis, R. A., 'Pitfalls in the application of discriminant analysis in business, finance and economics', *The Journal of Finance*, 22, 1977, 875–900.

Elizalde, A., 'Credit risk models I: default correlation in intensity models', 2005a, available at www.abelelizalde.com.

Geske, R., 'The valuation of compound options', *Journal of Financial Economics*, 7(1), 1979, 63–81.

Goldstein, R., Ju, N. and Leland, H., 'An EBIT-based model of capital structure', *Journal of Business*, 74(4), 2001, 483–512.

Hillegeist, S., Keating, E., Cram, D. and Lundstedt, K., 'Assessing the probability of bankruptcy', *Review of Accounting Studies*, 9(1), 2004, 5–34.

Hsu, J., Saá-Requejo, J. and Santa-Clara, P., 'Bond Pricing with Default Risk', *Working Paper*, UCLA, 2004.

Huang, J. and Huang, M., 'How much of the corporate-treasury yield spread is due to credit risk', *Working Paper*, Penn State University, 2003.

Kealhofer, S. and Kurbat, M., *The Default Prediction Power of the Merton Approach, Relative to Debt Ratings and Accounting Variables*, KMV, 2001.

Kealhofer S., Kwok S. and Weng W., *Uses and Abuses of Bond Default Rates*, KMV, 1998.

Kiefer, N. M., 'Economic duration data and hazard functions', *Journal of Economic Literature* 26, 1988, 646–79.

Kim, I. J., Ramaswamy, K. and Sundaresan, S. M., 'Does default risk in coupons affect the valuation of corporate bonds?: A contingent claims model', *Financial Management*, 22, 1993, 117–31.

Lancaster, T., *The Econometric Analysis of Transition Data*, New York, Cambridge University Press, 1990.

Leland, H. E., 'Corporate debt value, bond covenants, and optimal capital structure', *Journal of Finance*, 49, 1994, 987–1019.

Leland, H., 'Predictions of expected default probabilities in structural models of debt', *Journal of Investment Management*, 2(2), 2004.

Leland, H. and Toft, K., 'Optimal capital structure, endogenous bankruptcy, and the term structure on credit spreads', *Journal of Finance*, 51(4), 1996, 987–1019.

Longstaff, F. and Schwartz, E., 'Valuing risky debt: a new approach', *Journal of Finance*, 50, 1995, 789–820.

Mella-Barral P., and Perraudin W., 'Strategic debt service', *Journal of Finance*, 52(2), 1997, 531–66.

Mensah, Y. M., 'An examination of the stationarity of multivariate bankruptcy prediction models: a methodological study', *Journal of Accounting Research*, 22, 1984, 380–95.

Merton, R. C., 'Theory of rational option pricing', *Bell Journal of Economics and Management Science*, 4, 1973, 141–83.

Merton, R. C., 'On the pricing of corporate debt: the risk structure of interest rates', *Journal of Finance*, 29, 1974, 449–70.

Merton, R. C., 'On the Ppricing of contingent claims and the Modigliani–Miller theorem', *Journal of Financial Economics*, 5(2), 1977, 241–49.

Nielsen, L. T., Saá-Requejo, J. and Santa-Clara, P., 'Default risk and interest rate risk: the term structure of default spreads', *Working Paper*, 1993, INSEAD.

Ohlson, J., 'Financial ratios and the probabilistic prediction of bankruptcy', *Journal of Accounting Research*, Spring, 1980, 109–31.

Ronn, E. I. and Verma, A. K., 'Pricing risk-adjusted deposit insurance: an option based model', *Journal of Finance*, 41, 1986, 871–95.

Shumway, T., 'Forecasting bankruptcy more accurately: a simple hazard model', *Journal of Business*, 74(1), 2001, 103–24.

Vasicek, O., 'An equilibrium characterization of the term structure', *Journal of Financial Economics*, 5, 1977, 177–88.

Vasicek, O., *Credit Valuation*, KMV, 1984.

Vassalou, M. and Xing, Y., 'Default risk in equity returns', *Journal of Finance*, 59(2), 2004, 831–868.

Wang, W., 'The role of credit ratings in timing public debt issue, and debt maturity choice', *Working Paper*, Queen's University, 2005.

Wilcox, J. W., 'A prediction of business failure using accounting data', *Empirical Research in Accounting*, 2, 1973, 163–79.

Zavgren, C. V., 'The prediction of corporate failure: the state of the art', *Journal of Accounting Literature*, 2, 1983, 1–38.

Zmijewski, M., 'Methodological issues related to the estimation of financial distress prediction models', *Journal of Accounting Research*, Spring, 1984, 59–86.

7 Default recovery rates and LGD in credit risk modelling and practice: An updated review of the literature and empirical evidence*

Edward I. Altman

7.1. Introduction

Three main variables affect the credit risk of a financial asset: (i) the probability of default (PD), (ii) the 'loss given default' (LGD), which is equal to one minus the recovery rate in the event of default (RR), and (iii) the exposure at default (EAD). While significant attention has been devoted by the credit risk literature on the estimation of the first component (PD), much less attention has been dedicated to the estimation of RR and to the relationship between PD and RR. This is mainly the consequence of two related factors. First, credit pricing models and risk management applications tend to focus on the systematic risk components of credit risk, as these are the only ones that attract risk-premia. Second, credit risk models traditionally assumed RR to be dependent on individual features (e.g. collateral or seniority) that do not respond to systematic factors, and therefore to be independent of PD.

This traditional focus only on default analysis has been partly reversed by the recent increase in the number of studies dedicated to the subject of RR estimation and the relationship between the PD and RR (Fridson *et al.* 2000, Gupton *et al.* 2000, Altman *et al.* 2001, Altman *et al.* 2003, 2005, Frye 2000a, 2000b, 2000c, Hu and Perraudin 2002, Hamilton *et al.* 2001, Jarrow 2001 and Jokivuolle and Peura 2003). This is partly the consequence of the parallel increase in default rates and decrease of recovery rates registered

---

* This is an updated and expanded review of the original article by Altman *et al.* (2005).

during the 1999–2002 period. More generally, evidence from many countries in recent years suggests that collateral values and recovery rates can be volatile and, moreover, they tend to go down just when the number of defaults goes up in economic downturns.

This chapter presents a detailed review of the way credit risk models, developed during the last thirty years, have treated the recovery rate and, more specifically, its relationship with the probability of default of an obligor. These models can be divided into two main categories: (a) credit pricing models, and (b) portfolio credit value-at-risk (VaR) models. Credit pricing models can in turn be divided into three main approaches: (i) 'first generation' structural-form models, (ii) 'second generation' structural-form models, and (iii) reduced-form models. These three different approaches together with their basic assumptions, advantages, drawbacks and empirical performance are reviewed in sections 2, 3 and 4. Credit VaR models are then examined in section 5. The more recent studies explicitly modelling and empirically investigating the relationship between PD and RR are reviewed in section 6. In section 7, we discuss BIS efforts to motivate banks to consider 'downturn LGD' in the specification of capital requirements under Basel II. Section 8 reviews the very recent efforts by the major rating agencies to provide explicit estimates of recovery given default. Section 9 revisits the issue of procyclicality and Section 10 presents some recent empirical evidence on recovery rates on both defaulted bonds and loans and also on the relationship between default and recovery rates. Section 11 concludes.

7.2. First-generation structural-form models: the Merton approach

The first category of credit risk models are the ones based on the original framework developed by Merton (1974) using the principles of option pricing (Black and Scholes 1973). In such a framework, the default process of a company is driven by the value of the company's assets and the risk of a firm's default is therefore explicitly linked to the variability of the firm's asset value. The basic intuition behind the Merton model is relatively simple: default occurs when the value of a firm's assets (the market value of the firm) is lower than that of its liabilities. The payment to the debtholders at the maturity of the debt is therefore the smaller of two quantities: the face value of the debt or the market value of the firm's assets. Assuming that the company's debt is entirely represented by a zero-coupon bond, if the value of the firm at maturity is greater than the face value of the bond, then the bondholder gets back the face value of the bond. However, if the value of the firm is less than the face value of the bond, the shareholders get nothing and the bondholder gets back the market value of the firm. The payoff at maturity to the bondholder is therefore equivalent to the face value of the bond minus a put option on the value of the firm, with a strike price equal to the face value of the bond and a maturity equal to the maturity of the bond. Following this basic intuition, Merton derived an explicit formula for risky bonds which can be used both to estimate the PD of a firm and to estimate the yield differential between a risky bond and a default-free bond.

In addition to Merton (1974), first generation structural-form models include Black and Cox (1976), Geske (1977) and Vasicek (1984). Each of these models tries to refine the original Merton framework by removing one or more of the unrealistic assumptions. Black and Cox (1976) introduce the possibility of more complex capital structures, with subordinated debt; Geske (1977) introduces interest-paying debt; Vasicek (1984) introduces the distinction between short and long term liabilities which now represents a distinctive feature of the KMV model.[1]

Under these models, all the relevant credit risk elements, including default and recovery at default, are a function of the structural characteristics of the firm: asset levels, asset volatility (business risk) and leverage (financial risk). The RR is therefore an endogenous variable, as the creditors' payoff is a function of the residual value of the defaulted company's assets. More precisely, under Merton's theoretical framework, PD and RR tend to be inversely related. If, for example, the firm's value increases, then its PD tends to decrease while the expected RR at default increases (ceteris paribus). On the other side, if the firm's debt increases, its PD increases while the expected RR at default decreases. Finally, if the firm's asset volatility increases, its PD increases while the expected RR at default decreases, since the possible asset values can be quite low relative to liability levels.

Although the line of research that followed the Merton approach has proven very useful in addressing the qualitatively important aspects of pricing credit risks, it has been less successful in practical applications.[2] This lack of success has been attributed to different reasons. First, under Merton's model the firm defaults only at maturity of the debt, a scenario that is at

---

[1] In the KMV model, default occurs when the firm's asset value goes below a threshold represented by the sum of the total amount of short-term liabilities and half of the amount of long-term liabilities.

[2] The standard reference is Jones et al. (1984), who found that, even for firms with very simple capital structures, a Merton-type model is unable to price investment-grade corporate bonds better than a naive model that assumes no risk of default.

odds with reality. Second, for the model to be used in valuing default-risky debts of a firm with more than one class of debt in its capital structure (complex capital structures), the priority/seniority structures of various debts have to be specified. Also, this framework assumes that the absolute-priority rules are actually adhered to upon default in that debts are paid off in the order of their seniority. However, empirical evidence, such as in Franks and Torous (1994), indicates that the absolute-priority rules are often violated. Moreover, the use of a lognormal distribution in the basic Merton model (instead of a more fat-tailed distribution) tends to overstate recovery rates in the event of default.

7.3. Second-generation structural-form models

In response to such difficulties, an alternative approach has been developed which still adopts the original Merton framework as far as the default process is concerned but, at the same time, removes one of the unrealistic assumptions of the Merton model; namely, that default can occur only at maturity of the debt when the firm's assets are no longer sufficient to cover debt obligations. Instead, it is assumed that default may occur anytime between the issuance and maturity of the debt and that default is triggered when the value of the firm's assets reaches a lower threshold level.[3] These models include Kim *et al.* (1993), Hull and White (1995), Nielsen *et al.* (1993), Longstaff and Schwartz (1995) and others.

Under these models, the RR in the event of default is exogenous and independent from the firm's asset value. It is generally defined as a fixed ratio of the outstanding debt value and is therefore independent of the PD. For example, Longstaff and Schwartz (1995) argue that, by looking at the history of defaults and the recovery rates for various classes of debt of comparable firms, one can form a reliable estimate of the RR. In their model, they allow for a stochastic term structure of interest rates and for some correlation between defaults and interest rates. They find that this correlation between default risk and the interest rate has a significant effect on the properties of the credit spread.[4] This approach simplifies the first class of models by both exogenously specifying the cash flows to risky debt in the event of

---

[3] One of the earliest studies based on this framework is Black and Cox (1976). However, this is not included in the second-generation models in terms of the treatment of the recovery rate.

[4] Using Moody's corporate bond yield data, they find that credit spreads are negatively related to interest rates and that durations of risky bonds depend on the correlation with interest rates.

bankruptcy and simplifying the bankruptcy process. The latter occurs when the value of the firm's underlying assets hits some exogenously specified boundary.

Despite these improvements with respect to the original Merton's framework, second-generation structural-form models still suffer from three main drawbacks, which represent the main reasons behind their relatively poor empirical performance.[5] First, they still require estimates for the parameters of the firm's asset value, which is non-observable. Indeed, unlike the stock price in the Black and Scholes formula for valuing equity options, the current market value of a firm is not easily observable. Second, structural-form models cannot incorporate credit-rating changes that occur quite frequently for default-risky corporate debts. Most corporate bonds undergo credit downgrades before they actually default. As a consequence, any credit risk model should take into account the uncertainty associated with credit rating changes as well as the uncertainty concerning default. Finally, most structural-form models assume that the value of the firm is continuous in time. As a result, the time of default can be predicted just before it happens and hence, as argued by Duffie and Lando (2000), there are no 'sudden surprises'. In other words, without recurring to a 'jump process', the PD of a firm is known with certainty.

7.4. Reduced-form models

The attempt to overcome the above mentioned shortcomings of structural-form models gave rise to reduced-form models. These include Litterman and Iben (1991), Madan and Unal (1995), Jarrow and Turnbull (1995), Jarrow *et al.* (1997), Lando (1998), Duffie (1998) and Duffie and Singleton (1999). Unlike structural-form models, reduced-form models do not condition default on the value of the firm, and parameters related to the firm's value need not be estimated to implement them. In addition to that, reduced-form models introduce separate explicit assumptions on the dynamic of both PD and RR. These variables are modelled independently from the structural features of the firm, its asset volatility and leverage. Generally speaking, reduced-form models assume an exogenous RR that is independent from the PD and take as basics the behaviour of default-free interest rates, the RR of defaultable bonds at default, as well as a stochastic

---

[5] See Eom *et al.* (2001) for an empirical analysis of structural-form models.

process for default intensity. At each instant, there is some probability that a firm defaults on its obligations. Both this probability and the RR in the event of default may vary stochastically through time. Those stochastic processes determine the price of credit risk. Although these processes are not formally linked to the firm's asset value, there is presumably some underlying relation. Thus Duffie and Singleton (1999) describe these alternative approaches as reduced-form models.

Reduced-form models fundamentally differ from typical structural-form models in the degree of predictability of the default as they can accommodate defaults that are sudden surprises. A typical reduced-form model assumes that an exogenous random variable drives default and that the probability of default over any time interval is nonzero. Default occurs when the random variable undergoes a discrete shift in its level. These models treat defaults as unpredictable Poisson events. The time at which the discrete shift will occur cannot be foretold on the basis of information available today.

Reduced-form models somewhat differ from each other by the manner in which the RR is parametrized. For example, Jarrow and Turnbull (1995) assumed that, at default, a bond would have a market value equal to an exogenously specified fraction of an otherwise equivalent default-free bond. Duffie and Singleton (1999) followed with a model that, when market value at default (i.e. RR) is exogenously specified, allows for closed-form solutions for the term-structure of credit spreads. Their model also allows for a random RR that depends on the pre-default value of the bond. While this model assumes an exogenous process for the expected loss at default, meaning that the RR does not depend on the value of the defaultable claim, it allows for correlation between the default hazard-rate process and RR. Indeed, in this model, the behaviour of both PD and RR may be allowed to depend on firm-specific or macroeconomic variables and therefore to be correlated.

Other models assume that bonds of the same issuer, seniority, and face value have the same RR at default, regardless of the remaining maturity. For example, Duffie (1998) assumes that, at default, the holder of a bond of given face value receives a fixed payment, irrespective of the coupon level or maturity, and the same fraction of face value as any other bond of the same seniority. This allows him to use recovery parameters based on statistics provided by rating agencies such as Moody's. Jarrow et al. (1997) also allow for different debt seniorities to translate into different RRs for a given firm. Both Lando (1998) and Jarrow et al. (1997) use transition matrices (historical probabilities of credit rating changes) to price defaultable bonds.

Empirical evidence concerning reduced-form models is rather limited. Using the Duffie and Singleton (1999) framework, Duffee (1999) finds that these models have difficulty in explaining the observed term structure of credit spreads across firms of different credit risk qualities. In particular, such models have difficulty generating both relatively flat yield spreads when firms have low credit risk and steeper yield spreads when firms have higher credit risk.

A recent attempt to combine the advantages of structural-form models – a clear economic mechanism behind the default process – and the ones of reduced-form models – unpredictability of default – can be found in Zhou (2001). This is done by modeling the evolution of firm value as a jump-diffusion process. This model links RRs to the firm value at default so that the variation in RRs is endogenously generated and the correlation between RRs and credit ratings reported first in Altman (1989) and Gupton *et al.* (2000) is justified.

7.5. Credit value-at-risk models

During the second half of the 1990s, banks and consultants started developing credit risk models aimed at measuring the potential loss, with a predetermined confidence level, that a portfolio of credit exposures could suffer within a specified time horizon (generally one year). These were mostly motivated by the growing importance of credit risk management especially since the now complete Basel II was anticipated to be proposed by the BD. These value-at-risk (VaR) models include J.P. Morgan's *CreditMetrics*® (Gupton *et al.* 1997), *Credit Suisse Financial Products' CreditRisk+*® (1997), McKinsey's *CreditPortfolioView*® (Wilson 1998), KMV's *CreditPortfolioManager*®, and Kamakura's *Risk Manager*®.

Credit VaR models can be gathered in two main categories: (1) default mode models (DM) and (2) mark-to-market (MTM) models. In the former, credit risk is identified with default risk and a binomial approach is adopted. Therefore, only two possible events are taken into account: default and survival. The latter includes all possible changes of the borrower credit-worthiness, technically called 'credit migrations'. In DM models, credit losses only arise when a default occurs. On the other hand, MTM models are multinomial, in that losses arise also when negative credit migrations occur. The two approaches basically differ for the amount of data necessary to feed them: limited in the case of default mode models, much wider in the case of mark-to-market ones.

The main output of a credit risk model is the probability density function (PDF) of the future losses on a credit portfolio. From the analysis of such a loss distribution, a financial institution can estimate both the expected loss and the unexpected loss on its credit portfolio. The expected loss equals the (unconditional) mean of the loss distribution; it represents the amount the investor can expect to lose within a specific period of time (usually one year). On the other side, the unexpected loss represents the 'deviation' from expected loss and measures the actual portfolio risk. This can in turn be measured as the standard deviation of the loss distribution. Such a measure is relevant only in the case of a normal distribution and is therefore hardly useful for credit risk measurement: indeed, the distribution of credit losses is usually highly asymmetrical and fat-tailed. This implies that the probability of large losses is higher than the one associated with a normal distribution. Financial institutions typically apply credit risk models to evaluate the 'economic capital' necessary to face the risk associated with their credit portfolios. In such a framework, provisions for credit losses should cover expected losses,[6] while economic capital is seen as a cushion for unexpected losses. Indeed, Basel II in its final iteration (BIS, June 2004) separated these two types of losses.

Credit VaR models can largely be seen as reduced-form models, where the RR is typically taken as an exogenous constant parameter or a stochastic variable independent from PD. Some of these models, such as *CreditMetrics*®, treat the RR in the event of default as a stochastic variable – generally modelled through a beta distribution – independent from the PD. Others, such as *CreditRisk+*®, treat it as a constant parameter that must be specified as an input for each single credit exposure. While a comprehensive analysis of these models goes beyond the aim of this review,[7] it is important to highlight that all credit VaR models treat RR and PD as two independent variables.

7.6. Recent contributions on the PD–RR relationship and their impact

During the last several years, new approaches explicitly modelling and empirically investigating the relationship between PD and RR have been developed. These models include Bakshi *et al.* (2001), Jokivuolle and Peura (2003), Frye (2000a, 2000b), Jarrow (2001), Hu and Perraudin (2002), Carey

---

[6] Reserves are used to cover expected losses.
[7] For a comprehensive analysis of these models, see Crouhy *et al.* (2000) and Gordy (2000).

and Gordy (2003), Altman *et al.* (2001, 2003, 2005), and Acharya *et al.* (2003, 2007).

Bakshi *et al.* (2001) enhance the reduced-form models presented in section 4 to allow for a flexible correlation between the risk-free rate, the default probability and the recovery rate. Based on some evidence published by rating agencies, they force recovery rates to be negatively associated with default probability. They find some strong support for this hypothesis through the analysis of a sample of BBB-rated corporate bonds: more precisely, their empirical results show that, on average, a 4% worsening in the (risk-neutral) hazard rate is associated with a 1% decline in (risk-neutral) recovery rates.

A rather different approach is the one proposed by Jokivuolle and Peura (2003). The authors present a model for bank loans in which collateral value is correlated with the PD. They use the option pricing framework for modelling risky debt: the borrowing firm's total asset value triggers the event of default. However, the firm's asset value does not determine the RR. Rather, the collateral value is in turn assumed to be the only stochastic element determining recovery.[8] Because of this assumption, the model can be implemented using an exogenous PD, so that the firm's asset value parameters need not be estimated. In this respect, the model combines features of both structural-form and reduced-form models. Assuming a positive correlation between a firm's asset value and collateral value, the authors obtain a similar result as Frye (2000a, 2000b), that realized default rates and recovery rates have an inverse relationship.

The model proposed by Frye draws from the conditional approach suggested by Finger (1999) and Gordy (2000). In these models, defaults are driven by a single systematic factor – the state of the economy – rather than by a multitude of correlation parameters. These models are based on the assumption that the same economic conditions that cause defaults to rise might cause RRs to decline, i.e. that the distribution of recovery is different in high-default periods from low-default ones. In Frye's model, both PD and RR depend on the state of the systematic factor. The correlation between these two variables therefore derives from their mutual dependence on the systematic factor.

The intuition behind Frye's theoretical model is relatively simple: if a borrower defaults on a loan, a bank's recovery may depend on the value of

---

[8] Because of this simplifying assumption the model can be implemented using an exogenous PD, so that the firm asset value parameters need not be estimated. In this respect, the model combines features of both structural-form and reduced-form models.

the loan collateral. The value of the collateral, like the value of other assets, depends on economic conditions. If the economy experiences a recession, RRs may decrease just as default rates tend to increase. This gives rise to a negative correlation between default rates and RRs.

While the model originally developed by Frye (2000a) implied recovery to be taken from an equation that determines collateral, Frye (2000b) modelled recovery directly. This allowed him to empirically test his model using data on defaults and recoveries from U.S. corporate bond data. More precisely, data from Moody's Default Risk Service database for the 1982–97 period were used for the empirical analysis.[9] Results show a strong negative correlation between default rates and RRs for corporate bonds. This evidence is consistent with U.S. bond market data, indicating a simultaneous increase in default rates and LGDs for the 1999–2002 period.[10] Frye's (2000b, 2000c) empirical analysis allows him to conclude that in a severe economic down-turn, bond recoveries might decline 20–25 percentage points from their normal-year average. Loan recoveries may decline by a similar amount, but from a higher level. In all cases, Frye, and others, compare defaults and recoveries just after default, not the ultimate recovery after the restructuring, or recovery period.

Jarrow (2001) presents a new methodology for estimating RRs and PDs implicit in both debt and equity prices. As in Frye, RRs and PDs are cor-related and depend on the state of the macroeconomy. However, Jarrow's methodology explicitly incorporates equity prices in the estimation pro-cedure, allowing the separate identification of RRs and PDs and the use of an expanded and relevant dataset. In addition to that, the methodology explicitly incorporates a liquidity premium in the estimation procedure, which is considered essential in light of the high variability in the yield spreads between risky debt and U.S. Treasury securities.

Using four different datasets (Moody's Default Risk Service database of bond defaults and LGDs, Society of Actuaries database of private placement defaults and LGDs, Standard & Poor's database of bond defaults and LGDs, and Portfolio Management Data's database of LGDs) ranging from 1970 to 1999, Carey and Gordy (2003) analyse LGD measures and their correlation with default rates. Their preliminary results contrast with the findings of Frye (2000b): estimates of simple default rate-LGD correlation are close to zero. They find, however, that limiting the sample period to 1988–98,

---

[9] Data for the 1970–81 period have been eliminated from the sample period because of the low number of default prices available for the computation of yearly recovery rates.

[10] Hamilton *et al.* (2001) and Altman *et al.* (2003, 2005) provide clear empirical evidence of this phenomenon.

estimated correlations are more in line with Frye's results (0.45 for senior debt and 0.8 for subordinated debt). The authors postulate that during this short period the correlation rises not so much because LGDs are low during the low-default years 1993–6, but rather because LGDs are relatively high during the high-default years 1990 and 1991. They therefore conclude that the basic intuition behind Frye's model may not adequately characterize the relationship between default rates and LGDs. Indeed, a weak or asymmetric relationship suggests that default rates and LGDs may be influenced by different components of the economic cycle.

Using defaulted bonds' data for the sample period 1982–2002, which includes the relatively high-default years of 2000–2, Altman *et al.* (2005), following Altman *et al.* (2001), find empirical results that appear consistent with Frye's intuition: a negative correlation between default rates and RRs. However, they find that the single systematic risk factor – i.e. the performance of the economy – is less predictive than Frye's model would suggest. Their econometric univariate and multivariate models assign a key role to the supply of defaulted bonds (the default rate) and show that this variable, together with variables that proxy the size of the high-yield bond market and the economic cycle, explain a substantial proportion (close to 90%) of the variance in bond recovery rates aggregated across all seniority and collateral levels. They conclude that a simple market mechanism based on supply and demand for the defaulted securities drives aggregate recovery rates more than a macroeconomic model based on the common dependence of default and recovery on the state of the cycle. In high default years, the supply of defaulted securities tends to exceed demand,[11] thereby driving secondary market prices down. This in turn negatively affects RR estimates, as these are generally measured using bond prices shortly after default. During periods of low defaults, as we have observed in the 2004–6 cycle, recoveries increase.

The coincident relationship between high-yield bond default rates and recovery rates is shown in Figure 7.1. This graph shows the association of weighted average default rates and recovery rates over the period 1982–2006, using four bi-variate regression specifications. The actual regressions are based on data from 1982–2003 and the subsequent three years (2004–6) are inserted to show the regressions estimate compared to the actual. Note that

---

[11] Demand mostly comes from niche investors called 'vultures', who intentionally purchase bonds in default. These investors represented a relatively small (perhaps $100 billion) and specialized segment of the debt market. This hedge-fund sector grew considerably, however, in the 2003–6 period, perhaps more than doubling in size (author estimates).

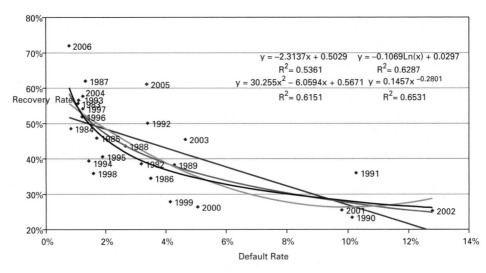

Figure 7.1   Dollar weighted average recovery rates to dollar weighted average default rates (1982–2006)
Source: E. Altman *et al.*, 'The link between default and recovery rates', NYU Salomon Center, S-03-4 and Altman and Ramayanmam (2006).

the degree of explanatory power is excellent with as much as 65% of the variation in aggregate bond recovery rates explained by just one variable – the aggregate default rate. These regressions include linear (53.6%), quadratic (61.5%), log-linear (62.9%) and power function (65.3%) structures. The clear negative relationship between default and recovery rates is striking with periods of excess supply of defaults relative to demand resulting in unusually low recoveries in such years as 1990, 1991, 2001 and 2002.

One can also observe, however, that the most recent years, 2005 and 2006, which are part of an extremely low default cycle, show estimates which are far below the actual results. For example, our model would have predicted an above average recovery rate of about 56% in 2006. Instead, the actual rate was almost 73% as of the end of the third quarter. And the 2005 estimate of about 45% compares to the actual recovery rate of over 60%. Either the model has performed poorly or the default market has been influenced by an unusual amount of excess credit liquidity, and perhaps other factors, which have changed, perhaps temporarily, the dynamics in the credit markets.

A recent report (Altman 2006), argues that there was a type of 'credit bubble' causing seemingly highly distressed firms to remain non-bankrupt when, in more 'normal' periods, many of these firms would have defaulted. This, in turn, produced an abnormally low default rate and the huge liquidity of distressed debt investors bid up the prices of both existing and newly defaulted issues. Time will tell if we will observe a regression to the long-term mean, i.e., lower recoveries, or whether a 'new paradigm' has evolved and the high recoveries will remain.

Using Moody's historical bond market data, Hu and Perraudin (2002) also examine the dependence between recovery rates and default rates. They first standardize the quarterly recovery data in order to filter out the volatility of recovery rates due to changes over time in the pool of rated borrowers. They find that correlations between quarterly recovery rates and default rates for bonds issued by US-domiciled obligors are 0.22 for post-1982 data (1983–2000) and 0.19 for the 1971–2000 periods. Using extreme value theory and other non-parametric techniques, they also examine the impact of this negative correlation on credit VaR measures and find that the increase is statistically significant when confidence levels exceed 99%.

7.7. Correlation results' impact and downturn LGD

The impact of the Altman *et al.* studies of 2001, 2003, as well as the Hu and Perraudin (2002) and Frye (2000a, 2000b, 2000c) studies, was almost immediate, resulting in suggested changes in Basel II's pillar I's guidelines. Specifically, the final BIS Accord (2004) suggested, via its paragraph 468 declaration, a 'downturn', or 'stressed' LGD for banks. According to this document, IRB banks are required to use estimates of LGD parameters, where necessary, to capture the relevant risks. The guidelines were in general terms only and left specific details of the quantification process to supervisors to develop in collaboration with the banking industry. The underlying theory was that recovery rates on defaulted exposures may be lower during economic downturns than during more normal conditions and that a capital rule be realized to guarantee sufficient capital to cover losses during these adverse circumstances. Paragraph 468 also stated that loss severities may not exhibit such cyclical variability, especially if based on ultimate recoveries, and therefore LGD estimates of downturn LGD may not differ materially from the long-run weighted average.

Many banks reacted negatively to this conservative approach and proposed more modest adjustments. Indeed, Araten *et al.* (2004) suggested that correlations are not usually material. All of this discussion and debate resulted in a set of more explicit guidelines and principles in the BIS (2005)

'Guidance on Paragraph 468 of the Framework Document'. In this report, the BIS found (1) that there is a potential for realized recovery rates to be lower than average during times of high default rates and failing to account for this could result in an understatement of the capital required to cover unexpected losses; (2) that data limitations pose a difficult challenge to the estimation of LGD in general and particularly in downturns; and (3) there is little consensus with respect to appropriate methods for incorporating downturn conditions in LGD estimates. The BIS was careful to state that any principles be flexible enough to allow for a range of sound practices and to encourage continued refinements. In other words, while requiring analysis and reports about 'downturn LGD' amongst its members, banks appear to be free to specify if there should be any penalty or not to their average assessments of LGD parameters.

The principles (2005) were that banks must have a rigorous and well documented process for assessing, if any, economic downturn's impact on recovery rates and that this process must consist of (1) the identification of appropriate downturn conditions for each asset class, (2) identification of adverse dependencies, if any, between default and recovery rates and (3) incorporating them to produce LGD estimates. The recovery cash flows should utilize a discount rate that reflects the costs of holding defaulted assets over the workout period, including an appropriate risk premium. These costs should be consistent with the concept of economic loss, not an accounting concept of economic loss (e.g., not the interest rate on the old loan). This can be accomplished either with a discount rate based on the risk-free rate plus a spread appropriate for the risk of recovery and cost of cash flows or by converting the cash flows to certainty equivalents (described in footnote 3 in BIS (2005) and discounting these by the risk-free rate, or by a combination of these adjustments to the discount rate.

By specifically referring to the stream of cash flows over the restructuring period, the BIS, and banks, are embracing the use of ultimate recoveries and not recoveries at the time of default. As such, the correlation between default and recovery rates observed in the bond markets by several researchers, discussed earlier, may not imply a negative correlation between default and ultimate recovery rates. Indeed, there is a timing disconnect which may be important, especially if the distressed loan market is not efficient and the discounted values of ultimate recoveries are materially different from the recovery values at the time of default. Finally, the BIS principles refer to the possibility that stress tests performed under normal expected values of recoveries will not produce different results than downturn LGD estimates under paragraph 468. It remains to be seen how bank regulators will respond to efforts by banks to assess downturn LGD estimates.

One regulator in the United States, the Federal Reserve System, has suggested that IRB banks in the United States use a simple formula to specify downturn LGD, of the form[12]

LGD in Downturn $= .08 + .92$ LGD,

Where LGD $=$ long-term LGD average. So, where the long-term LGD equals, for example, 0.3 (i.e., recovery rates of 0.7), the downturn LGD would increase modestly to 0.33 (about 10%). If this modification were applied to Foundation Basel II banks, not possible in the United States, then the downturn LGD $= 0.494$ on unsecured exposure $(.08 + .92\,(.45) = .494)$, again an increase of about 10% of the normal conditions' expected recovery. For secured loans, the analysis requires a stress test on the collateral itself.

Miu and Ozdemir (2006) analyse this downturn LGD requirement and suggest that the original LGD assessment by banks, without considering PD and RR correlation, can be appropriately adjusted by incorporating a certain degree of conservatism in cyclical LGD estimates within a point-in-time modelling framework. They find even greater impacts on economic capital than even Altman *et al.* (2001) did – with as much as an increase of 35–45% in corporate loan portfolios and 16% for a middle-market portfolio to compensate for the lack of correlations. Altman *et al.* had found, through simulations of loan portfolios, that about 30% needed to be added. Both studies, however, suggest that banks determine these penalties, if any, without abandoning the point-in-time, one-year perspective as to estimating LGD.

Some final references

A number of related studies on LGD can be found in Altman's *et al.* (2005) anthology. These include Chabane's (2004) credit risk assessment of stochastic LGD and correlation effects, Friedman and Sandow's conditional probability distribution analysis of recovery rates, Laurent and Schmit's estimation of distressed LGD on leasing contracts, DeLaurentis and Riani's further analysis of LGD in the leasing industry, Citron and Wright's investigation of recovery rates on distressed management buyouts and Dermine and Neto de Carvalho's empirical investigation of recoveries'

[12] From http://federalreserve.gov/GeneralInfo/Basel2/NPR_20060905/NPR/.

impact on bank provisions. Schuermann provides an overview on what we know and do not know about LGD, as well, in the volume.

Gupton and Stein (2002) analyse the recovery rate on over 1800 corporate bond, loan and preferred stock defaults, from 900 companies, in order to specify and test Moody's LossCalc® model for predicting loss given default (LGD). Their model estimates LGD at two points in time – immediately and in one year – adding a holding period dimension to the analysis. The authors find that their multifactor model, incorporating micro-variables (e.g., debt type, seniority), industry and some macroeconomics factors (e.g., default rates, changes in leading indicators) outperforms traditional historic average methods in predicting LGD.

Using data on observed prices of defaulted securities in the United States over the period 1982–99, Acharya et al. (2003, 2007) (referred to as ABH hereafter) find that seniority and security are important determinants of recovery rates. While this result is not surprising and is in line with previous empirical studies on recoveries, their second main result is rather striking and concerns the effect of industry-specific and macroeconomic conditions in the default year. Indeed, industry conditions at the time of default are found to be robust and important determinants of recovery rates. They show that creditors of defaulted firms recover significantly lower amounts in present-value terms when the industry of defaulted firms is in distress and also when non-defaulted firms are rather illiquid and if their debt is collateralized by specific assets that are not easily redeployable into other sectors. Also, they find that there is little effect of macroeconomic conditions over and above the industry conditions and the latter is robust even with the inclusion of macroeconomic factors. ABH suggest that the linkage, again highlighted by Altman et al. (2005), between bond market aggregate variables and recoveries arises due to supply-side effects in segmented bond markets, and that this may be a manifestation of Shleifer and Vishny's (1992) industry equilibrium effect. That is, macroeconomic variables and bond market conditions may be picking up the effect of omitted industry conditions.

Frye (2000a), Pykhtin (2003) and Dullmann and Trapp (2004) all propose a model that accounts for the dependence of recoveries on systematic risk. They extend the single factor model proposed by Gordy (2000), by assuming that the recovery rate follows a log-normal (Pykhtin, 2003) or a logit-normal (Dullmann and Trapp, 2004) one. The latter study empirically compares the results obtained using the three alternative models (Frye 2000a, Pykhtin

2003, and Dullmann and Trapp 2004). They use time series of default rates and recovery rates from *Standard and Poor's Credit Pro* database, including bond and loan default information in the time period from 1982 to 1999. They find that estimates of recovery rates based on market prices at default are significantly higher than the ones obtained using recovery rates at emergence from restructuring. The findings of this study are in line with previous ones: systematic risk is an important factor that influences recovery rates. The authors show that ignoring this risk component may lead to downward-biased estimates of economic capital.

7.8. Recovery ratings

There has been a debate in the practitioner literature about how recovery rates impact bond ratings ascribed to default risk estimates from the various major rating agencies. One agency, Moody's, has always maintained that it explicitly considered recoveries in the bond rating of a particular corporate issue. Others (S&P and Fitch), typically adjusted, through 'notching', the senior unsecured issuer rating based on whether the particular issue was investment grade or speculative grade given a certain seniority priority. For example, a subordinated issue of an investment grade company was typically 'down-notched' by one notch and a speculative grade issue was penalized by two notches if subordinated. The Moody's assertion was questionable since prior to the 1990s there simply was no reliable database on recoveries available.

Regardless of the 'ancient' approaches used, all three rating agencies have recently recognized the heightened importance of recoveries for a number of applications including Basel II, structured products, the credit default swap market, as well as traditional default analysis, and have introduced 'Recovery Ratings' as a complementary risk rating indicator.

Table 7.1 reviews these 'Recovery Ratings', first introduced by S&P on U. S. senior bank loans in December 2003 and discussed by Chew and Kerr in Altman *et al.* (2005). Fitch then introduced, in late 2005, their recovery analysis on all highly speculative grade issues rated B or below. Finally, Moody's in September 2006 introduced their rating of U.S. non-financial speculative grade issues and expected to do the same in Europe in 2007. We expect that all of the rating agencies will expand their coverage if the market deems this information valuable.

Table 7.1 Recovery ratings from the rating agencies

Agency	Moody's	Standard & Poor's	Fitch
Ratings Type	Loss Given Default Ratings	Recovery Ratings	Recovery Ratings
Ratings Scale	LGD1 0–9%	1+ 100%	RR1 91–100%
	LGD2 10–29%	1 100%	RR2 71–90%
	LGD3 30–49%	2 80–100%	RR3 51–70%
	LGD4 50–69%	3 50–80%	RR4 31–50%
	LGD5 70–89%	4 25–50%	RR5 11–30%
	LGD6 90–100%	5 0–25%	RR6 0–10%
Assets Rated	Non-financial corporate speculative-grade issuers in the US	US and Canadian secured bank loans to which it assigns bank loan ratings, to senior secured loans in Europe, and to any secured bonds issued along with rated bank loans	All corporate, financial institutions and sovereign issuers rated in the single B category and below
Methodology	1. Establish priority of claim a. Jr bonds are subordinated to Sr bonds, but may or may not be subordinated to other unsecured obligations b. Prioritize claims across affiliates 2. Assume a beta probability distribution for potential Enterprise Value (EV) outcomes	1. Review transaction structure 2. Review borrower's projections 3. Establish simulated path to default 4. Forecast borrower's free cash flow at default based on our simulated default scenario and default proxy 5. Determine valuation 6. Identify priority debt claims and value	1. Estimate the enterprise value (EV) a. Establish the level of cash flow upon which it is most appropriate to base the valuation b. Apply a multiple reflecting a company's relative position within a sector based on actual or expected market and/or distressed multiples

a. For most issuers, assume a beta distribution of EV relative to total liabilities

b. Corporate LGD distribution will have 50% mean and 26% standard deviation

3. For each EV outcome, calculate LGDs for each security class implied by absolute priority 4. Expected LGD equals the probability-weighted averages of LGDs across EV outcomes

7. Determine collateral value available to lenders

8. Assign recovery rating

9. Convey the recovery analytics to the issuer and investment community

2. Estimate the creditor mass, ie identify existing claims

a. Claims taken on as a company's fortunes deteriorate

b. Claims necessary to the reorganization process

c. Claims that have priority in the relevant bankruptcy code

3. Distributing the EV

a. The resulting value is allocated to creditors according to jurisdictional practice

Source: Moody's S&P and Fitch.

As shown in Table 7.1, each of the recovery rating classes, six in each case, has a quantitative estimate of the proportion of the issue that can be expected to be recovered given a default. These range from as high as 100% down to estimates of 0–10%. In addition to the recovery percentage estimates, Table 7.1 reviews each rating agency's methodology for arriving at their estimate. Fundamental valuation techniques are employed followed by priority analysis of each issue under consideration.

In all cases, the recovery ratings are available in addition to the traditional default ratings. It remains to be seen as to the market's acceptance of this second set of ratings and whether they will form a material part of their investment decisions.

7.9. Recovery rates and procyclicality

Altman *et al.* (2003) also highlight the implications of their results for credit risk modelling and for the issue of procyclicality[13] of capital requirements. In order to assess the impact of a negative correlation between default rates and recovery rates on credit risk models, they run Monte Carlo simulations on a sample portfolio of bank loans and compare the key risk measures (expected and unexpected losses). They show that both the expected loss and the unexpected loss are vastly understated if one assumes that PDs and RRs are uncorrelated.[14] Therefore, credit models that do not carefully factor in the negative correlation between PDs and RRs might lead to insufficient bank reserves and cause unnecessary shocks to financial markets.

As far as procyclicality is concerned, they show that this effect tends to be exacerbated by the correlation between PDs and RRs: low recovery rates when defaults are high would amplify cyclical effects. This would especially be true under the so-called 'advanced' IRB approach, where banks are free to estimate their own recovery rates and might tend to revise them downwards when defaults increase and ratings worsen. The impact of such a mechanism was also assessed by Resti (2002), based on simulations over a 20-year

---

[13] Procyclicality involves the sensitivity of regulatory capital requirements to economic and financial market cycles. Since ratings and default rates respond to the cycle, the new internal ratings-based (IRB) approach proposed by the Basel Committee risks increasing capital charges, and limiting credit supply, when the economy is slowing (the reverse being true when the economy is growing at a fast rate).

[14] Both expected losses and VaR measures associated with different confidence levels tend to be underestimated by approximately 30%.

period, using a standard portfolio of bank loans (the composition of which is adjusted through time according to S&P transition matrices). Two main results emerged from this simulation exercise: (i) the procyclicality effect is driven more by up- and downgrades, rather than by default rates; in other words, adjustments in credit supply needed to comply with capital requirements respond mainly to changes in the structure of weighted assets, and only to a lesser extent to actual credit losses (except in extremely high default years); (ii) when RRs are permitted to fluctuate with default rates, the procyclicality effect increases significantly.

7.10. Further empirical evidence

This section focuses on different measurements and the most recent empirical evidence of default recovery rates. Most credit risk models utilize historical average empirical estimates, combined with their primary analytical specification of the probability of default, to arrive at the all-important Loss-Given-Default (LGD) input. Since very few financial institutions have ample data on recovery rates by asset-type and by type of collateral, model builders and analysts responsible for Basel II inputs into their internal rate based (IRB) models begin with estimates from public bond and private bank loan markets. Of course, some banks will research their own internal databases in order to conform to the requirements of the Advanced IRB approach.

Early empirical evidence

Published data on default recovery rates generally, but not always, use secondary market bond or bank loan prices. The first empirical study, that we are aware of, that estimated default recovery rates was in Altman's *et al.* (1977) ZETA® model's adjustment of the optimal cutoff score in their second-generation credit scoring model. Interestingly, these bank loan recovery estimates did not come from the secondary loan trading market – they did not exist then – but from a survey of bank workout-department experience (1971–5). The general conclusion from this early experience of these departments was a recovery rate on non-performing, unsecured loans of only about 30% of the loan amount plus accrued interest. The cash inflows for three years post-default was not discounted back to default date. We will refer to this experience as the 'ultimate nominal recovery' since it utilizes post-default recoveries, usually from the end of the restructuring period.

In later studies, ultimate recovery rates refer to the nominal or discounted value of bonds or loans based on either the price of the security at the end of the reorganization period (usually Chapter 11) or the value of the package of cash or securities upon emergence from restructuring. For example, Altman and Eberhart (1994) observed the price performance of defaulted bonds, stratified by seniority, at the time of the restructuring emergence as well as the discounted value of these prices. They concluded that the most senior bonds in the capital structure (senior secured and senior unsecured) did very well in the post-default period (20–30% per annum returns) but the more junior bonds (senior subordinated and subordinated) did poorly, barely breaking even on a nominal basis and losing money on a discounted basis. Similar, but less extreme, results were found by Fridson *et al.*, Merrill Lynch (2000) when they updated (1994–2000) Altman and Eberhart's (1994) earlier study which covered the period 1981–93.

Other studies that analysed bank loans recovery rates were by Asarnow and Edwards (1995) and Eales and Bosworth (1998). The first study presents the results of an analysis of losses on bank-loan defaults based on 24 years of data compiled by Citibank; their database comprises 831 commercial and industrial (C&I) loans, as well as 89 structured loans (highly collateralized loans that contain many restrictive covenants). Their results (based on 'ultimate' recoveries) indicate a LGD of about 35% for C&I loans (with larger loans, above US$10 million, showing a somewhat lower loss rate of 29%); unsurprisingly, the LGD for structured loans is considerably lower (13%), due to the role played by collateral and covenants in supporting the early default-detection and recovery processes. In the second study, the authors report the empirical results on recovery rates from a foreign bank operating in the United States – Westpac Banking Corporation. The study focuses on small business loans and larger consumer loans, such as home loans and investment property loans.

Neto de Carvalho and Dermine (2003) analyse the determinants of loss given default rates using a portfolio of credits given by the largest private Portuguese bank, Banco Comercial Portugues. Their study is based on a sample of 371 defaulted loans to small and medium size companies, originally granted during the period June 1985–December 2000. The estimates of recovery rates are based on the discounted cash flows recovered after the default event. The authors report three main empirical results which are consistent with previous empirical evidence: (i) the frequency distribution of loan losses given default is bi-modal, with many cases presenting a 0% recovery and other cases presenting a 100% recovery, (ii) the size of the loan has a statistically significant negative impact on the recovery rate, (iii) while the type of collateral is statistically significant in determining the recovery, this is not the case for the age of the bank–company relationship.

More recent evidence

In Table 7.2, we present recent empirical evidence on bank loan recoveries (Emery *et al.*, Moody's 2006) and on corporate bonds by seniority (Altman and Ramayanam 2006) based on the average prices of these securities just after the date of default. Not surprisingly, the highest median recovery rates were on senior secured bank loans (73.0%) followed by senior secured bonds (59.1%).[15] Although the data from Moody's and Altman were from different periods and samples, it is interesting to note that the recovery on senior unsecured bonds (45.4%) was similar, but lower than senior unsecured bank loans (49.3%), with similar standard deviations. The estimates of median recoveries on the senior-subordinated and subordinated bonds were very similar. Similar recoveries on defaulted bonds can be found in Varma *et al.* (Moody's 2003). For example, Altman and Ramayanam's value weighted mean recovery rate on over 2000 bond default issues was 37.7% compared to Moody's value weighted mean of 33.8% and issuer-weighted mean of 35.4% on 1,239 issues.

Altman and Ramayanam (2007) further breakdown bond recoveries just after the default date by analysing recoveries based on the original rating (fallen angels vs. original rating non-investment grade ('junk') bonds) of different seniorities. For example, in Table 7.3, we observe that senior-secured bonds, that were originally rated investment grade, recovered a median rate of 50.5% vs. just 38.0% for the same seniority bonds that were non-investment grade when issued. These are statistically significant differences for similar seniority securities. Since fallen-angel defaults are much more prominent in some years in the United States (e.g., close to 50% in dollar amount of defaults in 2001 and 2002 were fallen angels prior to default), these statistics are quite meaningful. The median differential was just as great (43.5% vs. 31.2%) for senior unsecured bonds. Note that for

---

[15] Interestingly, the comparable median for defaults through 2003 was about 4.5% lower (54.5%), showing the considerable increase in default recovery rates on bonds in the period 2004–6.

Table 7.2 Recovery at default* on public corporate bonds (1978–2006) and bank loans (1989–2Q 2006)

Loan/Bond Seniority	Number of Issues	Median %	Mean %	Standard Deviation %
Senior Secured Loans	260	73.00	69.20	24.60
Senior Unsecured Loans	48	49.20	51.10	25.20
Senior Secured Bonds	330	59.00	59.50	27.70
Senior Unsecured Bonds	1012	45.40	36.70	24.40
Senior Subordinated Bonds	409	32.70	30.30	24.00
Subordinated Bonds	249	31.00	31.10	25.70
Discount Bonds	156	19.80	25.90	20.20
Total Sample Bonds	**2,156**	**41.77**	**37.65**	**25.56**

* Based on prices just after default on bonds and 30 days after default on losses.
Source: Moody's (Emery 2006) (Bank Loans) and Altman & Ramayanam, 2007 (Bonds).

Table 7.3 Investment grade vs. non-investment grade (original rating) prices at default on public bonds (1978–3Q 2006)

Bond Seniority	Number of Issues	Median Price %	Average Price %	Weighted Price %	Standard Deviation %
Senior Secured					
Investment Grade	134	50.50	54.91	59.63	25.62
Non-Investment Grade	263	38.00	41.58	42.02	27.39
Senior Unsecured					
Investment Grade	320	43.50	47.47*	46.38*	25.47
Non-Investment Grade	566	31.15	35.52	33.88	22.92
Senior Subordinated					
Investment Grade	15	28.00	38.91	36.36	27.44
Non-Investment Grade	396	27.50	32.4	29.14	23.81
Subordinated					
Investment Grade	10	35.69	37.67	25.29	32.99
Non-Investment Grade	214	29.00	32.03	28.77	22.30
Discount					
Investment Grade	1	13.63	13.63	13.63	–
Non-investment Grade	116	17.67	23.88	26.43	20.34
Total Sample	**2035**	**33**	**37.46**	**34.8**	**25.17**

* Including WorldCom, the Average and Weighted Average were 44.96% and 34.34% Non-rated issues were considered as non-investment grade.
Source: Moody's S&P and Fitch.

Table 7.4 Ultimate recovery rates on bank loan and bond defaults (discounted values, 1988–2Q 2006)

	Observations	Ultimate Discounted Recovery	Standard Deviation	Ultimate Nominal Recovery(1)
All Bank Debt	1324	77.20%	31.10%	87.32%
Secured Bank Debt	*1205*	*78.50%*	*30.00%*	n.a.
Unsecured Bank Debt	*119*	*64.20%*	*38.20%*	n.a.
Senior Secured Bonds	320	62.00%	32.90%	76.03%
Senior Unsecured Bonds	863	43.80%	35.10%	59.29%
Senior Subordinated Bonds	489	30.50%	34.10%	38.41%
Subordinated Bonds	399	28.80%	34.00%	34.81%

(1) 1998–2Q 2006.

Source: Standard & Poor's LossStates™ Database, 3395 defaulted loans and bond issues that defaulted between 1987–3Q 2006. Recoveries are discounted at each instruments' pre-default interest rate.

senior-subordinated and subordinated bonds, however, the rating at issuance is of little consequence, although the sample sizes for investment grade, low seniority bonds were very small. Varma *et al.* (2003) also conclude that the higher the rating prior to default, including the rating at issuance, the higher the average recovery rate at default. Apparently, the quality of assets and the structure of the defaulting company's balance sheets favour higher recoveries for higher quality original issue bonds.

In Table 7.4, we again return to the data on ultimate recoveries, only this time the results are from Standard & Poor's (2006) assessment of bank loan and bond recoveries. These results show the nominal and discounted (by the loan's pre-default interest rate) ultimate recovery at the end of the restructuring period for well over 3,000 defaulted loans and bonds over the period 1988–2006. Several items are of interest. First, the recovery on senior bank debt, which is mainly secured, was quite high at 87.3% and 77.2% for nominal and discounted values respectively. Senior secured and senior unsecured notes, which include loans and bonds, had lower recoveries and the more junior notes (almost all bonds) had, not surprisingly, the lowest recoveries. Note that the differential between the nominal and discounted recovery rates diminishes somewhat at the lower seniority levels.

Standard & Poor's (Keisman 2004) also finds, not shown in any table, that during the most recent 'extreme stress' default years of 1998 to 2002, the recovery rates on all seniorities declined compared to their longer

1988–2002 sample period. Since 1998 and 1999 were not really high default years, the results of S&P for 2000–2 are consistent with Altman's *et al.* (2001, 2003) predictions of an inverse relationship between default and recovery rates. Indeed, recovery rates were a relatively low 25% in the corporate bond market for both 2001 and 2002 when default rates were in the double-digits but increased to over 70% in 2006 when default rates tumbled to well below average annual levels (Altman and Ramayanam 2007).

Some recovery studies have concentrated on rates across different industries. Altman and Kishore (1996) and FITCH (2003) report a fairly high variance across industrial sectors. For Example, Verde (FITCH 2003) reports that recovery rates in 2001 vs. 2002 varied dramatically from one year to the next (e.g., Gaming, Lodging and Restaurants recovered 16% in 2001 and 77% in 2002, Retail recovered 7% in 2001 and 48% in 2002, while Transportation recovered 31% in 2001 and 19% in 2002) but returned to more normal levels in 2003.

Another issue highlighted in some studies, especially those from S&P (e.g., Van de Castle and Keisman 1999 and Keisman 2004) is that an important determinant of ultimate recovery rates is the amount that a given seniority has junior liabilities below its level; the greater the proportion of junior securities, the higher the recovery rate on the senior trenches. The theory being that the greater the 'equity cushion', the more likely there will be assets of value, which under absolute priority, go first in liquidation or reorganization to the more senior trenches.

7.11. Concluding remarks

Table 7.5 summarizes the way RR and its relationship with PD are dealt with in the different credit models described in the previous sections of this paper. While, in the original Merton (1974) framework, an inverse relationship between PD and RR exists, the credit risk models developed during the 1990s treat these two variables as independent. The currently available and most-used credit pricing and credit VaR models are indeed based on this independence assumption and treat RR either as a constant parameter or as a stochastic variable independent from PD. In the latter case, RR volatility is assumed to represent an idiosyncratic risk which can be eliminated through adequate portfolio diversification. This assumption strongly contrasts with the growing empirical evidence – showing a negative correlation between default and recovery rates – that has been reported in the

Table 7.5 The treatment of LGD and default rates within different credit risk models

	Main models & related empirical studies	Treatment of LGD	Relationship between RR and PD
Credit Pricing Models			
First-generation structural-form models	Merton (1974), Black and Cox (1976), Geske (1977), Vasicek (1984), Jones, Mason and Rosenfeld (1984).	PD and RR are a function of the structural characteristics of the firm. RR is therefore an endogenous variable.	PD and RR are inversely related (see Appendix A).
Second-generation structural-form models	Kim, Ramaswamy and Sundaresan (1993), Nielsen, Saà-Requejo, Santa Clara (1993), Hull and White (1995), Longstaff and Schwartz (1995).	RR is exogenous and independent from the firm's asset value.	RR is generally defined as a fixed ratio of the outstanding debt value and is therefore independent from PD.
Reduced-form models	Litterman and Iben (1991), Madan and Unal (1995), Jarrow and Turnbull (1995), Jarrow, Lando and Turnbull (1997), Lando (1998), Duffie and Singleton (1999), Duffie (1998) and Duffee (1999).	Reduced-form models assume an exogenous RR that is either a constant or a stochastic variable independent from PD.	Reduced-form models introduce separate assumptions on the dynamic of PD and RR, which are modeled independently from the structural features of the firm.
Latest contributions on the PD–RR relationship	Frye (2000a and 2000b), Jarrow (2001), Carey and Gordy (2003),	Both PD and RR are stochastic variables which depend on a	PD and RR are negatively correlated. In the 'macroeconomic

Table 7.5 (cont.)

	Main models & related empirical studies	Treatment of LGD	Relationship between RR and PD
	Altman, Brady, Resti and Sironi (2003 and 2005), Acharya Bharath and Srinivasan (2003, 2007), Miu and Ozdemir (2006).	common systematic risk factor (the state of the economy).	approach' this derives from the common dependence on one single systematic factor. In the 'microeconomic approach' it derives from the supply and demand of defaulted securities. Industry health is also a major factor. Downturn LGD studies.
Credit Value at Risk Models			
CreditMetrics®	Gupton, Finger and Bhatia (1997).	Stochastic variable (beta distr.)	RR independent from PD
CreditPortfolioView®	Wilson (1998).	Stochastic variable	RR independent from PD
CreditRisk+®	Credit Suisse Financial Products (1997).	Constant	RR independent from PD
PortfolioManager®	Crosbie (1999).	Stochastic variable	RR independent from PD

202

previous section of this paper and in other empirical studies. This evidence indicates that recovery risk is a systematic risk component. As such, it should attract risk premia and should adequately be considered in credit risk management applications.

Empirical results, especially demonstrated by historical record levels of recovery in the extreme benign credit environment of 2004–6, show the potential cyclical impact as well as the supply and demand elements of defaults and recoveries on LGD. Finally, we feel that the microeconomic/ financial attributes of an individual issuer of bonds or loans combined with the market's aggregate supply and demand conditions can best explain the recovery rate at default on a particular defaulting issue. An even greater challenge is to accurately estimate the ultimate recovery rate on individual issue as well as aggregate recoveries when the firm emerges from its restructuring.

REFERENCES

Acharya, V. V., Bharath, S. T. and Srinivasan, A., 'Understanding the recovery rates on defaulted securities', *Working Paper*, London Business School, 2003.

Acharya, V. V., Bharath, S. T. and Srinivasan, A., 'Does industry-wide distress affect defaulted firms – evidence from creditor recoveries', *Journal of Political Economy*, 2007 (forthcoming).

Altman, E., 'Measuring corporate bond mortality and performance', *Journal of Finance*, 44, 1989, 909–22.

Altman, E. and Eberhart, A., 'Do seniority provisions protect bondholders' investments', *Journal of Portfolio Management*, Summer, 1994, 67–75.

Altman, E. I., 'Are historically based default and recovery models still relevant in today's credit environment', *NYU Salomon Center Special Report*, October, 2006.

Altman, E. I., Brady, B., Resti, A. and Sironi, A., 'The link between default and recovery rates: theory, empirical evidence and implications', *NYU Salomon Center Working Paper Series #S–03–4*, 2003; *Journal of Business*, 78(6), 2005, 2203–27.

Altman, E., Haldeman R. and Narayanan, P., 'ZETA analysis: a new model to identify bankruptcy risk of corporations', *Journal of Banking & Finance*, 1(1), 1977, 29–54.

Altman, E. I. and Kishore, V. M., 'Almost everything you wanted to know about recoveries on defaulted bonds', *Financial Analysts Journal*, November/December, 1996, 57–64.

Altman, E. and Ramayanam, S., 'The high-yield bond default and return report: third-quarter 2006 review', *NYU Salomon Center Special Report* (November, 2006) and *2006 Annual Report*, January, 2007.

Altman, E. I., Resti, A. and Sironi, A., 'Analyzing and explaining default recovery rates', *ISDA Research Report*, London, December, 2001.

Altman, E. I., Resti, A. and Sironi, A., *Recovery Risk*, Risks Books, London, 2005.

Araten, M., Jacobs, M. and Varshny, P., 'Measuring LGD on commercial loans', *The RMA Journal*, May, 2004.

Asarnow, E. and Edwards, D., 'Measuring loss on defaulted bank loans: a 24 year study', *Journal of Commercial Bank Lending*, 77(7), 1995, 11–23.

Bakshi, G., Madan, D. and Zhang, F., *Understanding the Role of Recovery in Default Risk Models: Empirical Comparisons and Implied Recovery Rates*, Finance and Economics Discussion Series, Washington, DC. Federal Reserve Board of Governors, 2001, pp. 2001–37.

Basel Commission on Bank Regulation, International Convergence on Capital Measurement and Capital Standards, *BIS*, June, 2004.

Basel Commission on Bank Regulation, Guidance on Paragraph 468 of the Framework Document, *BIS*, July, 2005.

Black, F. and Cox, J. C., 'Valuing corporate securities: some effects of bond indenture provisions', *Journal of Finance*, 31, 1976, 351–67.

Black, F. and Scholes, M., 'The pricing of options and corporate liabilities', *Journal of Political Economics*, May, 1973, 637–59.

Carey, M. and Gordy, M., 'Systematic risk in recoveries on defaulted debt', *Mimeo*, Washington: Federal Reserve Board, 2003.

Chabane, A., Laurent, J.-P. and Salomon, J., 'Double impact: credit risk assessment and collateral value', *Revue Finance*, 25, 2004, 157–78.

CreditRisk+. A Credit Risk Management Framework, Technical Document, Credit Suisse Financial Products, 1997.

Crosbie, P. J., 'Modeling Default Risk', Mimeo, San Francisco, CA, KMV Corporation, 1999.

Crouhy, M., Galai, D. and Mark, R., 'A comparative analysis of current credit risk models', *Journal of Banking & Finance*, 24, 2000, 59–117.

Duffee, G. R., 'Estimating the price of default risk', *Review of Financial Studies*, Spring, 12(1), 1999, 197–225.

Duffie, D., 'Defaultable term structure models with fractional recovery of par', Writing Paper, Graduate School of Business, Stanford University, 1998.

Duffie, D. and Singleton, K. J., 'Modeling the term structures of defaultable bonds', *Review of Financial Studies*, 12, 1999, 687–720.

Duffie, D. and Lando, D., 'Term structure of credit spreads with incomplete accounting information', *Econometrica*, 2000.

Dullman, K. and Trapp, M., 'Systematic risk in recovery rates – an empirical analysis of U.S. corporate credit exposures', *EFWA Basel Paper*, 2004.

Eales, R. and Bosworth, E., 'Severity of loss in the event of default in small business and large consumer loans', *Journal of Lending and Credit Risk Management*, May, 1998, 58–65.

Emery, K., *Moody's Loan Default Database as of November 2003*, Moody's Investors Service, December, 2003.

Eom, Y. H., Helwege J. and Huang, J.-Z., 'Structural models of corporate bond pricing: an empirical analysis', *Mimeo*, 2001.

Finger, C., Conditional approaches for creditmetrics® portfolio distributions, *CreditMetrics® Monitor*, April, 1999.

Franks, J., and Torous, W., 'A comparison of financial recontracting in distressed exchanges and Chapter 11 reorganizations', *Journal of Financial Economics*, 35, 1994, 349–70.

Fridson, M. S., Garman C. M. and Okashima, K., 'Recovery Rates: The Search for Meaning', Merrill Lynch & Co., High Yield Strategy, 2000.

Frye, J., 'Collateral damage', *Risk*, April, 2000a, 91–4.

Frye, J., 'Collateral damage detected', *Federal Reserve Bank of Chicago Working Paper*, Emerging Issues Series, October, 2000b, 1–14.

Frye, J., 'Depressing Recoveries', *Risk*, November, 2000c.

Geske, R., 'The valuation of corporate liabilities as compound options', *Journal of Financial and Quantitative Analysis*, 12, 1977, 541–52.

Gordy, M., 'A comparative anatomy of credit risk models', *Journal of Banking and Finance*, January, 2000, 119–49.

Gupton, G., Finger, C. and Bhatia, M., *CreditMetrics™ Technical Document*, New York, J. P. Morgan, 1997.

Gupton, G. M., Gates, D. and Carty, L. V., *Bank Loan Loss Given Default*, Moody's Investors Service, Global Credit Research, November, 2000.

Gupton, G. M. and Stein, R. M., *LossCalc: Moody's Model for Predicting Loss Given Default (LGD)*, New York, Moody's KMV, 2002.

Hamilton, D. T., Gupton G. M. and Berthault, A., *Default and Recovery Rates of Corporate Bond Issuers: 2000*, Moody's Investors Service, February, 2001.

Hu, Y.-T. and Perraudin, W., 'The dependence of recovery rates and defaults', *Birkbeck College Mimeo*; February, and *CEPR Working Paper*, 2002.

Hull, J. and White, A., 'The impact of default risk on the prices of options and other derivative securities', *Journal of Banking and Finance*, 19, 1995, 299–322.

Jarrow, R. A., 'Default parameter estimation using market prices', *Financial Analysts Journal*, 57(5), 2001, 75–92.

Jarrow, R. A., Lando, D. and Turnbull, S. M., 'A Markov model for the term structure of credit risk spreads', *Review of Financial Studies*, 10, 1997, 481–523.

Jarrow, R. A. and Turnbull, S. M., 'Pricing derivatives on financial securities subject to credit risk', *Journal of Finance*, 50, 1995, 53–86.

Jokivuolle, E. and Peura, S., 'A model for estimating recovery rates and collateral haircuts for bank loans', *European Financial Management*, 2003, forthcoming.

Jones, E., Mason, S. and Rosenfeld, E., 'Contingent claims analysis of corporate capital structures: an empirical investigation', *Journal of Finance*, 39, 1984, 611–27.

Keisman, D., 'Ultimate recovery rates on bank loan and bond defaults,' *Loss Stats*, S&P, 2004.

Kim, I. J., Ramaswamy, K. and Sundaresan, S., 'Does default risk in coupons affect the valuation of corporate bonds a contingent claims model', *Financial Management*, 22(3), 1993, 117–31.

Lando, D., 'On Cox processes and credit risky securities', *Review of Derivatives Research*, 2, 1998, 99–120.

Litterman, R. and Iben, T., 'Corporate bond valuation and the term structure of credit spreads', *Financial Analysts Journal*, Spring, 1991, 52–64.

Longstaff, F. A., and Schwartz, E. S., 'A simple approach to valuing risky fixed and floating rate debt', *Journal of Finance*, 50, 1995, 789–819.

Madan, D. and Unal, H., 'Pricing the risks of default', *Review of Derivatives Research*, 2, 1995, 121–60.

Merton, R. C., 'On the pricing of corporate debt: the risk structure of interest rates', *Journal of Finance*, 2, 1974, 449–71.

Miu, P. and Ozdemir, B., 'Basel requirements of downturn loss-given-default: modeling and estimating probability of default and LGD correlations,' *Journal of Credit Risk*, 2(2), 2006, 43–68.

Neto de Carvalho and Dermine, J., 'Bank loan losses-given-default – empirical evidence', *Working Paper*, INSEAD, 2003.

Nielsen, L. T., Saà-Requejo, J. and Santa-Clara, P., 'Default risk and interest rate risk: the term structure of default spreads', *Working Paper*, INSEAD, 1993.

Pykhtin, M., 'Unexpected recovery risk', *Risk*, 16, 2003, 74–8.

Resti, A., *The New Basel Capital Accord: Structure, Possible Changes, Micro- and Macro-economic Effects*, Centre for European Policy Studies, Brussels, 2002.

Schleifer, A. and Vishny, R., 'Liquidation values and debt capacity: a market equilibrium approach', *Journal of Finance*, 47, 1992, 1343–66.

Schuermann, T., 'What do we know about loss given default', *Working Paper*, Federal Reserve Bank of New York, 2004; also in D. Shimko (eds.), *Credit Risk Models and Management*, 2nd edition, London, Risk Books, 2006.

Van de Castle, K. and Keisman, D., 'Suddenly structure mattered: insights into recoveries of defaulted,' *Corporate Ratings*, S&P, May 24, 1999.

Varma, P., Cantor R. and Hamilton, D., *Recovery Rates on Defaulted Corporate Bonds and Preferred Stocks*, Moody's Investors Service, December, 2003.

Vasicek, O. A., *Credit Valuation*, KMV Corporation, March, 1984.

Verde, M., 'Recovery rates return to historic norms', *FITCH Ratings*, September, 2003.

Wilson, T. C., 'Portfolio credit risk', Federal Reserve Board of New York, *Economic Policy Review*, October, 1998, 71–82.

Zhou, C., 'The term structure of credit spreads with jump risk', *Journal of Banking & Finance*, 25, 2001, 2015–40.

8 Credit derivatives: Current practices and controversies

Stewart Jones and Maurice Peat

8.1. Introduction

In this chapter we explore the rapid growth of the credit derivatives market over the past decade, including the most important economic and regulatory factors which have contributed to this growth. We explain and contrast a wide range of credit derivative instruments, including credit default swaps, credit linked notes, collateralized debt obligations (CDOs) and synthetic CDOs. Credit default swaps and synthetic CDOs have evidenced the greatest growth in recent years as these have emerged (inter alia) as a highly effective tool for hedging credit risk exposure and providing investors with a wide range of new investment and diversification opportunities. While many prominent commentators have touted the wide reaching benefits of credit derivatives in the financial markets, others have taken a more cautious view and have expressed concerns about the potential threats to financial stability when risk is too widely spread throughout the economy, particularly to counterparties who may not be subject to the same level of regulatory scrutiny as banking institutions. Other concerns have been voiced that credit derivative markets have not been tested in a serious economic downturn. This 'test' seems to have come a little sooner than expected with the 'sub-prime' meltdown in the United States, which first came into public prominence from June 2007. The sub-prime crisis had an immediate and devastating impact on world equity and debt markets generally, and credit derivative markets in particular. At the heart of the sub-prime collapse were the escalating default rates on sub-prime mortgages in the United States, which caused a sudden and rapid deterioration in the value of many CDOs, particularly those instruments having significant exposure the sub-prime lending market. Finally, this chapter examines credit derivative pricing models, including some implications for pricing which can be dependent on particular default probability methodology being selected.

As noted by Das (2005), credit derivatives are 'a class of financial instrument, the value of which is derived from the underlying market value driven by the credit risk of private or government entities other than the counterparties to the credit derivative transaction itself' (p. 6). The key feature of credit derivatives is the separation of credit risk, facilitating the trading of credit risk with the purpose of (a) replicating credit risk, (b) transferring credit risk, and (c) hedging credit risk (see Das 2005, p. 6).

Credit derivatives are commonly defined as a derivative contract which allows one party, the protection *buyer* or originator, to transfer defined credit risks of a reference asset or reference portfolio (such as a loan or bond or portfolio of loans or bonds) to one or more other counterparties, the protection *sellers*. The counterparty could be a market participant, such as a bank or insurance company, or it could be capital markets, through a process of securitization. In this situation, the counterparty to the transaction effectively becomes a synthetic lender e.g., the loan continues to be held on the accounts of the holder or originator, but the risks of default are effectively transferred to the counterparty.

The protection seller receives a periodic premium in return for incurring a contractual obligation to make payments to the protection buyer following a specified *credit event*. Credit default swaps, the most common form of credit derivative, are analogous to how an insurance contract might work. Consider an investor who takes a view on the Ford Motor company and believes the probability of Ford filing for bankruptcy protection over the next two years is very remote. As a result, the investor is willing to accept the potential default risk from Ford in exchange for a periodic payment. In exchange for taking on the risk of Ford defaulting, the protection seller (akin to the insurer) is contractually obliged to the protection buyer to make good any financial losses incurred should the company actually file for bankruptcy over the period of the default swap (either through cash settlement or through physical settlement of the underlying debt instrument).

Credit events are not confined to bankruptcy filings. Parties to a credit default swap contract can define any number of potential credit events – but in most cases parties to a credit default swap will use the master agreements sponsored by the International Swaps and Derivatives Association's (ISDA). The main advantage of using ISDA master agreements is that they can significantly reduce setup and negotiation costs in derivative contracts. Credit events are part of 1999 Credit Derivative Definitions which were revised in 2003 (published by ISDA on 11 February 2003). The Definitions are standard industry terms which are typically incorporated by contracting parties in their derivative agreements, and include the following definitions (see Harding 2004 for a detailed overview).

1. *Bankruptcy* (which is widely drafted by the ISDA to include a variety of events associated with bankruptcy or insolvency proceedings under English law and New York law).

2. *Obligation Acceleration* (which covers the situation, other than a Failure to Pay, where the relevant obligation becomes due and payable as a result of a default by the reference entity[1] before the time when such obligation would otherwise have been due and payable). For example, a breach of a covenant on one debt instrument by a company may make it possible for other obligations to be accelerated.

3. *Obligation Default* (covers the situation, other than a Failure to Pay, where the relevant obligation becomes capable of being declared due and payable as a result of a default by the reference entity before the time when such obligation would otherwise have been capable of being so declared).

4. *Failure to Pay* (this is defined to be a failure of the reference entity to make, when and where due, any payments under one or more obligations).

5. *Repudiation/Moratorium* (repudiation/moratorium deals with the situation where the reference entity or a governmental authority disaffirms, disclaims or otherwise challenges the validity of the relevant obligation. A default requirement threshold is specified).

6. *Restructuring* (under the 1999 definitions, restructuring covers events as a result of which the terms, as agreed by the reference entity or governmental authority and the holders of the relevant obligation, governing the relevant obligation have become less favourable to the holders than they would otherwise have been. These events include a reduction in the principal amount or interest payable under the obligation, a postponement of payment, a change in ranking in priority of payment or any other composition of payment. Under the 2003 revisions, parties to a credit derivatives transaction now have the choice of one of four alternative approaches in relation to the restructuring credit event.[2]

---

[1] That is the entity in respect of which credit protection is sold.

[2] These options include: (a) not to use Restructuring (i.e. a practice in Japan), (b) use Restructuring 'as is' (i.e. under the provisions under 1999 Credit Derivatives Definitions outlined above), (c) 'Modified' Restructuring (or 'Mod R' i.e. the position under the Restructuring Supplement Restructuring Supplement of the Credit Derivatives Market

8.2. Types of credit derivatives

Single-Name and Multi-Name Instruments. Single-name credit derivatives are the most common and provide protection against default by a single reference entity. Multi-name credit derivatives are contracts that are contingent on default events in a pool of reference entities, such as a portfolio of bank loans. The two most common forms of credit derivative products are replication products (such as total return swaps and credit spread transactions) and credit default products (such as credit default swaps). Furthermore, credit derivatives (such as credit default swaps) can be combined with other structured credit products to create financial instruments such as synthetic collateralized debt obligations and credit linked notes (see Bomfim 2005 and Gregory 2004 for discussion). Before discussing some broader issues relating to credit derivative markets, we first provide a brief description of each of these products.

Total return swap

In a total return swap, the investor (total return receiver) receives the total return generated by any credit asset including any capital gains accrued over the life of the swap. The credit asset may be any asset, index, or basket of assets (most TRORS, however, are on traded bonds and loans). The investor never actually takes possession of the reference asset. In return, the investor pays the owner of the asset (the total return payer) the set rate (either fixed or variable) over the life of the swap. If the price of the assets happens to depreciate over the duration of the swap contract, the investor will then be contractually obliged to compensate the asset owner for the full amount of the capital loss. A TRORS thus exposes the investor to all risks associated with the credit asset – credit risk, interest rate risk and other risks. TRORS have been widely used on bank loans, which do not have a liquid repo market.[3] TRORS allow one party to derive the same economic benefit as an ownership interest in the asset while keeping it off balance sheet, but allows

---

Practice Committee, dated 11 May 2001), (d) 'Modified Modified' Restructuring (or 'Mod Mod R'). Mod R is generally favoured in North America while Mod Mod R, is used more in the European markets. The main differences between these two approaches are in (i) the final maturity date of the Deliverable Obligation, and (ii) the (Fully Transferable) nature of the Deliverable Obligation.

[3] *Repos,* short for *repurchase agreements.* Essentially repos are contracts for the sale and future repurchase of a financial asset (usually Treasury securities). On the termination date, the seller repurchases the financial asset at the same price at which it was sold, with interest paid for the use of the funds.

the other party (the total return payer) to buy protection against potential diminution in value of the underlying credit asset.

Example. Two parties may enter into a one year total return swap where the total return payer receives LIBOR + fixed margin (3%) and the investor or total return receiver gets the total return of the ASX 200 (the index of Australia's largest 200 companies based on market capitalization) on a principal amount of $100,000. If LIBOR is 4% and the ASX 200 appreciates by 20%, the total return payer will pay the investor 20% and will receive 7%. The payment will be netted at the end of the swap contract with the investor receiving a payment of $13,000 ($100,000 × 20% − 7%). Conversely, the investor will have to make a payment of $13,000 of the ASX 200 lost value of 20% over the life of the swap.

Credit spread derivatives

The credit spread is the yield on a bond or loan minus the yield on a corresponding risk-free security (this can be the spread over a government security or the credit spread to LIBOR). Hence, the spread reflects the margin relative to the risk-free rate which compensates the investor for the risk of default. Credit spread options can protect the end user from unfavourable credit shifts which do not result in actual credit default. Spread option payoffs are generally specified in terms of the performance of a reference asset relative to another credit asset. The hedger can transfer the credit spread risk to the investor for a premium. The parties will agree on a *strike spread* which sets the upper or lower bound of acceptable movement for put or call options respectively before the option has value and allows the spread to be sold or bought. Credit spread options (similar to other options) allow investors to take synthetic positions on underlying assets rather than buying the assets in the market. Spread-forwards are like any other forward rate agreements on a certain credit spread of the underlying asset. At the maturity of the contract a net cash settlement is made, based on the agreed and actual spread (see Das 2005).

Credit default swaps

Credit default swaps (CDSs) are the most common form of credit derivative. The increasing liquidity for CDSs is evidenced by the more frequent availability of bid–ask spreads for these instruments in the market. Along with spreads in the corporate bond market, CDS quotes are increasingly becoming an important indicator of a company's creditworthiness and a key measure of investor willingness to shoulder this risk. As we have seen in the sub-prime meltdown (discussed below), CDS spreads are also becoming an important barometer of overall credit conditions in the wider economy.

In its basic vanilla form, a CDS is an agreement between a protection buyer and a protection seller whereby the buyer agrees to pay the seller a periodic premium (the credit default premium) in return for any financial losses associated with a specified credit event (such as a default or bankruptcy). The premium is usually quoted in basis points per annum on the notional value of the contract. However, in the case of highly distressed credits (as we have seen in the sub-prime collapse) it is becoming more common for protection sellers to demand payment of an upfront premium than a standard spread. In practice, contract sizes for CDSs are usually between $US10M and $US20M. Maturity dates can range between 1 and 10 years, but the most common maturity date in practice is 5 years. Most CDS contracts are *physically settled*, usually within 30 days of the credit event. With physical settlement the protection buyer has the right to sell or deliver the defaulted credit asset to the protection seller in exchange for the full face value of the debt. As the credit event will reduce the secondary market value for the loan or bond, this will usually result in losses to the protection seller. In a cash-settled arrangement, the protection seller is liable for the difference between the face and recovery values of the credit asset. However, cash settlement is less common because of difficulties associated with the pricing of distressed credit assets.

Example. An investor who takes a positive outlook on the Ford Motor Company might sell CDS protection. Suppose dealers quoted five-year credit default swap spreads on Ford at 31/33 basis points. This means the dealer quotes 31bp for a trade where the investor sells five-year protection and the dealer buys protection, and 33bp for a trade where the investor buys protection. On a typical trade size of $10 million, the protection seller would receive $31,000 a year, usually in four quarterly payments. Conversely, the investor could buy protection for 33bp, paying $33,000 a year. If Ford defaults during the life of the trade and, following the default, and the value of the company's debt falls to 40% of the face value (the 'recovery rate'), the protection seller will compensate the protection buyer for the $6 million loss.

Credit linked notes

A credit linked note is a security with an embedded CDS which allows the issuer to transfer the credit risk of the underlying note to investors. As with collateralized debt obligations discussed below, CLNs can be created through a Special Purpose Vehicle (SPV), usually a trust, which is collateralized with very highly rated securities. Investors then purchase securities from a SPV which in turn pays a fixed or floating coupon over the life of the note. At maturity, investors receive par unless there is a default event, in which case investors will only receive the recovery rate of the note. The SPV enters into a CDS with a dealer, and in the case of default the SPV pays the dealer par minus the recovery rate in exchange for an annual fee. This fee is passed on to the investors in the form of a higher yield on the credit linked note. Under this structure, the coupon or price of the note is linked to the performance of a reference asset. It offers borrowers a hedge against credit risk, and gives investors a higher yield on the note for accepting exposure to credit risk.

Example. An investor might want to take $20 million of exposure to Ford in a maturity or currency for which there are no outstanding Ford bonds. A dealer could issue a $10 million note in its own name, with Ford being the primary credit risk of the instrument. The investor would pay the dealer $20 million on the trade date to buy the note, the proceeds of which the dealer puts into his own deposit. The dealer issues a note which embeds a credit default swap in which the dealer buys $20 million of Ford protection from the investor. The note coupon would consist of the interest earned from the deposit plus the spread of the credit default swap, and would be paid to the investor quarterly. If there is no default, the credit default swap and deposit terminate on the maturity of the note, and the proceeds from the redemption of the deposit are paid back to the investor. If Ford experiences a default, the deposit is unwound and its proceeds used to pay the dealer the par amount. The dealer then pays the investor the recovery amount in the case of a cash-settled CLN or delivers deliverable obligations in the case of a physically settled CLN.

Applying the example above to an SPV-issued CLN, the dealer arranges for its SPV vehicle to issue $10 million of notes. The investor buys the note from the SPV and the proceeds are invested in high grade bonds. The SPV then sells protection on a $20 million Ford credit default swap to the dealer. The premium from the CDS along with the coupons from the collateral are paid to the investor quarterly. If there is no default, the credit default swap terminates and the collateral redeems on maturity, and the collateral redemption proceeds are paid back to the investor. If there is a default, the collateral is sold and its proceeds used to pay the dealer the par amount. The dealer either pays the investor the recovery amount or delivers deliverable obligations to the investor.

Collateralized debt obligations

A collateralized debt obligation or CDO is a security backed by a diversified pool of debt instruments which are spliced or 'tranched' on the basis of the underlying credit risks of each component of the debt. A collateralized debt obligation is termed a collateralized loan obligation (CLO) or collateralized bond obligation (CBO) if it holds only loans or bonds, respectively. A CDO has a sponsoring organization, which establishes a special-purpose vehicle (such as a trust) to hold collateral and issue securities. Sponsors can include banks, other financial institutions or investment managers, as described below. Expenses associated with running the SPV are deducted from the cash flows paid to investors. Often, the sponsoring organization retains the most subordinate equity tranche of a CDO.

The SPV acquires mortgages from a mortgage originator which are packaged and issued as mortgaged back securities (MBSs). This is known as a 'pass-through' structure as the mortgages are the only asset of the trust (i.e. investors are essentially investing in the mortgages via the trust) and are held on trust for the bondholders. There are a few steps to this process. First, a bank will package together and sell loans on its balance sheet to a special-purpose vehicle. The special-purpose vehicle then securitizes the loans. The credit risk is tranched (i.e. divided into triple A, double AA, triple B, etc.) and sold on to bondholders.

When this type of structure is applied to bonds as opposed to mortgages, it is known as a cash flow CDO. Cash flow CDOs are the earliest and simplest of CDO structures. They have evolved into the more common synthetic CDO structure. In a synthetic structure (discussed below) no legal or economic transfer of ownership of loans takes place. Instead, the bank that wishes to reduce its balance sheet risk will purchase a credit default swap from a CDO issuer.

Senior and mezzanine tranches of the CDO are typically rated by major credit rating agencies such as Standard and Poor's or Moody's. Senior tranches of the debt usually receive ratings from A to AAA and mezzanine tranches receive ratings from B to BBB. Equity tranches are usually unrated. The ratings reflect both the credit quality of underlying collateral as well as how much protection a given tranche is afforded by tranches that are subordinate to it. If there are four tranches, the first tranche is typically referred to as the equity tranche (first-loss notes), the second-loss notes as the subordinated mezzanine, the third-loss tranche as senior mezzanine, and the most senior notes simply as senior notes. This means that in the event of

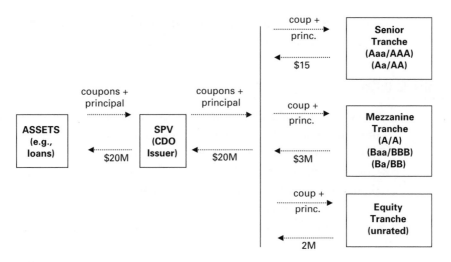

Figure 8.1   A CDO structure

default, equity tranches are first in line for losses and will absorb the full impact of losses before the second-loss tranches are impacted and so on up the hierarchy to the most senior notes. The returns paid to investors in a CDO reflect the various risk exposures. Investors in first-loss tranches normally receive the highest returns because they must bear the highest risk.

Figure 8.1 illustrates an SPV which has issued a CDO (having multiple classes of debt) to finance the acquisition of a pool of assets. The essential premise underlying the CDO issue is that the interest and principal generated by the acquired asset pool will be more than adequate to offset payment obligations on CDO issuer liabilities to investors. Figure 8.1 illustrates a CDO issuer with a portfolio of loans with a face value of $20M. To finance the purchase of the loan portfolio, the issuer (SPV) sells debt obligations (notes) to investors. The stream of payments to be paid by these notes is in turn backed by the cash flows generated by the loan portfolio. Suppose both the loans that make up the collateral and the resulting notes make quarterly payments. Each quarter the issuer (the SPV) receives the payments due on the loans and passes them through to the investors who bought the notes. As mentioned above, a key aspect of the CDO is that the notes have different coupons to reflect various levels of seniority and risk. Each quarter, any income paid by the underlying loans is first used to meet the payments of the most senior notes, followed by the next most senior notes, continuing until most first-loss notes are paid. In the absence of default, there will be sufficient cash flow to pay all investors. In the event of default, the coupon and principal of the first-loss notes will be what is left over after more senior investors and administrative fees are paid.

Synthetic CDOs

Synthetic collateralized debt obligations are structured products that closely mimic the risk and cash flow characteristics of traditional CDOs. This is achieved through the use of credit default swaps. Unlike traditional forms of securitization, synthetic CDOs do not involve any actual sale of assets by the originator – only the underlying *credit risk* of the reference assets is transferred to the counterparty. The originator remains the legal and beneficial owner of those assets. Figure 8.2 illustrates the structure of a basic synthetic balance sheet CDO, indicating a commercial bank (sponsoring bank) with a loan portfolio of 20M (the reference assets). The bank wants to mitigate the underlying credit risk of the portfolio, but does not want to sell the loans to a repackaging vehicle (the SPV). As a result, the bank chooses to sell the credit risk associated with the portfolio (i.e., the loans stay on the bank's balance sheet). The transfer of credit risk is achieved via a portfolio default swap (or a series of single-name default swaps) where the SPV is the counterparty and where the sponsoring entity buys protection against any losses (say) in excess of 3% of the portfolio. The bank in Figure 8.2 makes periodic payments to

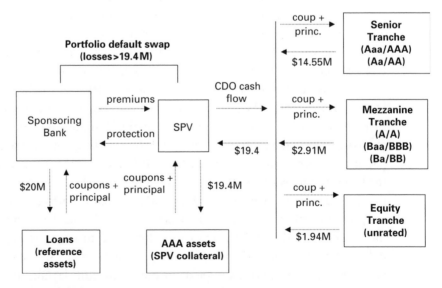

Figure 8.2   A synthetic CDO structure

the SPV, and the SPV is obliged to make good any default-related losses that exceed 3% of the portfolio. As in the traditional CDO structure, the SPV issues notes to investors who have claims to the SPV's cash flows based on the seniority of their claims. The default swap is an unfunded arrangement, and the cash flows it generates from protection premiums will not be enough to cover investors for their funding costs (the SPV-issued notes are fully funded) and for the credit risk associated with the reference portfolio. The SPV generates extra cash flow by investing the cash proceeds of the note sales in very highly rated investments. The SPV then uses these highly rated assets both as collateral for its obligations toward the sponsoring bank and the investors, and, through income that they generate, as a funding source to supplement the coupon payments promised by the notes. If there are no defaults at maturity date the portfolio swap is terminated and the SPV liquidates the collateral to repay the investors' principal in full. The CDO investors absorb all default related losses (in excess of the first-loss portion retained by the bank), starting with the equity investors.

In effect, through a synthetic CDO, the credit risk in a reference asset or portfolio is securitized – in contrast to a traditional CDO where both the credit risk and the debt are securitized. The rationale for using synthetic CDOs is that it does not require the sponsoring bank in a balance sheet CDO to sell any of its loans in a reference portfolio (which could entail customers problems, legal costs of sale and so on), or especially in the case of arbitrage CDOs, the SPV to source loans and securities in various markets. Synthetic CDOs allow a bank to sell anonymously the credit risk associated with the loans held on its books (see Bomfirm 2005).

8.3. Growth in credit derivatives market

The market for credit derivatives, particularly credit default swaps, has grown exponentially over the past decade. Initially, the first credit derivative transactions took place among a small group of pioneering investment banks in the early 1990s, with significant growth occurring in the latter part of that decade. As noted by the Report of the Joint Forum on *Credit Risk Transfer* (2004)[4] (published on behalf of the Basel Committee on Banking

---

[4] The Report represented a response to a request by the Financial Stability Forum (FSF) for the Joint Forum to undertake a review of credit risk transfer (CRT) activity. The report was prepared by the Joint Forum's Working Group on Risk Assessment and Capital and was based on several interviews with relevant market participants.

Supervision) the credit risk transfer market has been developing at a rapid rate and is 'characterized by significant product innovation, an increasing number of market participants, growth in overall transaction volumes, and perceived continued profit opportunities for financial intermediaries.' (p. 1).

However, a liquid market did not truly emerge until the International Swaps and Derivatives Association (ISDA) succeeded in standardizing documentation for these transactions in 1999. The year-end 2006 market survey by the ISDA indicated a rapid rise in the use of the complex financial instruments generally, amounting to a notional amount outstanding of US$327.4 trillion across asset classes. While credit derivatives still form a relatively small amount of the total derivatives markets (approximately 10.5%), the growth of this market has been remarkable. The 2006 survey indicated that the notional amount outstanding of credit default swaps (CDS) grew 32% in the second half of 2006, rising from US$26.0 trillion at June 30, 2006 to US$34.4 trillion at December 31, 2006. This compared with 52% growth during the first half of 2006. CDS notional growth for 2006 was 101%, compared with 103% during 2005.[5]

Collateralized debt obligations have also emerged as one of the fastest-growing areas of the asset-backed securities (ABS) market. According to the Securities Industry and Financial Markets Association (SIFMA), aggregate global CDO issuance totalled USD $157 billion in 2004 to $550 billion in 2006. See Table 8.1 which displays the annual growth figures for total CDO issuances, including breakdowns for the totals of (i) cash flow and hybrid CDOs, (ii) synthetic funded CDOs, and (iii) market value CDOs. Further breakdowns are provided for the total value of (i) arbitrage CDOs and (ii) balance sheet CDOs, with further breakdowns for the total amount of (i) long-term and (ii) short-term issuances. Table 8.1 also provides the SIFMA's definition of the different types of CDOs.

The rapid growth of the broader credit derivative markets is well publicized and has been spurred on by many factors, including the recent spate of high-profile corporate bankruptcies, and increasing turmoil of equity and bond markets over the past decade (such as the 9/11 event and the Latin American debt crisis, and more recently the sub-prime crisis which set in from June 2007). These events have fuelled a growing appetite among lenders and investors to manage and spread credit risk. While banks have been the predominant participant in these markets, activity has spread to a broad spectrum of market participants, including hedge funds, insurance

---

[5] The survey monitors credit default swaps on single-names, baskets and portfolios of credits and index trades.

Table 8.1 Global CDO market issuance data[1]

By Issuance type ($MM)

	Total issuance	Cash flow and hybrid[2]	Synthetic funded[3]	Market value[4]	Arbitrage[5]	Balance sheet[6]	Long term[7]	Short term[8]
2004-Q1	24,982.5	18,807.8	6,174.7	0.0	23,157.5	1,825.0	20,495.1	4,487.4
2004-Q2	42,861.6	25,786.7	17,074.9	0.0	39,715.5	3,146.1	29,611.4	13,250.2
2004-Q3	42,086.6	36,106.9	5,329.7	650.0	38,207.7	3,878.8	34,023.9	8,062.7
2004-Q4	47,487.8	38,829.9	8,657.9	0.0	45,917.8	1,569.9	38,771.4	8,716.4
2004 TOTAL	**157,418.5**	**119,531.3**	**37,237.2**	**650.0**	**146,998.5**	**10,419.8**	**122,901.8**	**34,516.7**
2005-Q1**	50,022.8	40,656.4	9,366.4	0.0	44,171,4	5,851.4	45,587.8	4,435.0
2005-Q2**	72,358.4	48,481.8	23,646.6	230.0	62,958.4	9,400.0	65,951.5	6,406.9
2005-Q3**	52,077.2	44,253.1	7,754.1	0.0	49,636.7	2,370.5	48,656.3	3,350.9
2005-Q4**	98,637.0	71,498.0	26,749.0	390.0	71,859.2	26,777.8	88,665.1	9,971.9
2005 TOTAL	**273,025.4**	**204,889.3**	**67,516.1**	**620.0**	**228,625.7**	**44,399.7**	**248,860.7**	**24,164.7**
2006-Q1**	107,858.9	83,790.1	24,068.8	0.0	100,975.8	6,883.1	94,916.3	12,942.6
2006-Q2**	125,395.5	97,721,7	24,764.6	2,909.2	103,005.7	22,389.8	120,124.6	5,270.9

Table 8.1 (cont.)

	Total issuance	Cash flow and hybrid[2]	Synthetic funded[3]	Market value[4]	Arbitrage[5]	Balance sheet[6]	Long term[7]	Short term[8]
2006-Q3**	138,630.8	102,154.4	14,718.9	21,757.5	125,915.3	12,715.5	122,767.4	15,863.4
2006-Q4**	178,384.4	130,727.6	25,389,6	22,267.2	141,108.3	37,276.1	169,158.9	9,225.5
2006 TOTAL	**550,269.6**	**414,393.8**	**88,941.9**	**46,933.9**	**471,005.1**	**79,264.5**	**506,967.2**	**43,302.4**
2007-Q1	158,428.7	130,902.4	14,603.9	12,922.4	130,758.4	27,670.3	138,972,1	19,456.6
2007 TOTAL	**158,428.7**	**130,902.4**	**14,603.9**	**12,922.4**	**130,758.4**	**27,670.3**	**138,972.1**	**19,456.6**

Source: Thomson Financial and Securities Industry and Financial Markets Association. As indicated by SIFMA, the totals may not foot due to rounding.

** Revised to reflect changes in classification or information submitted after prior cut-off date.

[1] Unfunded synthetic tranches are not included in this analysis. SME deals are classified as ABS and are not included in this analysis.

[2] Cash flow CDOs are structured to pay off liabilities with the interest and principal payments (cash flows) of their collateral. Hybrid CDOs combine the funding structures of cash synthetic CDOs.

[3] Synthetic CDOs sell credit protection via credit default swaps (CDs) rather than purchase cash assets. Synthetic CDOs use credit default swaps (CDS) to synthetically replicate cash flow CDO. Funded tranches require the deposit of cash to an SPV at an inception of the deal to collateralize portions of an SPV's potential swap obligations in the transaction; losses result in principal writedowns of the issued notes.

[4] Market value CDOs are structured to support liabilities through the value of the collateral.

[5] Arbitrage CDOs attempt to capture the mismatch between the yields of assets (CDO collateral) and the financing costs of the generally higher rated liabilities (CDO tranches).

[6] Balance sheet CDOs remove assets or the risk of assets off the balance sheet of the originator. Balance sheet CDOs may be cash or synthetic. In cash deals they are used to move assets off a balance sheet (frequently to reduce regulatory capital requirements, among other reasons, similar to traditional ABS securitizations). In synthetic deals, the risk is moved off balance sheet by the originator's purchasing protection from the SPV through CDS.

[7] Long-term tranches are defined as tranches with maturities of greater than 18 months.

[8] Short-term tranches are defined as tranches with maturities of less than 18 months.

companies, mutual funds, pension funds, corporate treasuries and other varying investor groups seeking to transfer credit risk, diversify their portfolios synthetically and increase their incremental returns. Banks in particular utilize credit derivatives to hedge credit risk, diminish risk concentrations, free up regulatory capital and improve the management of credit portfolios more generally (see Martellini 2003 and Das 2005 for discussion). However, institutional investors have several motivations for participating in these markets, such as the added flexibility gained from trading in credit without having to assume the ownership of the underlying credit assets or portfolios, wider participation in credit markets which would otherwise not be possible for traditional investors (such as loan markets), and the opportunity to arbitrage the pricing of credit risk across different markets.

Credit derivative markets may also perform a number of important roles in the world's financial markets. As noted in a 2005 speech by Alan Greenspan, the then Chairman of the Federal Reserve Board, 'the development of credit derivatives has contributed to the stability of the banking system by allowing banks, especially the largest, systemically important banks, to measure and manage their credit risks more effectively.'[6] These views have been echoed more recently by the Australian Reserve Bank governor, Glenn Stevens, following the sub-prime fallout in the United States, where he stated 'credit derivatives had dispersed the [credit] risk widely...exposure would probably not be fatal for any large financial institution or damage the core banking system in any significant country.'[7]

Many commentators have argued that the advent of credit derivatives have rendered the international financial system more robust or 'shock-resistant'. The Bank of England's publication *Financial Stability Review* (June 2001) observed: 'Credit derivatives are one of a number of markets for the transfer of credit risk. Development of these markets has clear potential benefits for financial stability because they allow the origination and funding of credit to be separated from the efficient allocation of the resulting credit risk...If banks hold more diversified credit portfolios, they will be less vulnerable to idiosyncratic or sectoral asset price shocks. If they can transfer credit risk more easily, the supply of credit to borrowers will be less

[6] Remarks by Chairman Alan Greenspan *Risk Transfer and Financial Stability* To the Federal Reserve Bank of Chicago's 41st Annual Conference on Bank Structure, Chicago, Illinois (via satellite) May 5, 2005 available at http://www.federalreserve.gov/boarddocs/speeches/2005/20050505/default.htm

[7] See 'Central bank chiefs keep lines humming' *The Australian*, 18 August 2007.

dependent on their willingness and ability to take credit risk, perhaps making credit crunches less likely.'

Some of the major advantages of credit derivatives can be summarized as follows:

A. *Vehicles for hedging credit risk.* Banking institutions in particular use redit derivatives (especially credit default swaps) as an effective mechanism to reduce or mitigate loan exposures and risk concentrations. As noted by the Basel Committee (2006) *Studies on Risk Concentration*, concentration of credit risk in particular asset portfolios has been one of the major causes of bank distress. For instance, the failure of large borrowers such as Enron, Worldcom and Parmalat were the source of sizeable losses to a number of banks. By purchasing credit default swaps, banking institutions can effectively reduce their risk concentrations, while still participating in the incremental returns of a credit asset or portfolio. For example, a bank with high exposure to the mining sector can potentially reduce this exposure by acquiring single or multi-name credit default swaps on reference entities having significant or predominant exposure to the mining sector. Furthermore, if a bank seeks to gain greater exposure to a particular industry without taking legal or beneficial ownership of the underlying credit assets, it can sell credit default swaps to counterparties having significant exposure to that industry. This allows a bank to participate in the underlying risk and return of a credit asset or portfolio while keeping the underlying credit exposures off the balance sheet.

Not only can credit default swaps be used to reduce a lender's exposure to a particular borrower, they can also be combined with multi-issuer swaps or other derivatives to create any number of flexible risk profiles. For instance, if the lender wishes to take on a borrower's firm-specific default risk, but not the risk related to the industry as a whole, the lender could purchase derivatives that would compensate the lender in the event of an industry downturn (such as a derivative linked to the share price index of a broad group of companies in that industry) (see Partnoy and Skeel 2007).

Credit default swaps have arguably served as a 'shock absorber' during the corporate crisis of 2001 and 2002. In the words of Alan Greenspan, 'New financial products have enabled risk to be dispersed more effectively to those willing, and presumably able, to bear it. Shocks to the overall economic system are accordingly less likely to create cascading credit failure. ... In addition, such instruments, more generally, appear to have effectively spread losses from recent defaults by Enron, Global Crossing, Railtrack, and Swissair in recent months.'[8]

B. *Liquidity and regulatory capital requirements.* Credit default swaps limit the bank's exposure to credit risk (by passing it on to other parties, such as insurance companies and pension funds). Hence, banks can potentially lend more money to other businesses which can improve overall liquidity in financial markets. Use of credit derivatives can also have important implications to a bank's regulatory capital requirements. Banks are bound by regulation to hold minimal levels of capital adequacy to cover potential default losses on their loan books. The 1988 Basel Accord requirements applied risk weightings to various types of loans and specified minimum capital adequacy reserves for each risk class. Most borrowers received a 100% risk weighting under the Accord (these are corporations and non-OECD banks and non-OECD governments), which attracted a minimum capital adequacy requirement of 8% of the total loan exposure. If a borrower had a risk weighting of 20% under the Accord (i.e., the borrower is an OECD bank) the capital charge would be much less, 1.6%. If the borrower is an OECD government, however, there is no risk weight applied (and hence no minimum capital adequacy requirements). These classifications are clearly very arbitrary (for example corporate debt, non-OECD banks and non-OECD countries are all lumped together as a single homogeneous risk class). Corporates are all assigned a 100% risk weight irrespective of the underlying creditworthiness of individual companies (in short, the same 8% regulatory capital requirement will be applied to an AAA-rated company as to a lower-rated company). It may make good economic sense for a bank to hold significantly more capital in reserve in respect of distressed or higher-risk companies, and less for an highly rated firm. Credit derivatives provide an effective means for banks to better manage their regulatory capital requirements. For example, the loans of highly rated borrowers, where the regulatory capital charge of 8% might be considered excessive, can be moved off balance sheet (by acquiring credit default swaps), while retaining the loans of lower-rated borrowers on balance sheet (which attract the 8% charge). This could also be achieved by a bank selling or securitizing loans made to highly rated borrowers. However, selling

---

[8] Remarks by Chairman Alan Greenspan *Finance: United States and Global* At the Institute of International Finance, New York, New York (via videoconference) April 22, 2002 available at http://www.federalreserve.gov/boarddocs/Speeches/2002/20020422/default.htm

loans is not always an attractive option for banks (e.g., there may be potentially adverse consequences with customers).

C. *Information content.* To the extent that the pricing of credit default swaps is disclosed or available to the market, default spreads provide an additional source of market-based information about a firm's credit-worthiness and the price that investors are prepared to pay to bear this risk. As market mechanisms develop to disseminate prices more widely, this has the potential to improve the efficient allocation of credit risk. Like the yield spreads of corporate bonds, credit default swap pricing may produce better and more timely information about a company's financial health. Market prices can capture more subtle and rapidly moving changes in borrower conditions than, say, the credit ratings provided by major rating agencies, which tend to react in a slower and (from time to time) a more idiosyncratic way to rapidly changing economic events. The price of credit default swap transactions can thus perform a valuable signalling function. One anecdote can be taken from the failure of Enron. Prior to its spectacular failure in December 2001, Enron was one of the most traded reference entities in the CDS market. When Enron's chief executive officer Jeffrey Skilling abruptly resigned on 15 August 2001 after only six months in the position, the default swap price on Enron moved up 18%, although there was no immediate impact on the stock prices. On that day, default swaps were priced at 185 basis points. As the company sank deeper into financial oblivion, by 25 October 2002, the default swap price sky rocketed to 9000 bps which essentially meant the protection seller would get 90% to guarantee a 100% repayment of Enron's debt.[9] Credit default swaps can also be a significant barometer of broader economic conditions. Following the sub-prime collapse, the bonds of many U.S. investment banks lost about $1.5 billion of their face value in the month of August 2007 alone. Credit default swaps tied to $10 million of bonds sold by Bear Stearns, the second-largest underwriter of mortgage bonds, were quoted as high as $145,000 in August, up from $30,000 at the start of June, which is a significant indication of growing investor anxiety about the sub-prime collapse. Further, prices of credit default swaps for Goldman Sachs (the largest investment bank by market value), Merrill Lynch and Lehman Brothers, equated to sub-investment grade

---

[9] See also 'Can Anyone Police the Swaps' *Wall Street Journal*, August 31, 2006 which discusses the information content of credit default swaps prior to significant company announcements.

rating of Ba1 in August 2007, which again is symptomatic of broader economic concerns with the sub-prime crisis.

D. *New investment and diversification opportunities.* Credit default swaps and structured credit products, such as CDOs, arguably generate investment opportunities that otherwise would not be available to investors. For instance, credit defaults and synthetic CDOs are unfunded credit derivative instruments. Unlike buying a corporate bond or extending a loan, which requires upfront funds, no cash flows actually changes hands in many credit derivative transactions. This allows protection sellers to leverage up their credit risk exposure. Consider an investor with relatively high cost of funds. That investor would probably not be attracted to investing directly in highly rated bonds, as the yield may even be lower than the investor's own cost of funds. However, the investor could enter a credit default swap with a highly rated dealer where it sells protection in exchange for a credit default premium paid by the dealer, thus avoiding some of the fund cost disadvantages but being subject to relatively low credit risk.

Structured products also provide many investment and diversification opportunities. In a standard cash flow CDO, a financial institution sells debt (loans or bonds) to a Special Purpose Entity (SPE), which then splits the debt into pieces or 'tranches' by issuing new securities linked to each piece. Some of the pieces are of higher quality; some are of lower quality. The credit rating agencies give investment grade ratings to most or all of the tranches. Because investments in cash flow CDOs often have credit ratings that are higher than the ratings of the underlying bonds, they provide a new opportunity for investors. For example, some investors might not be able to buy the underlying bonds, given their relatively low credit ratings. Other investors might be able to buy the underlying bonds, but would have to pay high capital charges due to regulations that depend on credit ratings. Thus, a cash flow CDO presents a new investment opportunity at potentially lower cost. Because synthetic CDOs – in contrast to cash flow CDOs – essentially create new instruments, instead of using assets already on the bank's balance sheets, they are not motivated by regulatory arbitrage, but instead by 'pure' arbitrage opportunities, because their tranches typically are priced at higher yields relative to other similarly rated fixed-income investments. Synthetic CDO tranches are popular because they offer investors a less expensive way of participating in the bond market, particularly the market for high yield debt.

Other opportunities to investors are the ability to devise strategies for shorting corporate bonds, synthesizing long positions in corporate debt, hedging investor financed deals and selling protection as an alternative to loan origination (see Bomfim 2005 for discussion).

Despite the many obvious benefits, credit derivatives markets do have their detractors. Warren Buffet famously remarked: 'Derivatives are financial weapons of mass destruction, carrying dangers that, while now latent, are potentially lethal.' Further, credit risk protection sellers have been likened to 'a foolish driver who launches his car into a busy road on the say-so of his passenger, without looking both right and left himself.' (*The Economist*, 9 February 2002). Some of the issues with credit derivatives relate to concerns with whether these instruments create clear transfers of risk, the broader economic and regulatory impacts of risk diffusion throughout the economy and financial stability considerations. We briefly discuss each of these issues.

The issue of clean transfer of risk relates to the presence of counterparty risk (whether the counterparty to a credit derivative transaction will be able to perform on its obligations); legal uncertainties associated with the transaction; the robustness of credit default swap matching and confirmation processes; how well market participants understand the risks to which they are exposed; and the potential build up of risk concentrations outside the banking sector. With respect to counterparty risk, the *Joint Forum on Credit Risk Transfer* (2004) noted this had not emerged as a significant issue in credit derivative markets. The report of the Joint Forum noted: 'Market participants address this risk in several ways. A number of transactions are effectively funded up-front, via issuance of securities, so that the counterparty risk is eliminated. Even in the case of unfunded transactions, frequent marking-to-market with transfer of collateral is common, particularly in relation to inter-dealer transactions and those involving lower quality counterparties. Market participants also stress the importance of proper credit due diligence with respect to credit derivatives counterparties.' (p. 2). The case of Enron has been held out as a major success story for credit derivatives, particular credit default swaps. Notwithstanding that credit default swaps (with Enron as the reference entity) were one of the most actively traded swaps on the OTC credit derivatives market prior to its collapse, obligations under these contracts were settled in an orderly way notwithstanding some popular speculation to the contrary. On the second issue, industry-standard documentation developed by the ISDA appears to have strengthened confidence in the market, notwithstanding some lingering uncertainties as to whether the contracts should cover restructuring events as well as bankruptcy or other more clear-cut default events. Another issue in relation to the documentation of transactions is whether the trade documents are matched and confirmed in a timely fashion. While many participants surveyed by the Joint Forum still report higher than desired levels of unmatched confirmations, they are optimistic that recent initiatives for automating credit default swap matching and confirmation processes will help alleviate this concern.

Other concerns with credit derivatives generally relate to risk diffusion and potential threats to the stability of the financial system. As banks attempt to reduce risk by deploying credit derivatives, they may be creating concentrations of risk outside the banking system that could prove a threat to overall financial stability. Some observers believe that credit risks are ultimately better managed by banks because they generally are more heavily regulated than the entities to which risk is being transferred. Further, banks are generally more experienced and adept at pricing and managing this risk. A counter-argument is that unregulated and less heavily regulated entities generally are subject to more effective market discipline than banks. Market participants taking on exposures to credit risk usually have strong incentives to monitor and control the risks they assume when choosing their counterparties. Using this argument, prudential regulation is supplied by the market through counterparty evaluation and monitoring rather than by regulatory authorities. As noted by the *Joint Forum on Credit Risk Transfer:* 'With regard to the role of unregulated market participants, the Working Group believes that market discipline as evidenced through effective counterparty risk management is an essential element of a well-functioning market place.' (p. 5). The report of the Joint Form also appeared to shrug off the concerns of risk concentration in the following terms: 'the aggregate amount of credit risk that has been transferred via credit derivatives and related transactions, particularly outside the banking system, is still quite modest as a proportion of the total credit risk that exists in the financial system. The Working Group has not found evidence of 'hidden concentrations' of credit risk.' (p. 3).

However, a point of vulnerability is that credit derivatives have never been seriously tested in major economic downturn, such As the U.S. sub-prime meltdown which came into prominence in mid-2007. Given the dramatic impact that the sub-prime crisis has had on world debt and equity markets in recent months, we will briefly cover these developments.

The sub-prime meltdown and impacts on global debt and equity markets

Sub-prime lending (sometimes referred to as *B-Paper* or near-prime lending), is the practice of extending loans (e.g., mortgages) to borrowers with elevated credit risks. Lenders seek to compensate for the high default risk by charging higher interest rates to these customers. Sub-prime loans have been pejoratively termed 'Ninja' loans – 'No Income, No Jobs or Assets'. Notwithstanding many detractors, the sub-prime lending market has grown very rapidly over the past decade. The development of the sub-prime market was described in a recent speech by the Chairman of the Federal Reserve Board, Ben Bernanke (May 2007): 'in the mid-1990s, the expansion was spurred in large part by innovations that reduced the costs for lenders of assessing and pricing risks. In particular, technological advances facilitated credit scoring by making it easier for lenders to collect and disseminate information on the creditworthiness of prospective borrowers. In addition, lenders developed new techniques for using this information to determine underwriting standards, set interest rates, and manage their risks ... The ongoing growth and development of the secondary mortgage market has reinforced the effect of these innovations. Whereas once most lenders held mortgages on their books until the loans were repaid, regulatory changes and other developments have permitted lenders to more easily sell mortgages to financial intermediaries, who in turn pool mortgages and sell the cash flows as structured securities. These securities typically offer various risk profiles and durations to meet the investment strategies of a wide range of investors.'[10]

According to the statistics of the Federal Reserve, about 7.5 million first-lien sub-prime mortgages are now outstanding, accounting for about 14% of all first-lien mortgages.[11] At the heart of the sub-prime crisis were the escalating default rates on sub-prime loans. The default rate on these mortgages has risen very sharply and recently stood at about 11% in August 2007 (double the default rate of the previous year) – with many defaults associated with customers not even making their first loan installment. This has led to a serious questioning of underwriting standards as well as the effectiveness of various credit rating models used by the larger rating agencies. The rapid development of structured credit products, particularly

---

[10] Remarks by Chairman Ben S. Bernanke at the Federal Reserve Bank of Chicago's 43rd Annual Conference on Bank Structure and Competition, Chicago, Illinois May 17, 2007

[11] So-called near-prime loans to borrowers who typically have higher credit scores than sub-prime borrowers but whose applications may have other higher-risk aspects account for an additional 8–10% of mortgages.

those products with significant exposure to the sub-prime lending market, may have also have contributed to a significant weakening in underwriting standards. When loans are repackaged and later sold as mortgage back securities (MBSs) to investors, they effectively transfer all the risks (including the risk of lax underwriting standards) on to investors. The moral hazard risk for investors can be significant when one considers the incentive structures of mortgage originators, which may well favour sales volume over credit quality standards.

The CDO market has played a central role in the sub-prime collapse. This in fact partly stems from the inherent ingenuity of these products. As MBSs linked to sub-prime lending markets are not considered investment grade, they will not attract high credit ratings (they are B paper), and hence they will not be palatable investment products for most professional fund managers or investors. CDOs have evolved as a more marketable alternative. By dividing up the MBSs into several tranches with different risk profiles, reflecting different investment grades, sub-prime mortgages (sometimes called the 'toxic waste') are packaged up with the higher grade debt. Many CDOs shelter a significant amount of sub-prime debt, but nevertheless get issued high credit ratings because there is a sufficient proportion of high quality debt to raise the overall investment grade. Hedge fund managers have been particularly active in trading equity and mezzanine tranches of the CDO. The value of the CDOs were 'marked up' in times when housing prices were booming in the United States, with the CDOs being used as collateral with banks to raise further cheap debt; which in turn allowed the hedge funds to leverage more heavily into the CDO market. However, as the mortgages underlying the CDOs collateral began to spiral downwards, banks and investment institutions holding CDOs witnessed a significant deterioration in the value of their CDO holdings. These problems were compounded by the relatively illiquid market for CDOs and the difficulties faced by hedge funds in pricing their losses in a rapidly declining market.

The general panic in the market resulted in many banks calling in their original collateral. However, with the escalating volume of CDO sales, the market quickly became saturated, particularly for the equity and mezzaine tranches of the CDOs. In some cases, this resulted in enormous book losses for a number of hedge funds and investment banks. With no buyers, the equity and mezzanine tranches literally have no value. As delinquencies and defaults on sub-prime mortgages continued to escalate (and no doubt will continue from the time this book was finished in early September 2007), CDOs backed by equity and mezzanine sub-prime collateral were experiencing dramatic rating downgrades.[12] For instance, on 10 July 2007, Moody's cut ratings on more than 400 securities that were based on sub-prime loan exposures. Around the same time, S&P announced that 612 securities were on review, and most were downgraded shortly after. This action has been likened by some commentators in the financial press as 'the equivalent of slapping food-safety warnings on meat that's already rotting in the aisles.'

The erratic shifts in ratings have compounded the nervousness in financial markets and has brought about a raft of criticism levelled at the Big Three ratings agencies, particularly for reacting too slowly to the crisis, for failing to downgrade mortgage bonds and related structured products in a timely manner and for failing to anticipate the escalating default rates on sub-prime mortgages in the first place. The adequacy of credit risk scoring models has also been widely questioned. Notwithstanding the critical role of ratings in the sub-prime crisis (obviously highly rated bonds can much more readily be disposed of than sub-investment grade or unrated bonds), ratings agencies have been seen to be taking a more passive role than they should have, particularly in rating mortgage bonds. This has resulted in some agencies putting their credit risk scoring methodologies under formal review and the launch of government enquiries into alleged conflicts of interests between ratings agencies and the issuers whose securities they rate.[13]

As for the capital market fall-out from the sub-prime collapse, the financial shock did not really begin to hit financial markets until June 2007, when two hedge funds managed by Bear Stearns Asset Management Inc. faced cash or collateral calls from lenders that had accepted CDOs backed by sub-prime loans as loan collateral. As a relatively late comer to the CDO market, Bear Stearns acquired many CDOs at the height of the property market in the United States, which largely explains why the firm was inflicted with such heavy losses. Similar events have spilled over into Australia. In late August, the Australian hedge fund Basis Capital (which had significant exposures to the CDO sub-prime market) applied to a U.S. court to have its Basis Yield master fund placed under bankruptcy protection after

---

[12] However, at the time of writing estimates on the fallout from the sub-prime meltdown varied from $75 to $90 billion (from Deutsche Bank AG), based on mortgages made from the previous year to borrowers with poor or limited credit records or high debt burdens. At the time of writing, Credit Suisse estimated the maximum potential losses for investors in CDOs is equivalent to about a tenth of the $513 billion of equity capital for the world's biggest 10 investment banks.

[13] Many commentaries have appeared in the popular press, see for example 'Credit Crisis Hurts Rating Agencies' *Forbes*, 14 August 2007; ' Credit-rating agencies feel heat' *USA Today*, 20 August 2007; and 'Ratings firms face sub-prime scrutiny', *The Australian*, September 13, 2007.

it failed to meet a series of margin calls. Basis Capital's other fund, the $355 million Basis Pac-Rim Opportunity Fund, has incurred substantial losses but has so far met all margin calls.

At the time of writing, the Federal Reserve Board Chairman, Ben Bernanke, took the unprecedented step of approving temporary changes to its primary credit discount window facility to ease the looming liquidity and credit crisis. The Board approved a 50 basis point reduction in the primary credit rate to 5.75%. The discount window is a channel for banks to borrow directly from the Federal Reserve rather than in the markets. With the markets widely expecting an interest rate cut at the September meeting of the Federal Reserve Board, a sense of stability seems to have been restored to financial markets around the world. However, with more than 90 mortgage companies failing or seeking buyers since the start of 2006,[14] and with many more casualties expected over coming months, it is difficult at this juncture to quantify how extensive the sub-prime meltdown is actually going to be and how long the sense of 'uneasy calm' will continue on the world's financial markets.

8.4. Credit derivative pricing models

Much of the growth of the credit derivatives market would not be possible without the development of models for the pricing and management of credit risk. It is clear that the compensation that an investor receives for assuming default risk and the premium that a hedger would need to pay to remove default risk must be linked to the size of the credit risk. This risk can be defined in terms of the probability of default and the recovery rate when a default occurs.

As an example, the pricing of a standard-form credit default swap is described and the effect of changes in the estimate of default probability investigated. A discrete-form pricing framework for a CDS is shown, then the impact of the default probability assumption in this framework is demonstrated through a sensitivity analysis of CDS prices to ratings-based and market-based default probability estimates. A standard CDS consists of two cash flow streams: (i) the fee premium cash flow stream and (ii) the contingent cash flow leg. The process for determining the par premium, in the absence of arbitrage, is to equate the present value of these cash flow streams.

---

[14] See commentary in 'U.S. Mortgage Contagion Spreads' *Australian Financial Review*, 22 August 2007.

Let us first look at the value of the premium leg. On each payment date the periodic payment made by the purchaser of the protection is the product of the annual CDS premium, S, and the fraction of a year between the payment dates, d_i. This payment will only be if the underlying credit object has not defaulted by the payment date, so the survival probability at time t, $q(t)$, will have to be taken into account. The expected payment at time t is given by

$$q(t_i)d_iS.$$

Using the discount factor for the payment date, $D(t_i)$, the sum of the present values of the premium payments is given by

$$\sum_{i=1}^{N} D(t_i)q(t_i)Sd_i. \tag{8.1}$$

If a default can occur between payment dates the preset value of the premium that would be payable from the partial period needs to be added to the value of the present value of the premium payments to find the total value of the premium leg. This payment is approximated by assuming that a default occurs at the mid-point of the interval between payments. If a default occurs between dates t_{i-1} and t_i the payment amount is $Sd_i/2$. This payment has to be converted into an expected payment by taking its product with the probability that the default occurs in this time interval $q(t_{i-1}) - q(t_i)$. So for any interval the expected accrual payment is given by $\{q(t_{i-1}) - q(t_i)\}Sd_i/2$.

The expected value of all the accrual payments is

$$\sum_{i=1}^{N} D(t_i)\{q(t_{i-1}) - q(t_i)\}S\frac{d_i}{2}. \tag{8.2}$$

Adding components (8.1) and (8.2) gives the present value of the premium leg:

$$PV[\text{premium leg}] = \sum_{i=1}^{N} D(t_i)q(t_i)Sd_i + \sum_{i=1}^{N} D(t_i)\{q(t_{i-1}) - q(t_i)\}S\frac{d_i}{2}.$$

Next, determine the value of the contingent leg. If the underlying bond defaults between payment dates $t-1$ and t the protection buyer will receive the contingent payment of $(1 - R)$ where R is the recovery rate. This payment to the buyer is only made if the underlying bond defaults, so the expected payment in any period is given by $(1 - R)\{q(t_{i-1}) - q(t_i)\}$. Discounting the expected payment and summing over the term of the contract gives

$$PV[\text{contingent leg}] = (1 - R) \sum_{i=1}^{N} D(t_i)\{q(t_{i-1}) - q(t_i)\}. \tag{8.3}$$

When a CDS is executed, the spread, that is the regular payment the protection buyer makes, is set so the that value of the premium leg is equal to the value of the contingent leg. Given all the parameters on the model (default probabilities, discount and recovery rates) the premium payment, S, is given by

$$S = \frac{(1 - R) \sum_{i=1}^{N} D(t_i)\{q(t_{i-1}) - q(t_i)\}}{\sum_{i=1}^{N} D(t_i)q(t_i)d_i + \sum_{i=1}^{N} D(t_i)\{q(t_{i-1}) - q(t_i)\}\frac{d_i}{2}}. \tag{8.4}$$

The determinates of the premium are the probability of default, $q(t_i)$, the recovery rate, R, and the discount factors, $D(t_i)$, that are derived from the term structure curve. When a CDS is initialized the value of the swap to both parties is zero, as the premium is derived by equating the value of the premium and contingent legs of the contract. Over the life of the swap, changes in the probability of default, recovery rate or discount factor can cause the value of the swap to move in favour of one of the parties, leaving the other party with a potential unfunded liability of the value of the swap.

To demonstrate the effect of changing parameters, the value of a CDS on the debt of Time Warner, in 2001, is computed with standard Moody's parameters and with default probabilities computed using structural and intensity models. Between 2000 and 2001 Time Warner had increased its debt level from 1,411M to 22,792M as a result of an acquisition transaction, the 'tech bubble' had burst and the Federal Reserve Board in the United States had begun the series of interest rate cuts that lead to historically low interest rates. Under these conditions the changes in the value of a CDS on Time Warner's debt and which party to the contract was 'in the money' would be important considerations to the parties of the swap contract. The debt of Time Warner was rated Baa1 in 2001; the annual default rate for this class of debt, from Table 8.2, is 0.06%. The debt is assumed to be subordinated, and the recovery rate on default is assumed to be 32.65%,[15] which lies within the interval for subordinated debt shown in Table 8.3.

---

[15] This is the recovery rate that is used by Jarrow *et al.* (1997) in their derivation of intensity based default probabilities.

Table 8.2 Average 1 year default rates 1983–2000 (Moody's)

Credit Rating	Default Rate (%)
Aaa	0.0
Aa1	0.0
Aa2	0.0
Aa3	0.08
A1	0.0
A2	0.0
Baa1	0.06
Baa2	0.06
Baa3	0.46
Ba1	0.69
Ba2	0.63
Ba3	2.39
B1	3.79
B2	7.96
B3	12.89

Table 8.3 Recovery rates on corporate bonds from Moody's Investor's Service (2000)

	Class Mean (%)	Standard Deviation (%)
Senior Secured	52.31	25.15
Senior Unsecured	48.84	25.01
Senior Subordinated	39.46	4.59
Subordinated	33.17	20.78
Junior Subordinated	19.69	13.85

Table 8.4 shows the calculation of the value of a base case 2 year CDS with quarterly payments. The term structure is assumed to be flat, so the 3 month treasury rate of 5.29% is used as the basis of the discount rates used in the calculation. Defaults are assumed to occur with a constant intensity λ per period of time given by the value for Baa1 debt and the recovery rate is 32.65%. Under these assumptions the value of the swap premium is 10.1 basis points, or $1013 per million covered. Two methods commonly used to estimate bankruptcy probabilities are described and implemented, and then the behaviour of the value of the CDS calculated using these probabilities is presented.

Table 8.4 CDS preimum calculation

Risk Free m	0.0529 Discount	Surv Prob	EV Fixed	Default Prob PV Fixed	0.006 Def Prob	E[Accrued]	PV (Accrued)	Recovery E[Contingent]	0.3265 PV(contingent)
0	1	1							
0.25	0.9872	0.9985	0.9985	0.9857	0.001503	0.000752	0.000742	0.001013	0.001000
0.50	0.9746	0.9970	0.9970	0.9716	0.001501	0.000751	0.000731	0.001011	0.000985
0.75	0.9621	0.9955	0.9955	0.9577	0.001499	0.000749	0.000721	0.001009	0.000971
1.00	0.9498	0.9940	0.9940	0.9441	0.001497	0.000748	0.000711	0.001008	0.000957
1.25	0.9376	0.9925	0.9925	0.9306	0.001494	0.000747	0.000701	0.001006	0.000944
1.50	0.9256	0.9910	0.9910	0.9173	0.001492	0.000746	0.000691	0.001005	0.000930
1.75	0.9137	0.9895	0.9895	0.9042	0.001490	0.000745	0.000681	0.001003	0.000917
2.00	0.9020	0.9880	0.9880	0.8912	0.001488	0.000744	0.000671	0.001002	0.000904
				7.5024			0.005648		0.007608

S (%) = 0.00101

$S per 1M = 1013.29

Obtaining default probabilities

There are several methods to obtain the probability of default of an institution on its obligations. However, two popular models in the literature are:
- KMV Expected default frequency (EDF) model,
- Reduced form (or intensity) models.

In this illustration we describe the application of the structural and reduced-form approaches to the calculation of bankruptcy probabilities for Time Warner. The procedure for estimating the bankruptcy probabilities using the structural approach, based on the simple Merton framework, is presented first. The procedure using the reduced-from approach based on Jarrow *et al.* (1997) is then presented. The bankruptcy probabilities computed under the each approach are then compared.

The Merton model is derived by treating the value of leveraged equity as a call option on the assets of the firm (see Chapter 6).

$$V_E = V_A N(d_1) - e^{-r(T-t)} D N(d_2) \tag{8.5}$$

where V_E is the value of equity, V_A is the value of assets and D is the face value of debt. $(T - t)$ is the time to maturity of the debt, r is the risk-free rate

$$d_1 = \frac{\ln(V_A/D) + (r + 1/2\sigma_A^2)(T - t)}{\sigma_A \sqrt{(T - t)}}, \quad d_2 = d_1 - \sigma_A \sqrt{(T - t)}$$

and $N(.)$ is the function for a normal distribution.

This approach also provides a relationship between equity and asset return volatility:

$$\sigma_E = \frac{V_A}{V_E} N(d_1) \sigma_A. \tag{8.6}$$

The risk-neutral probability of default in this framework is given by the expression

$$F(T|t) = \Pr[V_{A,T} < D | V_{A,0} = V_A] = \text{Student-}t \left[\frac{\ln\left(\frac{V_A}{D}\right) + \left(r - \frac{1}{2}\sigma_A^2\right)(T - t)}{\sigma_A \sqrt{(T - t)}} \right] \tag{8.7}$$

where $V_{A,T}$ is the value of the firms assets at the expiry of the debt contract, $V_{A,0}$ is the value of the firms assets at the beginning of the debt contract and probabilities are drawn from the Student-t distribution.

To compute the probability of bankruptcy using equation (8.7) we need to know the face value of debt, the length of the debt contract, the risk-free rate, the value of assets and the volatility of asset returns. What we can easily find is: the stock price, the face value of debt, the number of shares on issue and the risk-free rate. Using stock prices and the number of shares on issue, which is derived from 10Q SEC filings, we can calculate the value of equity, V_E, and equity returns. In this example the volatility of equity, σ_E, is calculated as the standard deviation of the previous month's equity returns. The face value of debt, D, is also taken from the companies 10Q SEC filing. The time to expiration in all the numerical examples is one year from the current date, that is $T = 1$ and $t = 0$. With these inputs the values of V_A and σ_A can be found by solving the nonlinear system of equations (8.5)–(8.6) using the Excel solver. The bankruptcy probability can then be found using equation (8.7). The values of the expression inside the probability function in equation (8.7) for Time Warner were in the range of 47 to 112; these values would result in zero probabilities under the normal distribution. To generate non-zero bankruptcy probabilities a Student-t distribution with one degree of freedom was used in this example.

Figure 8.3 is a time series plot of the bankruptcy probability, from the structural model, calculated on a daily basis over the 2001 calendar year.

The average bankruptcy probability is 0.00925 with a standard deviation of 0.00193. The variability apparent in the bankruptcy probability is driven by the asset volatility, the correlation between the volatility of assets, derived from the equity volatility, and the bankruptcy probabilities is 0.94.

Finding default probabilities using the reduced-form approach is based on the bond pricing formula and assumptions about the stochastic properties of the hazard function. Using the assumption of independence between the risk-free rate and the default process made in Jarrow *et al.* (1997), and a

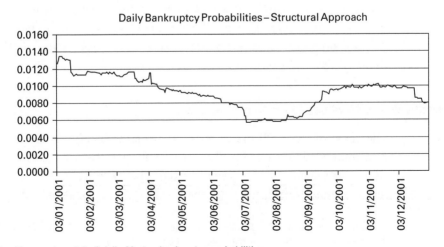

Figure 8.3   Time series plot of daily Merton bankruptcy probabilities

constant recovery rate for defaulted loans, the price of a risky zero coupon bond can be written as

$$p_r(T,t) = p_{rf}(T,t)[\delta F_r(T|t) + (1 - F_r(T|t))] \tag{8.8}$$

where $p_r(T,t)$ is the time t price of a risky zero coupon bond expiring at T, and $p_{rf}(T,t)$ is the time t price of a risk-free zero coupon bond expiring at T, with δ the constant recovery rate on default and $F_r(T|t)$ the probability of default for the risky bond. This pricing equation can be rearranged to provide an expression for the risk-neutral default probability:

$$F_r(T|t) = \frac{1 - \left(\frac{p_r(T,t)}{p_{rf}(T,t)}\right)}{1 - \delta}. \tag{8.9}$$

If the recovery rate δ is assumed to be constant, the only inputs required to calculate bankruptcy probabilities using (8.9) are zero coupon bond prices.

As most traded bonds are coupon bonds, a procedure for imputing the corresponding zero coupon bond prices is required. Hull (1997) provides a methodology for bootstrapping a zero coupon yield curve, Kwon (2002) presents an extension of the Nelson and Siegel approach which generates smooth zero coupon forward curves for risky bonds which always lie above the risk-free curve. Bond prices are calculated using the Nelson and Siegel parameters which describe the forward rate curve, as described in Bystrom and Kwon (2003).[16]

Bankruptcy probabilities corresponding to a recovery rate of 32.65%, the recovery rate used in Jarrow *et al.* (1997), which is the average recovery rate in 1991 for defaulted U.S. bonds, are calculated. The time to expiration in all the numerical examples is one year from the current date, that is $T = 1$ and $t = 0$.

Figure 8.4 is a time series plot of the bankruptcy probability, from the reduced-form model with $\delta = 0.3265$, calculated on a daily basis over the 2001 calendar year. The average daily bankruptcy probability is 0.017, with a standard deviation of 0.00296.

Sensitivity of CDS values to probability estimates

The value of the CDS premium is recalculated using the range or default probabilities derived from the Structural and Reduced-Form approach, while keeping all other parameters fixed. The CDS premium is calculated at seven default probabilities from the distribution of calculated values. At each

---

[16] The authors would like to acknowledge Dr Kwon's contribution of the estimated daily forward rate curve parametrizations used in the construction of zero coupon bond prices.

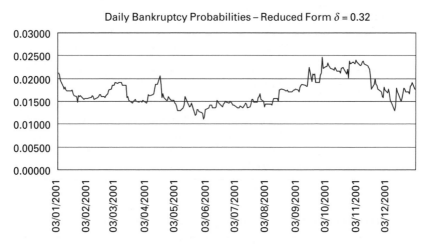

Figure 8.4   Time series plot of daily reduced form bankruptcy probabilities

probability value the premium for the given default probability is calculated, along with the difference between the calculated premium and the benchmark premium. Finally, the dollar value per million dollars of the swap, which is its value to the protection buyer and the unfunded liability for the protection seller, is calculated. The results for probabilities calculated using the structural approach are presented in Table 8.5.

For a CDS contract written using the base case parameters, then marked to market using the structural model probabilities in Table 8.5, the overall expected value to the protection buyer is $551 per million, and the corresponding mark-to-market expected loss for the protection seller is $551 per million. The probability of loss only drops below the 0.06% level used in the calculation of the base case for the $\mu-2\sigma$ and $\mu-3\sigma$ probabilities; in these two cases the protection buyer is under-protected and the protection seller would book a mark-to-market profit on the swap.

The results for probabilities calculated using the reduced-form approach are presented in Table 8.6.

For a CDS contract written using the base case parameters, then marked to market using the reduced-form model probabilities in Table 8.4, the overall expected value to the protection buyer is $1873 per million, and the corresponding mark-to-market expected loss for the protection seller is $1873 per million. The probability of loss does not drop below the 0.06% level used in the calculation of the base case. The swap contract has positive value to the protection buyer and the protection seller would book a mark-to-market profit on the swap at all probability values derived from the reduced-form model.

Table 8.5 CDS Premium under structural probabilities

	Default Prob	Premium (%)	Difference	Unfunded
$\mu+3\sigma$	0.01504	0.00255	0.00154	1538.30
$\mu+2\sigma$	0.01311	0.00222	0.00121	1208.70
$\mu+\sigma$	0.01118	0.00189	0.00088	879.74
μ	0.00925	0.00156	0.00055	551.42
$\mu-\sigma$	0.00732	0.00124	0.00022	223.75
$\mu-2\sigma$	0.00539	0.00091	-0.00010	-103.30
$\mu-3\sigma$	0.00346	0.00058	-0.00043	-429.71

Table 8.6 CDS Premium under reduced form probabilities

	Default Prob	Premium (%)	Difference	Unfunded
$\mu+3\sigma$	0.02588	0.00441	0.00340	3401.62
$\mu+2\sigma$	0.02292	0.00390	0.00289	2890.76
$\mu+\sigma$	0.01996	0.00339	0.00238	2381.46
μ	0.01700	0.00289	0.00187	1873.69
$\mu-\sigma$	0.01404	0.00238	0.00137	1367.44
$\mu-2\sigma$	0.01108	0.00188	0.00086	862.71
$\mu-3\sigma$	0.00812	0.00137	0.00036	359.49

These calculations show the sensitivity of the calculated CDS premium to the default probability that is used in the calculation. Reliance on historical default rates as benchmark parameters in the calculation of CDS premium, when the true probabilities are the market-based probabilities, has the potential to leave the protection writers with substantial unfunded liabilities arising from their CDS commitments. In the Time Warner case, if the default probabilities derived from the equity market using the structural approach are correct, writing CDS contracts over all of Time Warner's debt using the Moody's historical probabilities would lead to expected unfunded liabilities of 12.5 million dollars for the protection writers. Under reduced-form model probabilities the expected unfunded liabilities generated would be 42.7 million dollars.

Holders of large portfolios of CDS contracts are potentially exposed to large levels of unfunded liabilities. In the case of a downturn in the business cycle causing a sequence of defaults, these unfunded liabilities have the potential to affect the stability of institutions that have provided protection to lenders under these contracts.

REFERENCES

Basel Committee on Banking Supervision, Report of The Joint Forum, *Credit Risk Transfer*, October, 2004.

Basel Committee on Banking Supervision, 'Studies on credit risk concentration', *Working Paper No.15*, November, 2006.

Bank of England, *Financial Stability Review 12*, London, Bank of England, June, 2001.

Bomfim, A. N., *Understanding Credit Derivatives and Related Instruments*, San Diego, Elsevier, 2005.

Bystrom, H. and Kwon, O., 'A simple continuous measure of credit risk', *QFRG Working Paper 111*, School of Finance and Economics, University of Technology Sydney, 2003, in *International Review of Financial Analysis*, forthcoming.

Das, S., *Credit Derivatives: CDOs and Structured Credit Products*, International Swaps and Derivatives Association 2006 Year-End Market Survey, Hoboken, NJ, Wiley, 2007.

Gregory, J. (ed) *Credit Derivatives: The Definitive Guide*, Risk Books, London, 2004.

Harding, P. A., *Practical Guide to the 2003 ISDA Credit Derivatives Definitions*, Euromoney Books, 2004.

Hull, J., *Options, Futures, and Other Derivatives*, 3rd edn., Prentice Hall, 1997.

Jarrow, R., Lando, D. and Turnbull, S., 'A Markov model for the term structure of credit risk spreads', *Review of Financial Studies*, 10(2), 1997, 481–523.

Kwon, O., 'A general framework for the construction and the smoothing of forward rate curves', *QFRG Working Paper 73*, School of Finance and Economics, University of Technology Sydney, 2002.

Martellini, L., Priaulet, P. and Priaulet, S., *Fixed-Income Securities: Valuation, Risk Management, and Portfolio Strategies*, Chichester, Wiley, 2003.

Partnoy, F., and Skeel, D. A., 'The promise and perils of credit derivatives,' *University of Cincinnati Law Review 76*, 2007. (Invited symposium.)

Local government distress in Australia: A latent class regression analysis

Stewart Jones and Robert G. Walker

9.1. Introduction

The main focus of previous chapters in this volume has been on corporations in the private sector, and in particular, on those corporations whose securities are publicly traded (possibly because financial and market data about these firms were readily available). In this context, 'distress' has been variously interpreted as being evidenced by voluntary or creditor-induced administration (bankruptcy), default on a loan repayment, failure to pay a preference dividend (or even a reduction in the amount of ordinary dividend payments), share issues specifically to meet shortfalls in working capital, financial reorganization where debt is forgiven or converted to equity, and a failure to pay listing fees (see e.g. Foster 1986, Lau 1987, Ward 1994, Bahnson and Bartley 1992, Jones and Hensher 2004).

This chapter[1] is concerned with distress in the *public sector*, and focuses on local government in the state of New South Wales.[2] We interpret distress in terms of an inability of local governments to provide services at pre-existing levels. In order to provide services to the community, local governments are expected to invest in infrastructure and to maintain legacy infrastructure.

---

[1] This research is based on Jones and Walker (2007) 'Explanators of Local Government Distress', *Abacus*, 43:3, pp. 396–418. Permission to reproduce several parts of the Jones and Walker (2007) study was provided by Blackwell Publishing, the publishers of *Abacus*. In contrast to Jones and Walker (2007), this chapter employs a latent class analysis of local government distress (and include prediction outcomes), whereas Jones and Walker (2007) explore explanators of local government distress using a multiple regresson framework. We acknowledge funding support from the Australian Research Council (ARC) for this project.

[2] Australian local governments generally provide a more limited range of services than their counterparts in North America or the UK. Major responsibilities include provision of local roads, waste removal and maintenance of building controls – but not education, health services, or policing. Local councils in rural areas may also maintain water treatment and sewerage facilities, and other forms of transport infrastructure (such as regional airports).

Accordingly, we use the estimates developed by local governments of the cost of restoring infrastructure to a satisfactory condition as a measure of degrees of 'distress'. As such, the study uses a quantitative measure of distress, as opposed to the more limited (and less relevant) binary classification that characterizes private sector distress research.

There have only been limited applications of financial distress models to the not-for profit sector (e.g. Schipper's 1977 analysis of financial distress in U.S. private colleges). It is acknowledged that there has been extensive analysis of fiscal and financial crises in the local government sector, particularly in the United States in the wake of the financial problems facing New York city and Cleveland during the 1970s (see e.g. Gramlich 1976, Falconer 1991) and a subsequent spate of major financial crises in the early 1990s (see, e.g. Gramlich 1991, Honadle 2003). Commentators have also examined the financial crises experienced by local governments in a range of other countries (e.g. Carmeli and Cohen 2001, Bach and Vesper 2002, Carmeli 2003). In this context, a financial crisis could involve bankruptcy or loan default (see, e.g. the cases described in Cahill and James 1992) but has also been equated with a series of operating deficits (Cahill and James 1992, Bach and Vesper 2002).

Much of this literature has been concerned with exploring the *reasons* for fiscal crises – with some commentators attributing these problems to a lack of organizational resources and managerial skills leading to an incapacity to delivery quality services in an efficient manner or to adapt to changing conditions (Carmeli and Cohen 2001). Others have suggested that distress is a consequence of a failure to adapt to economic downturns in general, or the financial impact of unfunded mandates, as state governments shifted responsibilities to cities or municipalities without financial compensation or while restricting the capacity of local governments to increase revenues (Falconer 1991, Beckett-Camarata 2004). Still others sought to explain local government behaviour in times of financial stress (for a review, see Cooper 1996), or to describe state responses to municipal crises (see Cahill and James 1992, *Harvard Law Review* 1997).

While it appears there have only been limited attempts to predict local government financial distress in the research literature, those with a responsibility to monitor the performance of the local government sector have utilized a range of techniques to identify municipalities that may be facing difficulties. However, one contribution noted that while some jurisdictions have sought to establish early warning systems, 'they may not be functioning as planned' (Cahill and James 1992, p. 92). Another study reported the development of a simple index based on arbitrary weighting of nine variables (Kleine *et al.* 2003), and subsequently these authors reported the results of applying this to a sample of Michigan local governments – suggesting that it performed better than Michigan's current system of identifying potentially distressed local councils, apparently via financial statement analysis (Kloha *et al.* 2005). The claim of superior performance was based on the suggestion that it had 'theoretical validity', produced similar results to the assessments of a state agency, and was parsimonious. A 50-state survey by Honadle (2003) revealed that just under half of those states made some attempt to predict local government's fiscal crises, mainly through reviewing audit reports, local government reporting, or from information gleaned from discussions or regional workshops, with only some U.S. states using 'financial analysis methods' (p. 1454) – and apparently none using a statistical distress prediction model.

A recent Australian study proposed an econometric distress prediction model and (as with the approach used by Kloha *et al.* 2005) compared the findings with a 'watch list' compiled by a state government agency – in this case, concluding that the latter's selection of 'at risk' councils did not accurately identify municipalities that were (according to their model) in fact 'at risk' (Murray and Dollery 2005).

A number of commentaries have acknowledged that reviews of financial statement analysis alone may be a poor basis for predicting local government distress, because financial ratios may only show up problems 'too late'. Indeed, Clark and Ferguson (1983) provided extensive evidence to support their contention that fiscal strain reflects the degree to which governments fail to adapt to changes in the resources available to the taxpaying community. That observation in itself highlights the difficulties of applying distress prediction models to the public sector environment. It is well recognized that, in the private sector, a prediction of distress may not be fulfilled if management takes corrective action. It is also recognized that a major limitation of the distress literature is that many studies have modelled failure as a simplistic binary classification of failure or nonfailure (Jones 1987). This methodology has been widely questioned, because the strict legal concept of bankruptcy (or insolvency) may not always reflect the underlying economic reality of corporate financial distress. For instance, there is considerable documented evidence that corporations have, from time to time, misused bankruptcy provisions for their own strategic purposes, such as staving off creditors (Delaney 1991). Further, the two-state model can also conflict with underlying theoretical models of financial failure and this can potentially limit the extent to which empirical results can be generalized (see Chapter 2 of the volume).

If the archetypal two-state failure model is of dubious relevance in the private sector, its application may be even more severely limited in the public sector, where entities that are financially distressed may respond to falls in revenues or increases in costs by reducing the range and quality of services they provide to the community.

Against this background, the objective of this chapter is to fill a gap in the distress literature by developing a quantitative modelling approach to identify explanators of local council distress. As local councils typically do not fail in the sense of being unable to pay their debts, the aim is not to *predict* financial failure *per se* but rather to identify factors that explain local government distress – interpreted here as an inability of those entities to maintain standards of service.

A statistical modelling approach is arguably superior to more rudimentary and heuristic approaches (such as a financial statement analysis), because it allows the testing of formal hypotheses and an examination of the statistical and explanatory impact of a range of covariates in a multivariate setting. A quantitative model may have relevance in assisting state or commonwealth agencies oversighting the activities of the local government sector to develop robust early warning systems to identify potentially distressed councils. It may also assist in formulating policies regarding local council mergers or amalgamations, and (for jurisdictions that engage in rate pegging) assist in reviewing applications for special variations.[3] A quantitative modelling approach can also assist regulators back-test their own 'in house' distress ratings system (such as that undertaken by the NSW Department of Local Government in identifying councils that are 'at risk' of distress).

9.2. Measuring distress in local government

Previous literature has struggled to establish a satisfactory metric for local government distress. For instance, Clark (1977) discussed four indicators of municipal fiscal strain. These are: (a) probability of default, where default is defined as not meeting bond repayments, (b) ratio indicators, such as gross debt divided by the tax base or short-term debt to long-term debt, (c) social and economic base characteristics, such as population size and median

---

[3] Australian local governments are commonly subject to direction from state governments. NSW (alone amongst Australian states) subjects local government to a regime of rate pegging, whereby percentage increases in general income are subject to an upper limit unless applications for 'special rate variations' are approved by the Minister for Local Government (NSW Local Government Act, sections 505–13).

family income, and (d) funds flow measures. However, all of these measures have certain intractable problems when operationalized as a formal measure of local government distress (particularly in Australia). As noted by Clark (1977), bond defaults may not be useful given that actual default rates have historically been extremely low (see also Kaplan 1977). Furthermore, the link between bond ratings and financial condition presupposes that capital markets are provided with adequate financial information by local governments (which may be unrealistic given the lack of consistent and transparent financial disclosure in many U.S. local government authorities). Ratio indicators (such as debt to equity) are unsuitable as dependent variables in the modelling of distress, for many reasons, including (i) financial ratio indicators used as dependent variables are likely to be correlated, directly or indirectly, with other financial indicators used as independent variables and (ii) ratio metrics are not specifically related to the broader non-financial dimensions of local council distress (if interpreted as an inability to maintain the quality of service delivery to the community). Similarly, socio-economic factors (such as population size) are again more appropriately used as explanatory variables in modelling as these measures do not represent direct measures of local council distress.

Another dependent variable that can potentially indicate distress in local councils is the incidence of mergers and amalgamations. The NSW government has long encouraged voluntary local council mergers to encourage efficiencies and strengthen their financial well being. For instance, the Local Government Amendment (Amalgamations and Boundary Changes) Bill 1999 is designed to streamline the procedures laid down in the Local Government Act 1993 for voluntary amalgamations of council areas.[4] On the surface of it, the incidence of mergers and amalgamations represents a potentially attractive dependent variable, as merged councils can be readily identified[5] and typically such merger activity has been motivated in response to the financial viability of many local councils.[6] For instance, consider the proposal for creation of a New Capital City Regional Council incorporating

---

[4] Chapter 9 of the Local Government Act 1993 Part 1, Areas, and Part 3, Local Government Boundaries Commission, contain information on the constitution, dissolution and alteration of local government areas.

[5] Over the past 10 years, around 13% of councils have disappeared through mergers and amalgamations.

[6] Section 263 of the NSW Local Government Act requires that the Boundaries Commission has regard to (a) the financial advantages or disadvantages (including the economies or diseconomies of scale) of any relevant proposal to the residents and ratepayers of the areas concerned; (b) the impact of any relevant proposal on the ability of the councils of the areas concerned to provide adequate, equitable and appropriate services and facilities; (c) the impact of any relevant proposal on the employment of the staff by the councils of the areas concerned; (d) the impact of any relevant proposal on rural communities in the areas concerned.

several smaller councils (Cooma-Monaro, Gunning, Mulwaree, Queanbeyan, Tallaganda, Yarrowlumla and the Yass shire councils). A major rationale for the merger was motivated as follows (see p. 10 of the application):

'The substantial pool of funds (*through consolidating the revenues of all adjacent councils*) contrasts with the meagre financial bases that some of the existing Councils possess. It might be noted that two of the five Councils had deficits on ordinary activities in 2002. Gunning (southern half) had a small surplus in 2002, but a large deficit of $244,000 in 2001. Tallaganda had a deficit of $322,000 in 2001. It is clear that four out of the five Councils are operating on very slim margins between revenues and expenditure from ordinary activities.'[7] (*emphasis added*).

However, there are a number of issues to consider if council mergers and amalgamations are used as the distress metric. Public companies experiencing distress can seek out merger partners in any number of locations, and typically merge with business partners that are in a stronger financial position. However, mergers of local councils in NSW (and elsewhere) are constrained by geographic considerations (such as the statutory requirement to prepare a detailed cost benefit analysis of any proposed merger to regulatory authorities). Typically, distressed councils merge with adjacent councils that may only be marginally better off in financial terms themselves.[8] Merging two or more financially fragile councils does not necessarily create one larger 'healthy' council.[9] Most mergers over recent years in NSW have involved smaller regional councils, and the numbers have been comparatively small in absolute terms (not more than 13% in the past ten years).

Service delivery as the dependent variable

Given the difficulties in operationalizing an appropriate financial distress measure in local councils, this study focuses on constructing a proxy of distress linked to basic operating objectives of local councils, which is to provide services to the community. The major responsibilities of Australian local government are the provision of local infrastructure (such as roads,

---

[7] The application can be located at the following url:http://www.dlg.nsw.gov.au/Files/CommissionsTribunals/BC_ Proposal_Capital_City.pdf#xml=http://www.dlg.nsw.gov.au/Scripts/dtSearch/dtisapi6.dll?cmd=getpdfhits&DocId=67 6&Index=c%3a%5cdtsearch%5cuserdata%5cAllDocuments&HitCount=4&hits=6c + 70a + a64 + 1603 + &.pdf

[8] For example, consider the December 2000 proposal to create the new Gwydir Shire Council which combined the Yalloroi, Bingara and part of the Barraba shire councils (the new Gwydir Council was officially formed on 17 March 2004). This was a merger of three small regional councils, all of which were in a fairly fragile financial position.

[9] For instance, the Bingara and Yalloroi shire councils both showed a negative surplus on their 2002 financial statements. See their original petition at http://www.dlg.nsw.gov.au/Files/CommissionsTribunals/BC_ Proposal_Gwydir_Shire_Council.pdf#xml=http://www.dlg.nsw.gov.au/Scripts/dtSearch.

bridges and community facilities) and waste collection. Local councils are responsible for administering building controls (though in some circumstances these may be over-ridden by state authorities). In major metropolitan areas the provision of water and sewerage services is undertaken by state agencies, but in rural and regional areas these functions are generally provided by local councils (sometimes through joint ventures). While individual councils may provide some social welfare services, the provision of health, and education services is a responsibility of the states, with the commonwealth government providing earmarked grants to support some services (such as home care programmes for the aged or persons with disabilities).

Service delivery can be considered in terms of both the *quantity* or *quality* of services provided. In this exploratory analysis, the focus is on *qualitative* aspects of service delivery. A purely quantitative measure of service delivery can result in misleading interpretations of local council distress and may not be, for various reasons, strongly associated to explanators of distress (see Table 9.1). For example, road infrastructure can be provided and/or maintained by a local council, in spite of the fact that road quality itself can be steadily diminishing over time or left in a poor state of repair. Similarly, sewerage infrastructure may continue to operate, even though it is in such a poor state of repair that it can threaten public health standards and the local environment. An example of why a quantitative measure of service delivery may not be appropriate can be illustrated by the circumstances of Windouran Shire Council in New South Wales. The distress of this council was discussed in the NSW parliamentary debates as follows:

'Windouran's plan to get out of its financial distress was to significantly increase rates each year, rip up the bitumen on some roads and make them all gravel to save maintenance costs, sell all but essential plant and equipment and delay the purchase of new equipment, and consider further reductions in staff. This response demonstrates clearly the seriousness of the situation of Windouran council. Windouran Shire Council has an operating deficit amounting to $1,251 for each man, woman and child in the shire.' (*Hansard*, NSW Legislative Assembly, 11/11/1999, p. 2786).

It has been suggested that local government fiscal stress may lead to a decline in maintenance expenditure on infrastructure and a decrease in capital investment on infrastructure in order to finance other expenditures (Bumgarner *et al.* 1991). This chapter interprets a decline in expenditure on infrastructure – and a corresponding increase in the funding required to restore the functionality of infrastructure assets – as a proxy for distress, as

Table 9.1 Latent class regression analysis (1 class) for quantitative measures (i.e. physical output levels) of service delivery

Financial variables	Unstandardized Coefficients		Standardized Coefficients	t-value	p-value
	B	Std. Error	Beta		
(Constant)	5.572	5.171		1.078	.283
Current ratio	.518	1.087	.046	.477	.634
Cash flow operations to total assets	.425	1.235	.043	.344	.731
Long term interest bearing debt to total assets	.000	.002	.047	.265	.791
Cash resources to total assets	.100	.560	.018	.178	.859
Interest cover	.000	.000	−.097	−.536	.593
Gross debt to operating cash flow	−.190	.290	−.060	−.655	.514
Operating cash flow to total infrastructure assets	−.022	.263	−.008	−.085	.932
Ordinary revenue (less waste and sewerage charges) to total assets	.727	.977	.232	.745	.458
Total expenditure by total assets	−.912	.965	−.310	−.945	.347
Surplus to total assets	−.159	1.031	−.020	−.154	.878

local government entities fail to allocate sufficient funds to adequately maintain that infrastructure.

Information concerning the funding required to restore the functionality of infrastructure is available in NSW, since the 1993 legislation required local councils to assess and report to the Minister for Local Government whether their infrastructure (in four categories) was in a satisfactory condition, and if not, the estimated cost of bringing that infrastructure to a satisfactory condition. Further, councils were required to provide estimates of the (hypothetical) cost of maintaining those assets in a satisfactory condition, together with particulars of the current-year budgetary allocations for maintenance. A potential limitation of this dependent variable construct is that, in the absence of a standard methodology for defining and measuring 'satisfactory condition', local councils may have widely different interpretations of 'satisfactory condition'. We found that initially the information reported by councils varied in quality and coverage, and in the interpretations adopted for 'satisfactory condition' (see Walker *et al.* 1999). Our telephone interviews with several local council managers, accountants and engineers indicate that concepts have since been clarified and it appears that the majority of councils have improved the quality of the information reported (with some exceptions). While this has created more consistency in how 'satisfactory condition' is interpreted and reported by councils, there is still greater scope for local government regulators to develop more detailed and uniform definitions of 'satisfactory condition' as well as further clarifying an appropriate methodology or framework for estimating costs to get infrastructure assets into satisfactory condition.

Subsequently other standard-setting bodies – including the U.S. Federal Accounting Standards Advisory Board (FASAB, 1996), the Governmental Accounting Standards Board (GASB 1996) have introduced accounting standards that required some form of reference to infrastructure condition. The FASAB required disclosures related to the condition and the estimated cost to remedy deferred maintenance to property, plant and equipment, while prohibiting recognition of the dollar values of these items in the financial statements (FASAB 1996). The GASB introduced options for accounting for infrastructure by American states and municipalities: these entities were either to value and then depreciate infrastructure assets, or alternatively, demonstrate that infrastructure assets were being managed using an asset management system, and document that the assets were being preserved approximately at (or above) a condition level established by and disclosed by that government. Whereas the GASB required that state and municipal governments account for infrastructure either through asset recognition followed by depreciation, or through supplementary reporting on infrastructure condition, the NSW local government requirements required *both*, through a combination of the application of Australian Accounting Standards, and supplementary reporting.

9.3. Methodology

Much of the traditional corporate distress prediction literature has employed a variety of discrete-choice models, the most popular being linear discriminant analysis and binary logit and probit models (see e.g., Altman 1968,

Altman *et al.* 1977, Ohlson 1980, Zmijewski 1984, Duffie and Singleton 2003). There has also been a plethora of new modelling approaches in recent years, including structural (or 'distance to default') models and intensity (or reduced form) models (see Chapters 6 and 8 of this volume). Furthermore, new research has been conducted into the behavioural performance of advanced logit models, such as random parameters logit (or mixed logit), nested logit models, latent class MNL and error component logit models (see Chapters 2 and 3). This study uses the latent class methodology outlined in Chapter 3. However, in this case we employ a latent class regression model where the dependent variable is continuous.

Data collection and sample

The sample used in this study is based on the financial statements and infrastructure report data of 172 local councils in New South Wales over a two year period 2001–2. The data collected included local council characteristics (such as whether the council is large or small, or urban or rural based on formal classifications used by the DLG); service delivery outputs, condition of infrastructure and an extensive range of financial variables (described below). Data were collected from several sources. Infrastructure data were accessed from the 2002 infrastructure reports to the Minister on the condition of public infrastructure prepared by New South Wales councils in accordance with the Local Government Act of 1993. These reports were provided by the New South Wales Department of Local Government for the population of 172 councils then operating in the state in 2002.

Council background data were collected from a report of *Comparative Information on New South Wales Local Government Councils* prepared by the Department of Local Government (2002). This report contains comparative data for all councils in New South Wales across a series of key performance indicators for the years 1999/00, 2000/01 and 2001/02. This report was also used to source many of the financial and non-financial variables used in this study. Other financial variables were obtained from the 2001 and 2002 annual reports or financial statements of local councils.

The first stage in the annual report collection process involved searching the websites of the sampled local councils for downloadable copies of their 2001 and 2002 annual reports. The reports of 69 local councils were available online, and these reports were downloaded. The remaining 103 councils were contacted (either via email, telephone or mail) and requested to forward their 2001 and 2002 annual reports. This procedure resulted in 161 useable annual reports.

Data integrity checks of data relating to infrastructure condition that had been filed with the DLG identified some significant percentage variations between years. Follow-up enquires to individual councils resolved these; most reflected a failure to 'round' reported data to the nearest $1,000, while other amendments corrected typographical errors by those councils in one or other year.

Definition of distress

From the discussion above, the definition of distress used in this study incorporates a qualitative measure of service delivery. This definition is not linked to social service outputs per se but to the *condition* of infrastructure assets upon which the delivery of local council services is critically dependent. Levels of distress are defined for this purpose as being represented by the estimated cost expected to be incurred by local councils to get infrastructure assets into a 'satisfactory condition'. Specifically, the dependent variable in this study is a continuous variable defined as *the ratio of expected total costs to bring local council infrastructure assets to a satisfactory condition, scaled by total revenues*. Scaling (i.e., dividing) to total revenues is intended to control for size differences between local councils, and is appropriate as general revenue is the primary source of funds available to a local councils to maintain infrastructure in satisfactory condition. As noted above, many NSW councils (mainly those outside major metropolitan areas) received revenues from charges for water and sewerage services (and these charges are not subject to rate pegging). Accordingly, scaling involved use of total revenues (both excluding and including water and sewerage charges). It was found that scaling total costs to bring infrastructure assets to a satisfactory condition by other denominators (such as operating cash flows or total assets) was highly correlated with total revenues, suggesting that this measure is robust to choice of scale.[10]

Explanatory variables

A broad range of financial and non-financial measures were tested (see the Appendix for a list of variables and their definitions). The explanatory variables are in four categories: (1) council characteristics; (2) local service

---

[10] The total revenue measure and operating cash flow measure have a coefficient of 0.82, and the total revenue measure and total asset measure have a coefficient of 0.66 (both tests are based on a Pearson's *r* two-tailed test and are significant at the 0.01 level).

delivery variables; (3) infrastructure variables; and (4) financial variables. A brief description and explanation of the choice of variables follows.

Council characteristics

Local government areas in NSW vary considerable in terms of geography and demography, and encompass areas as small as 5.8 km^2 (the Sydney suburb of Hunters Hill) to as large as 26,268.7 km^2 (the local government area of Wentworth in the far west of the State) (DLG 2005). Population densities vary considerably – from 0.11 per km^2 in the rural areas of Brewarrina and Cobar, to 6,697.85 per km^2 in the Sydney suburb of Waverley. Such variations would affect both the volume of services to be provided to local communities, and the scale of revenues received by councils, mainly from 'rates' (property taxes based on unimproved capital values). Because of a combination of a lower rate base, smaller staffing levels and the challenge of having to service larger areas, it has been commonly suggested that the local government areas most exposed to financial stresses are in rural and regional areas (and, indeed, the Department of Local Government's 2002 'watch list' indicates that 24 of the 26 'at risk' councils are rural or regional).

Local councils were classified into eleven major categories in the DLG database:

1 = Capital City
2 = Metro Developed – small/medium
3 = Metro Developed – large/very large
4 = Regional Town/City – small/medium
5 = Regional Town/City – large/very large
6 = Fringe – small/medium
7 = Fringe – large/very large
8 = Agricultural – small
9 = Agricultural/Remote – medium
10 = Agricultural/Remote – large
11 = Agricultural – very large.

These variables included in the model to reflect council characteristics were as follows:

(i) whether the council is large or small (a dummy variable describing whether council is large/extra large or small/medium, based on the DLG classification summarized above, with large councils encompassing categories: 1, 3, 5, 7, 10, 11 and small councils encompassing 2, 4, 6, 8, 9);

(ii) whether the council is rural or urban (a dummy variable coded whether council is urban or rural, with urban councils being categories 1–7, and rural councils categories 8–11 in the DLG classification scheme);

(iii) number of equivalent full time council staff;

(iv) population serviced within local council boundaries;

(v) number of rateable farmland properties;

(vi) number of rateable business and ratable residential properties

Service delivery variables

It is commonly suggested that the main issues facing Australian local councils are the 3Rs – 'roads, rates and rubbish'. That label summarizes some of the major responsibilities of the 'third tier' of Australian government – councils are responsible for local roads, and the collection and disposal of waste; unlike local government in some other countries, they are not responsible for health, education, policing or public housing. Australian local governments may also provide a range of other services: some maintain libraries, swimming pools and sporting facilities, and provide care for the aged or disabled citizens (though the latter services are primarily funded by commonwealth and state governments). The provision of waste collection services constitutes a material expenditure for the sector. Other services (such as the provision of library facilities) are likely to be less significant.

Accordingly, service delivery variables (using data from the DLG database) were:

(i) domestic waste pickups per week;

(ii) number of residential properties receiving waste management services;

(iii) total kilograms of recyclables collected.

Infrastructure variables

Arguably the greatest expenditure of local governments is directed towards providing and maintaining infrastructure of varying kinds. While the maintenance of local roads, other transport infrastructure and drainage systems is a common responsibility, many local councils are also responsible for reticulation of potable water and sewerage (the exceptions being those local government areas serviced by state-owned authorities operating in areas surrounding Sydney and Newcastle).

With this background, the infrastructure variables examined in the analysis were:

(i) the carrying values for buildings, roads, other transport, water, sewerage and drainage infrastructure;

(ii) estimated costs to bring buildings, roads, other transport, water, sewerage and drainage infrastructure to a satisfactory condition;

(iii) budgeted maintenance expenditure for buildings, roads, water, sewerage and drainage infrastructure.

Financial variables

The financial measures used in the study are based on a number of ratio measures examined in the financial distress literature over the last three decades (examples include Altman *et al.* 1977, Ohlson 1980, Zemjewski 1984, Casey and Bartczak 1985, Gentry *et al.* 1985, Jones 1987, Altman 2001). More recent research has established the importance of operating cash flows in predicting corporate failure (see Jones and Hensher 2004). Previous U.S. research had only tested estimates of operating cash flows and such proxies have been found to be associated with significant measurement error (see Hribar and Collins 2002). As Australian accounting standards have required local councils to prepare detailed cash flow statements prepared using the direct method since the 1990s (see AAS 27 'Financial Reporting by Local Government', paragraphs 31–2 (1993), and AASB 1026 (1992)), it was possible to use reported cash flow measures). Financial ratio categories tested in this study include: operating cash flows (e.g. operating cash flows to total assets); cash position (e.g. cash and short-term investments to total assets); liquidity and working capital (e.g. current ratio); rate of return (e.g. reported surplus to total assets); financial structure (e.g. total debt to total assets); and debt servicing capacity (e.g. operating cash flow to interest payments). Further, several possible interactions of financial and council-specific and demographic variables were examined. The purpose of testing interaction effects is to determine whether contextual factors (such as population size or council type) have a moderating influence on the financial variables which enter the model. For instance, it is possible that the size of a council has a moderating influence on the level of indebtedness (larger councils might be more indebted than smaller councils or vice versa).

9.4. Empirical results

In this section, two latent class regression models based on a *quantitative* and *qualitative* measure of service delivery are compared. A quantitative measure of service delivery only considers changes in the physical level of output or services provided to the community by councils (such as the physical number of residential properties which receive a waste management service), whereas a qualitative measure of service delivery is based on the adequacy of services provided, as proxied by the physical condition of assets on which service delivery is critically dependent. As indicated earlier, a quantitative measure of service delivery can lead to misleading interpretations as it may only be spuriously linked to financial aspects of council distress and service quality itself. For example, local councils are obliged to collect residential waste products *irrespective* of their financial position or performance. Also, while councils can be maintaining services at current levels, a lack of investment in maintaining critical infrastructure can (potentially) result in a catastrophic drop in service quality in a later period.

In order to examine whether council financial performance is linked to a quantitative measure of service delivery, a service output measure was constructed, based on the annual growth of services provided by local councils over a two year period (2001–2). This measure of distress includes the following service output variables:[11] number of services (domestic waste pickups per week); total kilograms of recyclables collected; total kilograms of domestic waste collected; and number of residential properties receiving waste management service. A composite of growth in service delivery across these key measures was calculated, and then regressed onto a range of local council financial variables taken over the same period. Table 9.1 reports the parameter estimates and *t* values across a number of financial variables, including ratios based on working capital, cash flow from operations, cash position, interest cover, net surplus to total assets and total debt to total assets. As can be seen in Table 9.1, no statistically significant relationships were found between these variables and the quantitative measure of service delivery.[12] We found that this result held notwithstanding the number of latent classes specified in the model. Table 9.2 outputs were produced from a one-class regression model, which assumes the homogeneous parameter estimates over the sample.

In order to test the qualitative measure of distress, a series of latent class regression models were estimated ranging from 1–4 classes. Chapter 3 examines the major advantages of the latent regression model relative to the standard regression model. As was mentioned in Chapter 3, the number of classes specified is very important for model estimation. Specifying too

---

[11] Data were collected from Department of Local Government (NSW), *Comparative Information on New South Wales Local Government Councils*, 2002.

[12] The results were essentially the same when individual physical output measures (such as change in the number of residential properties receiving waste management service) were used as the dependent variable.

Table 9.2 Model fit and prediction statistics for a two-class latent regression model

Log-Likelihood Statistics			
Log-likelihood (LL)	−141.5		
Log-prior	−17.524		
Log-posterior	−159.02		
BIC (based on LL)	368.849		
AIC (based on LL)	332.999		
AIC3 (based on LL)	357.999		
CAIC (based on LL)	393.849		
R square	.82		
Classification Statistics	Classes		
Classification errors	0.1335		
Reduction of errors (Lambda)	0.7297		
Entropy R-squared	0.6884		
Standard R-squared	0.7002		
Classification log-likelihood	−148.19		
AWE	543.087		
Classification Table	Modal		
Probabilistic	Class1	Class2	Total
Class1	14.7741	0.9131	15.6872
Class2	3.2259	12.0869	15.3128
Total	18	13	31
Prediction Statistics			
Error Type	Baseline	Model	R^2
Squared Error	13409.7	36.0349	0.9973
Minus Log-likelihood	6.1708	3.2112	0.4796
Absolute Error	81.5532	4.7025	0.9423

many classes can improve model fit but cause the latent class model to become unstable. Specifying too few classes could result in the model failing to pick up important differences in latent classes in the sampled data.

Table 9.2 displays overall model-fit statistics and prediction errors. Table 9.3 displays parameter estimates and significance levels for a two-class latent regression model; including significance levels across latent classes. We found that a while a three- or four-class model improved model fit, individual parameter estimates were less significant overall.

The final model was selected based on its overall explanatory and statistical coherence. The two-class latent regression model displayed in Table 9.2

Table 9.3 Parameter estimates, wald statistics, Z values, means and standard deviations for latent class model

	Class1	Z value	Class2	Z value	Wald stat	Mean	Std.Dev.
Explanatory variables:							
Population within council boundaries	0.0006	2.8084	0.0018	5.908	9.8805	0.0012	0.0006
Road program costs over total assets	10798.4	7.5527	5467.78	1.9498	2.8993	8164.26	2665.11
Number of full-time (equivalent) staff	−0.0924	−1.6123	−0.142	−2.5771	0.3828	−0.1169	0.0248
Carrying value − total infrastructure	−0.0002	−4.9855	−0.0002	−3.5598	0.2364	−0.0002	0
Ordinary revenue less waste and sewerage to total assets	−28.178	−8.2598	−19.565	−6.3682	3.7376	−23.922	4.3061
Rates revenue to total ordinary revenue	−11.035	−11.9877	−0.0516	−0.0396	48.6002	−5.6076	5.4914
Local council large or small	−43.091	−4.5774	31.0418	2.4443	21.5065	−6.458	37.0636
Area serviced by Council (sqr kms)	−0.0162	−2.6118	0.0382	3.767	20.9529	0.0107	0.0272
Cash position to total assets	35.023	5.6373	22.352	4.9616	2.8665	28.7616	6.3351
Intercept	877.339	.0545	160.248	−.0545	42.5313	522.988	358.521
Error Variances							
Dependent variable	474.61	2.664	502.515	2.572		488.399	13.9515

has delivered a very good overall goodness of fit with an adjusted R^2 of 0.82. Importantly, when we estimated the model from 1–4 classes, there was a significant improvement in the log-likelihood ratio at convergence moving from 2–3 classes.

Table 9.2 also reports the Bayesian Information Criterion (BIC), the Akaike Information Criterion (AIC), Akaike Information Criterion 3 (AIC3), and the Consistent Akaike Information Criterion (CAIC) based on the L^2

and degrees of freedom (df) and number of parameters in the model. The BIC, AIC and CAIC scores weight the fit and parsimony of the model by adjusting the log-likelihood to take into account the number of parameters in the model. These information criteria weight the fit and the parsimony of a model: generally the lower BIC, AIC, AIC3, or CAIC values, the better the fit of the model. We found that the BIC score in particular was the most improved for a two-class model. Further, the R^2 value improved from 0.64 for a one-class model to 0.82 for a two-class model.

Classification statistics are also useful for interpreting model performance. When classification of cases is based on modal assignment (to the class having the highest membership probability), the proportion of cases that are expected to be misclassified is reported by the classification. Generally, the closer this value is to 0 the better; and the model has a relatively low classification error rate of 0.1335. Reduction of errors (lambda), Entropy R^2 and Standard R^2 are statistics which indicate how well the model predicts class memberships. The closer these values are to 1 the better the predictions as indicated in Table 9.2. Furthermore, AWE is a similar measure to BIC, but also takes classification performance into account. Finally, the classification table cross-tabulates modal and probabilistic class assignments.

The prediction statistics reported in Table 9.2 are based on the comparison between observed and predicted outcomes. This information can be used to assess prediction performance of the model. Table 9.2 provides the following measures of prediction error: mean squared error (MSE), mean absolute error (MAE), minus mean log-likelihood (−MLL), and for ordinal/nominal dependent variables, the proportion of predictions errors under modal prediction (PPE). For each error measure, we provide the prediction error of the baseline (or intercept-only model), the prediction error of the estimated model, and a R^2 value (which is the proportional reduction of errors in the estimated model compared to the baseline model).

Table 9.3 provides the parameter estimates for each predictor variable in the model, including the degree to which latent classes are statistically different from each other – this is shown by the Wald statistic (which is a test of the null hypothesis that parameter estimates are equal). Latent class parameters display the relative impact of the predictor variable on the local council distress variable. Interpreting the parameter estimates in Table 9.3, it can be seen that distress in local councils is *positively* associated with the population levels serviced within local council boundaries ($z = 2.80$ and 5.90 respectively for class 1 and 2). However, there are some differences in the statistical impacts across latent classes. Population levels in councils represented by latent class 2 has a stronger overall statistical impact on distress (0.0001 vs. 0.006), which is confirmed by the statistical significance of the Wald statistic reported in Table 9.3. Furthermore, the impact of local council size is strikingly different across the two classes (parameter estimates are −43.09 vs. 31.04). The opposite signs for this parameter indicate that among class 2 councils, larger councils have a positive impact on the distress of councils, but smaller councils are relatively more distressed among councils belonging to latent class 1. The area parameter also has opposite signs. For class 2 councils, the size of the local area service by councils has a positive impact on distress (0.038), but for class 1 councils smaller areas to service increase the probability of distress (−0.016). Again, the difference across classes is statistically significant. For both latent classes, lower numbers of full-time staff are associated with higher council distress, but this impact is higher for councils belonging to latent class 2; however, in this case the differences in class weights are not statistically significant.

It was found that distress is *negatively* associated with measures based on revenue generation capacity. Councils with lower percentages of rates revenue to total revenue were associated with higher distress; however, Table 9.3 indicates that this impact is much higher for councils belonging to latent class 1. Lower amounts of ordinary revenue to total assets are also associated with higher levels of council distress, and again this impact is much higher for councils belonging to latent class 1. In both cases, the difference between latent classes is statistically significant, although the differences on the rates revenue to total ordinary revenue variable is not as great across classes (the Wald statistics are 48.6 vs. 3.73 respectively).

Councils with lower carrying values for infrastructure assets were associated with greater distress ($z = -4.98, -3.55$ respectively for class 1 and 2). Lower written-down values could suggest that assets are older and possibly in poorer condition, however the parameter estimates for both latent classes are identical. Also, road maintenance costs featured prominently in results ($z = 7.55, 1.94$ respectively for class 1 and 2) – higher road programme costs are associated with higher council distress, although again the impact of this variable is stronger for class 1 than class 2 (the Wald statistic is only marginally significant, however). Cash resources to total assets was also significantly associated with council distress ($z = 5.63$ and 4.96 respectively for class 1 and 2), and once again the impact is slightly greater for class 1 (the Wald statistic is statistically significant across classes on this variable). The result on cash resources looks slightly counter-intuitive as higher cash resources appear to be associated with higher council distress. However, this result could indicate that councils are not committing cash resources to maintain infrastructure assets.

It can be seen from Table 9.3 that the highest z values (indicating a stronger statistical influence on distress) were variables associated with revenue generation ordinary revenue (less waste and sewerage charges) to total assets ($z = -8.25, -6.36$ respectively for class 1 and 2); rates revenue total revenue ($z = -11.03$ for class 1 but the parameter estimate is not significant on class 2). Again, this result could be directly related to legislative requirements for rate pegging among local councils in NSW, which can restrict the capacity of some councils to raise revenues to meet greater service delivery demands as well as finance the maintenance of infrastructure assets so that they remain in a satisfactory condition.

Overall, in terms of higher impacts on council distress, the profile of latent class 1 (which we call smaller lower-revenue generating councils), are smaller councils servicing smaller areas that are relatively less affected by population levels, but are highly impacted by road maintenance costs, and lower revenue generation capacity (particularly rates revenue generation). In terms of higher impacts on council distress, latent class 2 councils (which we call larger higher-revenue generating councils) are larger councils servicing larger areas with higher population levels and lower full-time staff. These councils are less impacted by their rates revenue base, but are impacted by lower overall revenue generation capacity. Compared to Class 1 councils, Class 2 councils are relatively less impacted by road programme costs, the carrying value of infrastructure assets.

There are some noteworthy findings that were *not* found to be significant in the results. For instance, the urban versus rural council classification did not yield any statistically significant findings in the model. This is despite a widely held belief that Australian rural councils are experiencing a relatively higher degree of distress, partly because they are required to service larger geographical areas coupled with smaller population sizes to generate rates revenue (as pointed out earlier, many council mergers and amalgamations in recent years have involved smaller rural councils). Table 9.4 provides a closer analysis of the financial performance of urban vs. rural councils in NSW across a wide range of financial indicators, including the current ratio, capital expenditure ratio, debt to assets, cash flow from operations, cash resources to total assets and revenue generation capacity. Also displayed are group differences in the distress construct used in this study (the costs to get infrastructure assets into satisfactory condition). It is noteworthy that neither the distress construct nor a range of financial performance variables

Table 9.4 Comparison of financial performance of urban vs. rural councils

Financial variables		N	Mean	Std. Dev	Std. Error Mean
Current Ratio	*Rural*	259	2.5978	1.64	.10
	Urban	65	2.4572	1.09	.13
Capital Expenditure Ratio	*Rural*	259	.3676	11.59	.72
	Urban	65	.9602	1.28	.15
Debt Ratio	*Rural*	259	6.06**	5.02	.31
	Urban	65	3.52	3.24	.40
Cash flow operations to	*Rural*	221	3.91*	6.72	.45
total assets	*Urban*	50	2.27	3.08	.43
Ordinary revenue to total assets	*Rural*	239	16.80*	42.67	2.76
	Urban	59	7.98	4.60	.60
Ordinary revenue less waste and	*Rural*	239	13.47*	38.46	2.48
sewerage to total asset	*Urban*	59	7.20	4.09	.53
Cash resources to	*Rural*	238	3.43*	6.02	.39
total assets	*Urban*	60	1.877	2.11	.27
Cash flow cover	*Rural*	98	54.93	38.01	38.85
	Urban	21	53.17	181.58	39.94
Rates to ordinary revenue	*Rural*	259	37.06**	10.83	.67
	Urban	65	57.73	8.24	1.02
Gross debt to operating	*Rural*	221	1.60	5.91	.39
cash flow	*Urban*	50	1.23	2.66	.37
Operating cash flow to total	*Rural*	105	5.2794	7.15	.69
infrastructure assets	*Urban*	26	5.2142	4.49	.88
Ordinary revenue less	*Rural*	121	17.6852*	31.91	2.90
water and sewerage to total	*Urban*	33	85.6761	375.58	65.38
infrastructure assets					
Operating cash flow to revenues	*Rural*	221	.3545*	.16	.01078
	Urban	50	.2614	.19	.02816
Net surplus to total assets	*Rural*	239	.4290	5.38	.34833
	Urban	59	.6366	1.13	.14819
Total costs to bring local council	*Rural*	121	144.8476	166.62048	15.14732
infrastructure assets into	*Urban*	33	114.7209	116.03305	20.19876
satisfactory condition scaled					
by total revenues (net of					
waste and sewerage charges)					

* Significant at .05 level
** Significant at .001 level

were found to be statistically significant between urban and rural councils. Table 9.4 indicates that rural councils have a significantly higher level of indebtedness relative to urban councils; however, rural councils appear to have a stronger revenue base relative to total assets (irrespective of whether waste and sewerage charges are included or excluded in revenues). Furthermore, rural councils have a significantly stronger cash position and operating cash flow performance relative to urban councils, as well as a lower proportion of rates to total revenue. Other financial indicators, such as the current ratio, debt servicing capacity, net surplus to total assets and gross debt to operating cash flows were not statistically significant between rural and urban councils.[13]

9.5. Conclusions

This chapter develops a latent class regression model to identify and predict factors most closely associated with local council distress in Australia. A major objective has been to develop a pragmatic and meaningful measure of council distress that can be readily operationalized for statistical modelling purposes.

The concept of distress used here is linked to the basic operating objectives of local government, which is to provide a basic range of services to the community. Specifically, the dependent-variable construct in this study is specified as a continuous variable, defined as the ratio of expected total costs to bring local council infrastructure assets into satisfactory condition scaled by total revenues (net of waste and sewerage charges). This dependent variable was modelled in a latent class regression framework using a wide range of performance indicators, including variables relating to council characteristics and demographics (such as council size and population size); service delivery; infrastructure variables and a wide range of financial indicators. The model that yielded the best model fit and predictive results was a two-class model. Overall, in terms of higher impacts on council distress, the profile of latent class 1 (which we call smaller lower-revenue councils), are smaller councils servicing smaller areas that are relatively less affected by population levels, but are highly impacted by road maintenance costs, and lower revenue generation capacity (particularly rates revenue generation). In terms of higher impacts on council distress, latent class 2

---

[13] Use of non-parametric tests (i.e. Mann–Whitney U for independent samples) did not alter the reported results significantly.

councils (which we call larger higher-revenue councils) are larger councils servicing larger areas with higher population levels and lower full-time staff. These councils are less impacted by their rates revenue base, but are impacted by lower overall revenue generation capacity. Compared to Class 1 councils, Class 2 councils are relatively less impacted by road programme costs, and the carrying value of infrastructure assets.

A major benefit of a statistically grounded distress model in the public sector environment is that they can be used as an effective screening device across a large number of councils to identify emerging financial difficulties and pressures among councils. Such models can also have important policy applications, such as providing an objective basis for assessing the financial circumstances of local councils in various rate pegging applications and/or in identifying distressed councils who are ripe for merger and/or amalgamation activity (as well as assessing whether the merger activity itself has been effective in reducing distress). Possibly triangulation of different distress measurement techniques (such as heuristic/descriptive and quantitative tests) may provide greater insights into the circumstances of public sector agencies than the use of one approach in isolation.

APPENDIX

Definition of Explanatory Variables

Variable   **Description**
Council characteristics

Variable	Description
Ccode	Council and year code.
Group	NSW Department of Local Government council group number.
Exist	Dummy variable describing whether council existed in a certain year.
Urban	Dummy variable describing whether council is urban or rural.
Large	Dummy variable describing whether council is large/extra large or small/medium based on the DLG's classification.
Popn	Estimated resident population within council boundaries.
Area	Area (sq km) at 30 June 2001.
Norrp	Number of rateable residential properties.

Norfp	Number of rateable farmland properties.
Norbp	Number of rateable business properties.
Staff	Number of equivalent full-time council staff.

Local service delivery variables

Dwpickup	Number of services (domestic waste pickups per week).
Wmsprop	Number of residential properties receiving waste management service.
Recyc	Total kilograms of recyclables collected.
Wastekg	Total kilograms of domestic waste collected.

Infrastructure variables

Cbldg	Carrying value of buildings infrastructure.
Cvroad	Carrying value of roads infrastructure.
Cvwatr	Carrying value of water infrastructure.
Cvsewr	Carrying value of sewerage infrastructure.
Cvdrn	Carrying value of drainage infrastructure.
Cvtot	Total carrying value of infrastructure assets.
Satbldg	Cost to bring buildings infrastructure to a satisfactory condition.
Satroad	Cost to bring roads infrastructure to a satisfactory condition.
Satwatr	Cost to bring water infrastructure to a satisfactory condition.
Satsewr	Cost to bring sewerage infrastructure to a satisfactory condition.
Satdrn	Cost to bring drainage infrastructure to a satisfactory condition.
Sattot	Total cost to bring infrastructure assets to a satisfactory condition.
Pmbldg	Programme maintenance expenditure for buildings infrastructure.
Pmroad	Programme maintenance expenditure for roads infrastructure.
Pmwatr	Programme maintenance expenditure for water infrastructure.
Pmsewr	Programme maintenance expenditure for sewerage infrastructure.

Pmdran	Programme maintenance expenditure for drainage infrastructure.
Pmtot	Total programme maintenance expenditure for infrastructure assets.

Financial Variables

Ordrev	Total ordinary revenue (including water and sewerage charges).
Ornows	Total ordinary revenue (excluding water and sewerage charges).
Raterev	Rates revenue (ordinary and special) and annual charges.
Rrrev	Residential rates revenue.
Frrev	Farmland rates revenue.
Brrev	Business rates revenue.
Racucf	Rates and annual charges plus user charges and fees.
Dwmchg	Total domestic waste management charges.
Ratesout	Outstanding rates and annual charges plus user charges and fees.
Ordexp	Total ordinary expenditure.
Oenows	Total ordinary expenses (excluding water and sewerage).
Wsopcost	Water supply operating costs including depreciation.
Ssopcost	Sewerage service operating costs including depreciation.
Depn	Depreciation.
Borrcost	Borrowing costs.
Ndscost	Net debt service cost.
Debtrat	Debt service ratio (*ndscost / revenue from ordinary activities*).
Empcost	Employee costs.
Ta	Total assets.
Cash	Cash assets.
Ca	Current assets (less external restrictions).
Cl	Current liabilities (less specific purpose liabilities).
Invsec	Investment securities.
Cibl	Current interest bearing liabilities.
Ncibl	Non-current interest bearing liabilities.
Cfo	Cash from operating activities.
Netopta	Net operating cash flow by total assets.
Netoptr	Net operating cash flow by sales revenue.
Cpta	Cash, deposits and marketable securities by total assets.
Cpcl	Cash, deposits and marketable securities by current liabilities.

Debtta	Total debt to total assets.
Tlta	Total liabilities to total assets.
Roa	Net income (surplus) to total assets.
Current	Current assets by current liabilities.
Workcta	Working capital (current assets – current liabilities) by total assets.
Nicover	Net income (surplus) by annual interest payments.
Cdebtc	Total debt by gross operating cash flow.
Cfcover	Net operating cash flow by annual interest payments.

REFERENCES

Altman, E., 'Financial ratios, discriminant analysis and the prediction of corporate bankruptcy', *Journal of Finance*, 23(4), 1968.

Altman, E., *Bankruptcy, Credit Risk and High Yield Junk Bonds*, Oxford, Blackwell, 2001.

Altman, E., Haldeman R. and Narayan, P., 'ZETA analysis: a new model to identify bankruptcy risk of corporations', *Journal of Banking and Finance*, 1(1), 1977.

Australian Accounting Standards Board, *Approved Australian Accounting Standard AASB 1026: Statement of Cash Flows*, Australian Accounting Research Foundation, 1992.

Australian Accounting Standard AAS 27, *Financial Reporting by Local Governments*, 1993 (first issued 1990).

Bach, S. and Vesper, D., 'A crisis in finance and investment – local government finance needs fundamental reform', *Economic Bulletin*, 39(9), 2002.

Bahnson, P. and Bartley, J., 'The sensitivity of failure prediction models', *Advances in Accounting*, 10, 1992.

Beckett-Camarata, J., 'Identifying and coping with fiscal emergencies in Ohio local governments', *International Journal of Public Administration*, 27(8/9), 2004.

Bumgarner, M., Martinez-Vazquez, J. and Sjoquist, D. L., 'Municipal capital maintenance and fiscal distress', *Review of Economics and Statistics*, 73(1), 1991.

Cahill, A. G. and James, J. A., 'Responding to municipal fiscal distress: an emerging issue for state governments in the 1990s', *Public Administration Review*, 52(1), 1992.

Carmeli, A., 'Introduction: fiscal and financial crises of local governments', *International Journal of Public Administration*, 26(13), 2003.

Carmeli, A. and Cohen, A., 'The financial crisis of the local authorities in Israel: a resource-based analysis', *Public Administration*, 79(4), 2001.

Casey, C. and Bartczak, N., 'Using operating cash flow data to predict financial distress: some extensions.', *Journal of Accounting Research* 23, 1985, 384–401.

Clark, T. N., 'Fiscal management of american cities: funds flow indicators', *Journal of Accounting Research*, 15, Supplement, 1977.

Clark, T. N. and Ferguson, L. C., *City Money: Political Process, Fiscal Strain and Retrenchment*. New York: Columbia University Press, 1983.

Cooper, S. D., 'Local government budgeting responses to fiscal pressures', *Public Administration Quarterly*, 20, 1996.

Delaney, K., *Strategic Bankruptcy: How Corporations and Creditors Use Chapter 11 to their Advantage*. Berkeley: University of California Press, 1991.

Department of Local Government (NSW), *Comparative Information on New South Wales Local Government Councils*, 2002.

Duffie, D. and Singleton, K., *Credit Risk: Pricing, Measurement and Management*, Princeton University Press, 2003.

Falconer, M. K., 'Fiscal stress among local governments: definition, measurement, and the state's impact', *Stetson Law Review*, 20(3), 1991.

Foster, G., *Financial Statement Analysis*, Englewood Cliffs, NJ, Prentice-Hall, 1986.

Gentry, J., Newbold, P. and D. Whitford., 'Classifying bankrupt firms with funds flow components', *Journal of Accounting Research* 23, 1985, 146–60.

Governmental Accounting Standards Board (GASB), *Statement No. 34, Basic Financial Statements – and Management's Discussion and Analysis – for State and Local Governments*, 1996.

Gramlich, E. M., 'The New York City fiscal crisis: what happened and what is to be done?', *American Economic Association*, 66(2), 1976.

Gramlich, E. M. and Gordon, R. J., 'The 1991 state and local fiscal crisis: comments and discussion', *Brookings Papers on Economic Activity*, 2, 1991.

Honadle, B. W., 'Fiscal health of local governments: the community economic development connection with implications for local and state government roles', *Community Economics*, December, 2003.

Hribar, P. and Collins, D., 'Errors in estimating accruals: implications for empirical research', *Journal of Accounting Research*, 40(1), 2002.

Jones, F., 'Current techniques in bankruptcy prediction', *Journal of Accounting Literature*, 6, 1987.

Jones, S. and Hensher, D. A., 'Predicting firm financial distress: a mixed logit model', *The Accounting Review*, 79(4), 2004.

Kaplan, R. S., 'Discussion of fiscal management of American cities: funds flow indicators', *Journal of Accounting Research*, 15, Supplement, 1977.

Kleine, R., Kloha P. and Weissert, C. S., 'Monitoring local government fiscal health', *Government Finance Review*, 19(3), 2003.

Kloha, P., Weissert C. S. and Kloha, P., 'Developing and testing a composite model to predict local fiscal distress', *Public Administration Review*, 65(3), 2005.

Lau, A. H., 'A five-state financial distress prediction model', *Journal of Accounting Research*, 25, 1987, 127–38.

Murray, D. R. and Dollery, B. E., 'Local council performance monitoring in New South Wales: are 'at risk' councils really at risk?', *Economic Papers*, 24(4), 2005, 332–45

Ohlson, J., 'Financial ratios and the probabilistic prediction of bankruptcy', *Journal of Accounting Research*, 18(1), 1980.

Schipper, K., 'Financial distress in local colleges', *Journal of Accounting Research*, 15, Supplement, 1977.

Walker, R. G., Clarke F. L. and Dean, G. W., 'Reporting on the state of infrastructure by local government', *Accounting, Auditing and Accountability*, 12(4), 1999.

Ward, T. 'An empirical study on the incremental predictive ability of Beaver's naïve operative flow measure using four-state ordinal models of financial distress', *Journal of Business Finance & Accounting* 21, 1994, 547–562.

Zmijewski, M., 'Methodological issues related to the estimation of financial distress prediction models', *Journal of Accounting Research*, 22, Supplement, 1984.

10 A belief-function perspective to credit risk assessments

Rajendra P. Srivastava and Stewart Jones

10.1. Introduction

Risk assessment in any field is a challenging problem whether it deals with assessing the potential loss of personal properties due to flood, the presence of material misstatements or fraud in the financial statements of a company, or assessing the likelihood of firm survival or loan default. There are two important general concepts related to risk assessment. One deals with the potential loss due to the undesirable event, such as loan default or corporate bankruptcy. The other deals with the uncertainty associated with the event, whether the event will occur or will not occur. There are two kinds of uncertainties. One kind arises purely because of the random nature of the event. For random events, there exist stable frequencies in repeated trials under fixed conditions.

For such random events, one can use the knowledge of the stable frequencies to predict the probability of occurrence of the event. For example, tossing a fair coin is purely a random process with stable frequencies in repeated trials where one would expect to get head 50% of the times and tail 50% of the times. This kind of uncertainty has been the subject of several previous chapters in this volume which has dealt with various statistical approaches to modelling default risk and corporate bankruptcy prediction.

The other kind of uncertainty arises because of the lack of knowledge of the true state of nature where we not only lack the knowledge of a stable frequency, but also we lack the means to specify fully the fixed conditions under which repetitions can be performed (Shafer and Srivastava 1990).

The present chapter provides a theoretical framework to deal with such situations. In the context of default risk, credit ratings and bankruptcy models, many statistical models attempt to exploit the regularities in empirical data in order to formulate probability estimates of the likelihood of such events in the future. Belief functions postulate that repetitions under fixed conditions which underlie many statistical models of default risk and bankruptcy prediction are often impossible, particularly where we even lack the means to specify fully the fixed conditions under which we would like to have repetitions. For example, the credit ratings issued by many large rating agencies, such as Standard and Poor's (S&P), are based on a raft of macroeconomic, industry and firm-specific information which are to a large extent unique to each particular firm being rated. For instance, S&P ratings (and revision of ratings) are usually based on detailed ongoing interviews with management, where dialogue with management tends to be more frequent in response to significant industry events, material announcements by the company or plans by the company to pursue new financings. Firm-specific information used by S&P includes the use of current and future-oriented financial information (both at the time of the rating and on an ongoing basis), assessments of the quality of management, the adequacy of corporate governance arrangements, the relationships with key suppliers and lenders, including a variety of confidential information (not disclosed to the public when a firm is rated), such as budgets and forecasts, financial statements on a stand-alone basis, internal capital allocation schedules, contingent risks analyses and information relating to new financings, acquisitions, dispositions and restructurings.[1]

This information is unique to each firm. What may happen in one firm cannot be generalized to another, hence there may be no observable empirical regularities in which statistical generalizations can be inferred.

This second kind of uncertainty is relevant in assessing default risk in many real-world situations. For example, consider a credit ratings agency which uses financial statement data (along with other factors) in assessing whether to upgrade or downgrade a firm's credit rating. Standard and Poor's is highly dependent on the integrity and quality of a company's financial disclosures, particularly as it stated ratings methodology is not designed to 'second guess' the auditor's report or replace the work of the auditor.[2] What is the risk that the audited financial statements of a company

---

[1] See for example the testimony of the Standard and Poor's rating agency in the public hearings before the U.S. Securities and Exchange Commission, November 15, 2002 on the *Role and Function of Credit Rating Agencies in the U.S. Securities Markets* (http://www.sec.gov/news/extra/credrate/standardpoors.htm).

[2] See testimony to the SEC, November 15, 2002. S&P also acknowledged that, in the context of recent corporate failures, it was misled by fraudulent and misleading financial statements which subsequently led to improvements in the methodology of the agency's ratings process.

fails to accurately portray the true going concern status of the firm, or even contains fraudulent and misleading information? The answers to these questions are not easy because the possibility of the presence of, say, fraud or misstatement in the financial statements of a S&P-rated company does not depend on the frequency of the presence of fraud or misstatement in the financial statements of other companies or industries. That is, it does not depend on the prior probability of fraud or misstatement. Rather, it depends on the unique characteristics of the company such as the management incentives to commit fraud, whether management has opportunities to perpetrate fraud, and whether management has compromising integrity to justify committing fraud. It is important to emphasize that the presence of fraud in the financial statements of a company is not a random process with a stable frequency in repeated trials under fixed conditions as argued by Shafer and Srivastava (1990). Thus, treating the presence of fraud or mis-statement in the financial statements of a company as a random process and trying to estimate the risk of its presence by assessing the prior probability may not be appropriate.

In this chapter, our objective is to demonstrate the use of the Dempster–Shafer theory of belief functions for assessing default and bankruptcy risk in situations where the event cannot be treated as a random variable; however, evidence exists which provides support for the presence or absence of such a variable.

This chapter is divided into six sections. Section 2 discusses problems with probability framework in modeling uncertainties. Section 3 presents an introduction to the Dempster–Shafer theory of belief functions. Section 4 demonstrates application of the belief functions in deriving a rudimentary default risk model based on some specified conditions which are used to derive the model. Section 5 discusses an approach to decision making under the Dempster–Shafer theory of belief functions and provides an economic analysis of cost and benefit to a credit rating agency in the presence of default risk. Section 6 provides a conclusion of the chapter.

10.2. Problems with probability frameworks

We want to introduce readers to some fundamental problems of probability theory in representing uncertainty judgments in common situations of decision-making, including one example in default risk and credit ratings.

Credit ratings

In deciding to issue a credit rating to a company (or to revise an existing rating), a credit rating agency (such as S&P) must assess a wide range of information, including macroeconomic, industry and firm-specific factors. Firm-specific factors might include the current and expectations of future financial performance, management style and ability, the existence of effective strategic plans, and the adequacy of corporate governance structures including a variety of confidential firm information used in the ratings process but not disclosed to the public. Suppose that all these factors lead to a positive decision from the credit rating agency towards issuing a favourable rating (say a rating of A or above using the standard S&P rating scale). The credit ratings agency wants to express this judgment and assigns a low level of support, say 0.2 on a scale of 0–1 that the overall firm-specific performance factors under consideration are adequate and no support that they are deficient. If we had to represent this judgment in terms of a probability then we would say that the credit rating agency has 0.8 (complement of 0.2) degree of support that there is deficiency in one or more of the firm-specific performance factors under review. But this interpretation suggests that the evidence is negative: i.e., 0.8 level of support that there are deficiencies. This would not make sense to the credit rating agency because it has no evidence in support of the fact that such a deficiency exists. The above evidence is easily expressed in terms of belief functions, as 0.2 level of support that the firm-specific performance factors are adequate to issue a positive or favourable credit rating, no belief that the firm-specific performance factors are deficient, and 0.8 degree of belief remaining uncommitted (see Section 3 for more details).

Just to illustrate a point, let us consider another case. Assume that the crediting rating agency thinks that all the environmental factors lead to a very strong positive support toward the firm-specific performance factors being adequate. Further, assume that the credit rating agency expresses this judgment by assigning a value of, say, 0.5 to the rating that it is correct. However, based on this assessment the rating agency still has some risk that the rating may have been issued incorrectly, i.e. $R = 0.5$. This value when interpreted in probability theory implies that the rating agency does not know what it is doing: i.e., the rating agency is ignorant because there is a 50–50 chance that the firm-specific performance factors are adequate or deficient. However, as it will be further elaborated in Section 4, under belief functions, $R = 0.5$ means that the rating agency has 0.5 level of support for the firm-specific performance factors being adequate, no support for the presence of deficiencies, and 0.5 level of support uncommitted.

Nature of evidence

Under a probability framework, one can define either a positive piece of evidence or a negative piece of evidence using the likelihood ratio (see Edwards 1984 and Dutta and Srivastava 1993, 1996). If the likelihood ratio is greater than one, then it is positive evidence. If the likelihood ratio is positive and less than one, then it is negative evidence. In both situations, by definition, the evidence is mixed: i.e., if the evidence is positive in support of a hypothesis, then it is also negative in support of the negation of the hypothesis. This implies that all items of evidence modelled under probability theory will always be mixed. However, it is quite common in the real world to find pure positive evidence or pure negative evidence. For example, suppose the rating agency finds that the company's management has exceptional ability and the financial statements have a high level of integrity based on the last several years of experience. The firm has never had any problems with these issues in the past. Also, the economic environment under which this firm's business operates is sound. Based on all these items of evidence the ratings agency believes it can trust the accuracy of the financial statements and supporting statements by the managers with some level of comfort: a low level of support, say 0.1, on a scale of 0–1. In the rating agency's judgment, it has no evidence to support a view that the financial statements are deficient (or the statements by the managers in the interview processes are untrustworthy in any way). This type of evidence can be easily expressed under belief functions in terms of the basic belief masses (see Section 3 for more details). However, if we use probability theory to model it, then we run into problems. For the above example, we will have the probability of trustworthy financial statements to be 0.1 and thus, by definition, we will have 0.9 probability that the financial statements are deficient in some way. This is not what the rating agency's judgment was; it had no information about the financial statements and accompanying management statements being inadequate.

Representation of ignorance

Representation of ignorance in probability theory, with 'n' mutually exclusive and collectively exhaustive states of nature, is to assign a probability of $1/n$ to each state of nature. If there are only two possible outcomes, then we assign 0.5 and 0.5 to each state to represent ignorance. However, this representation leads to a problem. Let us consider an example. A local infrastructure company under ratings review has started new operations in locations in the Middle East and China. It is exposed to two kinds of economic risk in two separate jurisdictions (let us say the risk of civil unrest and economic disruption in the Middle East location and the risk of an economic slowdown in China, both of which can impact on the financial performance and ultimately the creditworthiness of the company). Let us assume that the rating agency starts with no knowledge whether risk in any of the jurisdictions in which the entity operates is particularly high or low, but the risks are nevertheless present. The probability representation of this ignorance about the associated risks, say at just the two locations mentioned above (the Middle East and China), would be $P(f_1) = P(\sim f_1) = 0.5$, and $P(f_2) = P(\sim f_2) = 0.5$, where f_1 and f_2 represent the economic risks being low in jurisdictions 1 and 2, respectively, and $\sim f_1$ and $\sim f_2$ represent the economic risks being high in both jurisdictions.

Consider that we want to determine the probability that the economic risks in both jurisdictions 1 and 2 are low. We know in this case that the ratings agency will only consider the combined risk in the two jurisdictions to be adequate when both locations are judged to be low-risk. In other words, the combined risk would still be regarded as unacceptably high if the risk in one jurisdiction alone is too high. This yields a probability of 0.25 for the combined economic risk being low ($P(f_1 \cap f_2) = 0.5 \times 0.5 = 0.25$), and a probability of 0.75 for the combined economic risk being high. This result is counter-intuitive. We started with ignorance of the particular economic risk in each location, but when we combine the economic risks of both locations we seem to have gained some knowledge: 0.75 probability are that the combined economic risks are high. The probability result looks even worse if we consider a few more locations where economic risk is present for the company.

Knowledge versus no knowledge

Consider two urns, Urn 1 and Urn 2, each containing 100 balls. Urn 1 contains 100 balls of red and black colours, but we do not know the proportion. All may be red, all may be black, or in any proportion. Thus, Urn 1 is an urn where we have no knowledge about the proportion of red and black balls. Urn 2 contains 50 red and 50 black balls, i.e., we have complete knowledge about Urn 2. Einhorn and Hogarth (1985, 1986) conducted an experiment where they asked subjects to choose an urn from which they would pick a given colour ball, say red, and win $100, and get nothing if they pick the wrong colour ball. The subjects overwhelmingly chose to pick from Urn 2, the urn with complete knowledge. When we model the above situation using probability framework, then we get into a paradox. Einhorn and Hogarth refer to this paradox as Ellsberg's (1961) paradox. As discussed by them, the preference of Urn 2 over Urn 1 for picking a ball of either colour would mean the following probability inequalities:

P(Red from Urn 2) $>$ P(Red from Urn 1) $= 0.5$,
P(Black from Urn 2) $>$ P(Black from Urn 1) $= 0.5$,

or

P(Red from Urn 2) $= 0.5 > P$(Red from Urn 1),
P(Black from Urn 2) $= 0.5 > P$(Black from Urn 1).

The first condition implies that the probabilities for Urn 2 add to more than one and the second condition implies that the probabilities for Urn 1 add to less than one. This is the paradox. Einhorn and Hogath (1986) define these conditions, respectively, as 'superadditivity' and 'subadditivity'. They further state that (Einhorn and Hogarth 1986, p. S228)

... either urn 2 has complementary probabilities that sum to more than one, or urn 1 has complementary probabilities that sum to less than one. As we will show, the nonadditivity of complementary probabilities is central to judgments under ambiguity.

This paradox stems from the difficulty in distinguishing between the two urns under probability framework. The two urns, Urn 1, and Urn 2, are identical under probability framework, since the probability of picking a red ball from Urn 1 (complete ignorance) is 0.5 and the probability of picking a red ball from Urn 2 (complete knowledge, 50 red and 50 black balls) is also 0.5. However, decision makers clearly perceive the two situations to be different. Srivastava (1997) has shown that *super- or sub-additivity property is not needed to explain the decision maker's behaviour*. There is no paradox if the uncertainties were modelled using the belief-function framework. Also, probability is not a physical property that one urn would have super-additive probabilities and the other would have sub-additive probabilities. It is only a language to express uncertainties; it is our creation.

Rodeo paradox[3]

Consider a rodeo show in town. One thousand people go to see the show. However, one person buys the ticket to the show and the rest, 999, force their way into the show without a ticket. Police are called in for help. Police randomly pick up a person and take that person to the city judge for prosecution. We know that the probability of this person having entered the rodeo show without a ticket is 0.999. What should the judge do to this person based on this prior probability? Should the judge prosecute this person since the prior probability of being guilty is so high? Well, if you use common sense then you feel that there is no evidence to support that this person has entered the show without a ticket. Under belief functions, this situation is represented as having a zero belief that the person is guilty and also a zero belief that the person is not guilty. The judge cannot prosecute this person based solely on the prior probability even though the probability of this person being guilty is 0.999. Under such situations, the belief function framework becomes useful.

What if we now bring a piece of evidence into the story? If the person shows that he has the stub of the ticket, then what is the belief that he is not guilty? It depends on how he got the stub. Could it be that he had snatched it from the rightful owner of the ticket? What if a witness says that he saw this person purchase a ticket? The level of belief about whether the person in question is guilty or not guilty depends on these items of evidence and their credibility. It is important to note that the judge's decision to prosecute or not to prosecute the person does not depend on the prior probability of being guilty. Rather it depends on the belief that the judge can ascribe to the person the guilt or the lack of guilt through combining several pieces of evidence relevant to the case. A belief function treatment of such problems provides a richer framework for decision-making.

10.3. Introduction to Dempster–Shafer theory of belief functions

Although the current form of belief functions is based on the work of Dempster during the 1960s, Shafer (1976) made it popular through his book *A Mathematical Theory of Evidence*. Several authors have provided a basic introduction to the Dempster–Shafer theory of belief functions (e.g., see Srivastava 1993, Srivastava and Mock 2002a, and Yager *et al.* 1994). However,

---

[3] This example is described by Smets (1999).

Shafer's book (1976) is still the classic reference on this subject. In this section, we provide the basics of belief functions as an introduction.

The Dempster–Shafer theory of belief functions is similar to probability theory, however, with one difference. Under probability theory, we assign uncertainty to the state of nature based on the knowledge of frequency of occurrence. However, under the theory of belief functions, we assign uncertainty to the state of nature or assertion of interest in an indirect way based on the probability knowledge in another frame by mapping that knowledge onto the frame of interest. This mapping may not necessarily be one-to-one. For example, we may have probability knowledge of someone, say Joe, being honest, say 0.9, and not being honest 0.1, based on the observed behaviour over the years. If this person is making a statement that he saw the house on the northwest corner of Clinton Drive and Inverness Drive in the city on fire this morning, then one would believe, based on him being honest 90% of the time, that the house is on fire, with a level of support 0.9. However, Joe being dishonest does not give any evidence that the house is *not* on fire when he is saying that the house in on fire. The knowledge that he is dishonest 10% of the times suggests that he may or may not be truthful in what he is saying, which provides a level of support of 0.1 that the house may or may not be on fire.

We can provide further elucidation of the belief function concepts through another illustration. Suppose we have a variable, say A, with n possible mutually exclusive and exhaustive set of values: $a_1, a_2, a_3, \ldots, a_n$. These values define the frame $\Theta = \{a_1, a_2, a_3, \ldots, a_n\}$ of discernment for the variable A. Under probability theory, for such a set, we assign a probability mass, $P(a_i)$, to each state a_i such that the sum of all these probabilities equals one, i.e. $\sum_{i=1}^{n} P(a_i) = 1$. However, under the Dempster–Shafer theory of belief functions, uncertainties are assigned in terms belief masses to not only singletons, but also to all the sub sets of the frame and to the entire frame Θ. These belief masses add to one similar to probability masses. This will be elaborated further in the next section.

The basic probability assignment function (basic belief mass function)

As mentioned earlier, under the theory of belief functions, we assign uncertainties in terms of *belief masses* to all the sub sets of a frame Θ including the entire frame Θ. These belief masses define a function called the *basic belief mass function* (Shafer 1976 calls it the *basic probability assignment function*). In mathematical terms, we can write a belief mass assigned to a subset B as $m(B)$, where B could be a single element, or a subset of two, a subset of three, and so on, or the entire frame, Θ. The sum of such belief masses equals one, i.e. $\sum_{B \subseteq \Theta} m(B) = 1$. Thus, one can see that when the non-zero belief masses are only defined on the singletons, then the theory of belief functions reduces to probability theory. Thus, one can argue that probability theory is a special case of the Dempster–Shafer theory of belief functions.

Let us consider an example to illustrate the above concepts. Suppose a credit rating agency has performed an analysis on the financial statements of a firm to assess whether a ratings downgrade is appropriate. In analysing a particular variable of interest, say earnings quality over a five year period, the rating agency finds no significant difference between the recorded value and the predicted value: that is, based on this information, the rating agency thinks that the firm's earnings quality appears reasonable for a healthy entity, given its size, longevity and industry background. However, the rating agency does not want to put too much weight on this evidence given some inherent uncertainties with measuring earnings quality coupled with some known cases of earnings management practices in this particular industry, and so assigns a low level of assurance, say 0.3, on a scale of 0–1, that earnings quality is accurately represented in the financial statements. The rating agency has no evidence supporting the assertion that earnings quality is materially misstated or does not reflect acceptable industry averages. We can express this judgment in terms of belief masses as: $m(EQ) = 0.3$, $m(\sim EQ) = 0$, and $m(\{EQ, \sim EQ\}) = 0.7$, where the symbol EQ stands for the quality of earnings being a reasonable representation of reality and $\sim EQ$ stands for earnings quality being either materially misstated or not reflecting acceptable industry averages. The belief function theory interpretation of these belief masses is that the ratings agency has 0.3 level of support to EQ, no support for $\sim EQ$, and 0.7 level of support remains uncommitted, which represents ignorance.

However, if we had to express the above judgment in terms of probabilities, we get into problems, because we will assign $P(EQ) = 0.3$ and $P(\sim EQ) = 0.7$ which implies that there is a 70% chance that the earnings quality is materially misstated or does not reflect acceptable industry averages. However this is not what the rating agency's judgment is; it has no information or evidence that earning quality is materially misstated. Simply knowing the fact that the current year's earnings quality appears to be reasonable compared to the predicted values based on the industry average and prior years' performances provides no evidence that the current year's value is materially misstated. It only provides some level of support that the earnings quality is accurately stated.

Thus, we can use the belief masses to express the basic judgment about the level of support or assurance the rating agency obtains from an item of evidence for an assertion. An example of a negative item of evidence which will have a direct support for $\sim EQ$ would be the following set of inherent factors: (1) in the prior years earnings quality has been misrepresented, and (2) there are economic reasons for management to misstate earnings. In such a case we can express the rating agency's judgment as $m(EQ) = 0$, $m(\sim EQ) = 0.2$, and $m(\{EQ, \sim EQ\}) = 0.8$, assuming that the rating agency estimates a low, say 0.2, level of support for $\sim EQ$. One can express a mixed type of evidence in terms of the belief masses without any problems as: $m(EQ) = 0.4$, $m(\sim EQ) = 0.1$, and $m(\{EQ, \sim EQ\}) = 0.5$, where the judgment is that the evidence provides 0.4 level of support to EQ, 0.1 level of support to $\sim EQ$, and 0.5 level of support is uncommitted, i.e. unassigned to any specific element but to the entire set, representing ignorance. In probability theory, we cannot express such a judgment.

Belief functions

The belief in B, Bel(B), for a subset B of elements of a frame, Θ, represents the total belief in B and is equal to the belief mass, $m(B)$, assigned to B plus the sum of all the belief masses assigned to the set of elements that are contained in B. In terms of symbols:

$$\text{Bel}(B) = \sum_{C \subseteq B} m(C).$$

By definition, the belief mass assigned to an empty set is always zero, i.e. $m(\phi) = 0$.

In order to illustrate the above definition, let us consider our rating agency example discussed earlier. Suppose that the ratings agency has made the following judgment about the level of support in terms of belief masses for earnings quality being accurately represented (i.e., not materially misstated) and not accurately represented (i.e., materially misstated): $m(EQ) = 0.3$, $m(\sim EQ) = 0$, and $m(\{EQ, \sim EQ\}) = 0.7$. Based on analytical procedures alone, the belief that earnings quality is not materially misstated is 0.3, i.e. Bel(EQ) $= m(EQ) = 0.3$, no support that earnings quality is materially misstated, i.e., Bel($\sim EQ$) $= m(\sim EQ) = 0$, and the belief in the set $\{EQ, \sim EQ\}$ is $\text{Bel}(\{EQ, \sim EQ\}) = m(EQ) + m(\sim EQ) + m(\{EQ, \sim EQ\}) = 0.3 + 0.0 + 0.7 = 1$. In general, a zero level of belief implies that there is no evidence to support the proposition. In other words, a zero level of belief in a proposition represents lack of evidence. In contrast, a zero probability in probability theory means that the proposition cannot be true which represents impossibility. Also, one finds that beliefs for EQ and $\sim EQ$ do not necessarily add to one, i.e. $\text{Bel}(EQ) + \text{Bel}(\sim EQ) \leq 1$, whereas, in probability, it is always true that $P(EQ) + P(\sim EQ) = 1$.

Plausibility functions

Intuitively, the plausibility of B is the degree to which B is plausible given the evidence. In other words, $\text{Pl}(B)$ represents the maximum belief that could be assigned to B, given that all the evidence collected in the future support B. In mathematical terms, one can define plausibility of B as: $\text{Pl}(B) = \sum_{B \cap C = \emptyset} m(C)$, which can also be expressed as: $\text{Pl}(B) = 1 - \text{Bel}(\sim B)$, which is the degree to which we do not assign belief to its negation $(\sim B)$.

In our example above, we have the following belief masses and beliefs: $m(EQ) = 0.3$, $m(\sim EQ) = 0$, $m(\{EQ, \sim EQ\}) = 0.7$, and $\text{Bel}(EQ) = 0.3$, $\text{Bel}(\sim EQ) = 0$, and $\text{Bel}(\{EQ, \sim EQ\}) = 1$. These values yield the following plausibility values: $\text{Pl}(EQ) = 1$, and $\text{Pl}(\sim EQ) = 0.7$. $\text{Pl}(EQ) = 1$ indicates that EQ is maximally plausible since we have no evidence against it. However, $\text{Pl}(\sim EQ) = 0.7$ indicates that if we had no other items of evidence to consider, then the maximum possible assurance that earnings quality is materially misstated would be 0.7, even though we have no evidence that earnings quality is materially misstated, i.e., $\text{Bel}(\sim EQ) = 0$. This definition of plausibility that earnings quality is materially misstated represents the measure of risk that earnings quality could be materially misstated, even though there is no belief that earnings quality is materially misstated.

The measure of ambiguity

The belief function measure of ambiguity in an assertion, say B, is straightforward. It is the difference between plausibility of B and the belief in B (Wong and Wang 1993).

$$\text{Ambiguity}(B) = \text{Pl}(B) - \text{Bel}(B).$$

The belief in B represents the direct support for B, while the plausibility of B represents the maximum possible support that could be assigned to B if we were able to collect further evidence in support of B. The difference then represents the unassigned belief that could be assigned to B. This unassigned belief represents the ambiguity in B.

Dempster's rule

Dempster's rule (Shafer 1976) is the fundamental rule in belief functions for combining independent items of evidence similar to Bayes' rule in probability theory. In fact, Dempster's rule reduces to Bayes' rule under the condition when all the belief masses defined on the frame are zero except the ones for the singletons. For two independent items of evidence pertaining to a frame of discernment, Θ, we can write the combined belief mass for a sub set B in Θ using Dempster's rule as

$$m(B) = \sum_{C1 \cap C2 = B} m_1(C1)m_2(C2)/K, \tag{10.1}$$

where

$$K = 1 - \sum_{C1 \cap C2 = \emptyset} m_1(C1)m_2(C2). \tag{10.2}$$

The symbols $m_1(C1)$ and $m_2(C2)$ determine the belief masses of C1 and C2, respectively, from the two independent items of evidence represented by the subscripts. The symbol K represents the renormalization constant. The second term in K represents the conflict between the two items of evidence. The two items of evidence are not combinable if the conflict term is 1.

Let us consider an example to illustrate the details of Dempster's rule. Suppose we have the following sets of belief masses obtained from two independent items of evidence related to the accurate representation of earnings quality:

$m_1(EQ) = 0.3, \quad m_1(\sim EQ) = 0.0, \quad m_1(\{EQ, \sim EQ\}) = 0.7,$
$m_2(EQ) = 0.6, \quad m_2(\sim EQ) = 0.1, \quad m_2(\{EQ, \sim EQ\}) = 0.3.$

The renormalization constant for the above case is

$K = 1 - [m_1(EQ)m_2(\sim EQ) + m_1(\sim EQ)m_2(EQ)]$
$= 1 - [0.3 \times 0.1 + 0.0 \times 0.6] = 0.97.$

Using Dempster's rule in (1), the combined belief masses for EQ, $\sim EQ$, and $\{EQ, \sim EQ\}$ are given by

$$
\begin{aligned}
m(EQ) &= [m_1(EQ)m_2(EQ) + m_1(EQ)m_2(\{EQ, \sim EQ\}) \\
&\quad + m_1(\{EQ, \sim EQ\})m_2(EQ)]/K \\
&= [0.3 \times 0.6 + 0.3 \times 0.3 + 0.7 \times 0.6]/0.97 \\
&= 0.69/0.97 = 0.71134,
\end{aligned}
$$

$$
\begin{aligned}
m(\sim EQ) &= [m_1(\sim EQ)m_2(\sim EQ) + m_1(\sim EQ)m_2(\{EQ, \sim EQ\}) \\
&\quad + m_1(\{EQ, \sim EQ\})m_2(\sim EQ)]/K \\
&= [0.0 \times 0.1 + 0.0 \times 0.3 + 0.7 \times 0.1]/0.97 \\
&= 0.07/0.97 = 0.072165,
\end{aligned}
$$

$$
\begin{aligned}
m(\{EQ, \sim EQ\}) &= m_1(\{EQ, \sim EQ\})m_2(\{EQ, \sim EQ\})/K \\
&= 0.7 \times 0.3/0.97 = 0.21/0.97 = 0.216495.
\end{aligned}
$$

The combined beliefs and plausibilities that earnings quality is not misstated (EQ) and is misstated ($\sim EQ$) are:

$$Bel(EQ) = m(EQ) = 0.71134,$$

and

$$Bel(\sim EQ) = m(\sim EQ) = 0.072165,$$

$$Pl(EQ) = 1 - Bel(\sim EQ) = 0.927845,$$

and

$$Pl(\sim EQ) = 1 - Bel(EQ) = 0.28866.$$

10.4. Risk assessment

This section demonstrates the application of belief functions in assessing risk which can be applied to various situations. As discussed in the introduction, the belief function theory is appropriate for modelling uncertainties when we have partial knowledge about the state of nature. Also, it is useful for the situation when the event is not a random event with a given stable frequency in repeated trials under fixed conditions. Bankruptcy risk, audit risk, fraud risk, auditor independence risk, information security risk and business risk are examples of such situations where we do not have stable frequencies in repeated trials under fixed conditions.

The notion of risk in the theory of belief functions is represented in terms of plausibility function. For example, the plausibility of material misstatement in the financial statements is defined as the audit risk by Srivastava and Shafer (1990). The plausibility that fraud is present in the financial statements is defined to be the fraud risk by Srivastava *et al.* (2007). The plausibility of information being insecure is defined as information security risk by Sun *et al.* (2006). Similarly, in this chapter we define the plausibility of loan default or bankruptcies as loan default risk or bankruptcy risk respectively. An illustration follows.

Default risk

As an illustration of how a model could be developed, we derive a simple hypothetical default risk formula. Let us suppose that a major lender is evaluating the potential risks of a company in its loan portfolio defaulting on a loan. The lender is interested in continually monitoring the financial status of the company (including any relevant industry and economic risk factors) for any signs of deteriorating creditworthiness which may lead to loan default. Loan default can obviously result in economic losses for the lender; hence, identifying potential default risk as early as possible may give the lender some valuable lead time to take appropriate corrective or remedial action (such as increasing the amount of the security for the loan or even calling in the loan). Using belief functions, let us suppose that the following conditions must be present for loan default to occur: (1) the company must experience a deterioration in its current or expected future financial performance which will adversely impact its debt servicing capacity, (2) the industry in which the firm operates must experience some change which will adversely affect the risk profile of the company (e.g., a change in governmental regulation or policy that may expose the firm to greater competition), and (3) the firm must experience a significant adverse change in the macroeconomic environment which will adversely affect the risk profile of the company (such as an increase in interest rates which may affect the company's capacity to repay debt).

Figure 10.1 represents the evidential diagram of the default risk model where the three factors, adverse financial performance (AFP), industry risk factors (IRF), and adverse macroeconomic environment (AME) are related to the variable default risk (D) through an 'AND' relationship. The lower-case

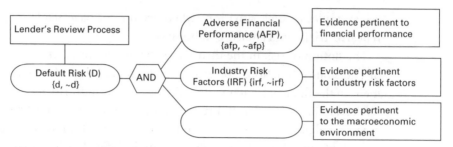

Figure 10.1 Evidential diagram for a rudimentary default risk model*

* The rounded boxes represent the variables and the rectangular boxes represent the items of evidence. The hexagonal box represents 'AND' relationship between ratings downgrade and the three influencing factors: adverse financial performance (AFP), Industry Risk Factors (IRF), and adverse macroeconomic environment (AME).

letters in the rounded boxes represent values that the corresponding variables are present or absent.

For example, 'afp' means that an adverse change in current or expected future financial performance is present and '~afp' means that this adverse change in current or expected future financial performance is absent. The 'AND' relationship implies that loan default will occur if and only if all these three factors or triggers are present. In terms of set notation, we can write $d = afp \cap irf \cap ame$. The evidence labelled 'lender's review process' pertaining to the variable 'D' includes all the procedures the lender would perform to assess whether default risk is likely to occur given the presence of AFP, IRF, and AME. Default risk would not occur (or can be avoided) if the lender's ongoing review procedures are effective.

In Figure 10.1, we have considered only one item of evidence for each default risk factor and one item of evidence at the default risk level for brevity.[4] However, several sets of evidence could be considered by the lender. For example, for adverse financial performance, the lender might consider the impact of a drop in sales growth, an unexpected increase in operating expenses in one of the business segments, or an analyst downgrade on future EPS estimates for the company. For industry risk factors, the lender might consider evidence relating to changed government policies pertinent to the sector as a whole, such as the removal of subsidies or an

---

[4] One can easily extend the current approach to multiple items of evidence for each variable; simply use Dempster's rule to combine these multiple items of evidence for each variable and then substitute the combined belief masses in place of the belief masses from the single item of evidence in the current approach.

increase in a special form of taxation, or a general decline in competitiveness of the industry owing to foreign competition. For macroeconomic effects, the lender may consider the impact of changes in interest rates, foreign currency rates, commodity prices and general inflation rates on the company's ability to service debt in the longer term.

We want to develop a formula for assessing default risk from the lender's perspective, given what we know about the presence of the three influencing risk factors and that the lender has performed appropriate review processes to assess a firm's default risk. Let us assume that we have the following belief masses (m) at AFP, IRF, AME, and D from the corresponding item of evidence:

Adverse Financial Performance (AFP) :

$m_{\text{AFP}}(afp), m_{\text{AFP}}(\sim afp), m_{\text{AFP}}(\{afp, \sim afp\})$

Industry Risk Factors (IRF) :

$m_{\text{IRF}}(irf), m_{\text{IRF}}(\sim irf), m_{\text{IRF}}(\{irf, \sim irf\})$

Adverse Macroeconomic Factors (AME) :

$m_{\text{AME}}(ame), m_{\text{AME}}(\sim ame), m_{\text{AME}}(\{ame, \sim ame\})$

Default Risk Present (D) :

$$m_{\text{D}}(d), m_{\text{D}}(\sim d), m_{\text{D}}(\{d, \sim d\}). \tag{10.3}$$

In order to develop the default risk formula, we proceed in two steps. First, we propagate the belief masses from the three default risk factors to D. Next, we combine the belief mass function at D (obtained from the lender's review processes) with the belief mass function (obtained from the three influencing risk factors). For the first step, we use a rudimentary default risk formula,[5] which yields the following belief mass function at variable D as a result of propagating belief masses from AFP, IRF, and AME:

$$m(d) = m_{\text{AFP}}(afp)m_{\text{IRF}}(irf)m_{\text{AME}}(ame),$$
$$m(\sim d) = 1 - (1 - m_{AFP}(\sim afp))(1 - m_{\text{IRF}}(\sim irf))$$
$$(1 - m_{\text{AME}}(\sim ame)),$$
$$m(\{d, \sim d\}) = 1 - m(d) - m(\sim d). \tag{10.4}$$

Next, we combine the above belief mass function with the belief mass function at D, given in (10.3) using Dempster's rule. This combination

---

[5] We use Srivastava *et al.* (1995) to combine the belief masses on AFP, IRF, and AME through 'and' relationship and marginalize them to variable D.

yields the following overall belief mass function at D:

$$m(d) = [m_D(d)m(d) + m_D(d)m(\{d, \sim d\}) + m_D(\{d, \sim d\})m(d)]/K,$$

$$m(\sim d) = [m_D(\sim d)m(\sim d) + m_D(\sim d)m(\{d, \sim d\})$$
$$+ m_D(\{d, \sim d\})m(\sim d)]/K,$$

$$m(\{d, \sim d\}) = m_D(\{d, \sim d\})m(\{d, \sim d\})/K, \tag{10.5}$$

$$K = 1 - [m_D(d)m(\sim d) + m_D(\sim d)m(d)]. \tag{10.6}$$

We obtain the following expression for the plausibility (Pl) of default risk from (10.5), by replacing the belief mass function defined in (10.4), and by simplifying:

$$Pl(d) = [m_D(d) + m_D(\{d, \sim d\})][m_{AFP}(afp) + m_{AFP}(\{afp, \sim afp\})]$$
$$[m_{IRF}(irf) + m_{IRF}(\{irf, \sim irf\})][m_{AME}(ame)$$
$$+ m_{AME}(\{ame, \sim ame\})]/K.$$

Using the definition of Plausibility function, we can rewrite the above expression as:

$$PI(d) = PI_D(d)PI_{AFP}(afp)PI_{IRF}(irf)PI_{AME}(ame)/K. \tag{10.7}$$

Since the plausibility of default risk represents the risk of a default (DR), we can express $Pl(d) = DR$. Similarly, the plausibility of the presence of adverse financial performance, $Pl_{AFP}(afp)$, is the risk of the presence of adverse financial performance (RAFP), i.e. $Pl_{AFP}(afp) = RAFP$. The plausibility of the presence of industry risk factors, $Pl_{IRF}(irf)$, is the risk of the presence of industry risk factors (RIRF), i.e., $Pl_{IRF}(irf) = RIRF$. The plausibility of the presence of adverse macroeconomic factors, $Pl_{AME}(ame)$, is the risk of the presence of adverse macroeconomic factors ($RAME$), i.e., $Pl_{AME}(ame) = RAME$. Also, the plausibility, $Pl_D(d)$, of loan default based on the lender's review processes can be expressed as the risk of a default going undetected by the lender ($Pl_D(d) = DPR$) (i.e., the lender's own ongoing review processes failed to detect the default risk). Thus, in terms of these individual risks, we can express the risk of default (DR) as follows:

$$DR = RAFP.RIRF.RAME.DPR/K, \tag{10.8}$$

where K is a renormalization (see equation (10.6)) constant because of the conflict between the belief mass function from the lender's review procedures and the belief mass function obtained from the three influencing factors. The default risk formula in (10.8) is logical formula; default risk will exist only when there is risk of adverse current or expected future financial performance, risk of adverse industry factors, the risk of adverse macro-economic factors, and the risk that the lender's review procedures will fail to detect default risk given the presence of one or more of the three influencing factors on loan default.

We can see from formula (10.8) that in situations where we do not have any information about the presence or absence of any of the variables, and also if the lender has not performed the appropriate review procedures on the company, then all the plausibilities would be unity and the default risk will be unity. However, after evaluating the evidence relating to the presence or absence of adverse financial performance, industry risk factors and macroeconomic events on a firm's overall creditworthiness, one might estimate the risk factors to a medium level, say RAFP to be 0.6, RIRF to be 0.7, and RAME to be 0.5. In this situation, without the lender performing any review procedures, it seems the default risk would still be quite high, about 16.8%. In order to reduce the default risk to an acceptable level, say 2%, it seems necessary that the lender perform effective review procedures with risk of only about 12% of failing to detect loan default problems for the company (DPR = 0.12).

One can use belief functions models for assessing various other kinds of risks. Because of shortage of space we do not discuss the other cases of risk assessment formulae. Readers are referred to Srivastava and Shafer (1992) and Srivastava and Mock (2002b) for applications in the audit risk area.

10.5. Decision making under belief functions

Traditionally, the utility maximization approach has been used to make decisions under uncertainty, especially when uncertainty is represented in terms of probabilities. However, the traditional approach does not work when uncertainties are not represented in terms of probabilities. There have been several approaches to decision making under belief functions (e.g., see Jaffray 1989, 1994, Nguyen and Walker 1994, Smets 1990a, 1990b, Strat 1990, 1994 and Yager 1990). All these approaches suggest a way to resolve the ambiguities present in the belief function framework and then perform the expected value or utility analysis. We use Strat's approach (1990, 1994), see also Srivastava and Mock (2000) and Sun et al. (2006), because it provides the worst and the best case scenarios of resolving ambiguity. We first discuss Strat's approach, then apply it to an example.

Strat's approach

Let us consider the same example of a Carnival Wheel #2 of Strat (1994) where the wheel is divided into ten equal sectors. Each sector is labelled by $1, $5, $10 or $20. Four sectors are labelled $1, two sectors $5, two $10, one $20, and one sector's label is masked, i.e., the label is not visible. Also, we are told that there could be any one of the following amounts: $1, $5, $10 and $20, under the masked label. In order to play the game, you have to pay a $6 fee. The question is: how will you decide whether to play the game?

Before we answer the above question, let us first express the distribution of labels on the carnival wheel using belief functions as

$$m(\$1) = 0.4, \ m(\$5) = 0.2, \ m(\$10) = 0.2, \ m(\$20) = 0.1$$
and $m(\{\$1, \$5, \$10, \$20\}) = 0.1$.

The above belief masses imply that we have direct evidence that $1 appears in four sectors out of ten on the wheel, $5 appears in two sectors out of ten, and so on. $m(\{\$1, \$5, \$10, \$20\}) = 0.1$ represents the assignment of uncertainty to the masked sector; it may contain any one of the four labels: $1, $5, $10, $20. It is interesting to note that such a clear assignment of uncertainty under probability framework is not possible.

Based on the above belief masses, we can express the beliefs and plau-siblities in the four outcomes as

Bel($1) = 0.4, Bel($5) = 0.2, Bel($10) = 0.2, Bel($20) = 0.1.

Pl($1) = 0.5, Pl($5) = 0.3, Pl($10) = 0.3, Pl($20) = 0.2.

Thus, we have 0.1 degree of ambiguity $(\text{Pl}(A) - \text{Bel}(A))$ in each label.

In order to determine the expected value of the outcomes or the expected value of the utilities of the outcomes, Strat resolves the ambiguity through the choice of a parameter, ρ. This parameter defines the probability of resolving ambiguity as favourably as possible. This implies that $(1 - \rho)$ represents the probability of resolving ambiguity as unfavourably as possible. After resolving the ambiguity, we obtain the following revised belief masses:

$$m'(\$1) = 0.4 + 0.1(1 - \rho), \ m'(\$5) = 0.2,$$
$$m'(\$10) = 0.2, \ m'(\$20) = 0.1 + 0.1\rho$$

The above belief masses are defined only on the single elements and, thus, they are equivalent to probability masses. Hence, we can now determine the expected value of the game using the traditional definition and obtain the following value:

$$E(x) = \$5.5 + 1.9\rho.$$

In order to decide whether to play the game, we need to estimate ρ. If we assume that the labels were put by the carnival hawker, we would be inclined to choose $\rho = 0$, which is the worst-case scenario. This choice implies that the decision maker is resolving the ambiguity as unfavourably as possible, i.e. assign the ambiguity of 0.1 to \$1.0. The expected value for this case is $E(x) = \$5.50$. Since this amount is less than the fee of \$6, one would not play the game. We can use a similar approach for determining the expected value of utility of the decision maker.

Economic analysis of cost of credit ratings versus reputation cost

As discussed earlier, predicting the ratings of a credit rating agency for a particular firm cannot be made in terms of probability because credit ratings are not a random process that has a stable frequency in repeated trials under fixed conditions. First, credit ratings agencies use a great deal of public and *private* information. Much of the private information is confidential and never released to the public at the time the rating is issued (or revised). As this information is not in the public domain, models to predict the ratings (and changes in ratings) of credit rating agencies tend to rely exclusively on publicly available information. At best, only indirect estimates of the impacts of private information can be inferred from statistical models. Second, the ratings process typically involves a close association between the ratings agency and the particular form being rated, which involves personal interviews with management on a regular basis, particularly if the company is attempting any new activities or ventures that may impact on the rating. Furthermore, the weights that credit rating agencies assign to different information inputs (particularly private information) is generally not known. It is unlikely that large-sample statistical models used to predict ratings and changes in credit ratings can capture such factors in model estimation.

Finally, the assessment of company's level of default risk by a credit ratings agency such as S&P is based on the effectiveness of the review procedures and methodologies and the quality of evidence gathered by the ratings agency. Suppose the rating agency has performed a detailed ratings review and has given a clean bill of health to a company (i.e., issued a positive rating).

However, there is always a possibility that the financial statements may contain material misstatements or even fraud even though the rating agency has not discovered it. This can lead to a spurious rating, which may only come to light if the company later defaults or goes bankrupt. Under the theory of belief functions, this risk is defined as the plausibility of the presence of default risk, $\text{Pl}(d)$, which is given by equation (10.8).

In this section, we want to perform an economic analysis of the cost of performing a credit ratings review with the potential reputation cost to the ratings agency if a company's default risk level is not accurately assessed by the ratings agency. Let us consider the following set of overall belief masses for the presence and absence of default risk:

$$m_D(d) = m^+, \quad m_D(\sim d) = m^-, \quad m_D(\{d, \sim d\}) = m^\Theta.$$

The belief that loan default risk is present or absent is, respectively, m^+ and $\tilde{m}$, i.e., $\text{Bel}(d) = m^+$ and $\text{Bel}(\sim d) = m^-$. The plausibility of default risk being present, i.e., the default (DR), is given by $\text{Pl}(d) = DR = m^+ + m^\Theta$. Let us assume that the rating agency has given a clean bill of health for the above case and also consider the following costs and benefits to the ratings agency on conducting the rating review. The rating agency gets 'RF' amount of fee revenue for issuing the rating, incurs 'RC' amount of cost in the conduct of the ratings review, expects to receive future benefits of 'FB' amount if the ratings review is of 'good quality' and there is no default (where a favourable rating has been issued), and incurs a loss of 'LC' as the reputation cost and loses all the future benefits if the rating turns out to be of a bad quality, (i.e., the rating agency did not accurately assess the level of default risk in a company and the company later defaults). In order to determine the expected benefit or loss to the ratings agency given that the agency has given a clean bill of health to a company, we need to use Strat's approach to resolve the ambiguity in the worst-case scenario and then determine the expected value of the costs and benefits to the ratings agency.

If we resolve the ambiguity of m^Θ against the ratings agency (worst-case scenario), the revised belief masses would be: $m_D'(d) = m^+ + m^\Theta$, and $m_D'(\sim d) = m^-$ In fact, by definition, $m_D'(d) = \text{Pl}(d) = DR$, and $m_D'(\sim d) = 1 - DR$. Thus, expected value of cost and benefits to the ratings agency for issuing a favourable rating can be written as

$$
\begin{aligned}
\text{Expected Benefit} &= (\text{RF} - \text{RC} + \text{FB})\, m_D'(\sim d) + (\text{RF} - \text{RC} - \text{LC})m_D'(d) \\
&= (\text{RF} - \text{RC} + \text{FB})(1 - \text{DR}) + (\text{RF} - \text{RC} - \text{LC})\text{DR} \\
&= \text{RF} - \text{RC} + \text{FB} - (\text{FB} + \text{LC})\text{DR}
\end{aligned}
$$

The rating agency will have positive benefit under the following condition:

$$\text{Default Risk}(DR) < (RF - RC + FB)/(FB + LC). \qquad (10.9)$$

Equation (10.9) determines the level of desired default risk by the rating agency given the ratings fee, cost of issuing (or revising) a rating, future benefits and the potential loss due to reputation loss for poor-quality ratings. In other words, Equation (10.9) can be interpreted as the acceptable or desired level of default risk needed for a rating agency to issue a favourable rating and be profitable.

To reduce the level of acceptable or desired default risk, a rating agency might choose to avoid rating certain companies where default rates are traditionally higher than industry averages or where there are greater uncertainties or difficulties in assessing information inputs to the rating. Alternatively, the agency might tighten its review processes and take a more conservative approach to ratings for companies and industries where ratings risk is perceived to be high.

For simplicity, we assume that reputation loss is expected to translate (in economic terms) to lost subscription revenues for the ratings agency's products and services (in reality, there may be other costs as well, such as litigation costs). Figure 10.2 shows a graph of acceptable default risk by the ratings agency versus reputation costs. We assume the following values for the other variables in (10.9): $RF = \$1,000,000$; $RC = \$800,000$;

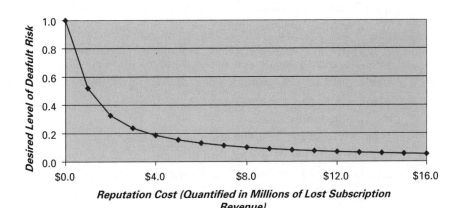

Figure 10.2 Effect of reputation cost on desired level of default risk [+]

[+] We have assumed the following costs for this graph: Ratings Fee (RF) = \$1,000,000; Ratings Cost (RC) = \$800,000; Future Benefits (FB) = \$670,000 (net present value of future cash flows of 20% of net income discounted at 15% over five years).

$FB = \$670,000$ (present value of the cash flow discounted at 15% over five years). It is interesting to see from Figure 10.2 that the ratings agency will not worry about default risk levels ($RR = 1$) if there is no reputation cost. However, as reputation cost increases, the desired level of default risk by the rating agency decreases as expected. For our example, for a reputation cost of $16,000,000, the ratings agency will perform the rating with 0.05 level of desired default risk. Of course, we have assumed the cost of the rating and rating fee to be fixed in the present calculation, which is not the case in the real world. However, we can analyse such a situation by considering the rating fee and the rating cost to be a function of the desired default risk; the lower the desired default risk of a company, the higher the cost of rating and, thus, the higher the credit rating fee.

10.6. Conclusion

This chapter provides a belief function approach to assessing default risk, along with a general introduction to belief functions. The chapter discusses two kinds of uncertainty. One kind arises purely because of the random nature of the event. For random events, there exist stable frequencies in repeated trials under fixed conditions. The other kind of uncertainty arises because of the lack of knowledge of the true state of nature where we not only lack the knowledge of a stable frequency, but we also lack the means to specify fully the fixed conditions under which repetitions can be performed. We have suggested that application of probability theory under these conditions can lead to inconsistent logic, spurious interpretations of evidence and ultimately poor or sub-optimal judgments. Belief functions provide a viable quantitatively grounded alternative to probability theory, particularly where statistical generalizations are not possible and/or not appropriate in the circumstances.

To demonstrate the application of belief functions we derive a default risk formula in terms of plausibility of loan default risk being present under certain specified conditions. The default formula suggests that if default risk exists, then the only way it can be minimized is for the lender to perform effective ongoing review activities, *ceteris paribus*. Finally, we discuss an approach to decision making under belief functions and apply this to perform an economic analysis of costs and benefits to a ratings agency when default risk is present.

REFERENCES

American Institute of Certified Public Accountants, *Statements on Auditing Standards, No. 47*, AICPA, New York, 1983.

American Institute of Certified Public Accountants, *Statements on Auditing Standards, No. 106*, AICPA, New York, 2006.

American Institute of Certified Public Accountants, *Statements on Auditing Standards, No. 107*, AICPA, New York, 2006.

American Institute of Certified Public Accountants, *Statements on Auditing Standards, No. 111*, AICPA, New York, 2006.

Dutta, S. K. and Srivastava, R. P., 'A Bayesian perspective on the strength of evidence in auditing', *Indian Journal of Accounting*, 27, June, 1996, 4–18.

Dutta, S. K. and Srivastava, R. P., 'Aggregation of evidence in auditing: a likelihood perspective', *Auditing: A Journal of Practice and Theory*, 12, Supplement, 1993, 137–60.

Edwards, A. W. F., *Likelihood: An Account of the Statistical Concept of Likelihood and its Application to Scientific Inferences*, Cambridge University Press, 1984.

Einhorn, H. J. and Hogarth, R. M., 'Decision making under ambiguity, *Part 2*', *The Journal of Business*, 59(4), 1986, 225–50.

Einhorn, H. J. and Hogarth, R. M., 'Ambiguity and uncertainty in probabilistic inference', *Psychological Review*, 92, 1985, 433–61.

Ellsberg, D., 'Risk, ambiguity, and the savage axioms', *Quarterly Journal of Economics*, 75, 1961, 643–69.

Jaffray, J.Y., 'Utility theory for belief functions', *Operations Research Letters*, 8, 1989, 107–12.

Jaffray, J.-Y., 'Dynamic decision making with belief functions', in Yager, R. R., Fedrizzi, M. and Kacprzyk, J. (eds.), *Advances in the Dempster–Shafer Theory of Evidence*, New York, Wiley, 1994.

Nguyen, H. T. and Walker, E. A., 'On decision making using belief functions', in Yager, R. R., Fedrizzi, M. and Kacprzyk, J. (eds.), *Advances in the Dempster–Shafer Theory of Evidence*, New York, Wiley, 1994.

Shafer, G., *A Mathematical Theory of Evidence*, Princeton University Press, 1976.

Shafer, G. and Srivastava, R., 'The Bayesian and belief function formalisms: a general perspective for auditing', *Auditing: A Journal of Practice and Theory*, Supplement, 1990, pp. 110–48.

Smets, P., 'The combination of evidence in the transferable belief model', *IEEE Transactions on Pattern Analysis and Machine Intelligence*, 12(5), May, 1990a, pp. 447–458.

Smets, P., 'Constructing the pignistic probability function in a context of uncertainty', in Henrion, M., Shachter, R. D., Kanal, L. N. and Lemmer, J. F. (eds.), *Uncertainty in Artificial Intelligence 5*, North-Holland, Elsevier, 1990b.

Smets, P., 'Practical uses of belief functions', in Laskey K. B. and Prade H. (eds.), *Uncertainty in Artificial Intelligence 15, UAI999*, 1999, pp. 612–621.

Srivastava, R. P., 'Belief functions and audit decisions', *Auditors Report*, 17(1), 1993, 8–12.

Srivastava, R. P., 'Decision making under ambiguity: a belief-function perspective', *Archives of Control Sciences*, 6 XLII (1, 2), 1997, 5–27.

Srivastava, R. P. and Mock, T. J., 'Introduction to belief functions', in Srivastava R. P. and Mock, T. (eds.), *Belief Functions in Business Decisions*, Heidelberg, Springer, 2002a, pp. 1–16.

Srivastava, R. P. and Mock, T. J., *Belief Functions in Business Decisions*, Heidelberg, Springer, 2002b.

Srivastava, R. P. and Mock, T. J., "Evidential reasoning for WebTrust assurance services', *Journal of Management Information Systems*, 16(3), 2000, 11–32.

Srivastava, R. P., Mock, T. J. and Turner, J., 'Analytical formulas for risk assessment for a class of problems where risk depends on three interrelated variables', *International Journal of Approximate Reasoning*, 45, 2007, pp. 123–151.

Srivastava, R. P. and Shafer, G., 'Belief-function formulas for audit risk', *The Accounting Review*, 67(2), 1992, 249–83.

Srivastava, R. P. and Shafer, G., 'The Bayesian and belief-function formalisms: a general perspective for auditing', *Auditing: A Journal of Practice and Theory*, Supplement, 1990, 110–48.

Srivastava, R. P., Shenoy, P. P. and Shafer, G., 'Propagating beliefs in an 'AND' tree", *International Journal of Intelligent Systems*, 10, 1995, 647–64.

Strat, T. M., 'Decision analysis using belief functions', *International Journal of Approximate Reasoning*, 4(5), 1990, 6.

Strat, T. M., 'Decision analysis using belief functions', in Yager, R. R., Fedrizzi, M. and Kacprzyk, J. (eds.), *Advances in the Dempster–Shafer Theory of Evidence*, New York, Wiley, 1994.

Sun, L., Srivastava, R. P. and Mock, T., "An information systems security risk assessment model under Dempster–Shafer theory of belief functions', *Journal of Management Information Systems*, 22(4), 2006, 109–42.

Wong, S. K. M. and Wang, Z. W., 'Qualitative measures of ambiguity', in Hackerman D. and Mamdani A. (eds.), *Proceedings of The Ninth Conference on Uncertainty in Artificial Intelligence*, San Mateo, CA: Kaufmann, 1993, pp. 443–50.

Yager, R. R., 'Decision making under Dempster–Shafer uncertainties', *Technical Report MII-915*, New Rochelle, NY, Iona College, 1990.

Yager, R. R, Fedrizzi, M. and Kacprzyk, J., *Advances in the Dempster–Shafer Theory of Evidence*, New York, Wiley, 1994.

Index